THE SOCIETY FOR POST-MEDIEVAL ARCHAEOLOGY MONOGRAPH 6

THE ARCHAEOLOGY OF POST-MEDIEVAL RELIGION

THE ARCHAEOLOGY OF POST-MEDIEVAL RELIGION

Edited by
CHRIS KING *and* DUNCAN SAYER

SOCIETY
for
CHURCH
ARCHAEOLOGY

A joint publication of the
Society for Church
Archaeology and the
Society for Post-
Medieval Archaeology

THE BOYDELL PRESS

Details of previously published titles are available from the Society

First published 2011
The Boydell Press, Woodbridge

ISBN   978 1 84383 693 3

The Boydell Press is an imprint of Boydell & Brewer Ltd
PO Box 9, Woodbridge, Suffolk IP12 3DF, UK
and of Boydell & Brewer Inc.
668 Mt Hope Avenue, Rochester, NY 14620, USA
website: www.boydellandbrewer.com

The publisher has no responsibility for the continued existence or accuracy
of URLs for external or third-party internet websites referred to in this book,
and does not guarantee that any content on such websites is,
or will remain, accurate or appropriate.

A CIP catalogue record for this book is available
from the British Library

Papers used by Boydell & Brewer Ltd are natural, recyclable products
made from wood grown in sustainable forests

MIX
Paper from
responsible sources
FSC® C013604
FSC
www.fsc.org

Printed in Great Britain by
CPI Group (UK) Ltd, Croydon, CR0 4YY

CONTENTS

FIGURES

TABLES

CONTRIBUTORS

Peter Benes
Director, The Dublin Seminar for New England Folklife

Anwen Cedifor Caffell
Department of Archaeology, Durham University

Rachel Clarke
Oxford Archaeology East

Chris King
Department of Archaeology, University of Nottingham

Jeremy Lake
English Heritage

Diana Mahoney-Swales
Department of Archaeology, University of Sheffield

Adrian Miles
Senior Archaeologist, Museum of London Archaeology

Rosie Morris
University of Birmingham

Harold Mytum
Centre for Manx Studies, University of Liverpool

Richard O'Neill
Wessex Archaeology, Sheffield

Greig Parker
Department of Archaeology, University of Sheffield

Natasha Powers
Head of Osteology, Museum of London Archaeology

Matthias Range
Department of History, Oxford Brookes University

Simon Roffey
Department of Archaeology, University of Winchester

Duncan Sayer
School of Forensic & Investigative Science, University of Central Lancashire

Andrew Spicer
Department of History, Oxford Brookes University

Claire Strachan
    Diocesan Advisory Committee, Diocese of Leicester

Hugh Willmott
    Department of Archaeology, University of Sheffield

Philippa Woodcock
    Department of History, Oxford Brookes University

ACKNOWLEDGEMENTS

This volume is the final product of a joint conference of the Society for Post-Medieval Archaeology and the Society for Church Archaeology on 'The Archaeology of Post-Medieval Religion', held in Norwich in 2008. The editors would like to extend their thanks to the past and current Presidents and Councils of both societies for their support of the initial conference proposal and subsequent publication. The presenters and attendees at the conference provided a stimulating range of papers and lively discussion, which is reflected in the quality of the final published works. We also thank Brian Ayers, Nicholas Groves and Ian Smith for their enthusiastic participation in showing delegates the wonderful post-medieval religious heritage of Norwich. Claire Strachan provided invaluable administrative assistance for the conference.

Preparing the papers for publication has been an enjoyable challenge. We extend our warmest thanks to Meredith Carroll for her much appreciated editorial help. We are also very grateful to David Gaimster for agreeing to provide a foreword for our volume. Finally, we would like to thank Sarah May (acting for SPMA) and Caroline Palmer and her editorial team at Boydell for their patience and support during the production process.

Chris King
Nottingham

Duncan Sayer
Preston

FOREWORD

I went to the Garden of Love,
And saw what I never had seen:
A Chapel was built in the midst,
Where I used to play on the green.

William Blake, *The Garden of Love*, 1794.

With the intensification of industry over much of the British Isles in the 18th century came a new social, cultural and religious landscape. The established topography of the parish church was no longer relevant to the shifting social and economic geographies of the factory, mine or dockyard. Chapels sprang up in towns, villages and across the countryside to serve the needs of the new local working community. Today many of them stand alone and forgotten in the post-industrial landscape and present a particular conservation challenge. Despite their frequently isolated position today, redundant churches and chapels serve to remind us of the dramatic consequences and turns in religious life following the schisms of the 16th century. We can observe a far more fragmented and pluralistic Christianity comprising new sects, denominations and movements often conflicting and competing with each other. Archaeologists of the modern period have tended to focus on economic, social and cultural change, exploring the various debates concerning production and consumption, wealth and poverty, trade and empire. It is fair to say that modernists have not given quite the same attention to religious concerns of the period with its increasingly diverse attitudes to salvation and the afterlife and their influence on the material record. The history of nonconformity was left to its committed chroniclers, for instance, and that of Anglicanism largely neglected, compared with the attention paid before 1660.

Despite the competing influences of capitalism, secularization, scientific enquiry and nation building, religious belief and identity continued to play a pivotal role in the lives of ordinary people across the post-Reformation Christian world. Late medieval Roman Catholic culture did not have a monopoly on the devotional fanaticism of ordinary men and women, as the confessional sectarianism and disputes of early modern Europe may attest. Equally, religious belief continued to have a powerful influence on the material world, on places of worship, on homes and in the realm of personal artefacts. Insight into personal religious identity and commemorative practice can also be gained most clearly in the post-medieval mortuary record, particularly the graveyards and cemeteries that proliferated following industrial and urban development, themselves a largely neglected primary historical resource until at least the 1990s (in contrast to the attention paid to medieval cemeteries). As the editors of this volume emphasise, as a discipline archaeology has a powerful contribution to make through the study of material remains towards our better understanding of post-medieval religious change in diverse communities on the ground. While the written record of personal religious experience is relatively richer than in the preceding centuries, the study of objects and the results of excavation have the ability to generate new and challenging perspectives on 'sacred economy' during an epoch of profound economic, social and cultural change. Future research, for instance, might explore the role of gender as a dynamic influence in the development of post-medieval religion. Did women, with their more prescribed family and domestic responsibilities, have different kinds of religious experience or develop alternative views of salvation, of death and the afterlife? The proliferation of nonconformist sects from the mid 17th century certainly gave women a more prominent role. Alongside a clearer insight into social dynamics of early modern and modern community life, the developing study of graveyard mortuary culture is beginning to expose some interesting gender differences here.

The growing importance of a systematic archaeological approach to the study of post-medieval religion was first explored in the joint Societies for Medieval Archaeology and Post-Medieval Archaeology conference exploring *The Archaeology of Reformation 1480–1580* in 2001 (proceedings edited by David Gaimster and Roberta Gilchrist and published as a Society for Post Medieval Archaeology Monograph in 2003). The editors of *The Archaeology of Post-Medieval Religion* (itself the product of a joint Societies for Post-Medieval Archaeology and Church Archaeology conference in 2008) are to be congratulated on producing a much-needed and excellent companion volume, maintaining a strong cross-disciplinary interest. As the editors make clear, the focus has shifted from questions of schism and iconoclasm to the creation of new religious identities within Protestant and Catholic Europe. As with the *Archaeology of Reformation*, the papers presented here ask more questions than they resolve. I look forward to participating in future discussions that further examine the complex and interconnected matrix of economic, social, cultural and religious experience that shaped the material world of ordinary men and women in early modern Europe.

DAVID GAIMSTER
Glasgow, August 2011

Conflict, Community and Custom:
The Material Remains of Post-Medieval Religion

CHRIS KING and DUNCAN SAYER

INTRODUCTION

The post-medieval centuries witnessed dramatic transformations in both the physical and mental landscapes within which life was lived. These were landscapes in which, by any standard, religion played a vital role. Religious beliefs and identities were both unifying and divisive as marks of political allegiance and community membership and as deeply profound and meaningful elements of collective and individual mentalities. This period saw the fragmentation of the world of medieval Christendom as distinctive and vibrant Protestant and Catholic religious cultures were forged in the wake of the European Reformation. Across the continent new denominations, sects and religious groups emerged to challenge religious and political hegemony within European states. As a dramatic cultural transformation the Reformation was in many ways a conflict over the use and meaning of religious spaces and objects; accordingly, the physical religious landscape was transformed along with the cultural and ideological landscape with which it was intimately bound.

But what was the nature of these changes? In 2001 the Societies of Medieval Archaeology and Post-Medieval Archaeology held a joint conference resulting in a major volume edited by David Gaimster and Roberta Gilchrist on *The Archaeology of Reformation 1480–1580*.[1] This important collection demonstrates the capacity of archaeological evidence to contribute to long-standing debates over the scale, chronology and impact of the religious and political revolutions of the 16th century. The papers address a series of key themes including iconoclasm and dissolution, the transformation of places of worship and the adaptation and reuse of religious objects and spaces. Archaeology as a discipline is well placed to identify the experience of religious change in different regions and communities *from the ground up*, as a counter to traditional narratives focusing on the top-down imposition of doctrinal and liturgical change. A decade on, *The Archaeology of Post-Medieval Religion* takes the Reformation as its starting point and seeks to explore the development of religious ideologies and practices across the 17th, 18th and 19th centuries. The present work brings together archaeologists and historians from a wide range of disciplinary sub-fields, all of whom share an interest in the changing spatial and material context of religious belief and identity in the post-medieval world.

This volume is the product of a Society for Post-Medieval Archaeology and Society for Church Archaeology conference held in Norwich in 2008. Our aim was to bring together new research on post-medieval religious buildings, landscapes, cemeteries and burials, and to provide a forum where the diversity and richness of this material could be explored in a cross-disciplinary context. The archaeological study of churches has a long history as a thriving sub-discipline concerned with the architectural development of church buildings and religious and mortuary practices, but has tended to focus on the medieval period and has only rarely considered the physical remains of post-Reformation religious sites.[2] Within archaeology, current work on more recent religious heritage is dominated by gazetteers and surveys of particular monument types, only rarely considered as elements within wider physical and cultural landscapes.[3]

Within the wider field of post-medieval or historical archaeology, broadly defined as the archaeology of the post-1550 world, religion remains a neglected topic, despite its obvious significance. Interpretive agendas have been dominated by issues of social class and consumption on the one hand, or (particularly in North American colonial and later historical archaeology) by ethnic and racial identities and power relationships.[4] However, in the past two decades many historical archaeologists have adopted a more sensitive approach to the role of religion in shaping communal and individual identities in past societies. Studies of institutions of reform and of religious settlements have shown that built landscapes and material culture can underpin powerful and pervasive religious ideologies within communities which may be alternately embraced or resisted by individuals.[5] Other historical archaeologists have examined religion as an element of cultural tradition and group identity within colonial or immigrant societies, such as the widespread continuity of West African religious and magical practices within enslaved and free African-American populations as a means of resisting the violence and oppression of slavery and racism.[6] Within British historical archaeology a handful of innovative new studies have addressed more wide-ranging questions of changing religious and cultural beliefs in the post-medieval period. These include Harold Mytum's work on the intersection of religious and ethnic identities as expressed through funerary monuments; Sarah Tarlow's exploration of attitudes to death and bereavement in post-Reformation society; and Nicola Whyte's study of the continuity of medieval religious sites as points of communal memory within the post-medieval rural landscape.[7]

Post-Reformation Religion: Spatial and Material Transformations
The changing material context of religious belief and practice has emerged as an important new area of shared interest in many disciplines, bringing together the concerns and approaches of religious history, social and cultural history, and art and architectural history.[8] Such work highlights the value of an interdisciplinary approach for the study of early modern religion, which must draw on architectural, material, cartographic, visual and documentary sources. Archaeology has a vital role to play in this endeavour, providing rigorous and detailed analyses of changing religious landscapes, buildings and material practices. The new interest in the wider transformation of religious spaces and practices has been informed by significant shifts in Reformation historiography, emphasising that this was neither a single, bounded event nor a unilinear process. Rather, the early modern period witnessed three centuries of drawn-out religious change across Europe, in which existing religious practices were appropriated in the service of new religious, political and cultural identities.[9] This makes the longer time-span covered by the present volume an important new direction in considering the archaeology of post-Reformation religion.

The later 16th and 17th centuries witnessed a hardening of confessional divisions across Europe and the expanding European colonial empires, as religion, dynastic politics and state-formation became inextricably intertwined. Accordingly, our focus has shifted from questions of iconoclasm and destruction to a broader concern with the creation of new religious cultures within Protestant and Catholic Europe. At one extreme of these changes, Calvinist churches rejected most traditional medieval religious practices and adopted a form of worship centred on written Scripture and its expostulation in preaching, while the Lutheran and Anglican churches arguably retained a greater sense of sacred space through the continuing importance of the sacraments.[10] Roman Catholic religious culture was equally a product of reform, initiated by the Council of Trent (1545–63) and advanced by the missionary orders, most notably the Society of Jesus. The increasing prominence of the pulpit alongside the elaboration of Eucharistic ritual, the ornamentation of churches and the gradual introduction of private confessional boxes transformed the experience of Catholic religious space in the service of Papal authority, doctrinal orthodoxy and personal devotion.[11] The early modern period has often been represented as an age of growing secularism, as advances in scientific knowledge, religious toleration and Enlightenment philosophy undermined faith and superstition.[12] Such a simplistic narrative is no longer tenable, however; even those Protestant churches which most strongly rejected the medieval 'sacred economy' centred on holy spaces and objects retained a profound sense of a moralised universe in which the divine and the diabolical were a continuous presence in human affairs.[13]

The new focus on the 'long Reformation' has produced important research on the ebb and flow of religious policy in 16th- and 17th-century England and its impact on the meaning and experience of religious spaces for ordinary people. Increasing religious divisions in early Stuart England brought the fragile *via media* of the Elizabethan Settlement under increasing pressure.[14] Deeper cultural divides had begun to open up in rural and urban communities, for instance over the repression of traditional folk customs and rituals in the name of civic order and moral regulation.[15] For a wide spectrum of churchmen and laypeople, of which the puritan movement represented only an advanced minority, the religious directives of the early Stuart monarchs represented a fundamental challenge to established doctrine and liturgy and were associated with the perceived threat of Roman Catholicism to the English constitution. This controversy reached a high point in the 'Arminian' crisis of the 1630s, as Charles I's archbishop of Canterbury, William Laud, sought to impose wide-ranging reforms on the Church.[16] These included a more ceremonious form of worship and the introduction of railed altars at the east end of churches, all of which were intended to stimulate awe and reverence for the house of God. Such a policy was anathema to many parishes, particularly those in which a puritan faction was dominant.[17] In the Civil Wars that followed – a conflict which was ignited by religious controversies between and within the Three Kingdoms of Britain – the destruction of church ornaments and iconography became a significant statement of the purification of the Church.

Archaeology can play a significant role here by mapping evidence for changes to church interiors across the period and considering these patterns in their wider socio-economic and cultural landscapes. Such an approach is hampered, however, by the difficulty of dating episodes of iconoclasm and by the relative paucity of surviving post-Reformation church fixtures.[18] While many of these were removed by 19th- and 20th-century 'restorers', there is a significant corpus of post-medieval pulpits, font covers, screens and church furniture which has never been comprehensively recorded. It is ironic that we know a good deal less about the appearance of many early modern churches than about their medieval phases, but this makes a rigorous archaeological approach to the fragmentary survivals arguably even more important.

Nonconformity and the Growth of Religious Pluralism

Despite continuing efforts to maintain religious cohesion as an instrument of state power, the post-Reformation centuries saw the emergence of a plurality of religious beliefs and new sects that could not ultimately be repressed or contained. Official toleration of religious difference was generally regarded as a highly iniquitous and dangerous doctrine in early modern Europe, where the 'charitable hatred' of persecution and conversion was commonly accepted as the duty of a Christian.[19] Nevertheless, recent scholarship has emphasised that *de facto* toleration on the ground may have been an important means of maintaining cohesion within local communities struggling to accommodate religious change, while formal toleration in several states (most notably the Dutch Republic) was an inevitable product of the growth of religious pluralism.[20]

In England, explicit toleration of groups outside the established Anglican Church was at first extended only to Continental Protestant refugees (the 'Strangers'), who were commonly granted disused medieval churches in which to worship.[21] Those groups who wished to see further Protestant reform of the Church formed a puritan clique within mainstream Anglicanism or joined small Separatist sects which faced considerable hostility, while Catholics remained a persecuted and shrinking minority. The breakdown of religious and political authority during the mid-17th-century Civil Wars opened the way for the emergence of a profusion of dissenting communities, often associated with radical political movements.[22] The temporary disestablishment of the Anglican Church during the Interregnum gave Independent, Presbyterian, Baptist and Quaker churches new freedom to worship openly, although Catholic and Anglican services were prohibited. It was also under Oliver Cromwell's Protectorate that Jewish communities were first allowed to worship openly in England after the expulsion of 1290. In fact, a small group of Portuguese crypto-Jews was present in London from the early 16th century, although archaeology has to date discovered evidence only for the post-Readmission community.[23] This advanced level of religious freedom could not be contained despite the reintroduction of severe penalties for nonconformity at the Restoration in 1660. Dissenting communities remained an active force in English society throughout the later 17th century, until the Act of Toleration of 1689 granted official toleration to Protestant dissenters.[24] Toleration in this instance was less the culmination of progressive Enlightenment secularism, as it was often presented in the teleological narratives of 19th-century liberal historiography, than a politically expedient measure to ensure the support of the broader Protestant community for the 1688 coup d'état of William of Orange and Mary Stuart against her father James II.

Studies of nonconformist places of worship have highlighted the use of plain architectural forms with a domestic character as an indicator of the modest means of early nonconformist communities, especially outside the major towns, but perhaps also a stricter concern with spiritual matters over worldly display.[25] Certainly the internal layout of their meeting houses with rows of pews and galleries centred on a prominent pulpit was a manifestation of their rejection of sacramental liturgy in favour of the Word. Arguably the austere aesthetic of their architecture can be read as a material creation of a distinctive and shared identity in opposition to the Anglican majority. Dissenters continued to exist under a series of legal and social restrictions, until these disadvantages were gradually removed over the 19th century. In spite of this, the 18th and 19th centuries witnessed a flourishing of nonconformity, particularly with the emergence of the 'new Dissent' led by the Baptist, Methodist and Unitarian churches under the influence of charismatic and passionate ministers and lay preachers.[26] Methodism emerged in the 1730s as a movement for renewal and spiritual awakening within Anglicanism, led by John Wesley and George Whitfield, and from the beginning was closely connected to the 'Great Awakening' in British America. The success of the nonconformists was dramatic in many regions; by the time of the religious census of 1851, 60% of the recorded attendances at a place of worship in England and Wales were nonconformists.[27]

The history of the nonconformist churches in England is one of a continuous succession of denominational changes, as churches split and re-formed around doctrinal and organisational disputes, while individual congregations also frequently divided or changed their affiliation. Arguably, it is this inherent flexibility within the dissenting tradition of independent congregations which enabled the nonconformists to respond to the radical social, economic and demographic shifts of the modern era. It gave them an appeal within both middle-class and working-class communities and opportunities to expand in urban centres and industrial districts which the established Church was less able to realise. The present volume highlights a new direction in the study of nonconformist places of worship which explicitly considers the varied physical, social and economic topographies within which congregations were founded and operated.[28] This broader approach stresses that chapels and meeting houses should be seen as elements within a wider religious and cultural landscape in which itinerant preachers, camp meetings, Sunday Schools and temperance gatherings created varied and responsive communities of faith and belonging in both towns and the countryside.

It would be wrong, however, to paint a picture of 18th- and 19th-century Anglicanism as either stagnant or narrowly conservative, despite the traditional stereotype of the gentrified, port-drinking, fox-hunting parson whose sacred duties were performed by an impoverished curate. In fact, the Church made considerable efforts to improve parochial provision though measures such as the 1711 'Commission for Building Fifty New Churches in London', the 1818 Church Building Act and the grant of additional funds for clerical support through Queen Anne's Bounty. The parish church remained a central part of the spiritual and ritual lives of rural and urban communities up and down the country. It was a focus for the expression of local pride and the negotiation of familial and personal social standing (made apparent in the continuing jockeying over seating hierarchies and investment in elaborate funerary monuments within churches and churchyards).[29]

From the late 18th century onwards the Evangelical movement met the dissenters on their own ground of spiritual and social regeneration inspired by Scripture, but this was countered from within by the growth of the powerful High Church tradition within 19th-century Anglicanism. The Oxford Movement and the Cambridge Camden Society affirmed the continuity of the English church from the early Church Fathers and sought to re-establish the sacramental theology and ceremonial worship of what they believed was an older and purer form of Christianity.[30] The logical culmination of High Church Anglicanism for some of its adherents was to convert to Roman Catholicism: most famously in the case of the leading light of the Oxford Movement, John Henry Newman (who was made a Roman Catholic cardinal in 1879). This period also saw the creation of a distinctive Anglo-Catholic tradition. The gradual extension of toleration to British Catholics in the later 18th and 19th centuries, culminating in the Catholic Relief Act of 1829, had been met with considerable hostility in many quarters. However, over the 19th century the Catholic Church was re-established as a prominent feature in many British urban and rural landscapes. These varied strands within 19th-century Christianity looked backwards to the Middle Ages, manifested in their concern to 'restore' churches to their medieval spatial and decorative conditions which has had such a dramatic and widespread effect on our surviving stock of medieval church architecture. They also inspired an innovative regeneration of neo-Gothic artistic and architectural styles in the service of a perceived need to provide a spiritual heart for a destabilising, divisive and alienating modern world. Arguably their success in this endeavour can best be seen in the widespread adoption of Gothic as the only naturally 'Christian' style by many Victorian nonconformist congregations.[31]

Burial and Commemoration

Burial provision was a contentious issue in the post-medieval period and the excavation of recent burials continues to be a subject of controversy.[32] Back in the 1990s many cemeteries were cleared with limited or no archaeological intervention.[33] However, today the outlook is not so bleak. Archaeologists work in tandem with cemetery clearance companies and on their own to excavate or recover post-medieval bodies and their coffins and clothing. Many of these sites are little windows into larger burial grounds – car parks in cathedral precincts, lighting sunk into graveyards to illuminate churches – but many sites have received more comprehensive excavation and analysis. Since the discovery of exceptionally well-preserved 18th- and 19th-century human remains and associated burial practices in the crypt of Christ Church, Spitalfields, in east London,[34] the value of a rigorous archaeological approach to the remains of the recent dead has been recognised not just for understanding the mortuary customs of the period but also for its wider application to scholarship by providing access to osteoarchaeological samples which can be closely dated and associated with documented gender, age and status categories. Once post-medieval burials within churches, churchyards and cemeteries were excavated because archaeologists were interested in earlier remains, and the post-medieval evidence was given only summary treatment at best. Now, large-scale cemetery excavations such as those undertaken at St Martin in the Bullring, during the construction of the Bullring shopping centre in Birmingham, are recognised as unique opportunities to investigate the lived experience and death rituals of 18th- and 19th-century urban communities.[35] Studies of post-medieval hospital cemeteries and skeletal remains that have been subjected to amputations or dissection have contributed further to histories of medicine and the post-mortem treatment of sailors or the criminal and marginal members of society.[36]

Cemetery studies have also been at the forefront of the ethical debate in British archaeology over the appropriate treatment of human remains. Nothing stirs up local outrage like a burial ground excavated without consultation or proper ethical guidelines, and there have been several cases (such as Bonn Square, Oxford) where archaeological work has been seen as invasive and offensive, and archaeologists subjected to abuse, being filmed or attacked on internet blogs.[37] Post-medieval archaeologists have been dealing with this sort of situation for over a decade, and would have been on the picket line themselves a few years earlier to prevent the unrecorded destruction of the archaeological record. Today, clear ethical structures exist to enable the sensitive excavation of more recent human remains, taking into account the legal and ethical responsibilities of the excavators and prioritising the development of research frameworks that can justify expensive archaeological intervention. Indeed, protest is far from the norm and many post-medieval bones from the Cross Bones cemetery in Southwark were publicly displayed in the Wellcome Trust's popular 2008 exhibition *Skeletons: London's Buried Bones*. However, it is perhaps unfortunate that many ongoing projects cannot contribute to standing research collections as the law requires reburial of Christian remains. What better way would there be of testing the isotope studies which are currently gripping pre- and proto-historical archaeologies than using a known group of French immigrants from London?

One area that has yet to be fully explored from an archaeological perspective is that of post-medieval funerary practice, including burial methods, the treatment of the corpse and artefacts such as coffin fittings and objects placed within burials. Historians such as Julian Litten have studied the design of funerary objects from an art historical perspective and within the context of the commercialisation of the funerary industry in the modern era,[38] and some commercial archaeologists are now developing a real interest in the realm of mortuary material culture. However, as yet there has been no wider attempt to synthesise the huge amount of data being generated by the commercial excavation of post-medieval cemeteries. A current project on beliefs about the body in early modern Britain, funded by the Leverhulme Trust and co-ordinated by Sarah Tarlow at the University of Leicester, will create a much-needed national database of post-medieval cemetery excavations which will hopefully stimulate further research.[39]

The archaeological study of post-medieval funerary commemoration has also expanded in significant new directions in recent years. Prehistoric archaeologists such as Cannon[40] and Parker Pearson[41] have used micro-studies of post-medieval monuments to make critical theoretical points about the complexities of relating monuments to social practices and identities, whose relevance is still recognised. Gravestones remain a popular choice for cheap, easily managed recording projects by amateur groups and students, and scholars such as Harold Mytum have assisted the development of such research by producing usable typologies and popular guides to the topic.[42] Meticulous period studies have provided rigorous archaeological analyses of post-medieval monuments that have contributed new understandings of the social and economic factors affecting monument provision and design in specific local contexts, and there remains considerable potential to further discuss the creation and negotiation of social, ethnic and religious identities as expressed through commemorative practice.[43] In addition, work on the emotional significance of bereavement and remembrance points to new ways in which archaeological studies can contribute to an understanding of attitudes towards death in the modern era.[44] Studies of post-medieval religious architecture, such as Stell's gazetteers of nonconformist chapels, frequently fail to recognise the association of chapels and private denominational cemeteries; yet burial practice could be a vital element of religious ideology, community cohesion and personal faith. Gravestones, like other cemetery data, should not be separated from our wider studies of religious and cultural change in this period.

To offer insight into the complexity of post-medieval religion this volume includes papers which discuss a wide spectrum of varied religious beliefs and denominations in Europe across the period from the late 16th to the late 19th century from scholars representing a range of disciplinary fields and drawing on a diverse set of architectural, archaeological, cartographic and documentary sources of evidence. Even so, they can touch on only a small number of key elements within such a broad topic. The chronological focus is on three and more centuries of changing religious beliefs, practices and identities following the mid-16th-century Reformations as they affected different regions and urban and rural communities within Britain and other western European countries. The papers deal almost wholly with Christianity, and the majority focus on aspects of institutionalised religion rather than evidence for magical and ritual practices which would certainly be amenable to archaeological analysis.[45] The expansion of Christian sects and non-Christian religious communities within Europe in the 19th and especially the 20th century has had a dramatic effect on our tangible and intangible cultural landscapes which is deserving of further study and will require new approaches to the recording and preservation of religious heritage in the future. It is hoped that the papers presented here will demonstrate the significant contribution that archaeology can make to a deeper understanding of the development of religion in the post-medieval world. It is only through the combination of archaeological and historical research frameworks that deploy landscapes, buildings, burials, monuments and artefacts in a sophisticated interdisciplinary approach that complex areas of past human life such as religion become open to further analysis.

THE ARCHAEOLOGY OF POST-MEDIEVAL RELIGION

The volume is divided into three sections, which together treat a range of different post-medieval religious groups and denominations and draw on varied material sources of evidence. The first section, 'Conflict and Conformity: Church and Society in the Early Modern World', investigates religious identities in post-Reformation Europe and the changing relationship between church and society in an age of increasing religious pluralism. The second, 'Nonconformity: Chapels, Landscapes and Community', explores the creation of religious communities outside the established church and explores the changing role of religious buildings in their physical, socio-economic and cultural landscape context. The third, 'Cemeteries: Funerary Custom, Burial and Identity', contains chapters looking at funerary material culture, cemeteries, funerary rites and the bodies of people found in burial grounds of different denominations. From this range of source material springs several themes that could just as easily have been used to understand the archaeology of post-medieval religion, such as religious conflict and accommodation, individual religious freedom and social cohesion, immigration and cultural diversity, and continuity and change in religious beliefs and practices. Religion is ultimately a truly dynamic field of human experience that is intimately bound up with political power, social relationships and individual personhood, which is why it remains a topic which must be seen as central to the wider archaeological study of the post-medieval period.

Part One: Conflict and Conformity: Church and Society in the Early Modern World
The first three chapters in this section present results from a major Arts and Humanities Research Council-funded project on 'The Early Modern Parish Church and the Religious Landscape',[46] and discuss the transformation of the material setting of public worship in the post-Reformation centuries. In the first chapter Andrew Spicer examines the redrawing of parish boundaries in post-Reformation Scotland. Focusing on the work of the 17th-century Parliamentary Commission for the Valuation of Teinds and the Plantation of Kirks, and using the example of the controversial but ultimately successful move to transplant the parish church of Bassendean to a new site at Westruther, he shows that varied local inter-

ests were carefully weighed in the concern to provide a church located centrally within the parish. Unlike in England, where there was a broad continuity in parish organisation, in Scotland the Kirk engaged in a wider redefinition of religious landscapes in order to ensure that churches were adequate for Reformed worship.

Philippa Woodcock examines the destruction and subsequent refitting of religious spaces during the French Wars of Religion, focusing on the diocese of Le Mans in the county of Maine. During the Huguenot ascendancy in Le Mans in 1562 iconoclastic attacks on the cathedral and parish churches were not directed by random violence but were an ordered process focused in part on the seizure of valuable metal items and in part on the control of sacred space. She argues that the refitting of churches by the Catholic hierarchy and local parishioners was both based on rescuing and purchasing items which had been looted, with as much concern for their monetary value as their sacred worth, and was an opportunity to commission new ornaments. This was a way not simply to reconstitute church fabric but to 'satiate the need for religious and physical security, represented by the church'. Matthias Range's investigation of Lutheran church interiors in early modern Schleswig, northern Germany, focuses on the introduction of purpose-built confessional boxes, often highly decorated, in the 17th and 18th centuries. Although commonly associated with the Tridentine Catholic Church, Range reminds us that confession remained a 'third sacrament' in addition to baptism and communion in Lutheran doctrine, and was an integral part of a wider concern to create a personal examination of faith within an institutional context. Significantly, the 'little boxes' of the Schleswig confessionals created small rooms that contributed to a individual's experience of church life and were designed to create a solemn, penitent environment for worship.

Simon Roffey extends the chronological scope of these themes by examining the reconstitution of ritual spaces, specifically private chantry and memorial chapels, in 19th-century English churches. These additions to the church fabric contributed to the distinctive liturgical arrangement of Catholic and High Church Anglican places of worship, but Roffey argues that 19th-century chantry chapels were ultimately commemorative monuments dedicated to the Victorian elite family and not to souls in purgatory, as their medieval predecessors had been. Chantry chapels may have enabled High Church Anglicans to redecorate or redesign church space to express a medieval Catholic aesthetic because purgatory itself had become an intellectual conundrum and not the issue of personal salvation it had once been.

The final two papers in this section examine the immigration of new religious communities into early modern English cities and their effect on the transformation of existing religious and social landscapes. Chris King provides an overview of the material legacy of the 'Strangers' in 16th- and 17th-century Norwich, one of the largest of the provincial communities of immigrants from the Low Countries which were established in southern and eastern towns in this period. The Strangers were initially invited to Norwich to revive the failing cloth industry, and were provided with religious buildings in which to worship according to Reformed Calvinist practice. Archaeological evidence reveals the distinctive lifestyles of the immigrant community and their often marginal socio-economic position, as they were concentrated in overcrowded tenements in the outer parishes of the city. Nevertheless, the urban landscape was not a static environment with distinct ethnic and religious zones, but a setting for dynamic interaction between immigrant and native English communities. Grieg Parker provides further insights into religious and cultural diversity in early modern cities through his examination of the temporal and spatial patterning of Huguenot churches in the west London suburbs in the later 17th and 18th centuries. He argues that supposed theological divides between churches which maintained a strict Calvinist doctrine and liturgy and those which adopted the Anglican form of service in French were not apparent in the foundation and location of churches, and cannot be argued to represent a move towards assimilation with the native community. Indeed, Parker argues that the French immigrant community did not have a homogenous religious identity and ties such as kinship and occupation may have surpassed those of religion.

Part Two: Nonconformity: Chapels, Landscapes and Communities
Jeremy Lake, working with Eric Berry and Peter Herring, discusses 18th- and 19th-century Methodist chapels in Cornwall and their position within the landscape using the detailed mapping approach provided by Historic Landscape Characterisation. Lake argues that nonconformist places of worship should be understood not simply as part of the built environment but as distinctive elements within developing patterns of land use and settlement, and the shifting social and economic geographies these represent. Methodist chapels were central to expanding agricultural and industrial settlements in western Cornwall. Indeed, by the late 19th century chapels were recognised as focal points for expressions of collective identity and performance where the success of the Methodism was sustained by the remoteness of the county from the Anglican core. Taking a similarly broad landscape perspective, Harold Mytum investigates the varied functions of both parish churches and nonconformist chapels as centres of activity in Welsh and Manx rural communities. The distribution of Anglican churches was inherited from the Middle Ages and was not always appropriate to the needs of later settlements. By contrast, nonconformist chapel builders may have been constrained by resources but could move or rebuild their structures to suit the needs of the active community. This in turn has created a problematic legacy of many small chapels which are no longer in use and which place demands on the management of the historic environment. Nevertheless, Mytum suggests that the historical significance of churches and chapels is greater than has often been recognised, as places of worship and their associated schools, halls and burial grounds created the spaces where people undertook social and spiritual activities.

Claire Strachan uses an analysis of the architectural complexity and the spatial locations of nonconformist chapels to discuss broader questions about protest and dissent in the urban centres of the woollen industry in south-west England. She argues that, although the 19th-century nonconformist movement served to promote a strict Protestant work ethic, the importance of group identities underpinned by chapel membership served to increase working-class confidence and resulted in a high degree of independent political activism. She highlights this trend by investigating the material elements of religious expression, particularly an increasing elaboration of chapel architecture in the first half of the 19th century, and the building of prominent new chapels in the commercial centres of towns. All of this occurred at a time when the woollen industry was experiencing a profound economic crisis, as chapel communities provided radical expressions of group belonging and permanence.

In an international perspective on nonconformist religious architecture, focusing on meetinghouses in Puritan New England, Peter Benes describes how the earliest 17th- and early 18th-century places of worship were derived from European Protestant buildings encompassing Scottish kirks, French Huguenot 'temples' and Reformed Dutch churches. However, he also argues that in New England the introduction of more traditional spatial arrangements and more elaborate decoration in Anglican churches in the 18th century had a profound effect on Congregational meetinghouses, many of which gradually adopted elements of these new styles. Benes suggests that this was part of broader shifts in the Congregational Church (which in New England formed the majority, established Church) as congregations grew and divided and younger generations rejected the austerity of their predecessors, so that 'before their parishioners knew it, stoves heated the bitterly cold New England interior spaces, and the stuffed cushion holding the Bible was now made out of fine Georgian cloth'.

Part Three: Cemeteries: Funerary Custom, Burial and Identity
Investigating identity in post-medieval burial practices is a complex topic that must incorporate many different elements of communal and personal life, such as religious denomination, group, familial and household identities, gender, lifecycle, social rank and wealth. Duncan Sayer opens this section of the volume with a broad overview of the range and diversity available in post-medieval burial practice. He looks at parish, non-parochial, private and planned cemetery sites and discusses vaults, grave cuts, grave trenches, pits and intramural burial spaces across Britain. He concludes that religious identity and social position often took priority over family and parish identities. He also describes the long-term trends in burial provision and suggests that the increasing variation visible in later post-medieval planned cemeteries is as much a product of the limitation of individual choices as it is about conspicuous consumption.

Diana Mahoney-Swales, Richard O'Neill and Hugh Willmott investigate another aspect of burial choice in the 18th and 19th centuries, specifically the material remains of coffin furniture, including grip plates, upholstery studs and escutcheons. They focus on recently excavated cemeteries in Sheffield, comparing two Anglican sites, Sheffield Cathedral and St Paul's Church, with two nonconformist chapels, Chapel Yard (Unitarian) and Carver Street (Methodist). They demonstrate the importance of studying the grave in a regional and multi-disciplinary context combining burial archaeology and osteoarchaeology to understand the socio-economic, religious, cultural and pragmatic factors which influenced access to and the desire for increasingly elaborate decorated coffins.

Natasha Powers and Adrian Miles compare two recently excavated London cemeteries, Bow Baptist Church (late 18th and 19th century) and the Catholic Mission of St Mary and St Michael (19th century). They present this preliminary examination of over 1,000 burials, coffin furniture and grave goods as a way to consider whether religious affiliation, location or social and economic situations had the greatest influence on burial provision. Bow Baptist Church was well ordered in contrast to St Mary and St Michael, which, they argue, seemed to be unprepared for the demands on burial space in the 19th century. Because of their multi-disciplinary approach they are able to identify differences in violence, child mortality and the numbers of smokers between the two populations, indicating that wealth as well as religion may have been important factors within the populations who choose to bury their dead in these two sites.

Anwen Caffell and Rachel Clarke discuss the excavation of the Norwich General Baptist's Priory Yard burial ground in 2002. The buried population at this site consisted of sixty-three individuals from the 18th and 19th centuries who showed a remarkable level of pathology and lifetime stress. Diseases present included maxillary sinusitis, tuberculosis, scurvy, rickets, dental caries and a significant degree of tooth loss. This, combined with the absence of expensive dental procedures, indicates that the buried population at Priory Yard was a poor working-class one, a factor which may have been exacerbated by their membership of a nonconformist congregation.

The final chapter examines a more ephemeral component of post-medieval burial custom: maidens' garlands, or funerary wreaths placed within churches to commemorate unmarried girls. Rosie Morris seeks to establish whether these were a sanctioned religious practice or a more popular folk ritual. She has been able to identify 140 surviving or recorded examples from across England, and argues that this was a widespread practice in the early modern period, continuing in some regions up to the First World War. The garlands were an ambiguous feature of post-medieval church interiors; while they could be seen as a celebration of purity and virginity in a continuation of the late medieval idealisation of chastity, they were also frequently condemned by churchmen as superstitious. Nevertheless, they endured as a significant and meaningful part of popular religious practice and identity in many rural communities into modern times.

CONCLUSION

Collectively, the chapters presented in this volume provide examples of a wide variety of original research that investigates many different aspects of the archaeology of religion in the post-medieval world. The 17th, 18th and 19th centuries were a period of continuous religious change, of sometimes violent religious conflict and of a dramatic growth in religious pluralism. These changes had a significant effect on the changing material and ideological landscapes through which religious beliefs and identities were forged, which in turn interacted with wider social, economic and cultural transformations and were firmly bound up with the intimate, everyday experiences of people in the past. The broad chronological and thematic perspective offered by these papers is a vital first step towards making religion a fundamental part of our understanding of post-medieval archaeology. We hope that this book will not just build on the contribution of others but will itself galvanise the further investigation of religion in later historic society. Religion is not simply an aspect of the early modern world; it is central to understanding it.

NOTES

1. Gaimster & Gilchrist 2003.
2. Dunbar 1996; Green 1996; Gilchrist & Morris 1996; Parkinson 1996 provide important statements of current knowledge and research priorities for post-medieval church archaeology.
3. Stell 1986; 1991; 1994; 2002; see Morris 1989 for a landscape perspective.
4. Crossley 1990; Newman 2001; Orser 1996.
5. De Cunzo 1994; Middleton 2008; Starbuck 2004; Tarlow 2002.
6. Ferguson 1992; Russell 1997; Wilkie 1995; 2003.
7. Mytum 1999; 2002; Tarlow 1999, 2011; Whyte 2009.
8. Coster & Spicer 2005; Hamling 2011; Hamling & Williams 2007; Spicer & Hamilton 2005; Walsham 2011.
9. MacCulloch 2003; Wallace 2004.
10. Spicer 2007.
11. Po-Chia Hsia 1998, 152–64; Tingle 2003.
12. Sommerville 1992; Thomas 1971.

13. St George 1998; Scribner 1993.
14. Fincham 1993; Tyacke 1998; 2001.
15. Hutton 1994; Underdown 1985.
16. The 'Arminian' movement grew from the 1590s, although it only reached the status of a comprehensive programme of reform in the late 1620s and 1630s. These high-churchmen rejected the doctrine of predestination and sought to re-emphasise the importance of the sacraments over preaching. It has been interpreted as a radical new challenge to a broad Calvinist consensus between conformists and puritans which characterised the Elizabethan and early Stuart Church: Tyacke 1987; Fincham 1993.
17. Fincham & Tyacke 2007; Lake 1993; Parry 2006.
18. See Oakey 2003.
19. Coffey 2000; Walsham 2006.
20. Kaplan 2007; Walsham 2006.
21. Goose & Luu 2005.
22. Watts 1978.
23. Nenk 2003; Pearce 1998.
24. Specifically, it applied to those who pledged to the oaths of Allegiance and Supremacy and rejected the doctrine of transubstantiation, so excluding Catholics and non-Trinitarians.
25. Stell 1999.
26. Watts 1995.
27. Snell & Ell 2000, 265.
28. Morris 1989; Lake et al. 2001.
29. Friedman 2004; Finch 2000, 145–81; Morris 1989, 377–450.
30. Nockles 1994.
31. Curl 2002.
32. Urban cemeteries were closed following health reforms in 1854 and 1855, and the 1857 Burial Act was passed to protect public decency when contemporary cemeteries were developed to make way for town infrastructure projects. Today these laws still affect archaeology and require excavators to obtain a licence to remove human remains. Indeed, many post-medieval sites have been developed without archaeological intervention (Sayer & Symonds 2004) or with public protest (Sayer 2010).
33. Sayer 2009; Sayer 2010.
34. Molleson & Cox 1993.
35. Brickley et al. 2006.
36. See, for example, the excavations at the Royal Hospital Greenwich: Boston et al. 2008.
37. Sayer 2010.
38. Litten 1991.
39. Tarlow 2011; Cherryson et al. forthcoming.
40. Cannon 1989.
41. Parker Pearson 1993.
42. Mytum 2000; Mytum 2004.
43. Finch 2000; Mytum 1999; 2002.
44. Tarlow 1997; 1999; Saunders 2003.
45. Merrifield 1987; Herva & Ylimaunu 2009.
46. Directed by Andrew Spicer at Oxford Brookes University, 2007–2010. See http://ah.brookes.ac.uk/research/project/parishchurch_and_religiouslandscape/ [accessed 01/08/10]

BIBLIOGRAPHY

Blair, J. & Pyrah, C. (eds) 1996, *Church Archaeology: Research Directions for the Future*. Research Report 104. York: Council for British Archaeology Research Report 104.
Boston, C., Witkin, A., Boyle, A. & Wilkinson, D.R.P. 2008, *Safe Moor'd in Greenwich Tier: A Study of the Skeletons of Royal Navy Sailors and Marines excavated at the Royal Hospital Greenwich*, Oxford, Oxford Archaeology.
Brandon, V. & Johnson, S. 1986, 'The Old Baptist Chapel, Goodshaw Chapel, Rawtenstall, Lancs', *Antiquaries Journal* 66: 330–57.
Brickley, M.B., Buteux, S., Adams, J. & Cherrington, R. 2006, *St. Martin's Uncovered: Investigations in the Churchyard of St. Martin's-in-the-Bull Ring, Birmingham, 2001*, Oxford: Oxbow.
Cannon, A. 1989, 'The historical dimension of mortuary expressions of status and sentiment', *Current Anthropol.* 30: 4, 437–58.
Cherryson, A., Crossland, Z. & Tarlow, S. forthcoming, *A Fine and Private Place: The Archaeology of Death and Burial in Post-Medieval Britain and Ireland*, Leicester: Leicester Archaeology Monograph.
Coffey, J. 2000, *Persecution and Toleration in Protestant England 1558–1689*, London: Longman.

Coster, W. & Spicer, A. (eds) 2005, *Sacred Space in Early Modern Europe*, Cambridge: Cambridge University Press.

Crossley, D. 1990, *Post-Medieval Archaeology in Britain*, Leicester: Leicester University Press.

Curl, J.S. 2002, *Piety Proclaimed: An Introduction to the Places of Worship in Victorian England*, London: Historical Publications.

De Cunzo, L.A. 1994, 'Reform, respite, ritual: an archaeology of institutions. The Magdalen Society of Philadelphia, 1800–1850', *Historical Archaeology* (special issue) 29: 3.

Dunbar, J.G. 1996, 'The emergence of the reformed church in Scotland c 1560–c 1700', in Blair & Pyrah 1996, 127–34.

Ferguson, L. 1992, *Uncommon Ground: Archaeology and Early African America, 1650–1800*, Washington DC: Smithsonian Books.

Finch, J. 2000, *Church Monuments in Norfolk Before 1850: An Archaeology of Commemoration*. British Archaeological Reports British Ser. 317. Oxford: Archaeopress.

Fincham, K. (ed.) 1993, *The Early Stuart Church, 1603–1642*, Basingstoke: Macmillan.

Fincham, K. & Tyacke, N. 2007, *Altars Restored: The Changing Face of English Religious Worship, 1547–c. 1700*, Oxford: Oxford University Press.

Finney, P.C. (ed.) 1999, *Seeing Beyond the Word: Visual Arts and the Calvinist Tradition*, Grand Rapids (MI): William B. Eerdmans Publishing.

Friedman, T. 2004, *The Georgian Parish Church: 'Monuments to Posterity'*, Reading, Berkshire: Spire Books.

Gaimster, D. & Gilchrist, R. (eds) 2003, *The Archaeology of Reformation 1480–1580*. Society for Post-Medieval Archaeology Monograph 1. Leeds: Maney.

Gilchrist, R. & Morris, R. 1996, 'Continuity, reaction and revival: church archaeology in England *c* 1600–1800', in Blair & Pyrah 1996, 112–26.

Goose, N. & Luu, L. (eds) 2005, *Immigrants in Tudor and Early Stuart England*, Brighton: Sussex Academic Press.

Green, S. 1996. 'Disruption, unification and the aftermath: the church in Scotland 1700–1990', in Blair & Pyrah 1996, 134–43.

Hamling, T. 2011, *Decorating the 'Godly' Household: Religious Art in Post-Reformation Britain*, New Haven (CT): Yale University Press.

Hamling, T. & Williams, R.L. (eds) 2007, *Art Re-formed: Re-assessing the Impact of the Reformation on the Visual Arts*, Cambridge: Cambridge Scholars Press.

Herva, V.-P. & Ylimaunu, T. 2009, 'Folk beliefs, special deposits, and engagement with the environment in early modern northern Finland, *J. Anthropol. Archaeol.* 28: 234–43.

Hutton, R. 1994, *The Rise and Fall of Merry England: The Ritual Year 1400–1700*, Oxford: Oxford University Press.

Kaplan, B.J. 2007, *Divided by Faith: Religious Conflict and the Practice of Toleration in Early Modern Europe*, Cambridge (MA): Belknap Press.

Lake, J., Cox, J. & Berry, E. 2001, *Diversity and Vitality: The Methodist and Nonconformist Chapels of Cornwall*, Truro: Cornwall Archaeological Unit.

Lake, P. 1993, 'The Laudian style: order, uniformity and the pursuit of the beauty of holiness in the 1630s', in Fincham 1993, 161–85.

Litten, J. 1991, *The English Way of Death: The Common Funeral since 1450*, London: Robert Hale.

MacCulloch, D. 2003, *Reformation: Europe's House Divided, 1490–1700*, London: Allen Lane.

McKinley, J. 2008, *The 18th Century Baptist Chapel and Burial Ground at West Butts Street, Poole*, Salisbury: Wessex Archaeology.

Merrifield, R. 1987, *The Archaeology of Ritual and Magic*, London: Guild Publishing.

Middleton, A. 2008, *Te Puna – A New Zealand Mission Station*, New York: Springer.

Molleson, T. & Cox, M. 1993, *The Spitalfields Project. Vol. 2 – The Anthropology: The Middling Sort*, York: Council for British Archaeology Research Report 86.

Morris, R. 1989, *Churches in the Landscape*, London: Dent.

Mytum, H. 1999, 'Welsh cultural identity in nineteenth-century Pembrokeshire: the pedimented headstone as a graveyard monument', in Tarlow & West 1999, 215–30.

Mytum, H. 2000, *Recording and Analysing Graveyards*. York: Council for British Archaeology Practical Handbook 15.

Mytum, H. 2002, 'A comparison of nineteenth and twentieth century Anglican and nonconformist memorials in north Pembrokeshire', *Archaeol. J.* 159: 194–241.

Mytum, H. 2004, *Mortuary Monuments and Burial Grounds of the Historic Period*, New York: Kluwer Academic/Plenum Publishers.

Nenk, B. 2003, 'Public worship, private devotion: the crypto-Jews of Reformation England', in Gaimster & Gilchrist 2003, 204–20.

Newman, R., with Cranstone, D. & Howard-Davis, C. 2001, *The Historical Archaeology of Britain, c.1540–1900*, Stroud: Sutton Publishing.

Nockles, P.B. 1994, *The Oxford Movement in Context: Anglican High Churchmanship, 1760–1857*, Cambridge: Cambridge University Press.

Oakey, N. 2003, 'Fixtures or fittings? Can surviving pre-Reformation ecclesiastical material culture be used as a barometer of contemporary attitudes to the Reformation in England?', in Gaimster & Gilchrist 2003, 58–72.

Orser, C. 1996, *A Historical Archaeology of the Modern World*, New York: Kluwer Academic/Plenum Press.

Parker Pearson, M. 1993, 'The powerful dead: relations between the living and the dead', *Cambridge Archaeol. J.* 3: 203–29.

Parkinson, A.J. 1996, 'Reformation, restoration and revival: churches and chapels in Wales 1600–1900', in Blair & Pyrah 1996, 144–58.

Parry, G. 2006, *Glory, Laud and Honour: The Arts of the Anglican Counter-Reformation*, Woodbridge: The Boydell Press.

Pearce, J. 1998, 'A rare delftware Hebrew plate and associated assemblage from an excavation in Mitre Street, City of London', *Post-Medieval Archaeology* 32: 95–112.

Po-Chia Hsia, R. 1998, *The World of Catholic Renewal, 1540–1770*, Cambridge: Cambridge University Press.

Russell, A.E. 1997, 'Material culture and African-American spirituality at the Hermitage', *Hist. Archaeol.* 31: 2, 63–80.

St George, R.B. 1998, *Conversing by Signs: Poetics of Implication in Colonial New England Culture*, Chapel Hill (NC): University of North Carolina Press.

Saunders, N.J. 2003, 'Crucifix, Calvary, and Cross: materiality and spirituality in Great War landscapes', *World Archaeol.* 35/1: 7–21.

Sayer, D. 2009, 'Is there a crisis facing British burial archaeology?' *Antiquity* 83: 184–94.

Sayer, D. 2010, *Ethics and Burial Archaeology*, London: Duckworth.

Sayer, D. & Symonds, J. 2004, 'Lost congregations: the crisis facing later post-medieval urban burial grounds', *Church Archaeol.* 5–6: 55–61.

Scribner, R.W. 1993, 'The Reformation, popular magic and the "disenchantment of the World"', *J. Interdisciplinary Hist.* 23: 475–94.

Snell, K.D.M. & Ell, P.S. 2000, *Rival Jerusalems: The Geography of Victorian Religion*, Cambridge: Cambridge University Press.

Sommerville, C.J. 1992, *The Secularization of Early Modern England: From Religious Culture to Religious Faith*, Oxford: Oxford University Press.

Spicer, A. 2007, *Calvinist Churches in Early Modern Europe*, Manchester: Manchester University Press.

Spicer, A. & Hamilton, S. (eds) 2005, *Defining the Holy: Sacred Space in Medieval and Early Modern Europe*, Aldershot: Ashgate.

Starbuck, D. 2004, *Neither Plain nor Simple: New Perspectives on the Canterbury Shakers*, Lebanon (NH): University Press of New England.

Stell, C. 1986, *Nonconformist Chapels and Meeting-Houses in Central England*, London: HMSO.

Stell, C. 1991, *Nonconformist Chapels and Meeting-Houses in South-West England*, London: HMSO.

Stell, C. 1994, *Nonconformist Chapels and Meeting-Houses in Northern England*, London: HMSO.

Stell, C. 1999, 'Puritan and nonconformist meetinghouses in England', in Finney 1999, 49–81.

Stell, C. 2002, *Nonconformist Chapels and Meeting-Houses in Eastern England*, London: English Heritage.

Tarlow, S. 1997, 'An archaeology of remembering: death, bereavement and the First World War', *Cambridge Archaeol. J.* 7/1: 105–21.

Tarlow, S. 1999, *Bereavement and Commemoration: An Archaeology of Mortality*, Oxford: Blackwell.

Tarlow, S. 2002, 'Excavating Utopia: why archaeologists should study "ideal" communities of the nineteenth century', *Int. J. Hist. Archaeol.* 6/4: 299–323.

Tarlow, S. 2011, *Ritual, Belief and the Dead in Early Modern Britain and Ireland*, Cambridge: Cambridge University Press.

Tarlow, S. & West, S. (eds) 1999, *The Familiar Past? Archaeologies of Later Historical Britain*, London: Routledge.

Thomas, K. 1971, *Religion and the Decline of Magic*, London: Weidenfeld & Nicolson.

Tingle, E. 2003, 'The Catholic Reformation and the parish: the church of Saint Thégonnec (Finistère, France) 1550–1700', in Gaimster & Gilchrist 2003, 44–57.

Tyacke, N. 1987, *Anti-Calvinists: The Rise of English Arminianism c.1590–1640*, Oxford: Clarendon Press.

Tyacke, N. (ed.) 1998, *England's Long Reformation, 1500–1800*, London: UCL Press.

Tyacke, N. 2001, *Aspects of English Protestantism, c. 1530–1700*, Manchester: Manchester University Press.

Underdown, D. 1985, *Revel, Riot and Rebellion: Popular Politics and Culture in England 1603–1660*, Oxford: Oxford University Press.

Wallace, P.G. 2004, *The Long European Reformation: Religion, Political Conflict and the Search for Conformity, 1350–1750*, Basingstoke: Palgrave Macmillan.

Walsham, A. 2006, *Charitable Hatred: Tolerance and Intolerance in England, 1500–1700*, Manchester: Manchester University Press.

Walsham, A. 2011, *The Reformation of the Landscape: Religion, Identity, and Memory in Early Modern Britain and Ireland*, Oxford: Oxford University Press.

Watts, M.R. 1978, *The Dissenters. Volume 1: From the Reformation to the French Revolution*, Oxford: Clarendon Press.

Watts, M.R. 1995, *The Dissenters. Volume 2: The Expansion of Evangelical Nonconformity*, Oxford: Clarendon Press.

Whyte, N. 2009, *Inhabiting the Landscape: Place, Custom and Memory, 1500–1800*, Oxford: Windgather Press.

Wilkie, L.A. 1995, 'Magic and empowerment on the plantation: an archaeological consideration of African-American world view', *Southeastern Archaeol.* 14/2: 136–48.

Wilkie, L.A. 2003, *An Archaeology of Mothering: An African-American Midwife's Tale*, London & New York: Routledge.

Part One

Conflict and Conformity:
Church and Society in the Early Modern World

'Disjoynet, Dismemberit and Disuneited'.[1] Church-building and Re-drawing Parish Boundaries in Post-Reformation Scotland: A Case Study of Bassendean, Berwickshire

ANDREW SPICER

The religious landscape of post-Reformation Scotland still reflected its medieval past, with the persistence of sacred sites and holy places as well as the continuance of the Catholic parochial system. The Kirk attempted to address these issues and this chapter focuses on the efforts to redraw parish boundaries and to relocate churches so that they accorded more to the needs of the local communities. Through the case study of Bassendean, Berwickshire, the chapter will illustrate the difficulties that the Kirk faced during the early 17th century in reordering the religious landscape for Reformed worship, which in this instance culminated in the erection of a new parish church at Westruther.

Following the collapse of the religious policies of Charles I in Scotland, with the establishment of the National Covenant and the abolition of the episcopacy at the Glasgow Assembly in 1638, the ecclesiastical authorities embarked on a further reformation of the Kirk to complete the work of their 16th-century predecessors. At the Reformation the Kirk had inherited a religious landscape which reflected the sacrality of medieval Catholicism, with holy places such as healing wells, wayside crosses and pilgrimage sites, as well as a religious infrastructure dedicated to the cure of souls through the system of parish churches or the contemplative and mendicant life of the religious orders. This was challenged by the religious changes of 1559–60, with iconoclastic assaults on some buildings and the conversion of others to accord with the demands of Reformed worship, in particular the preaching of the Word of God and administration of the sacraments.[2] The implementation of the Reformation and the suppression of what the Kirk regarded as superstitious practices took much longer to instil in the local population. Although parliament legislated in 1581 against 'passing in pilgrimage to chapels, wells and crosses, and the superstitious observing of diverse other popish rights', such customs continued to bring people to the attention of the kirk sessions into the 17th century.[3] There was a renewed attempt to deal with the remnants of the old religion which was undertaken in the wake of the General Assembly which had met in 1640. At their behest parliament passed an act with measures for local magistrates and officials 'to raze, demolish, abolish, cast down or deface all these idolatrous images, pictures and other idolatrous monuments', which led to a further purging of the realm.[4]

Besides this assault on the sacred landscape, there was also an increasing effort to deal with the problems posed by the parochial system that had remained largely unchanged since the 13th century and reflected not only the medieval Catholic landscape but an even older religious tradition associated with Celtic saints in some regions.[5] Although the Kirk had taken possession of the existing parish churches for Reformed worship, there were difficulties posed in some cases by the location of these churches within the parish and the natural landscape, as well as the actual size of some of the parishes that the ministers were expected to serve. There were over 1,000 parishes, which in some cases covered mountainous areas, desolate moorlands or island communities or were subdivided by rivers. During the later 16th century there had been an attempt to address the problems that were posed by the parochial landscape through individual initiatives by towns such as Arbroath, Forfar and Burntisland as well as by local lairds, such as John Shaw of Greenock, who erected new churches in the burghs or on their lands for the convenience of their tenants.[6] During the course of the early 17th century the location of churches and their boundaries increasingly attracted the attention of the authorities, which attempted to address the more serious cases, often through the Commission for the Plantation of Kirks and the Valuation of Teinds. Although the financial aspects of the work of these commissions, in particular relating to tithes, or teinds, as they were called in Scotland, has received some attention from historians in the past, the impact that they had upon the religious landscape and in particular on the location of parish churches has not been closely scrutinized.[7]

Legislation enacted during the early 17th century demonstrates the attempts to address the problems within the parochial landscape, which reached their peak in the period after the signing of the National Covenant (see Appendix). In total, sixty acts were passed between 1592 and 1649, of which twenty-six were enacted during the 1640s. In some cases the legislation was retrospective, as it granted permission for churches which had already been erected, as at Pitsligo, where the local laird had already built a new church for his tenants and separated this from the parish of Aberdour;[8] but in other instances it provided the necessary authorization for these measures to be undertaken. This parliamentary legislation included acts sanctioning the moving of the parish church to a more convenient location within the parish; the dividing of particularly large parishes and the erection of an additional church within the former bounds; the uniting of parishes, either assigning a new church to be built or designating an existing building to be the sole church, with any other places of worship being abandoned; and the removal of lands from one parish and the annexing of them to another so that they might be better served. (Acts which dealt with purely financial matters and did not relate to parish boundaries or the erection of new churches have not been included in this analysis.) It should also be noted that some acts dealt with more than one place, and so the extent of the church building or parochial changes being sanctioned was greater than might be assumed initially. The Act for the Infeftment of Lewis in 1600, for example, included provision for the erection of ten parish churches, while the 1609 Act for uniting certain kirks in Annandale dealt with ten cases in which two or three existing parishes were united into a single parish.[9] This assessment can give only a partial impression of the extent of the changes during the early 17th century, as not every case relating to the erection of a church or alteration of parish boundaries came before parliament; some, for example, were sanctioned by letters patent or were undertaken with the approval of the General Assembly of the Kirk. Nonetheless, the sheer number of acts illustrates the increasing efforts that were being made to address the problems posed by the location of churches and the extent of their parish boundaries.

Although a full analysis of the redrawing of the system of parishes and their boundaries in late 16th- and early 17th-century Scotland is needed, it lies outside the scope of this chapter. A micro-historical analysis of one particular case, however, provides the opportunity to look in closer detail at the problems that were faced by a local community and the processes which led to the erection of a new church on an alternative site within the parish. In March 1649, the Scottish parliament passed the 'Act anent the transplantation of the kirk of Bassendean', which sought to address the problems faced by a remote part of the border county of Berwickshire and the construction of a new church at Westruther in the centre of the parish.[10] Many of the records relating to the Commission for the Plantation of Kirks and the Valuation of Teinds were destroyed in a fire in the Teinds Office in 1700,[11] but the papers relating to the relocation of the parish church of Bassendean survive and offer an insight into the attempts to redefine parishes so that they accorded more with the demands of Reformed worship.

Some impression of the landscape and topographical features of the area is provided by an account of the parish entitled 'A Description of Berwickshire or the Mers'. This has been attributed to the 17th-century minister of Westruther, John Veitch, who took a prominent role in the transplantation of the church.[12]

The first parish on this Water [Blackadder river] is Westruther. Be west the church lyes Thorndikes a Gentleman's Dwelling of the name of Brown, of old, they were Frewhes, a considerable fertile ground both for Corn and Pasturage as any part of Scotland. Be north that, is SpotsWood [Spottiswoode], where, of old the lairds of that Ilk dwelt; of whom came the Superintendant and the Archbishop, thereafter Chancellour. To the north is Roecleuch, Flass and the lairdship of Weatherlie an ancient family of the name of Edgar. To the south Harelaw and Bassindean. That parish of old had great woods with wild beasts, fra quhilk [which] the Dwellings and Hills were designed as Woolstruther, Roecleuch, Hindside, Hartlaw and Harelaw.[13]

The scattered farmsteads identified in this account can still be located, but it also illustrates the contrasting landscapes of the parish, ranging from the remote hillsides and forested areas to tracts of fertile agricultural land. A simple rhyme about the area, which may date from the 17th century, makes allusion to the rivers and crops in the region but also hints at the remoteness of the area, with its description of the inhabitants of the neighbouring parish as simpletons.[14]

The church of St Mary at Bassendean had been founded and endowed by the Melvilles of Bassendean and reflected the Anglo-Norman influence on the development of parishes in southern Scotland. The church lies in the southern part of the parish but its close proximity to Bassendean House, with its remains of a fortified tower house, suggests that it conformed to the feudal model with the coincidence of parish and manor.[15] By the later 12th century the parish had been granted to the nunnery of Coldstream, which had been founded around 1166; this was confirmed by a papal bull in the early 13th century.[16] As was the case in the majority of Scottish parishes, the tithes (teinds) were appropriated by the religious house and a vicar was maintained to serve the cure of souls.[17] The parish remained in the possession of the religious house until after the Reformation; the last abbess, Elizabeth Hoppringill, died in the mid 1580s.[18] The priory of Coldstream was dissolved in 1621

Figure 1.1. Bassendean parish church, south side (photograph by A. Spicer).

and its possessions and financial rights were erected as a temporality by the crown and passed to Sir John Hamilton of Trabrown, a son of the Earl of Melrose.[19]

The surviving remains of the pre-Reformation church at Bassendean (Figs 1.1 and 1.2) show it to have been constructed as a defensive structure as well as a place of worship. The site is a raised promontory, with the land falling away to the south, and the evidence of the surviving entrance suggests that the building originally had a substantial and defendable door. It might also be for this reason that there are windows, which in part have been dated to the 14th century, only on the south side of the building.[20] The church is nonetheless a relatively modest rectangular structure built of rubble, just over fifty feet (15.25m) in length and twenty feet (6.1m) wide. In the walls either side of the east end of the church the recesses of the former piscina and sacrament house can be discerned; in addition, there are the remains of a font as well as an incised medieval tomb slab.[21] The importance of defence continued into the 16th century, as the Border region suffered from a series of English raids during the 1540s; the priory at Coldstream had been burnt by the English in November 1542 and again during Somerset's incursions during 1545.[22] The situation at Bassendean is less clear, but it was raided by an English garrison from Wark in November 1544.[23] These military attacks had a lasting effect on this part of Berwickshire. A survey of twenty-two churches in the Merse – although not Bassendean itself – undertaken by Archbishop Hamilton in 1556 revealed that:

Figure 1.2. Bassendean parish church from the north (photograph by A. Spicer).

a great many of the parish churches – their choirs as well as their naves – were wholly thrown down and as it were levelled to the ground: others were partly ruinous or threatening collapse in respect of their walls and roofs: they were without glazed windows and without a baptismal font and had no vestments for the high altars and no missals or manuals, so that their parishioners could not hear the divine services or masses therein as befits good Christians, neither could masses be celebrated nor the sacraments administered.[24]

The impact of the Reformation upon this particular church has left little evidence, but it was presumably adapted for the preaching of the Word and the administration of the sacraments; a later petition observed that 'the hole parish both before and after the Reformation of religion in Scotland' resorted to the church.[25] The parish does seem to have been provided with a minister for much of this period. In fact, Ninian Borthwick, who had been transferred to Bassendean from Lauder by 1574, was also responsible for the neighbouring parishes of Legerwood and Earlston, which were served only by readers.[26] Readers were not permitted to preach but only to read the Word of God, unlike ministers, and, furthermore, they were prohibited from administering the sacraments. The situation in this part of Berwickshire reflected the difficulties that the Kirk had generally in being able to establish a Reformed ministry across the kingdom during the later 16th century. The appointment of readers was only one solution to this problem; the General Assembly had considered as early as 1563 the benefits that could come from uniting neighbouring parishes under a single minister.[27] A more radical solution was proposed in 1581 with the creation of presbyteries which would have disciplinary oversight over a group of parishes, and their number would be reduced from over 1,000 to a mere 600. In the event, although presbyteries were established there was not such a drastic reduction in the parochial landscape.[28]

In 1617 the Commission for the Valuation of Teinds and the Plantation of Kirks was set up by statute by James VI. Its stated intention was to address the problem 'that there be diverse kirks within this kingdom not planted with ministers, through which ignorance and atheism abound amongst the people, and that many of those that are planted have no sufficient provision nor maintenance appointed to them, whereby the ministers are kept in poverty and contempt and cannot faithfully travel in their charges'.[29] Besides clerical provision, the Commission reflected the on-going attempt by the Crown to deal with the financial difficulties faced by the Kirk relating to ministerial stipends, and it was intended to examine cases where the stipend was below 500 marks and to increase the provision from the appropriated teinds which had passed from religious institutions into the hands of the lairds and nobility. The legislation was significant in granting powers to the commissioner to change the parochial structure in order to achieve a solution to the problem. They were permitted 'to unite such kirks, one or more, as may conveniently be united where the fruits of any one alone will not suffice to maintain a minister'.[30] These measures, therefore, permitted the reorganization of the parochial landscape principally for financial reasons concerning ministerial stipends rather than concerns about the location and suitability of the existing churches, which were issues considered only in passing.[31]

Although there are no records for the Commission at Bassendean, it apparently ruled on 18 February 1618 that the medieval church should be abandoned and the parish united with the neighbouring parish of Gordon, which lay to the south. The commissioners also settled the stipend for the minister of the conjoined parishes. Although the actual arrangements when the priory of Coldstream was dissolved and erected into a temporal lordship are unknown, Sir John Hamilton was bound to honour 'that part and portion of the stipend of the said united kirks which is appointed to be paid out of the teinds of the said kirk of Bassendean by the said act of the commissioners of Parliament'.[32] It was later alleged that the parishes had been united 'in the bishops' tymes' for purely financial reasons, because 'ane powerfull man callit Williame Home of Bassindane haveing gotten the teinds of that parochin and of the parochin of Gordon' and having therefore been responsible for the two parishes being joined, 'quhair [where] at the hole parochiners being greeved'.[33] The situation at Bassendean was far from unusual; David Calderwood argued in his *Historie of the Kirk of Scotland* that the work of the 1617 Commission satisfied neither the lairds nor the clergy, and that, in around 200 cases, two or three parishes had been united into one.[34]

There was also a questioning of the merits of some of these parochial unions when parliament established a further Commission in 1621. It argued that there had been 'sundry kirks united together and conjoined in one, albeit upon good considerations it may be found more expedient that the same union be dissolved and that the said kirks be provided severally with distinct functions and separate services at such places where the commodity may afford in the same manner as if no such union had been made'.[35] Nonetheless, this clause in the legislation had no impact on the situation at Bassendean because any changes made to 1617 settlements required the approval of all the parties involved and this seems not to have been forthcoming.

The 1621 legislation also marked a significant departure from the earlier measures relating to the parochial system. In the past the emphasis had dwelt principally on matters of pastoral provision, addressing the problem posed by the shortfall in the number of Reformed ministers and the value of stipends. These two concerns still remained a key part of the remit of the Parliamentary Commission, but for the first time the actual location of the parish churches and their accessibility were also to be seriously considered. The legislation acknowledged that:

> there be some kirks whereof the parish is of so large bounds that many parishioners, dwelling in rooms of the parish so remote from the kirk, who, for the great distance of the place or for the interjection of waters between their rooms and the kirks which often, especially in winter, are not passable or for some such other known impediment cannot have access and repair to the parish kirks at the ordinary times appointed for divine service and worship, and enjoy the comfort of the exercise thereof.[36]

The commissioners were therefore given permission to order the erection of churches in more convenient locations or even the establishment of new parishes with an adequate stipend in order to meet the needs of the local community.[37] This concern for the location of the parish church can be seen also in later commissions that were set up to deal with the valuation of teinds and the plantation of kirks. Even in the wake of the National Covenant, parliament returned to the terms of a Commission established by Charles I in 1633 and, after consultation, passed a new act in 1641. This again addressed fiscal matters but also gave the commissioners authority to erect churches in new locations and to alter parish boundaries:

> to disjoin too large and spacious kirks and plant them separately, and to cause the build and erect new kirks and appoint competent provisions for the ministers; to change kirks incommodiously situated to a more commodious part of the parish; to disjoin and dismember such parts and portions of the parish lying contiguous, and whereof one part of far distant from the proper parish kirk and more near and adjacent to the next adjacent and contiguous parish kirk from their own proper parish kirk from which the parts and portions are further distant and to unite and adjoin them to the other parish kirk to the which they are most adjacent; and also to unite kirks and parishes lying so near other and being so little bounds and small number of parishioners of that union of them shall be found more useful and conducible for the good and care of the parishioners of both the kirks and their edification ...[38]

Some sense of the impact of these commissions can be seen in the increasing legislation or referrals made by parliament relating to the alteration of parochial boundaries and the erection of new churches in more convenient locations.

The example of Bassendean is interesting because it provides some insights into not only the operation and workings of the Commission for the Plantation of Kirks and Valuation of Teinds but also the influence of vested interests and the local presbytery. In 1641, parliament had agreed that the uniting, dividing or dismembering of parishes should be done on the recommendation of the presbytery to the commissioners.[39] Unfortunately the records for the presbytery of Earlston, in which the parish lay, are not extant for this period but their role can be discerned in the surviving papers from the Teinds Office.[40] The minister of Bassendean, John Veitch, was also actively involved in the transplantation of the kirk. While the reasons that motivated him are not specified, he was in tune with the religious principles of the covenanting movement and was deprived after the Restoration for his refusal to conform to the reinstituted Episcopal structure within the Kirk.[41] Addressing the issue of the size of the parish and the location of the church was closely related to the need to ensure that there was adequate pastoral oversight for the community, which was ultimately achieved with the erection of the new kirk at Westruther.

After a period of nearly thirty years, on 30 June 1647 the Commission, after rehearsing the terms of the 1641 Act, resolved that the parishes of Bassendean and Gordon should be 'disjoynit, dismemberit and disuneited' as Bassendean had formerly been 'ane kirk of itself and servit be one minister'. The decision was made in spite of the opposition of some of the heritors, especially in the parish of Gordon, who as the local landowners were financially responsible for the parish and its church. The Act outlined the principal local estates of Evelaw, Thornydykes, Spottiswoode and Dirrington, together with other lands, which were assigned to the parish of Bassendean. The Commission ruled that there should be a new church built in the centre of the parish, and that all of the inhabitants should 'resort and ressave the benefit of the Word at the paroche kirk of Bassendean in all tyme comeing'. In spite of the resolution to build in the centre of the parish, which was favoured by the presbytery, after an appeal from some of the heritors the Commission decided instead that the new kirk should be built where the previous parish church stood.[42] The decision to return to this former religious site appears to have been because the walls of the old kirk were still standing and the burial ground had remained there; in addition, it was argued that there was a manse and glebe for the minister at Bassendean.[43] Rather than building a new church, the existing medieval structure was utilized; the rectangular windows in the south wall probably date from this period and conformed to the post-Reformation practice of allowing maximum light into the building for preaching the Word of God. It was later noted that the minister had preached for 'two yeres at a weill rebuilt kirk with pulpit and all other necesses'.[44] In spite of the Commission dividing the parish and addressing the matter of location, it seems that it did not make financial provision for the ministry at Bassendean. The heritors of the parish, therefore, agreed in early 1648, because 'a constant provision can not be had for the present because of the troubles and distractions of the tymes', to pay a stipend based on the value of the teinds they received until such time as an official settlement could be agreed.[45]

The agreement reached in 1647 to return parochial worship to its pre-Reformation site, 'because of an old chappell that was formerlie ther', was not universally accepted. Vietch referred two years later to 'our laitt sufferings because of our opposing the laitt unlawful judgement ... of those ... by whose preposterous industrie the kirke was seated at Bassen-deane'. He went on to characterize them as 'excluded from the Covenant because of their Malignancie'.[46] At the time of the dissolution of the united parish the presbytery had advised against it, arguing instead for the 'erecting of a new kirke in the upper end of that paroche in such a place as might best accommodat those who wer divided from the kirke of Gordonn'.[47] Two years later a supplication was submitted to parliament protesting about the decision reached by the Commission. The minister, John Veitch, and the parishioners

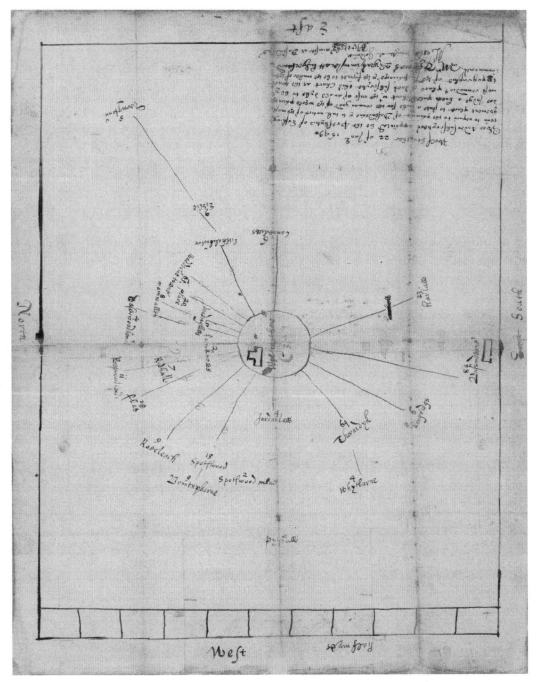

Figure 1.3. Map of the parish of Bassendean, 1649 (NAS TE5/112/12, reproduced courtesy of the National Archives of Scotland).

complained about 'the litlenesse and incapacitie of the said kirke as being no other then it that was the chappell of old and not above fyfteene footes wyde and so not able to conteine the on[e] halfe of the people'.[48] The inadequacy of the medieval church for accommodating the whole congregation was, however, only a secondary argument in the appeal for a new building to be erected; the main emphasis focused on the inappropriateness of the location.

In supporting the appeal the presbytery argued that Bassendean was at 'the outmost bounds of the paroche' and that 'almost all the parichioners ar very ill accommodate and put to a great deale of trouble and paines in attending divine service'. Veitch claimed that the remote location within the parish meant that the majority of the congregation were little better off than they had been when the parish had been united to Gordon. He observed that Bassendean was 'the remottest marche of the whole parioche not having so much as an house beyond it'.[49] When the case had been judged by the Commission in 1647 the presbytery had identified 'after perambulation' that Westruther was 'the most commodious and convenient place in regard of equal distance thereof from all the heritors and parishioners on all quarters of the said parish'.[50] The perambulation of the periphery and the identifying of the distances of townships within the parish by the presbytery was not unusual when it came to the transportation of the kirk to a new location or the redrawing of the boundaries. In the case of Bassendean, 'the said bounds of the parish extracted, drawn and subscribed by the commissioners of the said presbytery' were submitted to parliament with their supplication in 1649 and, remarkably, still survive.[51]

The map of the parish (Fig. 1.3) is subscribed by John Veitch and the ministers of the neighbouring parishes of Gordon and Legerwood.[52] It serves to show the relative location and distances of the farms and townships within the parish from Westruther, which appears in the centre, while Bassendean appears as the southernmost point in the parish. Comparison with a modern Ordnance Survey map has shown that these locations and distances were recorded fairly accurately by the ministers. In addition, the map also records the number of communicants in each of these scattered farms and townships, which can be seen in Table 1.

This detailed assessment of the distribution of the number of communicants confirms the claim of the presbytery that, unlike Bassendean, Westruther was the 'in the mids of the paroche and as they conceive the most convenient place as in all uther respects so also in regaird of the equall distance thereof from all the heritors and parochiners on all quarters of the paroche'.[53] What the map also shows, though, is that Bassendean was the largest single settlement in the parish in 1649, with eighty-four communicants, which makes the initial decision by the Commission to relocate the church there more understandable.

The petition to parliament for the relocation of the church to Westruther was supported not only by the presbytery but also the General Assembly of the Kirk, which appointed four of its members, including the prominent ministers John Livingstone and John Row, to assist them.[54] The transporting of the parish church was opposed by several of the local heritors, however, who argued that the decision of the Commission for the Plantation of Kirks and Valuation of Teinds could not be overruled.[55] They had earlier also complained both that Westruther was 'verie incommodious pairt within a moss' and about the cost of this move for such a poor parish, which they calculated as being between 8,000 and 9,000 marks for the building of a new church as well as the purchase of land for a manse and a glebe.[56] Parliament, influenced it would seem by the presbytery and its topographical depiction of the parish, ruled that the church should be 'transported from where it now

Table 1. Distribution of communicants and distance from Westruther in 1649*

Settlement	Distance from Westruther in miles	Number of communicants
Bassendean	2¼ (2½)	84
Bruntaburn	2 (2¼)	9
Cammerlaws	1½ (1½)	6
Dirrington	3¼	5
Dradinglaws	1	5
Easterwoodhead	1¾ (1¾)	4
Evelaw	2 (2¼)	9
Fauknows	¾	2
Flass	1¾ (1¾)	28
Harelaw	1¾ (1¾)	23
Jordonlaw	¾ (¾)	4
Langridgs	2	6
Litlhaliburton	1½	0
Mamwalles	1½	8
Pyatshaw	2½ (3¼)	0
Ridhall	1½	7
Raecleugh	1¾ (1¾)	9
Spottiswoode	1¾ (2)	2
Spottiswoode milne	1¾	15
Thornydykes	1½ (1½)	64
Wedderlie Place	1 ¼ (1)	20
Wedderlie Town	1 ¼ (1¼)	65
Westerwoodhead	2	11
Westruther	–	35
Whiteburn	2 (3)	4

* Where the modern township or farm can be identified the current spelling has been given and the distance from Westruther according to the Ordnance Survey map given in parentheses.

stands, being a remote part and nook of the parish, to that part of the parish called Wellstruther Green and to be built there as a commodious place and most equal and proportional distance to the whole heritors and parishioners of the parish of Bassendean'.[57] Perhaps in the light of the earlier concerns that had been raised, the Act went on to rule that 'the whole heritors and parishioners thereof to contribute proportionally for building the said new kirk and for buying and carrying materials and contribution to the expenses and everything necessary for building and completing thereof'.[58]

The aspirations to build a new church are reflected in 'the exact topographie of the paroche of Bassendean', which depicted the simple rectangular medieval church being replaced by a T-plan building at Westruther which accorded more to the needs of Reformed worship[59] (Figs 1.4 and 1.5). In fact, overleaf there was a very simple plan of the building, with windows at each gable end, two doors in the south wall and a centrally located pulpit with windows either side and facing the laird's aisle, which had its own door. The church

Figure 1.4. Westruther parish church, north side: site of the now-demolished laird's aisle
(photograph by A. Spicer).

erected at Westruther was altered in 1752 and abandoned during the mid 19th century for
a new site across the road, but the ruins of the earlier church have survived. There is no
longer a projecting laird's aisle – all that remains is a simple rectangular structure – but the
pattern of windows and doors in the south wall reflects the original design.

The transplantation of the church of Bassendean to a new site at Westruther represented a
triumph for the Reformed Kirk over the particular interests of the heritors, based on cogent
arguments about the greater accessibility of the new site for the majority of the parish and
the inadequate accommodation of the medieval structure. The former church, which was
built as much with defence in mind as the celebration of the mass, was replaced in the
mid 17th century with a new T-plan kirk which was characteristic of Scottish Reformed
kirks and better suited to the requirements for preaching the Word of God. This particular
case study demonstrates more widely the efforts which were undertaken across Scotland
to ensure that the location of churches accorded with the needs of Reformed worship.
Westruther was only one of a number of churches erected during the early 17th century
and, while not all of the proposed projects reached fruition, it is nonetheless indicative
of the attempts to redraw the religious landscape. This chapter has not focused closely on
the discussions over financial matters, but the correspondence between the parish and the
teinds it yielded meant that any attempt to alter the boundaries of the parish required

Figure 1.5. Westruther parish church, south side (photograph by A. Spicer).

careful negotiation and the cooperation of the heritors. This was an important element in the work of the Commissions for the Plantation of Kirks and Valuation of Teinds, which played a prominent part in effecting this reorganization of the parochial system. Its importance was reflected in the need to make adequate provision for this work when the Act of Union was debated in 1707.[60] Bassendean also illustrates the key role that was taken by the presbyteries in examining the location of existing churches, identifying alternative sites and working with the Commission, but also being prepared to challenge their decisions in the interests of spiritual oversight. In this case study, their topographical assessment seems to have played an important role in influencing parliament's decision. While in other states, such as England, a degree of continuity can be discerned in the parochial system after the Reformation,[61] in Scotland there was a more radical and concerted effort to overthrow that more ancient religious landscape and ensure that churches were in the most commodious and convenient places for Reformed worship.

APPENDIX

Legislation for the erection of new churches or the alteration of parish boundaries 1592–1649[62]

1592   For approving of the kirk built by John Shaw of Greenock
1592   For building of a second kirk within the parish of St Andrews
1594   Act regarding the kirk of Burntisland
1600   Ratification of the infeftment of Lewis
        (Included provision for building 10 parish churches)
1606   Act regarding the erection of the kirk of Leith to the north of the bridge in a parish kirk
1606   Act regarding the dismembering of certain towns from the kirk of Ellon and incorporating of the same to the kirk of Slains
1606   Erection of the kirk of Preston
1606   Act regarding the erection of the kirk of Portincraig
1609   Act for uniting certain kirks in Annandale
1609   Act regarding the kirk of Leith
1609   Act regarding the kirk of Carmyllie
1612   Act for translating of the kirk of Gullane to Dirleton
1612   Act regarding the kirk of Crailing, declaring the same to be a parish kirk
1617   Regarding the erection of the kirk of Ballantrae
1617   Act for changing of the kirk of Strageath
1617   For changing of the kirk of Lauder
1621   Regarding the plantation of kirks as yet unplanted
        (Included responses to nine supplications for disuniting parishes and erecting new churches)
1621   Act disjoining the parts lying within the ports of Edinburgh from St Cuthberts and Holyroodhouse
1621   Act in favour of the Laird of Buchanan
        (Lands of Buchanan dissolved from the parish of Luss)
1621   Act regarding the union of the lands of Kinninmonth to the kirk of Ceres
1633   Commission regarding the disjoining of Meikle and Little Daltons etc.
1633   Commission regarding the kirks of Nisbet and Crailing
1633   Act in favour of Sir James Hamilton of Priestfield
        (Lands of Priestfield to be annexed to the parish of Duddingston)
1633   Act in favour of [John Campbell], lord Loudoun
        (New parish and church of Muir established)
1633   Act in favour of [John Lindsay], lord Lindsay
        (Lands disjoined from Crail to the parish of Kingsbarns)
1633   Act in favour of [Alexander Forbes], laird of Pitsligo
        (Ratifies the erection of the new kirk at Pitsligo and separation from Aberdour)
1633   Act in favour of the ministers of Portpatrick
        (Ratifies the erection of the parish kirk at Portpatrick)
1633   Act in favour of the kirk of Pittenweem
1633   Act in favour of the kirk of Eyemouth

1633   Act of dissolution of Lugton and Melville from the parish of St Andrews, and union thereof to Dalkeith and Lasswade

1633   Act disuniting the kirks of Abdie and Newburgh

1633   Act regarding the parish kirk of Strichen

1633   Act uniting certain lands to the kirks of Corstorphine and Hailes

1633   Act regarding the re-edifying of the kirk of Beith

1641   Act regarding the ratification of the erection of the new kirk of Kilmarnock

1641   Act regarding the erection of the kirk of Elie

1641   Ratification and act regarding the erection of the kirk of Anstruther Easter

1641   Act regarding the disuniting of the kirk of Denny from Falkirk

1641   Act of erection of the kirk of Careston

1641   Ratification regarding the disuniting of Kirkmabreck and Kirkdale from Anwoth

1641   Act regarding the erection of the kirk of Longside

1641   Ratification in favour of South Queensferry
         (Erection into a separate parish)

1645   Act for transporting of the kirk of Kirkmabreck

1645   Act anent the erection of a new kirk of the landward parish of St Andrews

1645   Act anent the erection of the kirk of Carsphairn

1647   Act kirk of Glencorse

1647   Act kirk of Glenluce

1647   Act new kirk of Calder

1647   Act for transporting the kirks of Logie-Montrose and Pert

1648   Ratification disjoining the kirk of Ogston from St Andrews and uniting the same to Kynnedor

1648   Act erecting the kirk of Morvingsyde

1649   Act in favour of the inhabitants of the Chanonry of Ross

1649   Act anent the transplantation of the kirk of Bassendean

1649   Act in favour of the town of Bo'ness anent the erection of a new kirk

1649   Recommendation to the presbytery of Biggar in favour of Sir James Hope [of Hopetoun], knight, anent the erection of a kirk

1649   Act in favour of the ministers of the presbytery of Duns anent the parish of Eccles

1649   Act anent the transplantation of the kirk of Dunscore

1649   Act in favour of the parishes of Kilmadock and Kincardine

1649   Act anent the [presbytery] of Dumbarton anent dividing the parish of Kilpatrick

NOTES

1. NAS, TE5/112/10: Act of Parliament ordering the redrawing of the parish boundaries of Bassendean in 1641.
2. Spicer 2003, 31–4; Spicer 2007, 41–8.
3. Spicer 2005, 87–90. See also Walsham 2011.
4. *Records of the Kirk of Scotland*, 279; *APS*, V, 351.
5. Cowan 1961, 43–55.
6. Spicer 2007, 51, 57, 63. See also Spicer 2010 for a 17th-century case study.
7. On financial matters, see Connell 1815, I, 141–257; Cormack 1930, 79–108; Foster 1975, 156–72; MacInnes 1991, 49–76.
8. *APS*, V, 128.
9. *APS*, IV, 250, 441.
10. *APS*, VI pt. 2, 228–9. In the archives the new site is called variously as Wellstruther, Wellstruther Green, Woolstruther and Wolfstruther but for convenience the current name of Westruther has been used apart from in quotations.
11. Stephen 2007, 61.
12. Scott 1866–71, II, 165.
13. *Geographical Collections relating to Scotland*, III, 179.
14.

    Huntly Wood – the wa's down
    Bassendean and Barrastown
    Heckspeth wi' the yellow hair
    Gordon gowks for evermair

    Chambers 1870, 209. The rhyme is undated but the definition of 'gowk' as simpleton, dates from the 17th century, see *Dictionary of the Scots Language* at <http://www.dsl.ac.uk/>. As the poem relates to places within the parish of Gordon, it might even be conjectured that it could date to the early 17th century when the parishes were united.
15. Cowan 1961, 44–5, 50–1; Cowan 1967a, 15.
16. Cowan 1967a, 15, 215; Cowan & Easson 1976, 145.
17. Cowan 1961, 43–55; Cowan 1967a, iii–v; Cowan 1967b.
18. Cowan & Easson 1976, 146.
19. *APS*, IV, 647.
20. Brooke 2000, 10, 29, 362.
21. Robson 1896, 216–19; MacGibbon & Ross 1897, III, 412–13; RCAHMS 1915, 158; Cruft *et al.* 2006, 117; RCAHMS, Canmore Database No. 57337 at <http://canmore.rcahms.gov.uk/>.
22. Cowan & Easson 1976, 146. See also Merriman 2000.
23. *L&P Henry VIII* 21 Pt 1, 627, No. 1279.
24. NAS CH8/16.
25. NAS TE5/112/19.
26. Scott 1866–71, II, 165; Haws 1972, 22.
27. *Acts and Proceedings of the General Assemblies of the Kirk of Scotland*, I, 33.
28. *The Second Book of Discipline*, 104–5; *Acts and Proceedings*, II, 480–7; MacDonald 1998, 21.
29. *APS*, IV, 531.
30. *APS*, IV, 532; Foster 1975, 161–4.
31. 'For distance of place or others lawful causes may be found incommodious to be united' *APS*, IV, 532.
32. *APS*, IV, 649.
33. NAS, TE5/112/19; *APS*, III, 623–4.
34. Calderwood (1842–49), VII, 302–3.
35. *APS*, IV, 605–6.
36. *APS*, IV, 605–6.
37. *APS*, IV, 606–7.
38. *APS*, V, 401–2.
39. *APS*, V, 402, 689.
40. NAS TE5/112.
41. Scott (1866–71), II, 165–6. He was the brother of William Veitch, see *ODNB* at <http://www.oxforddnb.com/view/article/28174> [last modified May 2005].
42. NAS TE5/112/10.
43. NAS TE5/112/10, 18, 19.
44. NAS TE5/112/19; Robson 1896, 217.
45. NAS TE5/112/9.
46. NAS TE5/112/18.
47. NAS TE5/112/18.
48. NAS TE5/112/18.
49. NAS TE5/112/18, 20.
50. NAS TE5/112/18.
51. NAS TE5/112/12, 18.
52. NAS TE5/112/12.
53. NAS TE5/112/20.
54. *The Records of the General Assemblies of the Church of Scotland holden in Edinburgh the years 1648 and 1649*, 149.
55. *APS*, VI, pt. 2, 228–9.
56. NAS TE5/112/19.
57. *APS*, VI pt. 2, 229.
58. *APS*, VI pt. 2, 229.
59. NAS TE5/112/12.
60. Stephen 2007, 48, 61, 66, 87.
61. See Whyte 2007 and Hindle 2008.
62. This list records parliamentary legislation relating to the division of parishes, as well as the erection of new churches. Therefore it does not list legislation which was solely concerned with the financial aspects of the erection or division of parishes, or the provision of an additional minister without any changes to the structure of the parish. The

parliamentary records also include supplications, some of which were referred to the Commission for the Plantation of Kirks and Valuation of Teinds, but as these were requests rather than decisions made by parliament they are not listed. Multiple entries are also not included, with the exception of the case of a second church in the parish of St Andrews where further legislation was enacted fifty years later. Where the purpose of the legislation and its inclusion is not immediately clear from the title, a brief explanation has been included in parentheses. Source: *The Records of the Parliaments of Scotland to 1707*, K.M. Brown *et al.* (eds) (St Andrews, 2007–9), at <http://www.rps.ac.uk/> [Date accessed: 21 April 2009].

BIBLIOGRAPHY

Acts and Proceedings of the General Assemblies of the Kirk of Scotland, ed. T. Thomson, 1839–45, 3 vols, Maitland Club 49.

The Acts of the Parliament of Scotland, ed. T. Thomson & C. Innes, 1814–75, 12 vols, Edinburgh.

Brooke, C.J. 2000, *Safe Sanctuaries: Security and Defence in Anglo-Scottish Border Churches, 1290–1690*, Edinburgh: John Donald.

Calderwood, D. 1842–1849, *The History of the Kirk of Scotland*, ed. T. Thomson, Edinburgh: The Wodrow Society.

Chambers, R. 1870, *The Popular Rhymes of Scotland*, London: R. & W. Chambers.

Clarke, P. & Claydon, T. (eds) 2010, *God's Bounty? The Churches and the Natural World*. Studies in Church History 46. Woodbridge: Boydell & Brewer.

Connell, J. 1815, *Treatise on the Law of Scotland Respecting Tithes and the Stipends of Parochial Clergy*, Edinburgh: Peter Hill.

Cormack, A.A. 1930, *Teinds and Agriculture. An Historical Survey*, Oxford: Oxford University Press.

Coster, W. & Spicer, A. (eds) 2005, *Sacred Space in Early Modern Europe*, Cambridge: Cambridge University Press.

Cowan, I.B. 1961, 'The development of the parochial system in medieval Scotland', *Scottish Historical Review* 40: 43–55.

Cowan, I.B. 1967a, *The Parishes of Medieval Scotland*, Edinburgh: Scottish Record Society.

Cowan, I.B. 1967b, 'Vicarages and the cure of souls in medieval Scotland', *Records of the Scottish Church History Society* 16/2: 111–27.

Cowan, I.B. & Easson, D.E. 1976, *Medieval Religious Houses, Scotland*, London: Longman.

Cruft, K., Dunbar, J. & Fawcett, R. 2006, *The Buildings of Scotland: Borders*, New Haven (CT): Yale University Press.

Dictionary of the Scots Language <http://www.dsl.ac.uk/> [last modified 2004].

Foster, W.R. 1975, *The Church Before the Covenants: the Church of Scotland, 1596–1638*, Edinburgh: Scottish Academic Press.

Gaimster D. & Gilchrist, R. (eds) 2003, *The Archaeology of Reformation, 1480–1580*. Society for Post-Medieval Archaeology Monograph 1. Leeds: Maney.

Geographical Collections relating to Scotland, ed. A. Mitchell, 1906–8, 3 vols, Edinburgh: Scottish History Society, 51–3.

Halvorson, M.J. & Spierling, K.E. (eds) 2008, *Defining the Community in Early Modern Europe*, Aldershot: Ashgate.

Haws, C.H. 1972, *Scottish Parish Clergy at the Reformation, 1540–1570*, Edinburgh: Scottish Record Society, New Series No. 3.

Hindle, S. 2008, 'Beating the bounds of the parish: power, memory and identity in the English local community, c. 1500–1700', in Halvorson & Spierling 2008, 205–27.

Letters and Papers, Foreign and Domestic, of the Reign of Henry VIII, ed. J.S. Brewer *et al.* 1862–1932, 23 vols, London: HMSO.

Macdonald, A.R. 1998, *The Jacobean Kirk, 1567–1625: Sovereignty, Polity and Liturgy*, Aldershot: Ashgate.

MacGibbon, D. & Ross, T. 1896–97, *The Ecclesiastical Architecture of Scotland from the Earliest Christian Times to the Seventeenth Century*, Edinburgh: David Douglas.

MacInnes, A.I. 1991, *Charles I and the Making of the Covenanting Movement, 1625–1641*, Edinburgh: John Donald.

Merriman, M. 2000, *The Rough Wooings: Mary, Queen of Scots, 1542–1551*, East Linton: Tuckwell.

NAS CH8/16 Letter by John, Archbishop of St Andrews, to the dean of Christianity of the Merss, anent repair of churches there, 9 April 1556.

NAS TE5/112 Papers relating to Teinds and Teind Administration, Berwickshire: Parishes etc. of Westruther (Bassendean), 1631–1650.

Oxford Dictionary of National Biography, Oxford: Oxford University Press.

RCAHMS, 1915, *Sixth Report and Inventory of Monuments and Constructions in the County of Berwick*, Edinburgh: HMSO.

The Records of the General Assemblies of the Church of Scotland holden in Edinburgh the years 1648 and 1649, ed. A.F. Mitchell & J. Christie, 1896. Scottish History Society 25. Edinburgh.

Records of the Kirk of Scotland Containing the Acts and Proceedings of the General Assemblies, ed. A. Peterkin, 1838, Edinburgh: Sutherland.

The Records of the Parliaments of Scotland to 1707, ed. K.M. Brown *et al.* (St Andrews, 2007–9) at <http://www.rps.ac.uk/> [Date accessed: 21 April 2009].

Robson, J. 1896, *The Churches and Churchyards of Berwickshire*, Kelso: J. & J.H. Rutherford.

Scott, H. 1866–71, *Fasti Ecclesiæ Scoticanæ: The Succession of Ministers in the Parish Churches of Scotland, From the Reformation, A.D. 1560, to the Present Time*, Edinburgh: William Paterson.

The Second Book of Discipline, ed. J. Kirk, 1980, Edinburgh: St Andrew Press.

Spicer, A. 2003, 'Iconoclasm and adaptation: the Reformation of the churches in Scotland and the Netherlands', in Gaimster & Gilchrist 2003, 29–43.

Spicer, A. 2005, '"What kinde of house a kirk is": conventicles, consecrations and the concept of sacred space in post-Reformation Scotland', in Coster & Spicer 2005, 81–103.

Spicer, A. 2007, *Calvinist Churches in Early Modern Europe*, Manchester: Manchester University Press.

Spicer, A. 2010, '"God hath put such secretes in nature": The Reformed Kirk, church-building and the religious landscape in early modern Scotland', in Clarke & Claydon 2010, 260–75.

Stephen, J. 2007, *Scottish Presbyterians and the Act of Union 1707*, Edinburgh: Edinburgh University Press.

Walsham, A. 2011, *The Reformation of the Landscape. Religion, Identity and Memory in Early Modern Britain and Ireland*, Oxford: Oxford University Press.

Whyte, N. 2007, 'Landscape, memory and custom: parish identities c. 1550–1700', *Social History* 32, 166–86.

ABBREVIATIONS

APS	*The Acts of the Parliament of Scotland*
HMSO	Her Majesty's Stationery Office
L&P Henry VIII	*Letters and Papers, Foreign and Domestic, of the Reign of Henry VIII*
NAS	National Archives of Scotland, Edinburgh
ODNB	*Oxford Dictionary of National Biography*
RCAHMS	Royal Commission on the Ancient and Historic Monuments of Scotland

Was Original Best? Refitting the Churches of the Diocese of Le Mans, 1562–1598

Philippa Woodcock*

This chapter will consider the value placed on religious material culture during iconoclastic attack in the diocese of Le Mans, 1562–1598. It explores the methods used by the cathedral and parish churches to regain and restore their religious fabric and explains how this relates to the several different purposes of iconoclasm. It will ask if the return of original objects was of paramount importance, or whether the re-creation of an item of equivalent value or appearance was sufficient to re-create a Catholic religious landscape.

INTRODUCTION

The diocese of Le Mans in the *Ancien Régime* county of Maine has but a small place in the historiography of the French Wars of Religion (1562–98).[1] The region lay between the more turbulent regions of Normandy and the Loire valley, and witnessed skirmishes rather than significant battles between the Catholic and Protestant (or Huguenot) troops who traversed the area. It had few large, settled Huguenot congregations, in comparison with neighbouring regions, and after the Peace of Amboise of 1563 the Huguenots were deprived of places of public worship in Maine, removing a focus of tension and conflict. In the last forty years local historians such as Plessix and Bouton have reconstructed the political events surrounding the rise of the local Huguenot congregation and factional conflict.[2] They argue that, rather than seeking to find evidence of major religious change, the diocese is valuable for its history of continuity. It provides the story of how an early modern society coped with a sustained period of upheaval, the destruction of much of its religious treasures and sporadic iconoclastic attacks on the parish church for over thirty years. The policies adopted by faithful parishioners to defend their religious beliefs were successful, for in 1598 the diocese of Le Mans remained Catholic, and its cathedral (Fig. 2.1) and churches were busily engaged in rebuilding and re-creating their religious landscape.

Building on 19th-century antiquarian work on religious pluralism, local specialists such as Michel Ménard, Dominique Eraud and Geneviève Bresc-Bautier have developed the history of the diocese immediately after the Wars, using visual culture to explore popular piety and reactions to crises such as the plague and the Fronde. This work has rediscovered an artistic culture unique to Maine: in particular, they celebrate the grand retables installed at the east end of the diocese's churches, often in place of damaged altars, and the terra-cotta statues made by local masters to replace those destroyed in the Wars.[3] However, the immediate reaction to Huguenot activity and the issue of how, during the Wars, Catholic rebuilding was handled has received less attention. This chapter will examine the material

Figure 2.1. East end of the cathedral of St Julien, Le Mans (photograph by P. Woodcock).

culture of the earlier attacks upon the religious landscape of the diocese of Le Mans. What form did iconoclasm take, and what objects did Huguenots focus their attacks upon? Were these items that were essential to the sacramental or the physical life of the Church? In turn, was it necessary to regain every item for a Catholic church to feel itself whole and unpolluted after attack? If it was not possible to re-create the religious landscape of 1561, what other methods were available to rebuild the Church and its fabric throughout the Wars?

The sources for this work are varied. Antiquarian accounts include Abbé Piolin's six-volume history of the diocese of Le Mans, Abbé Ledru's *Histoire de la prise du Mans par les Calvinistes en 1562* and Anjubault and Chardon's reconstruction of the Huguenot congregation.[4] These accounts are largely seen from a Catholic position. They nevertheless draw on original material, in particular the cathedral of St Julien's *Plaintes et doléances*, the Consistory records of the Huguenot congregation and legal records from 1562–3.[5] The *Plaintes* were compiled after the cathedral of St Julien in Le Mans was desecrated in May 1562 and record exactly what was damaged, destroyed or stolen by the Huguenots, with an estimated total value of 256,537 *livres* and 6 *sous*.[6] This should in itself be treated with caution, as its authors may have sought to exaggerate the ferocity of the Huguenot attack to atone for the acquiescence of some of the canons in allowing the Huguenot leaders into the cathedral.[7] Members of the Le Mans congregation were easily identified, as when the Huguenots left the city on 11 July 1562 they left behind their church attendance registers.[8] This information was used to bring cases against followers of the Reformed faith for heresy and sacrilege. These legal cases should also be used with caution; both Ledru and Aubry question the veracity of some of the testimony.[9] However, they remind us that reaction can be as much about attempts to recoup a lost cellar of wine as about a desire to reconstruct the religious world.[10] Finally, parish *comptes des fabriques* speak of individual churches' experience of iconoclasm. These records are not widely extant, but the parish records used in conjunction with those of St Julien show that reconstruction could follow several impulses. It was not necessarily immediate, but reflected the political situation and the nature of the attack.

ICONOCLASM

Iconoclasm in the diocese was not random and had various distinct aims. It could be measured or disorderly, but it was never mindless. Le Mans, following the example of Orléans, was occupied and led by Huguenots for a period, so it is possible to speak of the city, if not the diocese, experiencing magisterial iconoclasm – that is, directed by the authorities.[11] For the diocese as a whole, iconoclasm can be classed into economic, psychological and sacrilegious attacks. It is important to remember that iconoclasm was not just about the destruction of an object. The evidence suggests that the idea of possession of an item made holy by belonging to a church, however quotidian, was as valid a tool for conveying messages of religious control as outright destruction of the same object.

The *Plaintes et doléances* were an equal riposte to the thorough destruction enacted in the cathedral and what appears to have been a carefully planned occupation of the town. The Huguenot congregation in Maine had been growing since the 1540s, and found protection in the châteaux of local nobles.[12] Centres of Reformed faith grew up at Bonnétable, Fresnay-le-Vicomte, Laval and Mamers, while the Consistory in Le Mans was founded on 1 January 1561 by Henri Salvert, a former monk, and strengthened under the pastorship of Pierre Merlin, sent later that year from Geneva. As the Consistory records illustrate, the Manceaux Huguenots included wealthy citizens and influential political figures such as Jean de Vignolles, the *lieutenant-particulier* of *la sénéchaussée du Maine*, and Thibault Bouju, *juge magistrat criminel au siège présidial*.[13] Reformed worship became increasingly visible as services were held in the main marketplace. The congregation reached around 4,000 members at the end of 1561.[14] After the massacre of Huguenot worshippers at Vassy in March 1562 and the hardening of religious factions the Huguenots of Le Mans took advantage of an absent bishop, Charles d'Angennes de Rambouillet, to ensure their survival.[15] On 3 April 1562 the Huguenot notables, under the command of de Vignolles, took control of the town gates and the château. Initially, the occupation was peaceful and controlled, but inevitably the rowdier and more extreme elements of the congregation demanded that no time be wasted in cleansing the religious landscape. The officers lost command of their brethren by early May, who commenced to attack the town's convents, including the Jacobins and Cordeliers.[16]

In response, the Huguenot elders and civic officers decided to identify the key treasures of the cathedral and protect them from destruction, not to preserve them but to convert these objects into cash and ingots of gold, following the Huguenot leader Condé's request.[17] An inventory was taken of the cathedral's treasures on 7 May, with the co-operation of the remaining canons, recording the 'ornaments, jewels, relics and other goods and riches of the said church'.[18] Two Huguenot goldsmiths evaluated and recorded each object. Precious treasures were removed from the cathedral, and controlled demolition began. This was a case of magisterial iconoclasm to prevent wastage of valuable resources and to fund the wider Huguenot war effort.

Huguenot goldsmiths were able to both advise of the value of materials and provide the expertise and networks to convert gold and jewels into money for waging war and defending Le Mans.[19] After the occupation Catholics expressed surprise that the same goldsmiths who had created the vessels of the mass would so readily destroy their works of art; devoted to the new Reformed faith, they were the ideal men to remove the visible richness of the Catholic church and convert it into money to do their God's will.[20] The work was ongoing when the Huguenots fled the town. When the Catholics returned they found abandoned ingots of gold, the melted-down cathedral treasures which the Huguenots had been unable to carry.[21]

Huguenots also removed baser metals from the cathedral. Iron railings, closures and copper decorations were stripped from altars, chapels, pillars, windows and doors.[22] The canons were jubilant to find in de Vignolle's splendid but abandoned house 'the greater part of the copper from the choir of St Julien, … [part] of the baptismal font, brass tomb plates and railings'.[23] These were practical removals, easily converted into cash and useful war materials, but also a work of God, for altar railings and tombs represented the Catholic hierarchical structure and beliefs about death. The destruction of these items was as much sacrilegious as economic iconoclasm.

However, it was only a matter of two days before the mob chaos took over the proceedings and 'the pillage' became 'systematic'.[24] St Julien was looted, its altars and imagery desecrated, its relics shattered, its books burnt, its cellar emptied and its glass smashed. It is against the *Plaintes et doléances* that the cathedral's inevitable subsequent destruction was later measured, and supported claims against the Huguenots who had committed 'pillages, robberies, demolition of altars and carrying away all the riches like chalices [and] ornaments'.[25]

On 11 July 1562 the Huguenots fled Le Mans. A royal army approached the town, and de Vignolles *et al.* decided to join their co-religionists in Normandy.[26] Accompanied by an 'indecent' number of women, they moved northwards, attacking the churches in their path and stripping them of their convertible wealth.[27] Their attacks were particularly ferocious in Beaumont-le-Vicomte and Fresnay-le-Vicomte, towns affiliated to the Protestant House of Navarre and where there were sizeable Huguenot communities.[28] As the Huguenots became organized into highly mobile military bands, the rest of the diocese found itself vulnerable to sacramental and economic iconoclastic attack.

Attacks on parish churches followed as on the cathedral; portable wealth was gathered, and the instruments of the mass and intercession of the saints destroyed – altars, statues, relics, vessels, chasubles and copes.[29] Considered planning is also present in the items that were stolen by the Huguenots. While the first-phase attacks on the cathedral and parish churches were arguably about massive destruction, later visits to the parishes can be read as carefully targeted 'shopping trips' for important items. Once again, metal objects dominate. Claxons were removed, but heavy bells were left to fall to the ground, smashed or shot. For example, in 1562 bells were destroyed at Beaumont, Fresnay and Pirmil.[30] As at St Julien, other small metal objects such as grilles and railings were also taken rather than destroyed, conjuring up an image of itinerant tinker Huguenots, roaming the countryside.

The robbery in particular of keys and claxons from both St Julien and parish churches can bear many interpretations. The theft of a relatively cheap key made an expensive lock redundant, while a beaterless bell was of little use; significant inconvenience was occasioned by the theft of these most portable of items. The *Plaintes* devote six pages of description to the theft of keys and closures alone: in the attack on St Julien, de Vignolles was noted to have deliberately taken the key to the bell tower, along with that to the room where the blacksmith made the keys to the church.[31] He was expressing his control over the security of the church and its ability to communicate to the parish and any friendly soldiers through the sonic landscape. Equally, this was another way to attack the belief in the intercession of the saints, as bells were christened with a patron's name and were most commonly dedicated to the Virgin Mary.[32]

The idea that beaters and keys were deliberately targeted for theft is evident in a variety of more psychological interpretations. The key was symbolic of St Peter, and hence Catholicism. By owning the key the Huguenots violated ideas about the apostolic succession and laid vulnerable the Catholic church and its buildings. Without the key to the great door, the protective function of any church was reduced and any remaining valuables exposed. It meant that the Huguenots could re-enter the church at will and effectively placed the Catholic congregation at their mercy. Other keys gave control over coffers of title deeds; the initial iconoclastic rage might destroy the documents, but without a key any future document was unsafe and the coffer rendered worthless, as well as leaving the church with little proof of its financial and property rights. This links closely with Aubry's thesis that the iconoclasm in Le Mans was aimed at destroying centuries-old titles to church land rented by Huguenot notables. 'The said Bouju, de Veignolles [their] accomplices and allies took, smashed, ripped and carried away the letters of foundation', eradicating both the financial relationship and the Church's social position over these rising men.[33] Iconoclasm had a social aspect too. The destruction of aristocratic heraldry by the *noblesse de robe* was a strike at the social domination of the *noblesse d'epée* as much as an attack on the Church.[34]

RESTORATION AND RE-CREATION

For Catholics, the focus on restoring the church, specifically to its pre-1562 status, became a long-lasting project frustrated by elusive peace treaties and rebel behaviour. The importance placed on restoring the original appearance of the church was the natural partner to the desire to free the site from all sullying Protestant influence. Churches attacked by the Huguenots had to be reconciled; the cathedral underwent the ceremony on 19 July 1562, while the canons tried to re-establish a holy precinct around the building by their ritual processions through Le Mans.[35] Physical cleansing went so far as to disinter the bodies of Huguenots buried within holy ground, as at Assé-le-Boisne.[36] Above all, parish church accounts speak of 'repairing' the church, but, as with iconoclasm, this could take many forms.[37]

The first and perhaps most successful tactic employed to return the church to its original appearance was prevention. If warned of imminent attack, church wardens could take their most precious objects and try to find a secure place to hide them. This was seen at Luché-Pringé, where early renaissance statues of the school of Michel Colombe were hidden in the walls of nearby houses.[38] At the chapel of St Michel de la Barre, the parish paid for statues to be taken to a place of safety.[39] The canons of Le Mans tried to hide the cathedral's treasures in the cellars under their houses, but these objects were found rather more quickly.[40] More frequently, restorative measures had to be taken after the pillage and destruction. The legal mechanisms followed by the cathedral as an institution widely demonstrate that iconoclasm did not necessarily mean destruction, and that rebuilding was as much a story of revenge and retribution as the re-creation of a religious world.

The *Plaintes et doléances* reflect a shared understanding with the Huguenots of the sacramental but also the financial value of the objects lost or destroyed during 1562. This catalogue does not concentrate upon the sacred nature of the objects lost; the language to describe the divine is minimal. Instead, the inventory focuses upon the objects' exact material composition and worth. This is unsurprising, for as with the unfortunately lost Huguenot estimate, the *Plaintes* were compiled with the assistance of experts: jewellers, goldsmiths, master glaziers and sculptors. This is evident in the precise description of an important altar to St Anne 'of rich craftmanship, having table and contretable and enriched at the top and at the bottom by niches filled with figures *à la moderne*, the entirety worth four hundred *livres tourn[ois]* ... with regard to the masonry'.[41]

This descriptive style suggests that the wealth of the Church during the French Wars of Religion should be thought of as both spiritual and fiscal – akin to the economic concept of the 'treasury of the Church' described by Sixtus IV in 1476.[42] The church building was evidence of the wealth of the second estate and proof of its links to the nobles of the first; the whole cathedral building was a corporate status symbol, stamped with badges of episcopal, noble and royal patronage.[43] These attitudes may have been sharpened in a period of war when wealth needed to be rapidly gathered to pay royal taxes or papal impositions. For example, in 1563 the canons of Le Mans were deemed liable for a third of the royal levy of 6,000 *livres*, raised to repair the town's defences, while in 1574 the cathedral was obliged to sell some pieces of silverware to pay another royal levy.[44] This was an avowedly mercenary interest in material riches, suggesting that rebuilding the cathedral was as much about re-creating its wealth, and the canons' status, as restoring a place of faith. The *Plaintes* functions as a record of what was lost, but also as a target for what had to be regained; if the original item was not available, then its estimate provided a target for payment to be extracted from those who had destroyed it.

This attention to material detail was translated into the cathedral's attack upon the iconoclastic malefactors. In the cases brought against the Huguenots in 1562–3 the accused could be tried and condemned in person or *in absentia* for committing 'pillage, sacrilege ... murder, conspiracy to take the town ... incitements, enrolments, contributions, sedition and rebellion demolition of the Church [and the] breaking of [its] images and altars'.[45] Frustratingly for the cathedral, the royal decree of September 1562 exempted the majority of the Huguenot congregation, except for their leaders and the main iconoclasts, from trial.[46] Most had of course fled into Normandy or England, and were tried *in absentia* and condemned to death. Those that remained were executed before the cathedral's west door, but their deaths did not restore the material wealth of the cathedral. In recompense, confiscation of all Huguenot property was authorized.[47] This restored some of the monetary wealth, as well as physical goods such as the wine and food which had been stolen from the cathedral and 'Catholic' houses. The determination to recoup value survived pacifications and truces, for the canons were still in pursuit of individual iconoclasts in 1574, and in 1587 issued a further call for stolen objects to be returned.[48] Of course, the canons were not only concerned with restoring the balance of material wealth. Their pursuit of items through legal cases clearly speaks of the perceived importance of restoring the cathedral to its appearance in 1561.

These cases were also built on the expectation that it was possible to recoup items. The cathedral's pursuit of those who had damaged their most precious items was almost an act of absolution; if they could be punished, then some sort of ritual cleansing of the icono-clastic pollution could be considered to have taken place. But the replacement of items also meant a return of the cathedral's wealth and, in turn, its prestige. We know from the *Plaintes* that some items were not destroyed, but remained in circulation as hostages of the Huguenots. These were preferred to recommissioning; but how to get them – and why would Huguenots relinquish them?

In the immediate aftermath of the attack the canons asked for a royal proclamation to track down stolen items, and specifically high-status surviving items such as fragments of the rood screen given to the cathedral by the cardinal-bishop Philip de Luxembourg. Denied access to de Vignolles, who had fled and was later pardoned, the canons' retribu-tive focus fell on one Huguenot who remained beyond the law, a man who had offended sensibilities not just as an iconoclast but as a war criminal. René de la Rouvraye, sieur de Bressault, known as *le diable*, was wanted by several dioceses for destruction and humani-tarian atrocities.[49] He was thought to have worn a necklace of ears hacked from the heads of monks, tethered other clergy behind his horses and castrated them.[50] The pursuit of de la Rouvraye became as important as the pursuit of fragments of the cathedral fabric.

His eventual arrest by officers of the diocese of Angers complicates our understanding of how a church might recuperate its goods. To whom did stolen items belong when they were found in another diocese? When the canons of Le Mans heard of de la Rouvraye's arrest they asked for him to be surrendered to their custody. Angers refused, wanting the prestige of his execution, but a diocesan representative from Le Mans was allowed to ques-tion him to try to extract the whereabouts of items stolen from St Julien.[51] There is further evidence of inter-diocesan co-operation in later legal devices: in October 1572 Le Mans asked the officials of Angers to publish proclamations against those still harbouring goods.[52]

Beyond official legal measures, the cathedral also had the power of its purse. A large diocese, before 1562 it had comparable wealth to such powerful bishoprics as Chartres.[53] It is testimony to the levels of destruction and impoverishment wrought by the Huguenots that when de la Rouvraye offered to sell items looted back to the cathedral, the canons had to refuse.[54] They were able to offer small rewards for the return of items: however, were the prices offered mediated with the concept of 'good work', with the donor or returnee of the item expected to give to the church as a Christian act? A sense of a just or market price supports the relatively significant payment of ten *ecus* for a model of the rood and the return of one of the Cardinal's pastoral books.[55]

The question of payment is particularly interesting when related to the more quotidian items that were systematically stolen from churches, here considered through evidence from the church of St Jouin at Pirmil (Fig. 2.2), founded by the abbey of St Vincent in the late 11th century.[56] It commands a hilltop site about 30km west of Le Mans. Attacks on this church reveal that rather than having recourse to powerful officials and legal devices, the limited amount of reacquisition that occurred was more about the cohesion of commu-nities, faith and trust. A pattern of entries indicating iconoclastic attack first appears in 1562, followed again in 1564, 1568 and 1575. In 1562 money was spent on repairing and re-creating the altars to St Catherine and Notre Dame. A new statue of St Jouin was

Figure 2.2. The south façade of the parish church of St Jouin, Pirmil
(photograph by P. Woodcock).

brought from Le Mans specifically to replace an image of the same saint. The bell was refounded and the defence of the religious landscape looked to: ditches were dug and trees removed from the sides of the road on the advice of the parishioners.[57] The repair of the church ornament was ongoing for several years; rich embroideries were replaced, the font repaired and assistance offered to other churches.[58] New locks and keys were commanded.[59] Yet in 1568 a new element in the refitting of the church emerges. Rather than replacement or repair, there was financial exchange between the Huguenots, the parishioners and the church of Pirmil, as at St Aubin des Coudrais.[60] The Huguenots had decided upon a readier and simpler way to raise money – the open market of the Catholic congregation. In return, the Catholic purchasers might hope to be rewarded by the church – financially, but also spiritually. After the 'Huguenots had polluted the church' in 1568, items were presented back to the church for purchase by named members of its congregation.[61] A surplice was bought for 3 *sous*, Etienne Brie was paid 10 *sous* for the keys to the west door, the chapel of Saint Barbara and one of the great coffers. Valentin Famelière was reimbursed 8 *sous* for 'the small stoop', while Bellenger was paid 5 *sous* for having found a claxon. Finally, and perhaps most interestingly, Michel Corm was paid 5 *sous* for 'metal which he said he bought from the Huguenots'.[62] Had this lump of metal really originally been an item looted from the church and melted down for reuse? When there was financial reward involved how could the church rely on the word of the Huguenot that it was of holy origin – or, indeed, even on the word of its parishioner, simply because he was a Catholic?

In the end, the test was of cohesion and trust. If the church were to refuse the lump of metal they doubted the word of one of their community and the Huguenot attack claimed a psychological victory, if not the money. The parish would be riven with doubt and weakened at a time when it loudly claimed that it was undefended by the local seigneur.[63] The repurchase was a chance to demonstrate unity; it represented a consensual decision; the two officers of the fabric, one lay, representing the parish, and the curate, worked together to administer the funds. Pirmil's monies were also augmented by donations from the prior of the neighbouring monastic house, representing further cohesion; the wooden crucifix in the apse was funded by such collaboration.[64]

If items were destroyed beyond repair, the initial enthusiasm was for immediate re-creation of destroyed items, as at Pirmil in 1563 when statues on the altars of St Catherine and St Jouin were replaced. The process could bind the community together as certain bands of parishioners would travel to workshops to collect new statues and altarpieces to replace those destroyed.[65] Equally, the church might forge renewed links with Le Mans or its patron house which might pay for replacement pieces, or at least recognize the dangers faced in the distant parishes. This characterizes the period of peace after the first iconoclastic attacks and was driven by a desire to return the church to its original appearance as soon as possible.

However, after repeated attacks – whether by different bands of Huguenots or in later phases of the Wars – churches were more reluctant to replace expensive votive statues or embroidery. Instead, money was diverted to protecting the church: locks and keys needed to be replaced, but to protect any surviving jewels and relics the physical building itself needed to be fortified. Parishes particularly prone to repeated attack strengthened their defences. Glass and doors were replaced in preference to statues and altarpieces. The church needed to be protected from secular depredations too. At St Jean des Echelles, Gabriel Thelys, a glazier, was paid to replace glass broken by 'thieves' who 'had in the year of the present account robbed the said church' in the aftermath of iconoclastic attack.[66]

There is evidence to suggest that defence of parish property came to include protecting the lives of parishioners and the church building itself as well as any remaining valuables. Elements of fortified architecture were added to churches; these can be seen most clearly near la Ferté-Bernard, in the north-west of the diocese.[67] This town, under the control of the ultra-montane de Guise, was besieged by royal troops in 1589–90. The commanders in this campaign made strategic use of the religious landscape. Gun loops were cut through nave walls, ditches thrown up around church precincts and fortified porches and cannon emplacements added to churches, as at St Aubin des Coudrais, Déhault and St Georges du Rosay.[68] New towers were built at St Jean des Echelles and la Ferté-Bernard to assist communications and defend approaches. Parish money was diverted from recommissioning to purchasing gunpowder, building materials and paying troops.[69]

CONCLUSION

Just as the Huguenots had several motives for destroying the fabric of Catholic worship, there were a variety of measures available to return the church to its pre-Reformation appearance: however, while the original appearance was sought it was often impossible to re-create exactly the fabric of 1562. Attempts to do so might be deferred until peacetime, when new fashions now influenced the appearance of the church. Depending upon the wealth and influence of the church, the law could be used to extract payment or exact retribution for damage incurred. Copies of the original furniture and decoration might be commissioned. Yet, iconoclasm did not have to mean destruction, and the survival of sacred material illustrates the way war transformed attitudes towards value and worth. The theft and ransom of 'corrupt' church possessions raised money for the Huguenots and demonstrated their control over the Catholic community's worship and security. At a time of war and emergency taxation, notions of material value drove iconoclasm as much as an attack on detested doctrines; equally, the process to refurnish the Church was about restoring its value as much as its sanctity. Above all, where possible, items were tracked down, purchased or negotiated for – whether across dioceses, or among rural parishioners. But this was not always possible, and the history of the Catholic Reformation in Maine suggests that new fittings could equally satiate the need for religious and physical security represented by the church. This is, however, the subject of another paper and others' research.[70] In Pirmil, the community came together to re-create, reclaim and rebuild their church; in Le Mans the cathedral was resurgent after the Wars, and commissioned new terracottas, rood screens, tabernacles and vestments through which to express the piety of the Catholic faith. The search for fragments of the past could only go so far, and particularly popular art forms such as the terracottas and the retables were a sign of a new response of the Church, creating the Catholic Reformation visual world.

NOTES

*   This chapter forms part of the Arts and Humanities Research Council-funded project 'The early modern parish church and the religious landscape', directed by Professor Andrew Spicer at Oxford Brookes University. Thanks also to the staff of the Archives départementales de la Sarthe, Archives départementales de la Mayenne and la médiathèque Louis Aragon, Le Mans for assisting my research.

1. This county lay on the border between France and its historical neighbour, the duchy of Normandy. It was formed of, roughly, the modern-day départements of Mayenne (Bas-Maine) and the Sarthe (Haut-Maine). The *ancien diocese* corresponded roughly with the county, but was split in the 19th century to more closely follow the départemental limits. A new bishopric was established at Laval for the western half of the diocese in 1855.

2. Plessix n.d.; Bouton 1970; in contrast Chardon 1880, 284, claimed that it is difficult to write a history of Protestantism in the area as, in contrast to Normandy or the Loire, most of the Huguenot consistory records were destroyed for Maine.

3. For terracottas see Bresc-Bautier *et al.* 2002; Bardelot *et al.* 2003. For the retables see Eraud

    et al. 1990; Ménard 1975; 1980; 1983; Sculpture en terre cuite du Maine XVIe et XVIIe Siècles 2003.

4. Piolin 1861; ADS 111 AC 998 Ledru, A. *Histoire de la prise du Mans par les Calvinistes en 1562*; Anjubault & Chardon 1867.

5. Ledru 1903, 167–256. The court records are held in ADS 111 AC 990–991. ADS 111 AC 985–986, 988–989 also hold original inventories of materials lost from the cathedral.

6. Piolin 1861, 445. He notes that a *livre* of 1562 was worth 4 F 50 in 1861.

7. Ledru 1903, 170 details complicit canons.

8. Alouis 1879, 58–70, discusses these events and political sympathies. Contemporaries attributed the Huguenots' departure to a miracle performed by St Sulpice, see ADS G 479.

9. Aubry 1998a, 103. Ledru notes the suspect dates in ADS 111 AC 991 and the information in sources such as ADS 111 AC 987 *Information faitte à la Requête des frères Prêcheurs par ordre du Parlement donné à Paris le 3 aoust 1562 contre les Huguenots.*

10. Ledru 1903, 256 details the 'pipes' of wine drunk from the cathedral cellar, worth 500 *livres.*

Further thefts are in ADS 111 AC 987, 1r–v: '*fut menée trois pipes de vin a la maison de Mr Louis Noüet Sr Duplessis rue St Flaceau*'.

11. Spicer 2007 for iconoclasm in Orléans.

12. See Dronne 1985 for a list of the Huguenot congregation and their noble patrons.

13. For de Vignolles' career see Aubry 1998a. This article discusses the background of other leading Huguenots. ADS 111 AC 990, 1r–v *Sentence criminelle rendue par les présidial du Mans*, 21 Nov. 1562 lists the professions of the key iconoclasts with political power and office.

14. For the Consistory see Conner 2003.

15. The bishops of Le Mans were noted absenteeists: see Biarne 1978, 110.

16. For destruction at the Jacobins see ADS 111 AC 987.

17. Ledru 1903, 170.

18. ADS 111 AC 990: '*ornements joyaux reliques et autres biens et richesse de la ditte église*'.

19. ADS 111 AC 990, 1 lists '*Etienne et Guillaume les De Louvignes, Nicola d'Antin, Michel Pishard, Francois Simon, Jean Bereaulis, Eutashe Piques Orfevres*' as goldsmiths among the iconoclasts.

20. Bouton 1970, 863–4: '*Il est curieux de recontrer parmi les farouches protestants Noël Huet qui avait construire entre 1553 et 1555 le célèbre jubé des Jacobins et presque tous les orfèvres du Mans, au nombre d'une dizaine, attirés par le pillage des richesses métalliques des églises.*'

21. Aubry 1998a, 105.

22. For example, see Ledru 1903, 179: '*Item auroient aussi … rompu et desmoly une belle grande cloyson de cuyvre eui estoit à l'entour du grant aultie*'.

23. ADS 111 AC 989, 2r: '*le plus grand part de la cuivriere qui estoit aud[ ] choeur de St Julian, et aussy fut trouvé le baston des fonds baptismaux d'icelle église, plusieurs tombes des cuivre meme la couverture de fer faite en facon de cage qui estoit sur la tombe de levesque du Mans appellé Gontier en la chapelle de N dame de choeur a plusieurs pieces tous de fer que de cuivre qui avoient été tirées des autres tombes et lieux dicelle église, quelles cuivrieres, epitaphes*'; for the architectural importance of the hôtel de Vignolles see Aubry 1998b and Castel & Chatenet 2008.

24. Aubry 1998a, 103: '*le pillage devient systematique*'.

25. ADS 111 AC 989, 3v: '*pilleries, voleries, demolissement d'autels et emportant toutes les richesses comme calices[et] ornemens*'.

26. Many Huguenots from Le Mans went to Alençon, see Blanchetière 2003, 49.

27. For comment on the number of camp followers, see Piolin 1861, 455.

28. For the Huguenot attack on Beaumont see Passe

1990, 39–40; for Fresnay, Assé and Sougé see Triger 1903, 15–16. For the attack on Fresnay 1562–3 see ADS 7 F 50, 140–150.

29. There were numerous parishes attacked. For 1562–3 examples see St Michel de la Barre, ADS 7 F 50, 202r–205r.

30. E.g for Pirmil see ADS 7 F 70, 234: '*Item payé au fondeur qui a refondre le d[ ] cloche 7 l 10 s*'. For Fresnay see ADS 7 F 50, 140v.

31. Ledru 1903, 238.

32. ADM *Mentions Trouvées dans les Registres Paroissiaux et D'état Civil* <http://ad53.lamayenne.fr/mentions/205_m_st-cenere.htm> cites the example of the parish of Saint Cénéré, 1618: '*Refonte et bénédiction d'une cloche, Potz laditte cloche a esté ointe et beniste par monsieur le curé de Saint Martin de Montseurs nommé Guillaume Barbes homme docte et sçavant et en icelle cloche y a le nom de Marye*'; also signalled in Angot 1998, 518.

33. Ledru 1903, 252: '*Lesdictz Bouju, de Veignolles [leurs] complices et alliez prins, brisé, laceré et transporté les lettres de fondation*'.

34. Aubry 1998a, 99–100; Ledru 1903, 228.

35. Piolin 1861, 457, 461.

36. E.g. exhumations at St Ouen de Mimbré and Assé-le-Boisne, ADS E supp.GG 1–16.

37. ADS 7 F 70, 230: *On repare l'eglise*.

38. Dufourcq 1990, 242. Dufourcq suggests that these statues may have been targeted because of their connection to Colombe.

39. ADS 7 F 50, 202r.

40. Piolin 1861, 437, 439; the same tactic was followed by the inhabitants of Le Mans when they were besieged by the League in 1589 – see Ledru 1880, 209–10.

41. Ledru 1903, 213: '*de faczon riche, ayant table et contretable et enrichissement tant hault que bas de mouleures enrichies de figures à la moderne, le tout vallant quatre cens livre tourn[ ], en l'esgard de la maczonnerie*'.

42. Kidd 1911, 3. *Salvator Noster* Sixtus IV, 3 August 1476: *de thesauro ecclesiae*.

43. E.g. Ledru 1903, 185, 192, lists embroideries donated by the 11th-century Queen Berthe valued at 20 *ecus* and a chasuble and tunics donated by Louis XI worth 200 *ecus*.

44. Piolin 1861, 511. See also Piolin 1861, 490 for 1565 tax and 501 for 1568 imposition.

45. ADS 111 AC 990, 1r: '*pilleries, sacrilege, … homicides, de conspirations de la prise de la ville …, concitoires, enrolements, contributions, sedictions et rebellions demolitions d'Eglise ruptures d'imaiges et autels d'icelles*'.

46. For the sentences against de Vignolles, de Bouju *et al.* see ADS 111 AC 990.
47. Piolin 1861, 479.
48. Piolin 1861, 517. ADS 111 AC 995 *Monitoire de l'official contre détenteurs des objets voles à la Cathédral, 1587.*
49. For his career see Joubert 1880; 1881.
50. Biarne 1978, 116. For the image of de le Rouvraye, see Piolin 1861, 447. This imagery of hacked ears recurs in descriptions of Huguenot atrocities, e.g. during the Michelade at Nîmes, 1567.
51. See letter of Julien Jamyn, 19 October 1572 to the canons and chapter of Le Mans in Chardon 1880, 319, and Piolin 1861, 506.
52. Piolin 1861, 506.
53. Bergin 1996, 10–116.
54. Piolin 1861, 494, shows that there was still enough money by October of this year to pay for armour for the canons when the city feared Protestant invasion.
55. Piolin 1861, 458.
56. Bergeot *et al.* 2006, 325–7.
57. ADS 7 F 70, 229–30: '*Item pour la despence de la journée que je suys allé allé [sic.] au Mans porter une commission au 4 esleux qu'ilz nous avoynt envoyée pour abattre les arbres au travers des chemins et y faire des fossés, laquelle je suys allé conseiller par l'advis des paroissiens ou j'ay despendre quinze sols xv s'.*
    1563 '*Item payé a Louis Lespine masson pour avoir refait l'authel de madame saincte Catherine xl s'*
    '*Item payé aud[ ] Lespine pour avoir refait l'aultel de Nostre Dame; Item pour la despence qui à esté faicte en marchandant celle qui avoir esté cassee durant les troubles par les Huguenotz v s'.*
    '*Item payé au fondeur qui a refondre la d[ ] cloche pour la peine seulement sept livres diz soubz; Item pour les aultres fraitz qu'il a fally faire a la d[ ] cloche, somme en suyt, chambre, cire, tonneau, carreaulx, charbon, souffletz que charrois payé cxviii sous vi d'.*
58. E.g. ADS 7 F 70, 235: '*Item, pour la reparacion des aornemens comme chapes, tronques et chasubles, payé a Pierre Grignart pour du Camelot rouge, toille negre et filnayr et peine dud[ ] Grynart et despens d'iceluy xx s vi d'.*
    '*Item pour ung muy de chaux promis a Parcé pour reparer les aultiers de lad[ ] église ay payé trente cinq soulz et pour le charon de lad[ ]chaux vingt et conq souls, lad chaux prins aux Pe-cherreries iii L'.*
    '*Item pour avoyr faict racoustrer la serure au la grant porte et une clef, et pour la serure de la ports de la sonnerie et une clef, et pour une clef a la serure des fons, ay payé a Jehan Rezé xvii s vi d'.*
    '*Item pour la serrure desd[] fons et base de fer avec*

les crampons a tenir icelle b/pare ay payé aud[ ] Rez viii s'.
    Repair can be found elsewhere in the diocese e.g. St Jean des Echelles, see ADS 7 F 51, 207r: '*Payé a Brice De la Planche macson dem[eurant] aud[it] S. Jehan des Eschell la some de huicts sols pour son sall[aire] d'avoir racoustré et rassemblé les ymages de St Jehan Bap[tis]te que avoyent estéz briséez des Huguenots pour ce viii s'.*
59. ADS 7 F 70, 230.
60. For St Aubin see ADS 7 F 51, 146v.
61. ADS 7 F 70, 238: '*Item après que les huguenoz eurent pullié l'eglise et achapté ung soupelis iii s'.*
62. ADS 7 F 70, 230: '*Item payé a Etienne Brie qui a achapté desd[] Huguenoz troys serrures savoyr est: la serure de la grand porte, et la serure de la porte de la chapelle saincte Barbe, et la sereure d'ung des grans coffres x s'.*
    '*Item ay payé à Valentin Famelière qui a achape desd[ ] huguenoz le petit benoistre et aultres besognes de lad[ ] eglise viii s'.*
    '*Item pour avir faict nectoyer l'eglise et renger les pierres des autiers rompuz apres que lesd[ ] huguenoz s'en furent allez iii s vi d'.*
    '*Item pour avoir fait racoustrer et remettre la serure de la porte de la chapelle Saincte Barbe v s'.*
    '*Item quant fut trouvé ung des bataulz des cloches au pres de Bellengier, fis chercher les aultres, pris de bois, pour savoyr si on pourroit trouver l'autre et pour les faire payé en un v s'.*
    '*Item a Michel Corm pour du métal qu'il disoyt avoir acheté des hugenoz v s'.*
63. ADS 7 F 70, 239.
64. Bergeot *et al.* 2006, 325.
65. ADS 7 F 70, 229: '*Item payé a deux hommes qui ont apporté l'ymaige de Sainct Jouyn qui le p[ro] cureur du Mans nous a donnée xii sous'.*
66. St Jean des Echelles ADS 7 F 51, 208–209: '*A gabriel Thelys vittrier dem[euran]t a la Ferté-Bernard pour avoir racoustré une des vittres de lad[ite] égl[is]e et du Tabernacle que avoyent esté cassées et brisées par les volleurs qui ont en l'an de ce p[rese]nt compte vollé la d[ite] égl[is]e xx s'.* There was similar rebuilding at Théligny: ADS 7 F 77, 101–110 (1591–1600) and Preval: ADS 7 F 51, 92r–v.
67. A summary of these fortifications can be found in Pioger 1967–68, 367.
68. For St Aubin see ADS 7 F 51, 127r.
69. E.g. St George du Rosay: ADS 7 F 74, 109–11.
70. For retables see n.3. For rood-screens see Bardelot *et al.* 2003, 108–9.

BIBLIOGRAPHY

ADM *Mentions trouvées dans les registres paroissiaux et d'état civil* <http://ad53.lamayenne.fr/
mentions/205_m_st-cenere.htm> [accessed 25 January 2009].

ADS 7 F 50.

ADS 7 F 51.

ADS 7 F 70.

ADS 7 F 74.

ADS 7 F 77.

ADS 111 AC 985–995.

ADS 111 AC 998 Ledru, A. *Histoire de la prise du Mans par les Calvinistes en 1562*.

ADS E supp. GG 1–16.

ADS G 479.

Alouis, M.V. 1879, 'Le Mans au mois d'Octobre 1562', *RHAM* 6: 58–70.

Angot, A. 1998, *Dictionnaire de la Mayenne* 3, Mayenne: Éditions Régionales de L'Ouest.

*Anjubault, M. & Chardon, H. (eds) 1867, Receuil de pieces inédits pour servir à l'histoire de la Réforme
et de la Ligue dans le Maine, Le Mans: Monnoyer.*

Aubry, V. 1998a, 'Jean de Vignolles, acteur des guerres de religion', *Province du Maine* 99/2: 97–114.

Aubry, V. 1998b, 'L'hôtel de Vignolles au Mans au XVIe siècle', *Province du Maine* 99/4: 291–337.

Bardelot, P., Bresc-Bautier, G., Chaserant, F., Guillaneuf, E., Le Boeuf, F., Mailho-Duboussi, L.
& Ménard, M. 2003, *Terre et Ciel: La Sculpture en Terre Cuite du Maine (XVIe et XVIIe siècles)*,
Paris: Monum.

Bergeot, K., Davoust, P., Leduc-Gueye, C., Le Hénaff, D., Masson, H., Niaussat, M. & Palanka-
Cohin, A. 2006, *Églises de la Sarthe*, Le Mans: Éditions de la Reinette.

Bergin, J. 1996, *The Making of the French Episcopate*, New Haven (CT): Yale University Press.

Biarne, J.E.A. 1978, *Histoire religieuse du Maine*, Le Mans: CLD Normand.

Blanchetière, J.-C. 2003, 'Les origines de la Réforme à Alençon (1520–1572)', *Societé Historique et
Archéologique de l'Orne* 122/4: 5–80.

Bouton, A. 1970, *Le Maine: histoire économique et sociale XIVe, XVe et XVIe siècle*, Le Mans: Imprimer
Monneyer.

Bresc-Bautier, G., Le Boeuf, F. & Loyrette, H. 2002, *Belles et inconnues: sculptures en terre cuite des
ateliers du Maine: XVIe–XVIIe siècles: étude iconographique*, Paris: Editions de la Réunion des
Musées Nationaux.

Castel, D. & Chatenet, M. 2008, 'Jacques Androuet du Cerceau et l'hôtel de Vignolles du Mans',
Bulletin Monumental 166/2: 117–34.

Chardon, H. 1880, 'Les Protestants au Mans en 1572, pendant et après la Saint Barthelemy', *RHAM*
8, 284–323.

Conner, P. 2003, 'Huguenot identities during the Wars of Religion: the churches of Le Mans and
Montauban compared', *Journal of Ecclesiastical History* 54, 23–39.

Dornic, F. (ed.) 1975, *Histoire du Mans*, Toulouse: Privat.

Dronne, M. 1985, *La Réforme et les Protestants dans le Maine*, Carnet-Rocheville: M. Dronne.

Dufourcq, N. 1990, 'Les statues de l'église de Luché-Pringé', *Province du Maine*, 92/4: 233–48.

Eraud, D., de Maynard, D., Perrin, J. & Salbert, J. 1990, *Retables de la Mayenne*, Paris: Inventaire
Général.

Joubert, A. 1880, *Un épisode des guerres de religion au Maine et en Anjou. René de la Rouvraye dit le
Diable de Bressault*, Le Mans: J. Gervais.

Joubert, A. 1881, 'René de La Rouvraye, sieur de Bressault', *RHAM* 10: 129–77.

Kidd, B.J. 1911, *Documents Illustrative of the Continental Reformation*, Oxford: The Clarendon Press.

Ledru, A. 1880, *Épisodes de la Ligue au Mans (1589)*, Mamers: G. Fleury et Dangin.

Ledru, A. 1903, 'Plaintes et Doléances du chapitre du Mans après le pillage de la cathédrale par les Huguenots en 1562', *Archiv. Historique du Maine* III, Le Mans: Société Historique de la Province du Maine, 169–256.

Ménard, M. 1975, 'Nouveautés du XVIe siècle', in Dornic 1975, 105–35.

Ménard, M. 1980, *Une histoire des mentalités religieuses aux 17 et 18 siècles: mille retables de l'ancien diocèse du Mans*, Paris: Beauchesne.

Ménard, M. 1983, 'Formes, espaces et sacré: les images favorites de saint Sébastien sur les retables des églises paroissiales de l'ancien diocèse du Mans', *Annales de Bretagne* 90/2: 357–75.

Passe, M. 1990, *Histoire de Beaumont-sur-Sarthe*, Paris: Res Universis.

Pioger, A. 1967–68, 'Le Fertois aux XVIIe et XVIIIe siècles', *BSASAS* 71: 332–449.

Piolin, P. 1861, *Histoire de l'église du Mans* 5, Paris: Julien et Lanier.

Plessix, R. n.d., *Permanences et évolutions. La Sarthe des origines à nos jours*, Le Mans: Éditions Bourdesoulles.

Sculptures en terre cuite du Maine XVIe et XVII siècles <http://www.sculpturesdumaine.culture.fr/fr/index.html> [accessed 25 January 2009].

Spicer, A. 2007, '(Re)building the sacred landscape: Orléans, 1560–1610', *French History* 21: 247–68.

Triger, R. 1903, *Le Canton de Fresnay Historique et Archéologique*, Le Mans: Imprimerie Sarthoise.

ABBREVIATIONS

ADM	Archives départementales de la Mayenne
ADS	Archives départementales de la Sarthe
BSASAS	*Bulletin de la société d'Agriculture, Sciences et Arts de la Sarthe*
RHAM	*Revue historique et archéologique du Maine*

The 'Third Sacrament': Lutheran Confessionals in Schleswig (Northern Germany)

Matthias Range[*]

This chapter examines the 16th- to 18th-century practice of confession in the Lutheran church and how it is reflected in material culture. For that purpose it looks at the example of the diocese of Schleswig in today's northern Germany and southern Denmark. As in other regions of Germany, confession was here described as a 'third' sacrament in addition to baptism and the Eucharist. In Schleswig a number of Lutheran confessionals have survived; their history, use and impact on the church building are examined.

INTRODUCTION

The 2001 SPMA/SMA conference *The Archaeology of Reformation* and the published conference proceedings were a clear sign of the developing interest in archaeology and material culture to complement 'traditional' archival sources for early modern historians.[1] While the majority of papers then dealt with Britain and Northern Europe in the period between 1480 and 1580, there has since been a growth in similar research stretching beyond this period. Research is now also undertaken on and in other regions, especially in Germany, the 'home-land' of the Reformation. In the German study *Archäologie der Reformation*, published in 2007, Barbara Scholkmann summarized the now widely accepted approach: 'Church archaeology [...] is able to record the material effects of the changed theological ideas on official rites, that is the re-organization and re-creation of church space that took place during the Reformation.'[2] More directly, it has been argued that 'it is in fact material culture which offers the most concrete and tangible remains of ephemeral and otherwise intangible beliefs during early Protestantism and its development through confessionalization'.[3] Indeed, it is the examination of material culture that allows historians to draw new conclusions and to see how church interiors contributed to parishioners' understanding of Lutheranism. After all, surviving objects draw attention to their purpose, to their origins, their use and their meanings; Wolfgang Brückner introduced the term 'Konfessionsarchäologie der Kasualien', or the 'denomination-archaeology of the church's official acts'.[4] Following this idea, based on recent findings the present study will look at confessionals as prominent features of Lutheran church interiors. The topic of confession and Protestantism is still very much a neglected one on the broader scale. As Alexander Wieckowski observes, 'the practice of private confession is well researched, but the studies are hardly known outside church history'.[5] Recently the topic has been taken up by scholars in a German context. Ronald Rittgers' notable comprehensive study *The Reformation of the Keys: Confession, Conscience and Authority in Sixteenth-Century Germany* focuses on the

Imperial city of Nuremberg, but also provides a good introduction to the general, theological background of confession.[6]

There is a remarkable amount of evidence for confessionals in the churches of the
Lutheran diocese of Schleswig, a significant area that has hitherto not been much considered by international scholars. The diocese of Schleswig comprised the northern part of
today's Schleswig-Holstein in Germany and the south-eastern part of the Danish peninsula,
otherwise known as Jutland. The duchies of Schleswig and Holstein were closely linked
to the kingdom of Denmark and Norway, and Schleswig played an important part in the
Scandinavian Reformation: it was in this duchy that the Reformation first gained ground
under Duke Christian before being introduced into Denmark after his coronation as King
Christian III of Denmark in 1537 (he had acceded to the throne in 1534). The Reformation in the diocese of Schleswig began relatively early, in the 1520s, and it ended with the
introduction of an official church ordinance for the two duchies of Schleswig and Holstein
in 1542. This church ordinance regulated nearly every aspect of church life and established
Lutheranism in the diocese; it was compiled under the advice of Johannes Bugenhagen,
close associate and friend of Luther's and pastor at the Wittenberg town church since 1523.
Bugenhagen had also helped to prepare the church ordinances for Hamburg and Lübeck
from 1529 and 1531 respectively, and the Latin church ordinance for Denmark in 1537.[7] In
Schleswig, long after the Reformation, the church authorities enforced strict adherence to
official Lutheranism by an oath in which priests had to swear not to follow Calvinism or
other Protestant movements.[8] This strict Lutheranism is reflected in the church interiors,
which show features that signify, enhance and support the official doctrine. Compared with
other regions of Germany, in Schleswig a considerable number of 16th- to 18th-century
church furnishings have survived the centuries.

THE PRACTICE OF CONFESSION IN LUTHERAN GERMANY

In Lutheran Germany, and especially in Schleswig, confession (usually named 'absolution', stressing the act of absolving from sins) was described from very early on as a 'Third
Sacrament'.[9] Indeed, the 1537 Danish church ordinance and the 1542 Schleswig church
ordinance explicitly count penitence (*Buße*) as a third sacrament in addition to Baptism
and Holy Communion: 'There are two sacraments, instituted by Christ, namely Baptism
and the Lord's Supper, on which the Catechism teaches us. To these one shall add the
third, which is penitence [...].'[10] While stressing that parishioners should not be forced to
confess all of their sins, as they would in the Catholic confession, the church ordinance
nevertheless underlines distinctly the importance of the individual's confession as a means
of relieving one's conscience.[11]

Most importantly, in the Lutheran church confession was closely linked with the celebration of the Eucharist. Luther himself criticized the custom of the Catholic church that
everybody could simply go to Communion without registration or an examination of the
faith beforehand.[12] Whereas he thought confession could remain voluntary, he asserted that
the examination of the faith should be compulsory before being allowed to receive Holy
Communion.[13] However, the practice of linking confession and examination in one rite
meant that confession eventually became compulsory, too.[14] In support of this demand
of confession and examination, and following Luther's critique of the Roman Catholic
practice, the Schleswig church ordinance strongly conveys the sense that only the worthy

or the prepared should take part in the Lord's Supper. So as to be allowed to receive Holy Communion, parishioners first of all had to signal their intent to the priest in advance. In preparation they then had to go to confession and had to be examined on the Lutheran catechism; both confession and examination were combined in one rite.[15] The church ordinance already allowed for exceptions in the case that 'one knows the people and does not think such questioning necessary'.[16] However, for the average parishioner, confession at least once a year could hardly be avoided: as before the Reformation, custom still required the taking of Holy Communion at least once a year, and in 1623 this minimum requirement was confirmed in an order from the authorities.[17] Such annual regularity would have been in accordance with Luther, who had pointed out:

> I admit that it is enough for this questioning and inquiring of one who wants to take the sacrament to happen once a year. Indeed, one who desires it [the sacrament] may be so well informed ['verstendig'] that he will be questioned only once as long as he lives, or even never. [18]

There is generally little information on the practicalities of confession in Lutheran Germany. Since the church ordinances contain few details on this, the main sources are depictions, most prominently the numerous so-called *Bekenntnisgemälde*, or 'confession paintings'.[19] From these paintings it appears that confession was a private affair between priest and parishioner. Even though they are not shown as sitting in a special, enclosed confessional, the private character is emphasized by the proximity of priest and parishioner. In contrast to this, the famous depiction of Bugenhagen himself hearing confession in Cranach the Elder's altarpiece in the Wittenberg town church shows confession seemingly taking place in public.[20] Bugenhagen sits on a chair with the parishioner kneeling in front of him, while two groups of people stand behind the chair on both sides. This arrangement for confession is similar in other 16th- and 17th-century depictions showing the Lutheran confessional practice at the time.[21] However, that Lutheran confession was nevertheless an 'auricular confession' – that is, a secret and private one – becomes clear from the fact that in this painting, as in many others, the priest and the parishioner confessing form a unit separated from their surroundings; indeed, occasionally the parishioner is distinctly shown speaking into the priest's ear, as in Andreas Herneisen's 1601 painting 'Das gantze evangelische Christentum', now in the Stadtgeschichtliche Museum Leipzig.[22] Furthermore, the private character of Lutheran confession is emphasized in another work from the Cranach workshop, the famous woodcut with the allegorical depiction of the evangelical teaching from after 1551.[23] In this Luther is shown together with the Elector Johann Friedrich ('der Großmütige') of Saxony. Both of them sit in a secluded corner of the stylized building, the Duke sitting in a chair while Luther sits to his side, probably on a simple bench. While the elector hits his chest with his right fist in a *mea culpa* gesture, Luther seems to be counting with his hands. The seemingly public character of confession in the Wittenberg altarpiece and other examples may simply have served to point out that it was publicly observed who took confession and when, as this was important for congregational discipline in relation to the celebration of Holy Communion.

Interestingly, for Schleswig there appears to be some evidence that the whole preparatory rite which the church ordinance subsumes under the term 'absolution' was still understood as two different parts: the actual confession and the examination of the catechism; it is possible that both were treated differently, the first taking place in private, the second in public. Between 1631 and 1633 there was a dispute between the parishioners and the 'pastor' of Schwabstedt, which was a residence of the bishop of Schleswig in the west of the diocese.[24] In the arguments against the pastor, the curate reports that he (the curate) had allowed two people at the same time to see him in the confessional, claiming that it had been busy and that this was the usual practice; however, the curate states that the pastor screamed out against this and accused that to be a 'public confession or even to be Calvinist'.[25] At the same time, however, the pastor allowed the examination in the confessional to be public, but this, on the other hand, the curate thought to be against the catechism.[26] A few years later, in 1637, King Christian IV of Denmark ordered that 'the public penitence sitting shall be re-introduced in our *amt* Hadersleben' – that is, in North Schleswig.[27] Thus parishioners' failings – at least the fact that they had had something to confess and to repent for – would have become public one way or the other.

THE 'ARCHITECTURE OF CONFESSION' IN LUTHERAN SCHLESWIG

Confession in Schleswig was to take place in the morning, just before the main service; however, in busy town churches, it was later moved to the preceding evening.[28] The 1542 church ordinance does not include much information on the practicalities of confession. There is no evidence for any special provisions in the churches for confession from the 16th century. It appears that priest and parishioner simply met in the church, and it is not clear when the confessionals were introduced. The church ordinance stipulated that, in the case of a communicant not passing the necessary examination to be allowed to take the sacrament, the priest should inform him/her about the refusal in the 'hemeliken Bicht', or 'secret confession', and Frauke Rehder concludes that telling people in secret confession was done 'so as not to embarrass the excluded one in front of the congregation'.[29] This indicates a somehow private meeting. At the same time, reports from the 17th century indicate that the practice of simply meeting with the priest in the church became increasingly impracticable, especially as many parishioners wanted to go to confession at the same time.[30] The demand for a secret confession in the church ordinance together with the busyness of the church at the times scheduled may have led to the development of a special 'architecture of confession', Lutheran confessionals, which in Schleswig survive from the 17th and 18th century.

It is difficult to give a definite number for the confessionals in Schleswig, as many inventories do not list them as such, but rather as priest's seats or sacristies. However, the number of the surviving confessionals is at least around a dozen. The earliest confessional now in existence in Schleswig is probably the one in the parish church of Welt, which is believed to date from around 1650 (Fig. 3.1). Most of the confessionals in Schleswig that have survived are found in churches of the peninsula of Eiderstedt, in the west of the diocese, on the North Sea coast (in the parish churches of Poppenbüll, Tönning, Tating, Westerhever, Welt, and Tetenbüll (two)). However, confessionals were not a peculiarity of this peninsula. Another surviving example is the confessional from 1691 in the Old Church (St Salvator) on the North Sea island of Pellworm (Fig. 3.2).[31] Furthermore, there is ample evidence that they existed in other parts of the diocese as well, and indeed before the mid 17th century. For instance, apart from the aforementioned example of Schwabstedt, where a confessional must have existed in the early 1630s, there is documentary evidence from

Figure 3.1. Welt (Eiderstedt), parish church of St Michael, confessional,
believed to date from *c.* 1650 (photograph by M. Range).

around 1650 of a restoration of the church of Enstedt in North Schleswig during which
the confessional was restored.[32] This in turn implies that the confessional had already been
in this church long enough to be in need of repair. A new confessional was donated to
the new church in Friedrichsberg, a suburb of the town of Schleswig, in 1650.[33] In 1671 a
confessional is reported as having been moved within the church of Brarup, in the north-
east of Schleswig, near the Baltic Sea coast.[34] In addition to these examples from Schleswig,
confessionals are also mentioned in visitation reports from 1635 from Dithmarschen and
from Eutin in Holstein, both of which shared the Schleswig church ordinance.[35]

There are no reports of how exactly priest and parishioner met in the confessionals in
Schleswig.[36] However, a close look at the surviving examples reveals interesting details and
allows comparison with Catholic examples. The Schleswig confessionals are mere 'little
boxes', providing a separate room in the church for a 'private' meeting of the priest and
his parishioners. It is noteworthy that, since confession was one prerequisite to be allowed
to take communion, it cannot have been an anonymous rite; the priest necessarily had to
know who exactly was confessing. Wieckowski observes that 'in contrast to Roman-Catholic
confessionals, evangelical confessionals normally do not have a separating grill'.[37] In the

Figure 3.2. Pellworm, Old Church (St Salvator), confessional from 1691
(photograph by M. Range).

Catholic church the 'type of confessional with two parts and separation wall' ('zweigeteilter Beichtstuhltypus mit Trennwand'), the wall dividing it into one area for the priest and one for the parishioner, was introduced after the Council of Trent.[38] Indeed, on the request of the Council it was developed by St Carl Borromaeus.[39] There is no evidence that any confessional in Schleswig had such a separation; in fact, the confessional in St Salvator (Pellworm), for instance, has only one entrance, underlining that it was not necessary to have a strict division into a cleric's and a parishioner's side (see Fig. 3.2). In addition, there is no special, original furniture in the Schleswig confessionals, such as chairs or benches (Figs 3.3 and 3.4), and no such furniture survives separately or is recorded to have existed.

Figure 3.3. Welt (Eiderstedt), parish church of St Michael; this second confessional in this church dates from 1703 and had originally been built for the church of the village St Peter (photograph by M. Range).

Ernst Feddersen assumes that 'undoubtedly', in accordance with Luther's catechism, parishioners would have knelt before the priest during confession.[40] This matches also with the aforementioned illustrations of confessions. Such a practice, however, implies that in the confessional there must at least have been one chair for the priest, and perhaps a kneeler or hassock for the parishioner. In any case, the arrangement in the confessional may in some churches have been quite comfortable, as this could be a concern for the authorities. For instance, in the late 18th century four new confessionals were built for the *Marienkirche* in Lübeck; the reason given for this was that the old ones had been 'too uncomfortable for the priest and the confessing parishioner'.[41]

As seen above, many people would have gone to Holy Communion only once a year; this meant that they also had to go to confession only once a year. There is not enough evidence to determine if people also went to confession without receiving communion afterwards,[42] which would theoretically have been possible. Altogether, it appears that the confessionals were probably not used as such very much throughout the year. However, apart from providing a room for confession, the confessionals may have served another purpose. It is possible that, if the church had no sacristy, the priest used the confessional to change his liturgical vestments during the celebration of the mass.[43] Such a secondary

Figure 3.4. Welt (Eiderstedt), parish church of St Michael, confessional from 1703, originally from St Peter, interior (photograph by M. Range).

Figure 3.5. Tetenbüll (Eiderstedt), parish church of St Anna, second confessional, 1787 (photograph by M. Range).

use may also explain why the confessionals from the 18th century are considerably bigger than the ones from the 17th century. A good example of these 'oversized' confessionals is the second confessional in the parish church of Tetenbüll in Eiderstedt, which dates from 1787 (Fig. 3.5). Most of the confessionals have inscriptions referring explicitly to confession, and the 18th-century confessionals especially have lavish painted ornamental decoration. However, it is noteworthy that, apart from the inscriptions, the decorations of the confessionals do not refer to their use. The second confessional in Welt has a crest with keys at the top (see Fig. 3.3). This could be read as an allusion to the keys that often symbolically represent confession and absolution.[44] In this case, however, the reason for the crest with keys is simply that the confessional originally belonged to the church of the village St Peter, which had this crest.

In northern Germany Lutheran confessionals like the ones in Schleswig were built and used throughout the 18th century. New confessionals were built, especially in richer parishes. As already seen, the *Marienkirche* in Lübeck acquired new confessionals at the end of the 18th century. Also in Lübeck, the cathedral had new confessionals from 1743 and 1785.[45] Their appearance and use was the same as that of the Schleswig confessionals. But confessionals were in no way restricted to the north: for instance, in Saxony, confessionals belonged to church life up until the 19th century.[46]

CONCLUSION

On the example of altars and pulpits, Luther himself had pointed out the importance of interiors in churches, explaining that these furnishings were 'built not only to meet a need but also to create a solemn atmosphere' ('Haec non necessitatis tantum causa, sed etiam solennitatis facta sunt').[47] The confessionals in the Schleswig churches may be good examples of this; they point out that Lutheranism paid much attention to the sacraments and held them in high esteem. The requirement of confession and examination of the catechism before being allowed to take communion underlines the reverence with which Holy Communion was approached. Bridget Heal summarized that, 'for Lutheran commentators, church furnishings were not simply utilitarian'.[48] Indeed, even when the confessionals where not actually used, this permanent architecture of penance in the church, normally clearly visible to the congregation throughout the service, brought confession to parishioners' awareness whenever they visited their church; in this way the confessionals reminded them constantly of their duties.[49]

Wieckowski states that today confession is often held to be 'a specific of the Roman-Catholic church' and that confessionals 'are seen as the classic distinguishing feature between the Protestant and the Roman-Catholic denominations'.[50] This observation underlines once more the importance of the archaeology of the Reformation, the importance of studying the material culture of churches; for it is the study of the surviving material culture that brings to attention aspects otherwise easily overlooked. The surviving material may improve the modern understanding of the changes introduced by the Reformation, and it may provide new insights into everyday church life in the early modern period. The confessionals as part of the interiors of Schleswig's Lutheran churches are a clear reminder of the fact that confession was an integral part of Lutheran theology; indeed, a part that directly formed people's personal experience of church life for centuries after the Reformation. Overall, the Schleswig confessionals manifest the sacramental character of staunch Lutheranism very clearly; they show how this sacramental character was reflected in the material culture and could thus help to evoke a 'solemn atmosphere' in church. In allusion to the wording in the Schleswig church ordinance, the confessionals may truly be called the materialization of the 'Third Sacrament'.

NOTES

*   The research for this study was undertaken as part of the Arts and Humanities Research Council-funded project 'The Early Modern Parish Church and the Religious Landscape' at Oxford Brookes University.

1.   Gaimster & Gilchrist 2003.

2.   Scholkmann 2007, 14: 'Kirchenarchäologie [...] kann die materiellen Auswirkungen der veränderten theologischen Vorstellungen auf die offizielle Kultausübung, also die im Zuge der Reformation erfolgte Neuorganisation und Neugestaltung der Kirchenräume, erfassen.' Unless otherwise stated, all translations are the author's.

3.   Lee 2008, 149.

4.   Brückner 2007, 159.

5.   Wieckowski 2008, 43, fn. 4, which also provides an overview of the literature. For more literature on confessionals see Brückner 2007, 189; more generally, for confession in Lutheranism see also Karant-Nunn 1997, 94, fn. 17.

6.   Rittgers 2004. For the pre-Reformation practice and more details and literature on the development of early modern confessionals see Karant-Nunn 1997, 94, esp. fn. 17.

7.   See Herbst 1992, 88. See also Karant-Nunn 1997, 119–20.

8.   The oath was introduced by the first super-

intendent, Paul von Eitzen in 1574. For the original manuscript with Eitzen's signature see Landesarchiv Schleswig-Holstein (LAS), Abt. 7, no. 2057 'Eidt der Prediger in den kirchen des Durchleuchtigenn Hochgebornen Fürsten vnd Hern, Herrn Adolff …'. In 1557 there had already been a 'Confessio und Bekenntnis' to be signed by priests during visitations, and this had probably also been written by von Eitzen. See Feddersen 1938, 268.

9. Cf. Brückner 2007, 188, who refers to Luther's Great Catechism, and Rittgers 2004, 119, who refers to Philipp Melanchton's interpretation.

10. *Die Schleswig-Holsteinische Kirchenordnung von 1542*, ed. Göbell 1986, 36–9. For details and the decline of this nomenclature see Feddersen 1938, 253. For Luther's view on this topic see Karant-Nunn 1997, 94: 'The Wittenberg Reformer at one and the same time preserved tradition and broke with it. For several years he retained penance within a group of three scripturally warranted sacraments, and then he abandoned it, leaving baptism and the Eucharist as those rites that were made up of the sacramental requisites, a sign instituted by God and accompanied by His promise.' For more literature on the topic see the same, fns 17 and 18.

11. *Die Schleswig-Holsteinische Kirchenordnung von 1542*, ed. Göbell 1986, 90f. This can also be traced back to Luther's *Formula Missae*, see Herbst 1992, 36–9.

12. Herbst 1992, 35.

13. For this and the following see Wieckowski 2008, 45.

14. See also Klein 1961, 164.

15. *Die Schleswig-Holsteinische Kirchenordnung von 1542*, ed. Göbell 88–95. For the prerequisites for the Eucharist, see also Karant-Nunn 1997, 127.

16. See *Die Schleswig-Holsteinische Kirchenordnung von 1542*, ed. Göbell 98–9. For the consequences that this exception meant see Feddersen 1938, 483, who observes that this rule allowed the pastor to make a difference 'between first class and second class Christians'. See also Rehder 1989, 11–165, here 48.

17. See Feddersen 1938, 538, and Rehder 1989, 44, who refer to an order dating 14 December 1623.

18. Luther 1522, 21: 'Nun halt ichs dafür/ daß diese frage/ oder erforschung gnügsam sey/ wenn sy ain mal imm jar geschee gegen dem/ der das Sacrament nemen will. Ja es kann ayner der sein begert so verstendig seyn/ daß er entweder nur ain mal sein leben lang/ oder aber gar nymmer gefragt werd.' See also Herbst 1992, 34–5, who

19. refers to Luther's more prominent *Formula Missae et Communionis* from 1523.

20. See Brückner 2007.

21. For illustrations and more details see Koerner 2004, which focuses particularly on this altar. See also Brückner 2007, 66–7.

22. For examples from Saxony see Wieckowski 2008, 43–5, 52–3. For examples from other parts of Germany (mainly northern Bavaria) see Brückner 2007, 188–90.

23. See Wieckowski 2008, 45.

24. See Brückner 2007, 206, 274–5.

25. For this and the following see LAS Abt. 162, no. 40 ('Acta betr. den Pastor Gabriel Herman zu Schwabstedt, seine unterschiedlichen gravamina und die deshalb eingesetzte kgl. Commission etc. de 1631–1633'), complaint letter against Hermann to the 'Amtmann von Schwabstedt' dated 13 March 1632, written by 'Bartholomeus Milius Vicarius ibidem': 'Neuwe ein gesicherte ['eingesickerte'] Ceremonien so sich der Pastor Zu Schwabstet Gabriel Herman vnterstanden der gemeinde auff Zu dringen vnd ob scandalum inde ortum necessario abgeschaffet werden mussen, weil sie niemals hir in gebrauch gewesen.'

26. Point 9: '… confessionem publicam oder wol gar für Calerinisch ['Calevinisch'?] anklagt.'

27. Point 11: '… daß Examen im Beichtstul publice & con cione', which would be against the 'principal Stucke eins'.

28. LAS Abt. 65.1, no. 115 'Königs Christian IV. Zu Dännek [sic] Resolution, die Verbeßerung der Kirchen=Ordnung betreffend. Glücksburg d. 26. Oct. 1637', point 7: 'Die affentliche Bußsitzung soll auch in unser amt Hadersleben, Krafft Mandati wierüm introduciret werden'.

29. For the shift of time for confession see Feddersen 1938, 536–7. See also Rehder 1989, 41–4.

30. *Die Schleswig-Holsteinische Kirchenordnung von 1542*, ed. Göbell 1986, 90–91, and Rehder 1989, 42.

31. Cf. Feddersen 1938, 536.

32. Koehn 1954, 291.

33. Christensen 1962, 10.

34. See Bejschowetz-Iserhoht 2003, 9.

35. See, for instance, LAS Abt. 167.2, no. 158: 'Kirchenbuch / der / Kirchen zu Brarup', p. 18: 'Anno 1671 ist der Beicht=Stuhl beßer nach dem Altar hinauf gesetzet und synd an doselbigen Stete 5 Newe Frawen Stule der Kirchen Zum besten gesetzet worden …'.

36. Rehder 1989, 44–6.

37. For the pre-Reformation practice and more

details and literature on the development of early modern confessionals see Karant-Nunn 1997, 94.

37. Wieckowski 2008, 53. The 'type of confessional with two parts and separation wall' ['zweigeteilter Beichtstuhltypus mit Trennwand'] was introduced into the Catholic church after the Council of Trent. See Brückner 2007, 188.

38. See Brückner 2007, 188. For a detailed study of the development and use of Catholic confessionals see also Schlombs 1965, esp. part B.

39. Schlombs 1965, 37.

40. Feddersen 1938, 481.

41. *Die Bau- und Kunstdenkmäler der Freien und Hansestadt Lübeck* 1906, 302, which refers to the custodians' protocol from 16 April 1787: 'für den Priester als für die Beichtenden sehr unbequemen [Beichtstuhl]'. For a photograph of the confessionals see Hasse 1983, 9.

42. See Klein 1961, 165.

43. See Wilckens 2003, 108–9.

44. See Rittgers 2004.

45. *Die Bau- und Kunstdenkmäler der Freien und Hansestadt Lübeck*, 1920, 197.

46. See Wieckowski 2008, 43. On p. 44, he states that about 100 Protestant confessionals have survived complete or in parts in Saxony.

47. See Luther 1958, 95. For the original Latin see Luther 1911, 42, 72b. See also Heal 2005. 45. For early Protestant discussions on church buildings see Michalski 1994, 44–6.

48. Heal 2005, 45.

49. Cf. Dürr 2004, 388, who points out that the confessionals were also a reminder of the priest's authority, as he alone had the power to absolve parishioners and thus allow them participation in Holy Communion.

50. Wieckowski 2008, 43–4. See also Brückner 2007, 188–9.

BIBLIOGRAPHY

Bejschowetz-Iserhoht, M. 2003, '"… in der Vorstadt Cratzenberg … ein Gotteshaus an zu richten und zu verfertigen": 350 Jahre Dreifaltigkeitskirche in Schleswig-Friedrichsberg', in Bejschowetz-Iserhoht & Witt 2003, 7–19.

Bejschowetz-Iserhoht, M & Witt, R. (eds) 2003, *Kirchliches Leben in Schleswig-Holstein im 17. Jahrhundert: Vortäge zu einer Ausstellung im Landesarchiv*. Veröffentlichungen des Schleswig-Holsteinischen Landesarchivs 78. Schleswig: Landesarchiv Schleswig-Holstein.

Brückner, W. 2007, *Lutherische Bekenntnisgemälde des 16. bis 18. Jahrhunderts. Die illustrierte Confessio Augustana*, Regensburg: Schnell und Steiner.

Christensen, F. 1962, *Aus der Geschichte des Kirchspiels Enstedt*, Schriften der Heimatkundlichen Arbeitsgemeinschaft für Nordschleswig 5.

Coster, W. & Spicer, A. (eds) 2005, *Sacred Space in Early Modern Europe*, Cambridge: Cambridge University Press.

Die Bau- und Kunstdenkmäler der Freien und Hansestadt Lübeck, 1906, ed. by the Baudeputation, 2: Petrikirche, Marienkirche, Heil.-Geist-Hospital, Hirsch, F., Schaumann, G. & Bruns, F. (eds), Lübeck: Bernhard Nöhring.

Die Bau- und Kunstdenkmäler der Freien und Hansestadt Lübeck, 1920, ed. by the Baudeputation, 3: Kirche zu Alt-Lübeck, Dom, Jakobikirche, Ägidienkirche, Joh. Baltzer & F. Bruns, Lübeck: Bernhard Nöhring.

Die Schleswig-Holsteinische Kirchenordnung von 1542, ed. by Walter Göbell, 1986, publ. as 'Schriften des Vereins für Schleswig-Holsteinische Kirchengeschichte', series 1, 34, Neumünster: Wachholtz.

Dürr, R. 2004, 'Private Ohrenbeichte im öffentlichen Kirchenraum', in Rau & Schwerhoff 2004, 383–411.

Feddersen, E. 1938, *Kirchengeschichte Schleswig-Holsteins*, vol. 2: 1517–1721. Schriften des Vereins für Schleswig-Holsteinische Kirchengeschichte 19. Kiel: Kommissions-Verlag Walter G. Mühlau.

Gaimster, D. & Gilchrist, R. (eds) 2003, *The Archaeology of Reformation 1480–1580*. Society for Post-Medieval Archaeology Monograph 1. Leeds: Maney.

Hasse, M. 1983, *Die Marienkirche zu Lübeck*, München: Deutscher Kunstverlag.

Heal, B. 2005, 'Sacred image and sacred space in Lutheran Germany', in Coster & Spicer 2005, 39–59.

Herbst, W. 1992, *Evangelischer Gottesdienst. Quellen zu seiner Geschichte*, 2nd edn, Göttingen: Vadenhoeck und Ruprecht.

Jäggi C. & Staecker, J. (eds) 2007, *Archäologie der Reformation. Studien zu den Auswirkungen des Konfessionswechsels auf die materielle Kultur*. Arbeiten zur Kirchengeschichte 104. Berlin: de Gruyter.

Karant-Nunn, S.C. 1997, *The Reformation of Ritual: An Interpretation of Early Modern Germany*, London: Routledge.

Klein, L. 1961, *Evangelisch-Lutherische Beichte, Lehre und Praxis*. Konfessionskundliche und kontroverstheologische Studien 5. Paderborn: Bonifacius-Druckerei.

Koehn, H. 1954, *Die Nordfriesischen Inseln. Die Entwicklung ihrer Landschaft und die Geschichte ihres Volkstums*, 4th edn, Hamburg: Cram, de Huyter.

Koerner, L. 2004, *The Reformation of the Image*, Chicago: University of Chicago Press.

LAS, Abt. 7, no. 2057: 'Eidt der Prediger in den kirchen des Durchleuchtigenn Hochgebornen Fürsten vnd Hern, Herrn Adolff …'.

LAS, Abt. 65.1, no. 115 'Königs Christian IV. Zu Dännek [*sic*] Resolution, die Verbeßerung der Kirchen=Ordnung betreffend. Glücksburg d. 26. Oct. 1637'.

LAS, Abt. 162, no. 40: 'Acta betr. den Pastor Gabriel Herman zu Schwabstedt, seine unterschiedlichen gravamina und die deshalb eingesetzte kgl. Commission etc. de 1631–1633'.

LAS, Abt. 167.2, no. 158: 'Kirchenbuch / der / Kirchen zu Brarup'.

Lee, B.B. 2008, 'Communal transformations of church space in Lutheran Lübeck', *German History* 26/2: 149–67.

Luther, M. 1522, *Die weyße der Meß / vnnd geniessung des Hochwirdigē Sacraments / für die Christliche Gemayn verteütscht*, Wittenberg.

Luther, M. 1911, *D. Martin Luthers Werke. Kritische Gesamtausgabe*, 120 vols, 42: 'Genesisvorlesung (cap. 1–17) 1535/38', Weimar: Böhlau.

Luther, M. 1958, *Luther's Works*, ed. by Jaroslav Pelikan, 55 vols, 1: Lectures on Genesis, Chapters 1–5, Saint Louis: Concordia Publishing.

Magirius, H. (ed.) 2008, *Die Dresdner Frauenkirche: Jahrbuch zur ihrer Geschichte und Gegenwart*, vol. 12, Regensburg: Schnell & Steiner.

Michalski, S. 1994, 'Einfache häuser – prunkvolle kirchen: zur topik der frühen protestantischen debatten um den kirchenbau', in Raschzok & Sörries 1994, 44–6.

Raschzok, Kl. & Sörries, R. (eds) 1994, *Geschichte des protestantischen Kirchenbaus. Festschrift für Peter Poscharsky zum 60. Geburtstag*, Erlangen: Junge.

Rau, S. & Schwerhoff, G. (eds) 2004, *Zwischen Gotteshaus und Taverne. Öffentliche Räume in Spätmittelalter und Früher Neuzeit*, Köln: Böhlau.

Rehder, F. 1989, 'Volksfrömmigkeit und Kirchenzucht: Beispiele aus Schleswig-Holsteinischen archivalischen Quellen', in Seminar für Volkskunde der Christian-Albrechts-Universität Kiel 1989, 11–165.

Rittgers, R.K. 2004, *The Reformation of the Keys: Confession, Conscience, and Authority in Sixteenth-Century Germany*, Cambridge (MA): Harvard University Press.

Schlombs, W. 1965, *Die Entwicklung des Beichtstuhls in der katholischen Kirche. Grundlagen und Besonderheiten im alten Erzbistum Köln*. Studien zur Kölner Kirchengeschichte 8. Düsseldorf: L. Schwann.

Scholkmann, B. 2007, 'Forschungsfragestellungen, Möglichkeiten und Grenzen einer Archäologie der Reformation in Mitteleuropa', in Jäggi & Staecker 2007, 3–25.

Seminar für Volkskunde der Christian-Albrechts-Universität Kiel (ed.) 1989, *Volksleben, Kirche und Obrigkeit in Schleswig-Holstein von der Reformation bis ins 19. Jahrhundert*. Studien zur Volkskunde und Kulturgeschichte Schleswig-Holsteins 21. Neumünster: Wachholtz.

Wieckowski, A. 2008, 'Evangelische beichtpraxis in Sachsen und in der Dresdner Frauenkirche', in Magirius 2008, 43–56.

Wilckens, N. 2003, '"Sieg über Tod und Teufel" – Theologische Programme der Originalausstattung der Friedrichsberger Dreifaltigkeitskirche', in Bejschowetz-Iserhoht & Witt 2003, 101–13.

ABBREVIATION

LAS   Landesarchiv Schleswig-Holstein

Romantic Anachronisms?
Chantry Chapels of the 19th Century

SIMON ROFFEY

The 19th century witnessed a religious revival in England and an attempt to recover the original Catholic heritage of the Church, as exemplified by the highly ritualized practices of the medieval period, and supported by the elaborately decorated interiors of churches often replete with chantry foundations. Previously abolished at the Reformation, chantry chapels were thus resurrected as a distinct element of space and plan in Catholic and High Anglican churches. This chapter will consider the nature of such institutions in the Victorian period and examine some examples that emerged in the preceding centuries. Overall it will reflect upon the extent to which chantries had a relevant role to play in the religious practice of the 19th century.

INTRODUCTION

Chantry chapels, along with related practices concerning death and the afterlife, were one of the most fundamental elements of pre-Reformation religion. The Reformation, and specifically, the acts for the dissolution of the monasteries in the 1530s and the dissolution of the chantries in 1547, did much to obliterate the physical presence of the chantries both as the physical representation of Catholic beliefs in the afterlife and as symbols of traditional orthodoxy. Thus, to speak of a post-Reformation chantry chapel is somewhat of a misnomer. However, having played such a formative role in the development of church space, art and architecture, as well as both public and private piety and memorial practice, for almost 400 years, the broad influence and the architectural legacy of the medieval chantry chapel was not so easily diminished. This chapter will provide a contextual examination of post-medieval chapels.[1] It will consider the continuing influence of the medieval chantry on the churches of the post-medieval period and particularly in the time of orthodox revival in the mid 19th century, as well as their meaning in the context of the revitalization of religious practice. Furthermore, it will evaluate their particular function in the resurgence of one of medieval England's most important religious institutions.

First, we must define the form and function of the medieval chantry chapel. The chantry was a foundation and endowment of a mass by one or more benefactors, to be celebrated at an altar, for the souls of the founders and other specified persons. Thus it was a direct strategy for the medieval afterlife and a mechanism to benefit souls in purgatory. The majority of such foundations were of a temporary duration. However, a number of chantries, founded usually by wealthier men and women, but also by collectives such as guilds and fraternities, were intended to last in perpetuity. These perpetual chantries were often in the form of dedicated chapels that appropriated or added to existing church space. These chapels ranged from the impressive cage-chantries of the cathedrals and greater churches, such as the 16th-century Markham and Meyring chapels at Newark, Nottinghamshire, to the undoubtedly more common parclosed chapels of the parish churches, as at Lavenham, Suffolk, for example.[2] Some were colleges – essentially 'superchantries', such as the royal foundation of St George's, Windsor, which drew on the prayers and observances of a dedicated religious community, as well as, in some cases, such as Winchester College, having educational responsibilities. Chantry chapels were often sumptuously decorated and those rare survivals such as the intricately decorated Greenway chapel at Tiverton, Devon, hint at the scope and breadth of similar works that are now lost to us through the ravages of reformation and time.

THE REFORMATION OF CHAPELS

By 1548 all chantries, colleges, religious brotherhoods and hospitals were surrendered to the king. As well as the removal of the monuments themselves, the dissolution of the chantries also involved the effective dismantling of many of the institutions associated with chantry foundation, such as schools, hospitals and almshouses. Many former chantry chapels were, however, converted to more secular purposes. At the former Augustinian priories at Smithfield and Southwark in London, the spaces of former chantry chapels were employed as blacksmiths and stables respectively,[3] while at Salisbury Cathedral the remarkable Hungerford and Beauchamp chapels, at the east end of the cathedral church, were taken down as part of a general 'restoration' in the 18th century.[4] At Wakefield, West Yorkshire, the bridge chantry chapel was put to a variety of secular uses, including a water store, warehouse, library, merchant's office and cheesecake shop. In the 19th century, its decorated western façade was removed to nearby Kettlethorpe Hall and became the façade of a folly boathouse.[5]

In many parish churches the spaces formerly occupied by chantries survived, and retained their family connections: examples include the 15th-century Spencer chapel at Great Brington, Northamptonshire, and the Bardolph chapel at Mapledurham, Oxfordshire, which was sealed off from its church during the 16th century.[6] At Great Brington a polygonal apse leading from the chapel was rebuilt by Edward Blore in 1846.[7] The Long chapel at South Wraxall, Wiltshire, became the Long family pew in 1566, and the chantry of the Bretts, a family of notable recusants, at Whitestaunton, Somerset, survived as a family chapel with an elaborate portal entrance added in 1588.[8] However, such chapels were often dramatically reorganized and ritually 'sanitized'. This form of spatial iconoclasm included the removal of screens, the setting-up of private pews and, in some cases, the effective sealing-off or obstruction of former ritual areas and features by tombs and memorials. The placement of large and ostentatious tombs such as the Hungerford tomb in the former chapel of St Anne at Farleigh Hungerford, Somerset, and the Wriothsley monument at Titchfield, Hampshire, appropriated virtually the whole floor space of the chapels.[9] In effect, the occupation and appropriation of former chantry chapel space in the decades after the Reformation marked the transition from the communally valued chantry to wholly exclusive space.[10]

These post-Reformation chapels of Protestant England were distinctly different from their Catholic precursors. Architecturally they were similar and their overall function was

still concerned with religious practice and memorial, but intercession and the formal peti-
tioning for souls in the afterlife were no longer factors. Furthermore, they were sterilized
of all forms of orthodox decoration, imagery and liturgy. In some cases, such as the former
chantry, 'Southampton', chapel at Titchfield, their proprietors still held to Catholicism,
although their chapels clearly did not. It would be rather imprudent for those chapels held
by Catholics to be anything like their medieval precursors. The significance of Catholic-
held chapels such as Titchfield lay not in their function or form but in their heritage value
as a link to a once-Catholic past. In fact, as we shall see when we come to discuss the
Victorian examples, this 'link' may have been of significant symbolic value.

The religious changes wrought by the Reformation dictated that the fate of the soul
was sealed at death, so there was no need for prayers for the dead or petitions for souls in
purgatory. However, the forms of visual reminder confirming, celebrating and publicizing
the status, deeds and ultimately the morality of the deceased were important. Therefore,
special emphasis was placed on the tomb or memorial as an indicator of social status, not
just with regard to decoration, inscription and the quality of construction and materials
but also with regard to the setting, appropriation of space and visibility. Whereas it was
not essential for the body (and therefore a tomb) to be an element of medieval chantry
chapels – as the foundation was often for the benefit of souls – now special emphasis was
placed on the tomb as a mechanism for the evocation of memory of the dead by the living.
Increased importance was placed on the memorial as being a designator of familial prestige,
status and rank in life. Whereas the former chantry mass was mutually beneficial to both
patron and parishioner, now any benefit was strictly one-way.

Thus many of these private chapels functioned as both repositories for family memorials
and as status symbols for local families in the context of the local church. Pews were often a
feature of these chapels. In some instances, as at Cartmell Fell and Whalley parish churches
in Lancashire and Gaddesby, Leicestershire, pews were constructed from the screens of
former chantry chapels.[11] The period after the Reformation still witnessed the building of
family chapels such as the Protestant Knollys chapel at Rotherfield Greys, Oxfordshire,
built around 1605.[12] However, those former chantry chapels that survived were now shorn
of any orthodox decoration and became more exclusive contexts for private piety and, in
particular, family memorial and commemoration. Hence some Protestant chapels were
now often off-limits and detached both visually and physically from the rest of the church.
The Hoare family pew at Stourton, Wiltshire, was sealed off from the nave and its interior
could be viewed only by the priest in the pew. The former Darrell chantry at Ramsbury,
Wiltshire, had a private entrance inserted into its north wall and stalls introduced for the
local Popham family.[13] Such changes forced the tearing-out of a tomb from its recess and
the blocking of the entrance from the north aisle to the chapel, effectively sealing off the
chapel from the rest of the church. At Rycote, Oxfordshire, two large enclosed wooden
pews were erected in the chapel of St Michael in the early 17th century.[14] Their location at
the east end of the nave would have obstructed vision to the east end of the church and
they thus imposed themselves visually on the congregation seated behind. Each pew was
canopied and enclosed by decorated screens with well-furnished interiors and would have
made outstanding additions to the church interior.[15]

In certain cases, chapels may have been designed so as to directly imitate the medieval chantry chapel and thus provide themselves with some sort of antique credibility or
implied family longevity. The 18th-century Poley chapel at Boxted, Suffolk, provides a

Figure 4.1. The brick-built Poley Chapel, Boxted, Suffolk (photograph by S. Roffey).

unique example comprising a brick north chancel chapel with an adjoining north aisle containing two sets of box pews (Fig. 4.1). That to the east was for the use of the family, with a prime view to the pulpit to the south, and that to the west was possibly for the use of servants and retainers. Thus the entire north side of the church was appropriated by the Protestant Poley family.[16] Significantly, this arrangement was probably influenced by medieval chantry chapels at nearby Somerton and particularly the impressive Clopton chantry chapel at Long Melford, which comprised a north chapel with adjoining chancel chantry chapel to the east.

THE REBIRTH OF PURGATORY

Essential to the function of the medieval chantry chapel was the belief in purgatory, a very Catholic doctrine. It was still a mainstream belief within 19th-century Catholicism, but a doctrine that, while being courted by certain High Church Anglicans, was traditionally eschewed by their more conservative brethren. However, generally speaking, as Rowell and Wheeler note, the doctrine of an intermediate state of some form or other was of growing importance during the 19th century. Furthermore, belief in a level of spiritual progress in an intermediate state was 'remarkably widespread among nineteenth-century Protestants of widely different theological positions'.[17] These beliefs ranged from a tentative reappraisal of traditional purgatory; a foreshortened hell, and a place of 'moral progress and expansion of the mind'.[18] We shall continue to explore these theological developments later but first of all we shall examine the rebirth of that monument most associated with purgatory – the chantry chapel – before moving on to see what the reinvention of these chapels can tell us about contemporary associated belief in Victorian England.

ROMANTIC ANACHRONISMS?

The centuries prior to the 19th century, therefore, witnessed the destruction of many chantry chapels but also, in other cases, their transformation into private and family mortuary chapels. Though an important aspect of parish church layout they were wholly exclusive, often replete with private pews and elite monuments celebrating the status and deeds of the dead. Naturally, these chapels and monuments contained little in the way of wall painting, sculpture or decoration – those elements so essential to the religious symbolism of the medieval chantry. However, the 19th century was to reintroduce more emotive elements to contemporary religious practice and the architectural contexts within which this was experienced.

The 19th century witnessed the introduction of various acts and bills, in particular the Catholic Relief Act of 1829, which led to greater freedom for Catholics in Great Britain and Ireland. Furthermore, this period also heralded the so-called 'Gothic Revival', behind which were various attempts to get back to the roots of the Christian tradition and recover the original Catholic heritage of the Church of England. In particular, groups such as the Oxford Movement, initiated in 1833,[19] worked tirelessly to promote the reintroduction of a more emotive element to contemporary religious practice in the Anglican church as exemplified by the highly ritualized practices of the medieval period and supported by the iconographic and symbolic interiors of the churches. While theologians such as John Henry Newman and John Mason Neale were establishing contexts for theological debate, and societies such as the Cambridge Camden Society were providing a platform for the dissemination of high church ideas, many architects, such as Augustus Pugin and William Butterfield, were beginning to build and rebuild ecclesiastical buildings that were heavily influenced by medieval principles relating to design, decoration and the use of space, such as the early example of All Saints, Margaret Street, London, built in 1849.[20] Pugin himself from as early as the 1830s had worked on the restoration of a medieval building in Salisbury and had designed his own Neo-Gothic mansion, St Marie's Grange, at Alderbury, Wiltshire, where he built one of his first medieval-style chapels.[21] Many parish churches around the country were once again furnished with medieval-style stained glass, images and wall paintings. At Highnam, Gloucestershire, for example, the chancel arch was painted with a florid depiction of the Day of Judgment, a painting that would not have looked out of place some 400 years earlier.[22] At Asthall, Oxfordshire, the chancel of the church was redecorated completely in gothic style.

Many revivalists, such as Neale and Pugin, believed that the architecture of many Protestant churches was purely functional and overtly secular in design. Likewise, religious symbolism, where used, was, to them, too simplistic and easily understandable, lacking the mystic complexity and deeper meanings of the medieval. These people believed that the remedy lay in the re-introduction of the medieval gothic, particularly the so-called genius of pointed architecture, a style in which Neale himself believed 'all conditions of beauty, of detail, of general effect, of truthfulness, of reality are so fully answered'.[23] Architecture, it was held, should be a metaphor for higher spiritual principles. Additionally, Pugin believed that it should synthesize the natural with the mystical. For example, he perceived the natural function of pinnacles as 'upper weathering', but also as mystical symbols of the Resurrection.[24] Fundamentally, he believed that architecture should be used to represent a 'moral life', a life of beauty and higher values. Importantly, Pugin emphasized the inter-visibility of church space, its order and aesthetic compartmentalization where, he believed, the spectator moving through the church should see new views at each stage in his passage and could at once perceive its purpose.[25] The progress from one space to the next was ultimately directed towards the central drama of the sanctuary, its power enforced on the mind of the laity by being partly hidden from their sight. In contrast to what some now believe of medieval religious practice,[26] Pugin believed that 'seeing' was not as important as 'experiencing' and compared it with the contemporary Protestant need to 'hear'.[27] Screens, many of which were destroyed at the Reformation, were particularly essential in that they set apart the spaces of altars from less sacred areas.[28] Overall, Pugin felt that chapels were an integral element of church layout, stating that 'where there are lateral aisles, these should be terminated towards the east by altars, either erected against the wall, and protected by open screen work, or in chapels'.[29] John Mason Neale criticized the Protestant church for holding the view that church chapels obstructed the interior of churches. This, he argued, was due to the fact that planners and architects were thinking in terms of a layout perceived from a drawing or plan. The contribution of chapels to the interior landscape of churches could only be appreciated by the spectator, one who moves around the church and experiences it at first-hand. Furthermore, one writer of the time, writing for the Camden Society publication *The Ecclesiologist*, emphasized the importance of church ritual and particularly chapels as places for communion, and, as we shall see, as essential for burial ritual.[30]

Thus, this period witnessed the rebirth of the chantry chapel – at least in its architectural form – both as an important element of church ritual space and as a natural expression of medieval aesthetics and religious sensibility and, importantly perhaps, authenticity. The construction of chapels at this period was nowhere near as prolific as in the medieval period; however, many were founded as essential elements in revival-inspired ecclesiastical building programmes. St George's Cathedral, Southwark, the first Catholic cathedral since the Reformation, housed two chantry chapels: the Petre chantry, designed by Augustus Pugin, and the Knill chantry, by his son Edward.[31] The cathedral itself, constructed in 1848, was originally planned by Augustus Pugin to have a tower, transepts and clerestory and therefore provide a light and spacious interior to the church – a fitting environment for the establishment of side altars and chapels. This initial plan was, however, eventually rejected and Pugin was forced to omit these elements.[32] Although the cathedral was much damaged by bombing in the Second World War the chapels survived and are testament to both the quality of workmanship and the religious sensibility of the period.

In its report of the opening the Catholic newspaper, *Tablet*, remarked that it was the intention of the Cathedral to 'erect chantries outside the church in the spaces between the confessionals'.[33] The first, erected before his death in 1849, was that of the prominent and wealthy Catholic, Edward Petre, who requested that a chantry chapel be erected in the cathedral in which his 'remains should repose after his death'.[34] Accordingly, masses were still being said in this chantry for the repose of Petre's soul some twenty years later.[35] It is likely that the chapel was originally planned to have been placed close to the west

Figure 4.2. The Petre Chapel, St George's Cathedral, Southwark (photograph by S. Roffey).

door. However, it was felt that the monument would have been a rather overt symbol of traditional orthodoxy, and would thus, for some observers, represent the excesses of traditional Catholicism. Thus Petre's family requested that the chapel should be placed at a safe distance from the public thoroughfare of St George's Road.[36] It was placed within an arcade between the Lady Chapel and the east end of the nave, in close proximity to the high altar. Inside, the vaulted chapel includes a richly decorated altar and reredos. Petre's tomb sits within an open arch and is constructed of Caen limestone with black marble inlaid with a brass cross and an inscription exhorting prayers for the soul. The windows of the chapel once contained stained glass by John Hardman and included depictions of St George the Martyr, St Lawrence, St Robert and St Germanus.[37] In its design and location the chapel clearly echoes the medieval cage chantry, like those still extant in many medieval cathedrals such as Salisbury and Winchester, close to where Pugin lived and worked early in his career. However, despite its internal grandeur, the decoration on the outside is rather plain in comparison, suggesting a certain reserve or even caution in its display in the public context (Fig. 4.2).

In 1857 Pugin's son, Edward, designed the Knill chantry. This beautifully decorated chapel sits at the east end of the north aisle, again in close proximity to the high altar. Likewise, the design is reminiscent of medieval cage chantries but, unlike his father's Petre

Figure 4.3. The Knill Chapel, St George's Cathedral, Southwark (photograph by S. Roffey).

chapel, Edward's monument was sumptuously decorated not only inside but externally also, and featured open screen work adorned with ball flowers, ornamented pinnacles and the images of angels (Figs 4.3 and 4.4). It was not without its own controversy, however. A report by the cathedral provost of the time states that the chapel 'projected into the church by two feet', causing some offence as it partially intruded into the archway leading into the chapel of the Blessed Sacrament.[38] The Knill chantry was reported to be in disrepair by 1907, though masses were still being celebrated at its altar.[39] Another chantry, for George Talbot, was proposed in 1854 at a princely sum of £1000. Although some work was started on this monument, it was held up owing to the death of Talbot's kinsman, the earl of Shrewsbury, and the fact that the recently vacant earldom was taken up by a Protestant. The chapel later became the Relic Chapel.[40]

Edward Pugin also designed a number of other chantry chapels, including the Catholic Weedall chantry at St Mary's Oscott, in the West Midlands, refounded as a college in 1838. Originally, the chantry wall was decorated with the mystical theme of the angel of death standing on a tomb from which the tree of life emerged. This was later replaced with memorial brasses commemorating past presidents of the college.[41]

As in the medieval period, the collegiate design was one that was particularly popular with those who had the influence and wealth to adopt it. But it was a design that was not just reserved for the new monasteries and training colleges, such as Oscott and Ramsgate,

Figure 4.4. Interior of Knill Chapel, St George's Cathedral, Southwark
(photograph by S. Roffey).

Kent. At Pontefract, North Yorkshire, Augustus Pugin designed a collegiate-style private chapel for the Catholic Tempest family. This foundation consisted of a chapel, with nave, chancel and north chantry chapel, connected to the house via an elaborate cloister.[42] The windows of the chantry chapel, now demolished, contained stained glass featuring the Evangelists and the Virgin and Child as well as the armorial bearings of the Tempest family. In true medieval style there was an open 'niche' between the chancel and chapel within which was a tomb/Easter Sepulchre. The whole monument, to Pugin, resembled 'a small religious edifice of the fine period of Edward III'.[43]

Perhaps the one building that exemplified the High Church movement was Keble College, Oxford. The Anglican college was founded in memory of John Keble (1792–1866), a founding member of the Oxford Movement who, unsurprisingly, believed that decorated gothic architecture was a style that was 'by far most in harmony with the mysteries of religion'.[44] The college was designed by William Butterfield, a man seemingly of more practical temperament than many of his contemporaries, who believed that the true power of gothic lay not in its mystical associations, espoused by the likes of Pugin, but in its structural integrity: its longevity and the power of its bricks and mortar. True enough, Keble College impressed with its monumental proportions and Gothic authenticity. Based on medieval collegiate design, it consisted of a large open cloister with associated buildings centring on the large neo-Gothic chapel. Inside, the chapel was sumptuously decorated with sculpture, images, furniture and wall paintings, much of which survives today.

Chantry chapels were also constructed in parish churches. A late, but nonetheless interesting, example is the Bateman Mausoleum at Morley, Derbyshire, constructed in 1897. The chapel is independent but was built into part of the medieval church wall and was suitably furnished with sculpture and stained glass. At its centre is the tomb of Hugh Alleyn Sacheverell Bateman. The cross on the tomb chest is set with small crystal inserts through which the coffin may be seen. The monument has recently been sensitively restored by the Mausolea and Monuments Trust.[45] Another particularly impressive example can be seen at the Anglican church of West Tofts in Norfolk. Here there is an Augustus Pugin-designed parclosed north chapel with painted screen and recess tomb. The north transept chapel is highly carved and decorated and the walls were once originally stencilled. The church clearly illustrates how Pugin believed a medieval church should be experienced, with its light, open and decorated space containing distinct liturgical compartments.

An important feature of many of the revivalist architects' work was the synthesis, where possible, of original work with new. This relationship Pugin considered at some length in his written treatise *Contrasts* (1836). At Oscott, for example, the chapel altar was reconstructed from fragments of an original altar. At Bicton, Devon, the Rolle mortuary chapel was built using surviving material from the original church itself, including the roof, which was sumptuously decorated in revival style. The medieval church itself was left as a ruinous folly paying testament to the authenticity of the new-built chapel (Fig. 4.5). The Protestant Rolle family was clearly sympathetic to High Church ideology and saw such vestiges of the past as the ideal reflection of contemporary spirituality. The chapel was also tiled and has stained glass featuring images of, among others, St Lazarus.[46] Inside are two tombs, the earliest being that of Dennis Rolle Esq. (1638), which pre-dates the construction of the chapel. Its inclusion may indicate a desire to provide the chapel with some antiquity. The second tomb, against the north wall and framed by an elaborate stone reredos containing images of saints, is that of the second Lord Rolle (*c.* 1842).

Figure 4.5. The Rolle Chapel, Bicton, Devon. The rebuilt chapel sits at the south-east corner of the ruined medieval church. Note the remains of a church *piscina* in the north wall of the chapel and the churchyard cross marking the former location of the high altar (photograph by S. Roffey).

The 19th century, therefore, witnessed the rebirth of the chantry chapel as a distinct architectural feature within the church. However, the question remains as to what exactly the function of these monuments was. It is clear that those architects influenced by the Gothic revival felt that the chantry chapel was an integral element of the ritual spaces they were designing. However, their medieval precursors were designed as strategies for intercession: monuments that would both evoke memories of their founders and provide a context for both intercessory masses and prayers for the dead. They also contributed greatly to the religious experience of the medieval period by providing multiple and often unique masses in a period of Eucharistic popularity. To ascertain the function of the 19th-century chantry chapel we have to first examine the theological underpinning behind the Gothic revival as it applies to notions of purgatory and the afterlife.

'PURGATORY' IN THE 19TH CENTURY

Purgatory was a belief that was central to the make-up of the late medieval church. It was, however, a subject that was treated with some ambivalence and uncertainty by 19th-century theologians and revivalists. Some, such as John Henry Newman and those involved with the Oxford Movement, viewed it as a 'a time of preparation for heaven'; a sort of 'school-time of contemplation'.[47] However, many, including Henry Edward Manning, still recognized the intercessory value of human prayer in this process. In 1877 Manning and Bishop Grant of Southwark, supported by Newman, invited to England representatives of the Society of the Helpers of Holy Souls.[48] Originally founded in France in 1856, the Society's mission was to actively help souls in purgatory through prayers and supplications and the transference of personal spiritual merit. Thus the Society added a fourth, 'heroic', vow to the three traditional ones of Poverty, Chastity and Obedience by promising 'complete surrender for the souls in purgatory of all the merits I can acquire'.[49] At this time, however, there were also many who believed in and promulgated purgatory as a place of pain and fire. The most notorious of these was perhaps the Catholic evangelist Reverend Joseph Furniss, with his series of *Books for Children*. In one tract, *The Sight of Hell*, he described the six dungeons of purgatory which included a burning dress, a red-hot floor and a coffin complete with imprisoned child.[50] Thus were the many extreme and conflicting ideas of the time.

What was clear, however, was that some theologians, such as Newman, firmly believed in the existence of a purgatory but not the various Roman doctrines that concerned it. Certainly, the Tracts, conceived within the Oxford Movement, largely in the 1830s, were keen to encourage a belief that purgatory was a place of refreshment, a type of peaceful antechamber to heaven. Here, death was not an exit, but a passage, a travelling to things eternal, when time has been journeyed through, hence 'who would not hasten to what is better?'[51] This was a very different view from that of the English medieval period and had, in fact, more in common with continental romantic ideas of purgatory as espoused by the medieval Italian poet Dante, for example. Furthermore, the Tractarians were keen to take the advice of the 17th-century Archbishop Ussher in believing that prayers for the dead were very different from prayers for those in purgatory.[52] The former, it seemed, catered more for a sense of bereavement and evocation of memory rather than as a unit of merit which could actually help souls in purgatory. Newman's poem *The Dream of Gerontius* perhaps gives us one singular insight into a perception of purgatory held by at least one 19th-century churchman. The *Dream*, first published in 1865, recounted the death of an old man and the journey of his soul to judgement. In the later stages of the journey an angel proclaims to the dead man: 'In my most loving arms I now enfold thee, And, o'er the penal waters, as they roll, I poise thee, and I lower thee, and hold thee.'[53] Intriguingly, this poem also refers to 'Masses on the earth and prayers in heaven ...' which shall 'aid thee at the Throne of the most Highest',[54] which may suggest the perceived spiritual relevance of chantries at this time.

CONCLUSION

From the Reformation, therefore, the chantry chapel ceased to function as a strategy for the medieval afterlife: a monument dedicated to providing intercessory masses for souls in purgatory. The post-Reformation chapels of the late 16th to 18th centuries were very different. Whereas the medieval chantry chapels provided a contribution to church space and ritual, often contributing directly to the increasingly complex and popular Eucharistic-based liturgy of the period, post-medieval chapels were often shorn of decoration.

Furthermore, many were sectioned off to become wholly private family pews and memorial chapels. Some chapels, such as that at Boxted, may have been designed to imply family longevity. Others, as at Rycote, compartmentalized and privatized the space of former chantry chapels. In some ways, though, the chantry chapels of the 19th century, many founded in the context of Gothic revivalism and Catholic emancipation, were more similar to their medieval precursors. Significantly, they were used as memorials, though more often than not for the wealthy. Many were highly decorated with religious themes and replete with altars and founder's tombs. And, importantly, they were an integral element of church ritual space. In the increasingly religiously liberal times of the mid 19th century they were seen as once important components of the medieval church – a church that was to some a symbol of the purity of Christian tradition; a representation of beauty and higher values; in a sense a vision of heaven on earth. They were components of an ordered ritual landscape. Victorian chantry chapels were also, importantly, a strategy for evoking memories of the individual deceased, but, significantly, not specifically for souls in purgatory. Here, fundamentally, they were different from their medieval predecessors. While adding much to the aesthetic of church spaces and providing a symbolic link to a particular form of medieval religious piety and expression, they were ultimately monuments dedicated to a Victorian elite, in a sense acting as a sort of 'religious folly'; a memorial novelty. Those found in Catholic institutions had little appeal to the majority of common churchgoers – mostly poor and of Irish immigrant stock. To the high church Anglicans their appeal must have been little more than sentimental, at most giving a certain amount of authority to often newly decorated or designed church spaces. Chapels such as that at Bicton were in form very much like the medieval chantry chapels of old. But they were often highly exclusive monuments and, in this sense, differed little from the post-Reformation chapels. At Bicton, emphasis was clearly on the chapel and its setting as a piece of memorial architecture, not as a context for the rituals of intercession or, indeed, Eucharistic piety. Furthermore, whereas many medieval chantry endowments included regular cycles of alms-giving or the foundation of hospitals and schools, the Victorian examples provided little active charity.

In addition, 19th-century views of purgatory were subtly different from the medieval ideal where prayers and particularly masses were an important intercessory mechanism and verified doctrinally. The former view was of purgatory as a place of repose, an antechamber for heaven, rather than a fiery realm of purgation and suffering. It is also questionable as to what extent the common man or women dwelt on such mysteries during a period of economic growth and the development of scientific and industrial innovation. It does appear, at times, that to the likes of Neale and Newman the issue of purgatory was not one of personal and impending salvific import, but rather an intellectual conundrum: a fascinating and knotty subject for theorizing, contemplation and convivial debate.

Thus, the role of chantry chapels in the 19th century was to offer a natural expression of medieval religious sensibilities and aesthetics, and to provide a crucial element of authenticity to church spaces. To some, they linked the values of the past with those of the present, indicative of a time of loftier spiritual ideals. But these were the ideals and aesthetic values of a Victorian elite, and unlike their medieval predecessors they had little formal, practical role for the overall laity. In another sense they also represented a shift in emphasis from a traditional celebration of family status and memory to a more individualistic, aesthetic monumentalization. The Victorian 'chantry', while being authentic in architectural form, was largely symbolic in function and was shorn of much of the complex liturgy and indeed wider social implications of its medieval precursors. Thus they were romantic anachronisms; monuments that were testaments to a rich period of religious revival, as well as nostalgic and artistic sensibility, but which ultimately drew inspiration from a very different age, long since departed.

NOTES

1. A method of archaeological interpretation, originally pioneered by the archaeologist Ian Hodder (i.e. 1986), in which emphasis is placed on the study of contexts in order to understand wider meanings.
2. Roffey 2008.
3. Roffey 2008, 169.
4. Brown 1999.
5. Green 2002.
6. Roffey 2003, 349.
7. Pevsner 1973, 230.
8. Dunning 1978, 210–24.
9. Roffey 2003, 350.
10. Roffey 2007, 144–5.
11. Roffey 2008, 171.
12. Sherwood and Pevsner 1974, 734.
13. Roffey 2007, 134.
14. English Heritage 2004.
15. Roffey 2008, 172.
16. Pevsner 1974a, 106.
17. Wheeler 1994, 78.
18. Rowell 1974; Wheeler 1994, 78.
19. Smart 1989, 5.
20. Smart 1989, 2.
21. Stanton 1971, 14.
22. Roffey 2008, 177.
23. Neale and Webb 1843, i.
24. Pugin 1841, 8.
25. Curl 2002, 34.
26. Cf. Graves 2000; Roffey 2006.
27. Pugin 1851, 4.
28. Pugin 1851, 3.
29. Pugin 1969, 13 (originally published in *Dublin Review* 1841/42).
30. *Ecclesiologist* 1845, 10.
31. The cathedral also housed many other memorial and side chapels, such as the Weld family chapel and the chapel of the Blessed Sacrament.
32. Stanton 1971, 57.
33. Bogan 1958, 230.
34. Clarke 1899, 14.
35. Bogan 1958, 278.
36. Bogan 1958, 138.
37. Anon. 1850.
38. Bogan 1958, 241.
39. Bogan 1958, 324.
40. Darlington 1955.
41. Champ 1988.
42. Pugin 1969, 96 (originally published in *Dublin Review* 1841/42).
43. Pugin 1969, 97 (originally published in *Dublin Review* 1841/42).
44. Curl 2002, 35.
45. Mausolea and Monuments Trust.
46. Stanton 1971, 170.
47. Newman's Sermon 25 'the Intermediate State' quoted from Rowell 1974, 100.
48. Rowell 1974, 169.
49. Rowell 1974, 169.
50. Rowell 1974, 171.
51. Tract Number 79 – Against Romanism No III. *On Purgatory:3.*
52. Tract Number 79 – Against Romanism No III. *On Purgatory:3.*
53. Newman 1869, Part 6, 369.
54. Newman 1869, Part 6, 370.

BIBLIOGRAPHY

Anon. 1850, *A Complete Description of St George's Cathedral*, London: Thomas Richardson.

Bogan, B. 1958, *The Great Link: A History of St George's Cathedral, Southwark, 1786–1958*, London: Burns and Oates.

Brown, S. 1999, *Sumptuous and Richly Adorn'd: The Decoration of Salisbury Cathedral*, London: HMSO, RCHME.

Champ, J.F. 1988, *Oscott College 1838–88*, Birmingham: Oscott College.

Clarke, A.M. 1899, *Life Of The Hon. Mrs Edward Petre*, London: Benziger Bros.

Curl, J.S. 2002, *Piety Proclaimed: An Introduction to the Places of Worship in Victorian England*, London: Historical Publications.

Darlington, I. 1955, *Survey of London: St George's Fields*, volume 25, English Heritage: <http://www.british-history.ac.uk/source.aspx?pubid=741> [2008].

Dunning, R.W. 1978, *Victoria History of the Counties of England: Somerset 4*, 210–24.

Ecclesiologist 1845, volume 4 (volume 2 New Series), Cambridge: Cambridge Camden Society.

English Heritage 2004, *Rycote Chapel, Oxfordshire*. <http://www.english-heritage.org.uk/upload/pdf/rycote_chapel.pdf > [last modified 2004].

Gaimster, D. & Gilchrist, R. (eds) 2003, *The Archaeology of Reformation, 1480–1580*. Society for Post-Medieval Archaeology Monograph 1. Leeds: Maney.

Graves, C.P. 2000, *Form and Fabric of Belief: The Archaeology of Lay Experience in Medieval Norfolk and Devon*. British Archaeological Report British Series 311. Oxford: J. & E. Hedges.

Green, E. 2002, 'Bridge chapels', *Historic Churches* 9: 6–9.

Hodder, I. 1986, *Reading the Past: Current Approaches to Interpretation in Archaeology*, Cambridge: Cambridge University Press.

Mausolea and Monuments Trust <http://www.mausolea-monuments.org.uk> [last modified 15 November 2008].

Neale, J.M. & Webb, B. (eds) 1843, *The Symbolism of Churches and Church Ornaments: A Translation of the First Book of the Rationale Divinorum Officiorum by William Durandus*, Leeds: T.W. Green.

Newman, J. 1869, *The Dream of Gerontius* <http://www.newmanreader.org/works/verses/gerontius.html> [last modified 2007].

Pevsner, N. 1973, *Buildings of England: Northamptonshire*, 2nd edn (revised by B. Cherry), Harmondsworth: Penguin.

Pevsner, N. 1974a, *Buildings of England: Suffolk*, 2nd edn (revised by E. Radcliffe), Harmondsworth: Penguin.

Pevsner, N. 1974b, *Buildings of England: Oxfordshire*, 2nd edn (revised by J. Sherwood), Harmondsworth: Penguin.

Pugin, A.W.N. 1841, *Contrasts and True Principles of Christian or Pointed Architecture*, Reading: Spire Books.

Pugin, A.W.N. 1851, *A Treatise on Chancel Screens and Rood Lofts: Their Antiquity, Use and Symbolic Significance*, Leominster: Grace Wing.

Pugin, A.W.N. 1969, *The Present State of Ecclesiastical Architecture in England (1843)*, Oxford: Blackwell.

Roffey, S. 2003, 'Deconstructing a symbolic world: the Reformation and the English medieval parish chantry', in Gaimster & Gilchrist 2003, 342–55.

Roffey, S. 2006, 'Constructing a vision of salvation: chantries and the social dimension of religious experience in the medieval parish church', *Archaeology Journal* 163: 122–46.

Roffey, S. 2007, *The Medieval Chantry Chapel: An Archaeology*, Woodbridge: Boydell.

Roffey, S. 2008, *Chantry Chapels and Medieval Strategies for the Afterlife*, Stroud: Tempus.

Rowell, G. 1974, *Hell and the Victorians: A Study of the Nineteenth Century Theological Controversy Concerning Eternal Punishment and the Future Life*, Oxford: Clarendon Press.

Sherwood, S. & Pevsner, N. 1974, *Buildings of England: Oxfordshire*, Harmondsworth: Penguin.

Smart, C.M. 1989, *Muscular Churches: Ecclesiastical Architecture of the High Victorian Period*, Fayette-ville (AR): University of Arkansas Press.

Stanton, P. 1971, *Pugin*, London: Thames and Hudson.

Tract Number 79 – Against Romanism No III. *On Purgatory:3*. <http://www.newmanreader.org/works/times/tract79.html> [last modified 2007]

Wheeler, M. 1994, *Heaven, Hell, and the Victorians*, Cambridge: Cambridge University Press.

ABBREVIATIONS

HMSO   Her Majesty's Stationary Office
RCHME   Royal Commission on Historic Monuments (England)

'Strangers in a Strange Land': Immigrants and Urban Culture in Early Modern Norwich

CHRIS KING*

This chapter considers the material legacy of the 'Stranger' community of Norwich: Dutch and Walloon immigrants who settled in the city in large numbers in the later 16th century, for a time forming over one-third of the city's total population. Archaeological evidence provides a view of increasingly crowded conditions in the areas of the city where the majority of the Strangers lived, and gives us an insight into distinctive cultural practices within immigrant households with regard to cooking and serving food. The Strangers were granted the use of prominent medieval churches to hold their services and received a considerable degree of public support from the civic authorities and leading churchmen, who saw their advanced Calvinist religious doctrine as an inspiration for the future direction of the English Church. Many wealthy Low Countries mercantile families maintained close social ties with the native population as well as their own community, as shown by the presence of elaborate Stranger funerary memorials within several of the city's parish churches. Ultimately, the urban landscape was a dynamic locale where these complex social and religious identities could be expressed and negotiated.

INTRODUCTION

In the mid 16th century the Norwich worsted weaving industry was in severe depression as a result of increasing competition from Low Countries producers combined with the short-term economic upheavals of inflation, epidemic disease, poor harvests and the collapse of the Antwerp market.[1] In response to this crisis, in 1565 Mayor Thomas Sotherton obtained (through the efforts of the Duke of Norfolk, a patron of the city) royal letters patent giving him licence to invite thirty Dutch and Walloon craftsmen with their households (numbering a maximum of 300 persons in total) to the city, with the explicit aim that they should introduce the manufacture of 'Bayes Arras Sayes Tapestry Mockadoes Staments Carsay and such other outlandish com'odities as hath not bene used to be made w'hin this our Realme of England'.[2] Over the next forty years the Stranger community revitalised the city's failing economy and rapidly expanded to form a substantial proportion of the early modern urban population.

There was a long history of merchants and craftspeople of Low Countries origin residing in medieval English towns and cities, particularly the eastern coastal ports. These included the self-governing communities of Hanseatic merchants in London and other major ports, including King's Lynn and Boston.[3] Medieval immigrant communities were much more extensive than this, however; it has been estimated that there were *c.* 3,400 resident aliens in London in the 15th century, comprising up to six per cent of the total population.[4] They lived and worked among the native English population, worshipped in the same parish churches and practised a wide range of occupations. Particular concentrations were settled in Southwark and other poorer suburban areas, and immigrant names are prominent among many of the luxury crafts and artistic trades.[5] Norwich, as one of the largest provincial cities in England, had particularly close trading connections with the Low Countries through its out-port at Great Yarmouth. Flemish merchants and craftspeople are recorded as residents from the early 14th century, and were no doubt present in some numbers before this time.[6]

However, immigration to England took on a new significance in the turmoil unleashed by the European Reformation in the 16th century. Increasing numbers of Protestants from various regions of Continental Europe sought refuge in England from the 1530s; the first exile Calvinist church was established in London under the leadership of the Polish minister Jean à Lasco in the reign of Edward VI, being granted the nave of the church of Austin Friars for their place of worship.[7] Although they suffered persecution along with other Protestants during the reign of Mary I, the accession of Elizabeth I brought a new wave of immigration, coinciding as it did with an intensification of confessional divisions across Europe, although many no doubt sought new economic opportunities as well as religious freedom.[8] The overall number of immigrants in 16th- and 17th-century England is difficult to establish with any certainty. Pettegree suggests that between 40,000 and 50,000 aliens may have arrived in London between 1550 and 1585 alone.[9] However, urban populations were highly fluid as a result of the impact of epidemic disease and continuing in- and out-migration, while numbers of aliens were often under-reported. The total size of the alien population living in England at any one time would be much smaller than this; Goose has recently argued that by the 1590s the resident population of aliens living in England is likely to have been in the region of 23,000–24,000.[10]

The 1560s and 1570s saw an upsurge in the arrival of Protestant refugees from the southern Netherlands, occupying both Dutch/Flemish- and Walloon/French-speaking areas of what are now Belgium, Luxembourg and northern France, where the Dutch Revolt against Spanish rule resulted in decades of warfare, persecution and economic disruption.[11] The majority of these incomers joined the established communities in London or founded a series of new immigrant churches in other major southern and eastern provincial cities, including Norwich, Canterbury, Colchester, Sandwich and Southampton.[12] They were officially supported by the Crown and Privy Council, as well as local urban Corporations, as co-religionists fleeing persecution. They were also welcomed as bringing important new craft skills to revive England's economy, particularly in the textile industries, although native English craftsmen often resented the competition the aliens represented.[13]

The historical study of the immigrant or, to use a common contemporary term, 'Stranger'[14] communities of early modern England was initially pioneered by the Huguenot Society. Although the Society's interests focus on the more famous French Huguenot diaspora which occurred after Louis XIV's revocation of the Edict of Nantes (which had granted limited toleration) in 1685, from the start they recognised the significance of the early refugee communities and published extensive collections of their surviving records.[15] W.J.C. Moens presented a comprehensive analysis of the history and registers of the French Church of Norwich in the first volume of the Society's Publications in 1887–8; this remains the most detailed account of the Norwich Dutch and Walloon communities.[16] The Norwich Strangers have also been the subject of more recent historical research by Raingard Esser, who addresses a range of topics relating to their social, economic and cultural lives.[17]

The early immigrant communities have received a notable increase of attention in the past decade from a new generation of historians, reflecting the influence of broader cultural and political interest in issues of immigration and diaspora in an era of increasing globalisation. This has resulted in several detailed case studies of individual Stranger churches and a series of edited collections and thematic works on the growth, organisation and occupations of early modern immigrant communities.[18] It is now possible to gain a much clearer understanding of the social and economic impact of immigrants within early modern towns and cities.[19] Scholars have explored the attitudes of native English inhabitants to their presence, which ranged from the welcome of persecuted co-religionists to outright xenophobia.[20] We have also begun to address the more complex issues of the nature of a distinctive 'Stranger' cultural identity and how this may have developed through the generations, and the eventual process of integration with their English 'host' communities.[21]

To date, however, there has been very little archaeological interest in the presence of these sometimes large immigrant communities who lived and worked in early modern towns and cities. In part the reasons for this are easily understood. The excavation of whole urban tenements with good associated domestic assemblages is comparatively rare in medieval and post-medieval urban centres, making social interpretation of the archaeological record a challenging endeavour. Furthermore, while the Strangers may have worshipped in their own churches and spoken a different language, they were broadly part of the same European cultural tradition and it is difficult to identify and isolate distinctive material culture or social practices associated with them alone. The extensive excavations of urban tenements in Norwich which have been undertaken and published since the 1970s provide some of our best urban sequences and assemblages from a city with a prominent Stranger community, and archaeologists have achieved some success in identifying immigrant Low Countries households here. However, the lead excavators of the Norwich Survey remained somewhat sceptical of the value of this evidence for discussing any distinctive cultural identity.[22]

This chapter argues that archaeologists should bring into play the widest extent of material evidence for the early modern immigrant community, including excavations of urban tenements, the fragmentary remains of their places of worship and funerary monuments, and consider their place within the wider urban landscape. In this way, a holistic approach can make a distinctive contribution to the understanding of the lifestyle of this community, their visibility within the urban landscape and their varied social and cultural relationships with the wider urban population.

THE STRANGER COMMUNITY OF NORWICH

The royal letters patent which permitted the establishment of a Stranger community in Norwich in 1565 allowed for the settlement of twenty-four Flemish-speaking (known as the 'Dutch') and six French-speaking Walloon households of up to ten persons, who were then residing in the established immigrant communities in London and Sandwich.[23] However, the number of immigrants in the city expanded rapidly. A census of resident aliens in the city of 1568 records over 300 Dutch and 64 Walloon households, containing 1,446 and 339 individuals respectively, and in a second listing of 1571 there were nearly 4,000 aliens living in the city.[24] To put these figures in context, the muster of 1569 and the Census of the Poor of 1570 suggest that the English population of Norwich was approximately 8,000.

Throughout the 1570s and 1580s the Strangers formed over one-third of the city's total population, reaching a peak of 6,000 on the eve of the plague of 1579–80, in which they suffered heavy losses.[25] The numbers of the Dutch and Walloon congregations seem to have fallen off to *c.* 3,000 in 1600 and were just *c.* 2,000 by 1635, at a time when the urban population as a whole was expanding from a figure of *c.* 14,000 in 1600 to over 20,000 in the 1630s.[26] The decline is accounted for in part by diminishing immigration to England from the Low Countries with the declaration of a truce between the United Provinces and Spain in 1609, which also led to the return of some Stranger families to the Continent.[27] The decline must also be a result of the gradual integration of third- and fourth-generation immigrants with the native English population. However, the Stranger communities did continue to maintain a distinctive and visible presence within the wider urban population, with their own language, customs and church organisation, well into the 18th century. Services at the French and Dutch churches continued to be held for a dwindling number of congregants until 1832 and 1921 respectively.

The large influx of aliens received a mixed reception from the native English inhabitants. Many members of the civic elite supported them as persecuted Protestant refugees, as well as pointing to the economic stimulus brought about by the revival of the weaving trade and their occupation of rental properties. However, native English craftsmen often resented their competition and frequently argued that the Strangers were breaking the strict economic regulations placed upon them.[28] In 1567 Mayor Thomas Walle threatened to expel the Strangers, and in 1570 a more serious rebellion was plotted among several Norfolk Catholic gentlemen and townspeople to drive out the Strangers and overthrow Elizabeth's government.[29] The central government remained concerned about the number of aliens residing in Norwich and other cities, and required frequent censuses of their numbers and assurances of their good behaviour. In 1575, while noting the significant increase in the alien population over the past ten years, the Norwich Corporation offered a strong testament of support for the Strangers in their midst to the Privy Council, declaring:

> they for the moste parte feare God, and do diligently and laborously attende upon their severall occupations, they obey all magistrates and all good lawes and ordynaunces, they lyve peaceablie amonge themselves and towarde all men, and we thinke our cittie happie to enjoye them.[30]

The Stranger communities were placed under strict economic and social regulation in an attempt to prevent friction with the native inhabitants. Like all aliens in early modern England, they were forbidden to own, inherit or bequeath any real property, engage in retail trade or send their children to be apprenticed; and, as they were not freemen of the city, they could not join the city's guilds or participate in civic government.[31] The 1571 'Book of Orders' for the Strangers, drawn up in the aftermath of the upheavals of 1570, laid down clear procedures for the government of the Stranger community and strict regulations for the searching and sealing of Stranger cloths, which could be sold only in an appointed public sale hall. Artisans who were perceived as being in competition with native Englishmen such as bakers, cobblers and tailors were permitted to sell their goods only to members of their own community, and were obliged to fix a lattice one yard high before their windows.[32] The Strangers operated under several additional financial burdens. They were forced to pay poor rates and watch money to their English parish of residence, but were not entitled themselves to receive parish relief and so had to maintain the poor and orphans of their communities from their own reserves. They had to pay fees to the city whenever they travelled abroad, and resident aliens were generally required to pay taxation and customs duties at double the rate of native Englishmen, so that in the Tudor and Stuart lay subsidies even the poorest Stranger households paid the minimum amount of 4d, later 8d, rather than the English minimum payments of 2d and 4d.[33]

In the context of this social and economic segregation, the Stranger churches emerged as strong points in the social lives and regulation of their communities.[34] In common with the practice of Reformed Calvinist churches on the Continent, the Dutch and Walloon congregations were governed by a Consistory of ministers and community elders, which was responsible for enforcing strict moral standards as well as organising poor relief. In addition, from 1568 the system of 'Politic Men' was instituted, through which the Stranger communities were governed by a committee of twelve respectable men (eight for the Dutch and four for the Walloons) annually elected from within the community and approved by the Mayor's Court. They were charged with maintaining law and order and arbitrating disputes, keeping a register of their numbers and representing their interests to the Corporation. Raingard Esser argues that this 'separate but integrated' system of justice shows a high level of support for the autonomy of the leaders of the immigrant communities as allies of the Corporation in the fight against urban crime and disorder.[35]

From the beginning the majority of the Strangers were involved in the production of fashionable light colourful woollen and mixed fabrics collectively known as the 'New Draperies'. The textile industry of the city and region was transformed, as the number of cloths produced by the Strangers increased from 1,200 in 1567 to 38,700 in 1586, although in the early period there was only a limited amount of transfer of new skills to the English population.[36] The two communities specialised in different types of cloth, and while the making of heavier bays and serges declined with the shrinking of the Dutch community from the early 17th century, the 'caugeantry' made by the Walloons (closely related to the worsted cloths already produced in the city) flourished. This laid the foundation for the dramatic expansion of the trade in 'Norwich Stuffs' which underpinned the city's remarkable expansion and prosperity in the later 17th and 18th centuries.[37]

The censuses of Strangers taken at several points in the late 16th century, combined with the mention of Dutch and Walloon households in taxation returns and muster rolls in the 16th and 17th centuries, provide an overview of the wealth and occupational structure of the immigrant communities. They are found as residents in all of the city's parishes, but with relatively higher numbers in two of the four great wards: Wymer, on the south bank of the river Wensum, and 'Over-the-Water', on the north bank.[38] The clustering on either side of the river is natural, as this was the traditional centre of the city's cloth industry. There were particular concentrations in some of the more marginal parishes in the western and northern districts of the city. Here, the majority of Strangers were relatively poor, being taxed at the minimal sum for wage labourers who owned little or no property.[39] As will be shown below, archaeological excavations in these areas have revealed the increasing intensification of occupation and declining standards of living in the 16th and 17th centuries. Properties were subdivided and courtyards infilled with housing to accommodate the rapidly expanding urban population (of both alien and English migrants). However, the Stranger community always had a broad occupational base. A return of 1622 lists the occupations of 298 Stranger men (Table 5.1).

Table 5.1. Occupations of adult men in the Return of the Strangers, 1622
(after Moens 1887–8, 189–93)

78 Weavers	9 Bakers	2 Sellers of Small Wares
25 Journeymen Weavers	8 Gardeners & Farmers	2 Chair Makers
28 Woolcombers	8 Merchants	1 Pinner
38 Journeymen Woolcombers	6 Tailors	1 Tanner
27 Hosiers	4 Turners	1 Cutler
20 Spinners	3 Grocers	1 Claspmaker
6 Dyers	2 Schoolmasters	1 Shoemaker
1 Journeyman Dyer	2 Brokers	1 Cordyner
3 Combmakers	1 Factor for Merchants	1 Brazier
2 Fullers	1 Usufer	1 Seller of Pots
2 Says Makers	2 Surgeons	1 'Heartel' Maker
1 Bays and Says Measurer	1 Physician	1 Slay Maker
1 Hose Stamper	2 Aqua Vitae Distillers	1 Sojourner
1 Hose Skoure	1 Aqua Vitae Seller	
Total in cloth manufacture (column 1): 233		
Overall total: 298		

Over three-quarters worked in the cloth industry, but there were a number of other craftsmen catering to the basic needs of the immigrant community and a small number of luxury or specialist tradesmen. Several Stranger craftsmen are known to have played a prominent role in the city's economic and cultural life. Between 1567/68 and 1572 Anthony de Solempne of Brabant ran the first printing press in the city, producing mainly religious works in French, Dutch and English and gaining some of his commissions from the city authorities; several other booksellers and bookbinders are listed among the early immigrants.[40] In an early attempt at economic diversification, in 1567 two Dutchmen, Jasper Andries and Jacob Janson, established a workshop producing tin-glazed earthenware, the first of its kind in England. Waster sherds providing evidence of this activity have been discovered in archaeological excavations on Ber Street, but the workshop seems to have been short-lived, decamping to London by the 1580s.[41] More long-lasting was the impact of Dutch and Walloon merchants, who made good use of their contacts and experience of Low Countries trade to maintain strong commercial links between Norwich and the Continent. Throughout the history of the Stranger community such wealthy merchants and professionals, such as the prominent Dutch physician Martin von Kurnbeck and the successful Low Countries merchant Jacques de Hem, both discussed further below, maintained close links with the native English merchant community.

In 1598, the Norwich Corporation granted resident aliens the right to become freemen of the city on the same terms as the native English, through apprenticeship, inheritance or purchase. Their aim was to encourage wealthy Dutch and Walloon families to take on a fuller share of the burden of civic office and taxation, and a few wealthy merchants (including Jacques de Hem) did purchase the freedom for themselves and their children. Nevertheless, very few Stranger families took up this offer of full citizenship, despite continuing pressure to do so.[42] Even wealthy men such as de Hem did not generally follow the accepted route to full membership of the urban civic community, usually consisting of minor parish office followed by election to the Common Council, and then perhaps the aldermanic bench. Only one member of the Dutch or Walloon community is know to have held public office in the 16th century, and only a small number of others took this route in the 17th century, none rising above the rank of constable. Raingard Esser persuasively argues that this reflects the strength of the internal networks within the immigrant communities and the continuing importance of membership of their own church and civic institutions as an alternative route to social and economic success.[43]

ARCHAEOLOGICAL EVIDENCE FOR STRANGER HOUSEHOLDS

Extensive archaeological excavations of urban tenements in Norwich have revealed some important, although ambiguous, evidence for Stranger households in the city and their distinctive material culture and lifestyles. It is necessary to stress that the mere presence of imported Low Countries ceramics in a domestic assemblage is by no means a marker of the ethnic or cultural identity of the household; they are ubiquitous in late medieval and post-medieval excavated assemblages in Norwich, and distinctive vessel forms including cauldrons and skillets or frying pans were being imitated in locally produced earthenware from the 15th century.[44] Nevertheless, a series of assemblages have been identified in Norwich dating to the early–mid 17th century which contained a significantly higher proportion of imported Low Countries ceramics, constituting around twenty-five per cent of the total assemblage compared to a more usual three to five per cent.[45] These assemblages were all excavated in the outlying parishes in the wards of 'Over-the-Water' and 'West Wymer', areas where the Strangers are known to have been concentrated (Fig. 5.1). They are also associated with some distinctive vessel forms and other items of imported material culture which are less common across the city as a whole, notably slip-decorated fire covers and burnished clay pipes,[46] which lend support to the interpretation of these assemblages as belonging to immigrant households.

Some of the best-known examples are found in excavations on the north and south sides of Botolph Street in the northern parish of St Augustine's, in one of the poorest quarters of the city where high numbers of immigrant households are known to have lived. On site 170N (south side of Botolph Street) large quantities of imported Low Countries pottery were found in pits located in the rear yards behind street-front dwellings, which were filled in c. 1640.[47] These included several examples of near-complete vessels, suggesting that this may represent a 'household clearance' deposit. The vessels included North Holland slipware steep-sided bowls with collared rims (known as 'cockerel bowls', from one common motif found in the base of the bowl) and a rare North Holland slipware pipkin; Dutch tin-glazed earthenware; and Werra ware dishes from Northern Germany.[48] Werra slip-decorated wares have been linked by John Hurst and David Gaimster to the presence of immigrant communities in southern and eastern English ports.[49] The finds included a Werra dish dated 1625 and a North Holland slipware bowl dated 1614, suggesting that they were in use for several decades before being discarded in c. 1640.[50] On site 281N (north side of Botolph Street), a large cesspit (possibly shared) associated with a row of small houses rebuilt in c. 1625 contained a similar range of imports in levels dating to c. 1625–50.[51] Also present was a residual fragment (from a later, intercutting, pit) of a 17th-century North Holland slip-decorated firecover of a type that has also been found on other sites with possible immigrant connections.[52]

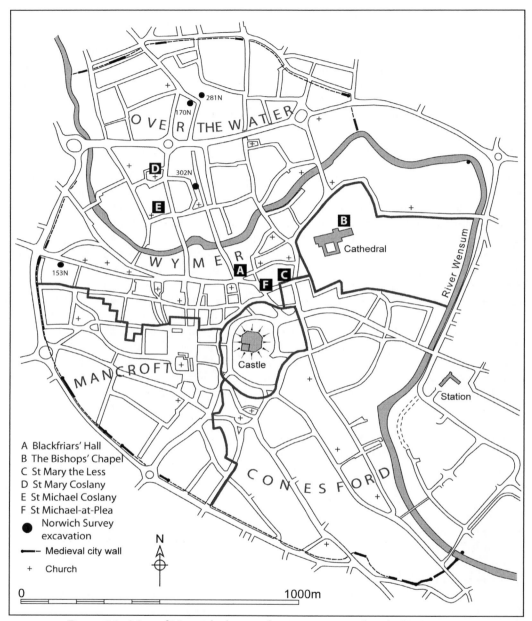

Figure 5.1. Map of Norwich showing key sites associated with the Strangers
(base map courtesy of NAU Archaeology).

Similar evidence was identified at Alms Lane (Site 302N), north of Colegate in 'Over-the-Water', where a group of tenements with street-front buildings and rear yards was excavated, producing a sequence of occupation from the 15th to the early 18th century showing the increasing intensification of building and the subdivision of properties to accommodate the expanding population of this quarter in the early modern period.[53] The principal evidence for immigrant households was discovered in tenement A in the late 16th and 17th centuries. Fragments of a North Holland slipware firecover were found in the yard in levels dating to the last quarter of the 16th century (period 8),[54] and in periods 9–10 (*c.* 1600–1750), after the buildings had been subdivided into smaller rental units, the midden deposits in the yard (along with material of the same date redeposited in the fill of an adjacent cesspit in the mid 18th century in period 11) contained a high proportion of Low Countries ceramics.[55] The finds included vessels forms such as cauldrons which were uncommon in local wares by the 17th century and a rare fragment of a Westerwald stone-ware jug from the early 17th century. Other possible imported items from these deposits include a buckle with close parallels to an early 17th-century example from Amsterdam[56] and a Dutch clay pipe stem with a floral design.[57] The occupant of the tenement in 1725 was Jacob Votier, a member of the Walloon church, perhaps indicating a long-term presence of immigrant households in this location.

A fourth site that confirms the interpretation of these distinctive assemblages of imported material culture is Site 153N, Nos 104–106 St Benedict's Street, located in West Wymer ward. Here, pits excavated in the rear yards contained a high proportion of imported Low Countries pottery including North Holland cockerel bowls, a Werra ware dish dated 1621 and a Westerwald stoneware chamber pot. Vessel forms in Dutch and Dutch-type red earthenwares included cauldrons, pipkins, skillets and dripping pans, which are comparatively rare within the local earthenware tradition, and an unstratified fragment of a North Holland slipware firecover.[58]

It is striking that there is only limited evidence for Stranger households in the city in deposits dating to the late 16th and early 17th centuries, when we know immigrants formed a significant proportion of the city's population. However, rather than being surprised that the bulk of our evidence comes from the mid–late 17th century, we should perhaps consider that this is telling us something important about the role of material culture and the domestic sphere for immigrant populations.[59] We must refocus the questions we ask of our evidence to explore the active role of material culture in social practices that may have contributed to the maintenance and negotiation of a distinctive yet fluid community identity within the Stranger population.

The high proportion of imported pottery found on these sites is important but it is the range of vessel types and forms that is suggestive of a distinctive mode of life within the Stranger community, indicated by the material culture associated with food preparation and serving. The predominance of ceramic cauldrons and bowls is perhaps particularly significant, as meat stews were a central part of everyday diet in the early modern Netherlands and the '*hutsepot*' was in many ways a symbol of emergent national identity.[60] Surviving letters from Norwich immigrants to their families in the Low Countries also reveal the importance of domestic goods, clothing and familiar foods and cooking methods; for instance, Clais Van Wervekin wrote to his wife on 21 August 1567: 'When you come, bring a dough trough, for there are none here ... Buy two little wooden dishes to make up half pounds of butter, for all Netherlanders and Flemings make their own butter, for here is all pigs fat.'[61] Stranger merchants are recorded as importing a range of material goods in the late 16th and early 17th centuries, including 'earthen potts' and 'drinking vesselles',[62] both for wholesale trade within the city and also, presumably, for sale within the community. The presence of relatively high-status ceramics such as Werra ware and Westerwald stoneware in tenements in the poorer districts of the city can perhaps be interpreted in this light. Given that there were significant restrictions on aliens owning property until the early 17th century, and considering that even after this date the majority of the Strangers remained relatively poor and so are unlikely to have owned their own houses, the ownership of decorative moveable goods and their display within the home may have been a particularly valued mark of status within the immigrant community. It is also significant that many of the items which were discarded in the mid–late 17th century on Alms Lane and Botolph street were produced in the first quarter of the 17th century, indicating that they may have been preserved as valued household possessions for several decades, perhaps across generations. As Atkin and Evans suggest, it is likely that these late deposits represent the 'clearance' of Stranger households, either when they were returning to the Continent, or simply because they no longer felt the need to keep these distinctive and decorative objects.[63] Far from being surprised at the lack of evidence for late 16th and early 17th century Stranger households, we must recognise that it is in fact only when these objects leave the active realm of the social world and the cultural value placed on them is diminished that they appear in the archaeological record in increasing numbers.

THE STRANGER CHURCHES

The Stranger churches, beginning with the first established congregation in London in 1550, were the only religious communities to be granted freedom to worship outside the Church of England until 1689, although nominally under the ecclesiastical authority of Anglican bishops. Puritan reformers often looked to the Stranger churches as visible models of Reformed Calvinist worship which should inspire further reform of the established Church.[64] Norwich has long been recognised as an early centre for the spread of advanced Protestantism, and from the later 16th century the magistrates were increasingly under the influence of radical Puritan ministers and espoused a cause of moral and spiritual reform among the citizens. A new generation of religious historians (notably Muriel McClendon and Matthew Reynolds) have stressed that the dominance of Puritanism was far from total and that Norwich was marked by ongoing conflicts and tensions between conservative and radical elements within the magistracy and the wider population.[65] Nonetheless, the Corporation showed continued favour to the Calvinist exile congregations living in their midst.

Stranger congregations were commonly granted public buildings as dedicated places of worship in English towns and cities. In Canterbury the French church was permitted to worship in the crypt of the Cathedral; in Sandwich the Stranger community used St Peter's parish church, sharing it with the English parishioners; while in Southampton the French congregation was granted the chapel of God's House hospital on the edge of the town.[66] In Norwich the corporation showed a marked degree of public support for the immigrant community when they granted the Dutch congregation the old choir of the Dominican Friary (now known as Blackfriars' Hall), which had been in use as a civic chapel from the time of its purchase by the city in 1540 (Fig. 5.2).[67] The nave of the Friary at that time had

Figure 5.2. The choir of the Dominican Friary (Blackfriars' Hall), Norwich, used as the Dutch church between the 16th and 19th centuries (photograph by C. King).

Figure 5.3. Mural monument to Johannes Elison (1581–1639), pastor of the Dutch community, in the centre of the north wall. A brass plaque mounted on the wall beneath commemorates his son Theophilus Elison (1609–1676) (photograph by C. King).

been converted into the 'Common Hall' or 'New Hall' of the city and was used for the annual feasts of the civic Company of St George and the city's craft guilds. The rest of the Friary complex was converted into a range of public functions, including a granary and a sale hall for the Strangers' cloth. The whole complex was located in the commercial heart of the city, on the south bank of the River Wensum opposite St Andrew's parish church. This was one of the wealthiest parishes in Norwich and a recognised centre for radical Protestant preaching throughout the late 16th and early 17th centuries, initially under the Puritan minister John More, known as the 'Apostle of Norwich'. The city Corporation often attended public worship as a civic body in St Andrew's, where seats for the magistrates and ministers were erected within the medieval chancel, and they also maintained a public preaching yard on St Andrew's Plain outside the Common Hall, where sermons were preached on lecture days and Protestant civic festivals.[68]

Very little is known of the internal layout and furnishings of Blackfriars' Hall during its use as the Dutch church, but it is likely that it was made to conform to the requirements of Reformed Calvinist practice, with a tall pulpit, fixed pews or benches and perhaps a raised bench for the consistory, as were recorded in the Stranger churches at Austin Friars and Threadneedle Street, London.[69] The only visible reminder of this important period of the building's history is a mural monument to Johannes Elison (1581–1639), pastor of the Dutch community. The monument has a plain architectural surround containing an inscription in Latin and Dutch, and its prominent position in the centre of the north wall may reflect the central position of the pulpit in the Dutch church (Fig. 5.3). Beneath the monument is mounted a brass plaque with an inscription to his son Theophilus Elison (1609–1676), who followed his father in the role of pastor; this is likely to have been removed from a floor-slab monument at a later date.

The much smaller Walloon congregation was granted the use of the private chapel in the bishops' palace adjacent to the cathedral in 1566 by Bishop Parkhurst, who was a moderate Puritan and sympathetic to the needs of the refugee communities.[70] However, by the early 17th century the position of the Stranger churches in relation to the established Church was increasingly contentious in the context of widening religious and cultural divisions within mainstream Anglicanism. The 1620s and 1630s saw moves to reinforce ecclesiastical authority over Puritan elements in the parishes and corporations, culminating in Charles I and Archbishop Laud's drive to impose conservative Anglican doctrine and a more ceremonious liturgy across the kingdom.[71] As part of this campaign, in 1634–5 Laud made a concerted effort to impose the Anglican liturgy within the Stranger churches and to force members who were born in England to leave the congregations and worship in their English parishes of residence, moves which were strongly resisted by many within the Stranger communities.[72]

In Norwich, as early as 1610 Bishop Jegon gave notice to the Mayor and aldermen that he required the palace chapel for his own use, and it was proposed that an old chapel at the New Hall beside the Dutch church be fitted up for the French church. The Walloons, however, argued that the proposed building was too small for their community and the two congregations in such proximity would disturb one another's worship, so their petition to remain in the bishops' chapel was granted on this occasion.[73] In 1633–4 Bishop Corbett pressed the congregation to repair the chapel and remove themselves, writing in December 1634:

> You have promised me from time to time, to restore my stolen bell, and to glaze my lattice windows. After three years' consultation (beysides other pollution), I see nothing mended. Your discipline, I know, care not much for a consecrated place, and anye other roome in Norwich, that hath but bredth and length, may serve your turne as well as the chappel, wherefore I say unto you without a miracle, *Lazare prodi foras*, depart and hire some other place for your irregular meetings.[74]

This is a striking denunciation of the Reformed Calvinists' apparent lack of concern for the concept of sacred space and due reverence to the 'beauty of holiness' that was at the core of the growing concern of the Caroline Church to return to ceremonial forms of worship over preaching and disputation.

Bishop Corbett, who died soon after this order, was replaced by the Laudian appointee Matthew Wren, whose campaign to enforce conformity and ceremony led to an escalation of confessional divisions across the city. Wren's episcopal visitation of 1636 resulted in the suspension of eleven Norwich ministers for nonconformity and led to an exodus of Puritan ministers and citizens to the Low Countries and Massachusetts.[75] Wren also succeeded in finally ejecting the Walloon congregation from the bishops' chapel in 1637. The bishop then attempted to claim up to £200 for repairs, accusing them of leaving the roof timbers in a decayed state, defacing figurative stained glass windows and removing furnishings, while they countered that they had found the chapel in gross disrepair ('more like a dove-house than a church') and had restored the windows and roof timbers at their own cost.[76] Whatever the true state of the chapel fabric when they first occupied it, it seems clear that the Walloon congregation had invested considerable sums in making it fit for their services and had replaced figurative imagery in the windows with plain glass more suitable for a Reformed Protestant church interior.

The magistrates extended their support to the Walloon congregation at this time by granting them the use of the old parish church of St Mary the Less, on Tombland, which had been closed at the Reformation and used since then as a public hall for the sale of the Strangers' goods and more recently for the city's yarn market.[77] The Walloons spent £160 on refitting the church as a place of worship, although very little evidence of this survives. The door in the north chancel wall has a decorative arched head carved with the date 1637, the year the Church entered possession. The roof of the nave has been ceiled at some point in its history, in a similar fashion to that at the London Dutch church at Austin Friars, and this may reflect an attempt to improve the acoustics of the space as a venue for preaching.[78] The church today also contains several monuments to members of the French congregation dating from the 18th and 19th centuries.

The public support of the magistrates for the immigrant communities in their midst had wider resonance at a time of ongoing controversy over the shape and future direction of the doctrine and liturgy of the Anglican Church. A prominent faction of the 'godly' within the Corporation continually resisted the efforts of Jacobean and Caroline bishops to close down Puritan lectureships, enforce conformity, introduce religious ceremonies and re-build and 'beautify' parish churches.[79] The Stranger churches provided a visible model of Reformed Calvinist worship which Puritan ministers urged the ecclesiastical authorities to follow; it was precisely because of this that there was increasing concern to bring the immigrant congregations under stronger episcopal authority. The Norwich Dutch church had been granted space within a prominent civic building in the heart of the city for their services, making their distinctive religious practices unusually visible to the wider civic community, and when the Walloons came under considerable pressure to conform from Bishop Wren in 1637 they were provided with a place in which to continue their own forms of worship. Financial and military support for embattled Protestants on the Continent was an important mark of identity for 'godly' citizens in 17th-century English towns;[80] in Norwich, this took the form of public maintenance of the Reformed Protestant communities living within their midst, and thus connected their city to the wider community of European Protestantism.

IMMIGRANTS AND EARLY MODERN URBAN CULTURE

Raingard Esser, in a recent overview of the 'cultural impact' of Dutch immigrants focused mainly on literary culture and their visibility in public discourse through participation in national and civic festivals, emphasises that in the early years of settlement they were able to maintain and display a shared cultural identity through reference to their Calvinist faith, their role in England's economic development and their Dutch language and history.[81] The broader material legacy of the immigrant communities of Norwich points to both cultural distinctions and social interaction with the native English population in different spheres. The complexities of civic position, social status and religious and cultural identity in early modern Norwich can be highlighted through examination of a third class of archaeological monument created by the Stranger community: the funerary monuments of immigrant families contained within the city's Anglican parish churches. Only a small number of these now survive among Norwich's impressive collection of post-medieval funerary monuments, although many other examples are recorded in antiquarian sources. Jonathan Finch has discussed these distinctive Dutch monuments as the products of a Norwich masons' workshop operating in the late 16th and early 17th centuries, producing funerary sculpture for both the immigrant and English elite. These monuments use a repertoire of shared architectural elements and decoration, many of which are strongly influenced by Low Countries sources, and it is possible, although not certain, that the workshop was run by immigrant craftsmen, or at least included them in the workforce.[82]

Two of the earliest surviving examples are located in the ward of 'Over-the-Water'. The first, in the church of St Mary Coslany, is a large mural monument to Dr Martin van Kurnbeck (d. 1578) and his wife Joan (d. 1579), which has a recess under a four-centred arch and triangular pediment containing an effigy of the couple kneeling on either side of a covered table; rather than being sculpted, the effigy is incised into the stone rear wall of the monument and infilled with pitch.[83] A second, smaller Stranger monument in the church of St Michael Coslany consists of a blue-black marble ledger slab (Fig. 5.4), now mounted on the wall, commemorating wealthy merchant Franchoys van der Beke (d. 1592). The material and the presence of an armorial roundel are unique for 16th-century ledger slabs in the region, leading Finch to suggest that this is likely to have been imported from the Continent.[84]

A second prominent group of Stranger funerary monuments survives in St Michael at Plea parish church in the ward of Mid-Wymer, in the central populous district south of the river. These commemorate the family of Jacques de Hem, already mentioned as one of the wealthiest Dutch merchants in late 16th- and early 17th-century Norwich, who was well connected to the city's native English governing and commercial elite. De Hem was one of only two aliens to be assessed on goods worth £8 in the Lay Subsidies of 1597 and 1599.[85] He was a prominent merchant with extensive trading connections in the native English population and contacts in the Low Countries; records show him as the most active Stranger merchant importing valuable cargoes through Great Yarmouth between 1587 and 1601,[86] and during the dearth of 1596 being commissioned by the Corporation to purchase grain on behalf of the city.[87] In 1602, de Hem was one of the few aliens to purchase citizenship for himself and his seven children for the sum of £50.[88] Strikingly, even in the last decade of the 16th century, although at least some of his children were baptised in the Dutch church, they were also recorded in the parish registers of St Michael at Plea, enabling them to prove an established connection to their parish of residence.[89]

The earliest monument in the group is a striking mural monument to Anna de Hem, the wife of Jacques de Hem, who died in childbirth in 1603 (Fig. 5.5a). The monument is prominently placed in the re-entrant north-west angle of the nave, surrounding and visibly

Figure 5.4. Blue marble ledger slab, now mounted on the wall, commemorating Franchoys van der Beke (d. 1592) in St Michael Coslany parish church (photograph by C. King).

dominating the font, which has a decorative wooden canopy dating to the same period. The monument contains two panels surrounded by a pedimented architectural frame. An inscription in the left-hand panel praises Anna as a wife and mother, and on the right an incised effigy shows husband and wife in an identical manner to that of the Kurnbecks, at prayer on either side of a desk or table surmounted by a large hour-glass, but in this case surrounded by their ten children.[90] These two Stranger monuments are the only ones surviving in Norwich to depict effigies using the incision technique, and to show them kneeling against a table rather than the more typical fald-stool or *prie-dieu*, which may reflect the strict Calvinist sensibilities of those commemorated.

Jacques de Hem himself, who died in 1624, is commemorated by a large black marble ledger slab with a finely carved strapwork border surrounding an inscription and roundel containing his merchant's mark, placed in a prominent position in the centre of the nave beneath the chancel arch (Fig. 5.5b). Although black marble ledger slabs are a common 17th-century monument type in Norwich the majority are plain without any border, and Finch again suggests that this unique highly decorated example was imported from the Continent.[91] De Hem's eldest son Tobias (d. 1629) is commemorated by a more modest brass plaque, although he too had strong connections to the mercantile elite of the city, marrying the daughter of an English doctor and serving as ward constable in 1621.[92]

a

Figure 5.5. De Hem family monuments, St Michael at Plea parish church: a) incised mural monument to Anna de Hem (d. 1603); b) black marble ledger slab with a strapwork border commemorating Jacques de Hem (d. 1624) (photographs by C. King).

b

The location of these monuments within the city's parish churches demonstrates the strong connections between at least some members of the Dutch and Walloon communities and the parishes in which they lived. Jacques de Hem recognised the importance of his connections within the city's merchant community, but he remained a prominent member of the Dutch congregation, acting as a church elder in 1610 and 1615.[93] Esser's analysis of the surviving wills of Norwich Strangers shows that more prosperous members of the community made more frequent use of English witnesses, particularly from the second and third decades of the 17th century, presented more regular bequests to English men and women and made donations to English parish ministers and the poor as well as to the Stranger churches. Jacques de Hem left 40s to the minister of St Michael at Plea and £3 to the poor of the parish, as well as a further bequest of £10 to the poor of the city, alongside generous donations to the Dutch church.[94] The de Hem family were thus prominent members of both communities and their commemorative strategies were a means of negotiating these complex social relationships and identities. Like their English counterparts, the de Hems placed their funerary monuments in prominent positions that demonstrated social rank within the wider urban community; the placement of Anna de Hem's monument, overlooking the font, located the family at the heart of parish life, in a poignant manner given her death in childbirth. Yet the subtle distinctions in decorative style, technique and iconography between the small number of surviving Stranger monuments and those of the native English elite also suggest an attempt to publicly maintain an element of cultural distinctiveness which displayed their European origins and connections. As has already been commented upon, even a wealthy merchant such as Jacques de Hem chose not to follow the established career trajectory of public office that would have been expected of an English man of his rank and fortune, instead remaining more closely connected to the parallel networks of power and influence exercised within the Stranger community.

The material legacy of the immigrant community in early modern Norwich is varied and complex, yet in the final analysis it reveals the urban landscape not as a fixed domain occupied by homogenous and bounded ethnic and religious groups, but as a site of cultural diversity, religious pluralism and ongoing community interactions. Urban populations in late medieval and early modern England are likely to have always been more culturally diverse than is often considered by archaeologists and historians, particularly in the larger commercial centres with their extensive European contacts. Nevertheless, the experiences of immigrants in late 16th- and early 17th-century Norwich were qualitatively different, driven in part by the rapid expansion of their numbers and the prominence of their distinctive Reformed Calvinist doctrines within ongoing religious controversies that took place in the broader body politic. Social and economic tension between the Strangers and the ordinary craftspeople and tradesmen of the city was always present, despite the public support, both political and material, provided by the city Corporation, and the ability of wealthy professional and mercantile families to establish close connections with their native English counterparts. The archaeological evidence for the maintenance of distinctive cultural practices and lifestyles within Stranger households, most of whom remained relatively poor and lived in crowded tenements in the marginal parishes of the city, shows a familiar pattern among immigrant communities of the need to maintain familial and community cohesion through shared rituals and practices across the generations. These began to break down only in the mid 17th century, as the Strangers' grandchildren and great-grandchildren became increasingly integrated into the wider urban population. Even in these dense urban neighbourhoods, however, interaction between natives and Strangers is likely to have been commonplace, as Strangers increasingly worked alongside, traded with and intermarried with the English population.

NOTES

* The research on which this chapter is based was initially pursued as a doctorate funded by the Arts and Humanities Research Council at the University of Reading. It has been further developed within a British Academy Postdoctoral Research Fellowship held at the University of Leicester (2007–2010) entitled: *Voices of Dissent: The Cultural Landscapes of Urban Nonconformity 1580–1780*.

1. Allison 1960.
2. Moens 1887–88, 17–19, 244–5; Priestly 1990, 9.
3. Bratchel 1984; Bolton 1998, 6–7.
4. The majority of these were Dutch- and French-speaking immigrants from the Low Countries: Bolton 1998, 5–9, 28–34.
5. Bolton 1998, 11–24; Pettegree 1986, 9–22.
6. Moens 1887–88, 1–2; 160–61.
7. Pettegree 1986, 23–37.
8. Goose 2005a; Esser 2007, 64.
9. Pettegree 1986, 299.
10. Goose 2005a, 14–18.
11. Fagel 2005. These decades also brought a significant influx of French Huguenot refugees fleeing the first wave of the Wars of Religion.
12. Goose 2005a, 14–29. Smaller and more transitory immigrant communities were found in a host of smaller towns, including Great Yarmouth, Thetford and Kings Lynn (Norfolk), Halstead (Essex), Dover and Maidstone (Kent), Rye and Winchelsea (West Sussex), and the Lincolnshire and Cambridgeshire fens. There was also a sizeable immigrant community in the West Country ports, although these have been neglected in recent historiography in favour of the southern and eastern regions.
13. Goose 2005b; Goose 2005c, 136–39.
14. 'Stranger' and 'alien' were used interchangeably from the mid-14th century to refer to foreign-born residents and their descendants, who had only limited political and economic rights; 'foreign' was more broadly used in early modern towns to refer to anyone who was not a freeman, including English migrants: *Oxford English Dictionary* <http://www.oed.com/> [accessed 20/06/2010]. Luu 2005a, 58–71, and Esser 2006, 237–41, discuss the legal status of aliens and the restrictions they faced in early modern England.

15. Early volumes of the Huguenot Society Publications dedicated to provincial communities of the 'first refuge' include Cross 1898; Hovenden 1891–98; Moens 1905; the Society's annual *Proceedings* also contain relevant material.
16. Moens 1887–88; the French church which is Moen's chief subject was much the smaller of the two Norwich immigrant churches, but his work also includes material relating to the larger Dutch congregation.
17. Esser 1995; 2006; 2007.
18. Backhouse 1995; Goose & Luu 2005; Grell 1989; 1996; Pettegree 1986; Spicer 1997; Vigne & Littleton 2001.
19. Goose 1982; 2005c; Luu 2005c.
20. Yungblut 1996. Recent work stresses that despite considerable hostility from native artisans who feared competition, blind xenophobia and violent reprisals against immigrant communities were rare extremes of behaviour: Goose 2005b; Esser 2007, 67–9.
21. Esser 2005; Grell 1996, 1–33.
22. Evans & Atkin 2002, 245.
23. Moens 1887–88, 17–19.
24. Moens 1887–88, 25–7, 34.
25. Pound 1988, 28, 126–7.
26. Pound 1988, 28–9.
27. Like all early modern urban populations affected by high death rates, the Stranger communities would not have been able to maintain their number without continued in-migration. Stranger families often maintained strong links with their countries of origin and many of the first and second generations of immigrants may well have considered their time in England as a temporary refuge: Esser 1995; Grell 1996, 1–33. Return immigration from England to the Netherlands intensified in the first half of the 17th century: Luu 2005b.
28. Goose 2005b, 124–9.

29. Moens 1887–88, 20, 27; Reynolds 2005, 48–56.
30. Moens 1887–88, 262. Similar statements of support were returned in 1569, 1571, 1583, 1606 and 1611 (Moens 1887–88, 27, 34–5, 45, 246–9); their chief objective was no doubt to reassure the central authorities that the city was well governed and to avoid further external scrutiny.
31. Luu 2005a, 59–60. Aliens could become 'adopted subjects' or denizens by acquiring letters patent from the crown; this enabled them to keep a shop and send their children to English masters as apprentices, but they were still unable to own real property: Esser 2006, 240. The royal letters patent which permitted the initial settlement in Norwich was more generous in allowing aliens to enter into leases of property for a term of years, notwithstanding the existing statutes against this from the reigns of Richard III and Henry VIII: Moens 1887–88, 244–5. Wealthy aliens seem to have been quickly able to circumvent the ban on owning real property: Esser 2007, 72; Luu 2005a, 66.
32. Moens 1887–88, 28–30, 255–61. Despite these strict regulations, complaints from native artisans that Strangers were ignoring the restrictions on retail trade were common: Esser 2007, 67; Luu 2005a, 63–8.
33. Esser 2006, 240–41; Moens 1887–88, 161–87.
34. Pettegree 1986, 182–214; Spicer 2005.
35. Esser 2006, 241–2; Esser 2007.
36. Allison 1961; Priestly 1990, 10–11.
37. Corfield 2004; Martin 1997; Priestly 1990.
38. Moens 1887–88, 161–93.
39. Moens 1887–88, 162–81.
40. Moens 1887–88, 72–4; Esser 2005, 163–5.
41. Ayers 2009, 146.
42. In 1614 and 1615 the Corporation attempted to force Stranger practitioners of the flourishing hosiery trade to take up citizenship, but most initially preferred to pay a fine instead: Esser 2006, 243.
43. Esser 2006, 243–4.
44. Jennings 1981, 61–74, for late medieval and early post-medieval local wares copying Continental vessel forms; 78–147 for imported slip-decorated earthenware, stoneware and glazed red earthenware.
45. Evans & Atkin 2002, 242–5.
46. Jennings 1981, 93–4. However, the copper-alloy 'head dress pins' which were originally identified as a Low Countries female dress item (Margeson 1993, 8–10) have now been re-interpreted as ordinary bodkins: Beaudry 2006, 66–70.
47. Evans 1985, 96–111.
48. Jennings 1981, 78–87.
49. Hurst & Gaimster 2005.
50. Evans 1985, 105–11.
51. Davison 1985, 122–4; Jennings 1985a, 132–5.
52. Jennings 1981, 93–4.
53. M. Atkin 1985.
54. M. Atkin 1985, 163–4; Jennings 1985b, 193–4.
55. M. Atkin 1985, 165–8; Jennings 1985b, 193–8.
56. Margeson 1985, 203.
57. S. Atkin 1985, 215.
58. Evans 2002, 89–93.
59. Evans & Atkin 2002, 243–5.
60. Schama 1987, 176–7.
61. Moens 1887–88, 220–24; Esser 1995, 143–4.
62. Rickwood 1970, 90–93.
63. Evans & Atkin 2002, 245.
64. Spicer 2005, 93.
65. Collinson 1988, 28–59; McClendon 1999; Reynolds 2005.
66. Spicer 2005, 96.
67. Moens 1887–88, 23; Blomefield 1806, 339–42.
68. Collinson 1982, 141–5.
69. Spicer 2005, 97–8.
70. Moens 1887–88, 21.
71. Lake 1993; Fincham & Tyacke 2007, 126–273.
72. Luu 2005b, 199–200.
73. Moens 1887–88, 21–2.
74. Moens 1887–88, 22.
75. Reynolds 2005, 186–213; 217–30.
76. Moens 1887–88, 22, 277–8.
77. Moens 1887–88, 22–3.
78. Spicer 2005, 99.
79. Reynolds 2005.
80. Underdown 1992, 168–78.
81. Esser 2005, 161–9.
82. Moens 1887–88, 130–37; Finch 2000, 96–9.
83. Finch 2000, 86.
84. Finch 2000, 80.
85. Moens 1887–88, 177, 182.
86. After becoming a freeman in 1602 he no longer appears in the records of customs levied on Strangers' goods: Rickwood 1970, 93–108.
87. Esser 1995, 149.
88. Esser 2006, 243.
89. NRO PD 66/1(S), 1591; 1594; 1606; 1612; 1618.
90. Finch 2000, 86.
91. Finch 2000, 81.
92. Esser 1995, 150 and n. 38.
93. Esser 1995, 149.
94. Esser 1995, 146–50.

BIBLIOGRAPHY

Allison, K.J. 1960, 'The Norfolk worsted industry in the sixteenth and seventeenth centuries. Part I: The traditional industry', *Yorkshire Bulletin of Economic and Social Research* 12/2: 73–83.

Allison, K.J. 1961, 'The Norfolk worsted industry in the sixteenth and seventeenth centuries. Part II: The new draperies', *Yorkshire Bulletin of Economic and Social Research* 13/2: 61–77.

Atkin, M. 1985, 'Excavations on Alms Lane (Site 302N)', in Atkin *et al.* 1985, 144–260.

Atkin, M. & Evans, D.H. 2002, *Excavations in Norwich 1971–78 Part III*, East Anglian Archaeology 100.

Atkin, M., Evans, D.H. & Carter, A. 1985, *Excavations in Norwich 1971–78 Part II*, East Anglian Archaeology 26.

Atkin, S. 1985, 'The clay pipes', in M. Atkin 1985, 213–17.

Ayers, B. 2009, *Norwich: Archaeology of a Fine City*, 3rd edn, Stroud: Amberley Publishing.

Backhouse, M. 1995, *The Flemish and Walloon Communities at Sandwich during the reign of Elizabeth I (1561–1603)*, Brussels: Koninklijke Academie voor Wetenschappen, Letteren en Schone Kunsten.

Beaudry, M.C. 2006, *Findings: The Material Culture of Needlework and Sewing*, New Haven (CT): Yale University Press.

Blomefield, F. 1806. *An Essay Towards a Topographical History of the County of Norfolk*, Volume 4, London: William Miller.

Bolton, J.L. 1998, *The Alien Communities of London in the Fifteenth Century: The Subsidy Rolls of 1440 and 1483–4*, Stamford: Richard III and Yorkist History Trust/Paul Watkins.

Bratchel, M.E. 'Alien merchant colonies in sixteenth-century England: community organisation and social mores', *Journal of Medieval and Renaissance Studies* 14: 39–62.

Collinson, P. 1982, *The Religion of Protestants: The Church in English Society 1559–1625*, Oxford: Clarendon Press.

Collinson, P. 1988, *The Birthpangs of Protestant England*, Basingstoke: Macmillan.

Corfield, P.J. 2004, 'From second city to regional capital', in Rawcliffe & Wilson 2004, 139–66.

Cross, F.W. 1898, *History of the Walloon and Huguenot Church at Canterbury*, Publications of the Huguenot Society Vol. 15, Canterbury.

Davison, A.H. with Evans, D.H. 1985, 'Excavations on 49–63 Botolph Street (Site 281N)', in Atkin *et al.* 1985, 114–43.

Ellis, S.G., Hálfdarnarson, G. & Isaacs, A.K. (eds) 2006, *Citizenship in Historical Perspective*, Pisa: University of Pisa Press.

Esser, R. 1995, 'News across the Channel: contact and communication between the Dutch and the Walloon refugees in Norwich and their families in Flanders', *Immigrants & Minorities* 14/2: 31–46.

Esser, R. 2005, 'Immigrant cultures in Tudor and Stuart England', in Goose & Luu 2005, 161–74.

Esser, R. 2006, 'Citizenship and immigration in 16th- and early 17th-century England', in Ellis *et al.* 2006, 237–53.

Esser, R. 2007, '"They obey all magistrates and all good laws … and we thinke our cittie happie to enjoye them": migrants and urban stability in early modern English towns', *Urban History* 34/1: 64–75.

Evans, D.H. 1985, 'Excavations on 44–56 Botolph Street (Site 170N)', in Atkin *et al.* 1985, 92–112.

Evans, D.H. 2002, 'Excavations at 104–106 St Benedict's Street (Site 153N)', in Atkin & Evans 2002, 79–106.

Evans, D.H. & Atkin, M. 2002, 'General discussion', in Atkin & Evans 2005, 235–46.

Fagel, R. 2005, 'Immigrant roots: the geographical origins of newcomers from the Low Countries in Tudor England', in Goose & Luu 2005, 41–56.

Finch, J. 2000, *Church Monuments in Norfolk before 1850: An Archaeology of Commemoration*. British Archaeological Reports Brit. Ser. 317, Oxford: Archaeopress.

Fincham, K. (ed.) 1993, *The Early Stuart Church, 1603–1642*, Basingstoke: Macmillan.

Fincham, K. & Tyacke, N. 2007, *Altars Restored: The Changing Face of English Religious Worship, 1547–c. 1700*, Oxford: Oxford University Press.

Goose, N. 1982, 'The Dutch in Colchester: the economic influence of an immigrant community in the sixteenth and seventeenth centuries', *Immigrants and Minorities* 1/3: 261–80.

Goose, N. 2005a, 'Immigrants in Tudor and early Stuart England', in Goose & Luu 2005, 1–38.

Goose, N. 2005b, "Xenophobia' in Elizabethan and early Stuart England: an epithet too far?', in Goose & Luu 2005, 110–35.

Goose, N. 2005c, 'Immigrants and English economic development in the sixteenth and early seventeenth centuries', in Goose & Luu 2005, 136–60.

Goose, N. & Luu, L. (eds) 2005, *Immigrants in Tudor and Early Stuart England*, Brighton: Sussex Academic Press.

Grell, O.P. 1989, *Dutch Calvinists in Early Stuart London: the Dutch Church in Austin Friars 1603–1642*, Leiden: Sir Thomas Browne Institute.

Grell, O.P. 1996, *Calvinist Exiles in Tudor and Stuart England*, Aldershot: Scolar Press.

Harte, N.B. (ed.) 1997, *The New Draperies in the Low Countries and England, 1300–1800*. Pasold Research Fund Publications Vol. 10. Oxford: Oxford University Press.

Hovenden, R. 1891–98, *The Registers of the Walloon or Stranger's Church in Canterbury (3 volumes)*. Publications of the Huguenot Society of London Vol 5. Lymington.

Hurst, J.G. & Gaimster, D. 2005, 'Werra ware in Britain, Ireland and North America', *Post-Medieval Archaeol.* 39/2: 267–93.

Jennings, S. 1981, *Eighteen Centuries of Pottery from Norwich*, East Anglian Archaeology 13.

Jennings, S. 1985a, 'The pottery', in Davison 1985, 130–36.

Jennings, S. 1985b, 'The pottery', in M. Atkin 1985, 178–201.

Lake, P. 1993, 'The Laudian style: order, uniformity and the pursuit of the beauty of holiness in the 1630s', in Fincham 1993, 161–85.

Luu, L. 2005a, 'Natural-born versus Stranger-born subjects: aliens and their status in Elizabethan London', in Goose & Luu 2005, 57–75.

Luu, L. 2005b, 'Alien communities in transition, 1570–1640', in Goose & Luu 2005, 192–210.

Luu, L. 2005c, *Immigrants and the Industries of London, 1500–1700*, Aldershot: Ashgate.

McClendon, M. 1999, *The Quiet Reformation: Magistrates and the Emergence of Protestantism in Tudor Norwich*, Stanford (CA): Stanford University Press.

Margeson, S. 1985, 'The small finds', in M. Atkin 1985, 201–13.

Margeson, S. 1993, *Norwich Households: Medieval and Post-Medieval Finds from Norwich Survey Excavations 1971–79*, East Anglian Archaeology 58.

Martin, L. 1997, 'The rise of the New Draperies in Norwich, 1550–1622', in Harte 1997, 245–74.

Moens, W.J.C. 1887–88, *The Walloons and their Church at Norwich (Parts I and II)*. Publications of the Huguenot Society Vol. 1. Lymington.

Moens, W.J.C. 1905, *Register of Baptisms at the Dutch Church at Colchester*. Publications of the Huguenot Society Vol. 12 Lymington.

NRO PD66: 'Parish Registers of St Michael at Plea, 1538–1966'.

Pettegree, A. 1986, *Foreign Protestant Communities in Sixteenth-Century London*, Oxford: Clarendon Press.

Pound, J.F. 1988, *Tudor and Stuart Norwich*, Chichester: Phillimore.

Priestly, U. 1990, *The Fabric of Stuffs: The Norwich Textile Industry from 1565*, Norwich: Centre for East Anglian Studies, University of East Anglia.

Rawcliffe, C. & Wilson, R. (eds) 2004, *Norwich Since 1550*, London: Hambledon & London.

Reynolds, M. 2005, *Godly Reformers and their Opponents in Early Modern England: Religion in Norwich, c.1560–1643*, Woodbridge: Boydell Press.

Rickwood, D.L. 1970, *The Norwich Accounts for the Customs on Strangers' Goods and Merchandise 1582–1610*. Norfolk Record Society Vol. 39. Norwich.

Schama, S. 1987, *The Embarrassment of Riches: An Interpretation of Dutch Culture in the Golden Age*, London: Collins.

Spicer, A. 1997, *The French-Speaking Reformed Community and their Church in Southampton 1567–c. 1620*. Southampton Record Series Vol. 39. Stroud.

Spicer, A. 2005, "A place of refuge and sanctuary of a holy Temple': exile communities and the Stranger Churches', in Goose & Luu 2005, 91–109.

Underdown, D. 1992, *Fire From Heaven: Life in an English Town in the Seventeenth Century*, London: Fontana.

Vigne, R. & Littleton, C. (eds) 2001, *From Strangers to Citizens: The Integration of Immigrant Communities in Britain, Ireland and Colonial America, 1550–1750*, Brighton: Sussex Academic Press.

Yungblut, L.H. 1996, *Strangers Settled Here Among US: Policies, Perceptions and the Presence of Aliens in Elizabethan England*, London & New York: Routledge.

ABBREVIATION

NRO   Norfolk Record Office

Expressions of Conformity: Identifying Huguenot Religious Beliefs in the Landscape

Greig Parker*

This chapter examines the extent to which the religious beliefs of the Huguenot refugees of early modern London were visible in the landscape. It argues that the temporal and spatial patterning of Huguenot church establishment and duration in the western suburbs cannot be used as evidence of either the community's theological preferences or that conformism was associated with assimilation. In addition, it discusses the significance of intra-denominational variation in religious practices and their potential archaeological correlates.

INTRODUCTION

This chapter examines the extent to which differences in the religious practices of the Huguenot refugees of early modern London were visible in the landscape. In particular, it compares the pattern of church establishment and duration between conformist and nonconformist churches in the west London suburbs during the late 17th and early 18th centuries. In so doing, it critically reviews Robin Gwynn's argument that the temporal and spatial patterning of Huguenot church establishment can be used as evidence of the community's theological preferences.[1] Additionally, it examines the evidence for there having been a difference in the rate of assimilation between the eastern and western suburbs and the subsequent claim that there was an association between conformist religious practices and assimilation.[2] Finally, it discusses the extent to which the material correlates of Huguenot religious practices provide evidence of a substantive theological division within the community.

The relationship between material culture, theology and religious practice has been a focus of recent research within archaeology.[3] The current chapter is particularly concerned with the degree of variation in religious practices that can exist both within and between different denominations. A difficulty for archaeologists and historians is in determining the degree to which disputes between theologians and church elders corresponded to the attitudes of those they sought to represent. Gwynn's claim that the community's preference for a particular form of worship was visible in the material environment appears to offer an independent line of evidence to balance that given in church records and correspondence.

Gwynn's suggestion that changes in religious practices are associated with more rapid assimilation also has implications for archaeological models of migration, which often fail to adequately address the role of religion in immigrant settings.[4] Religious refugees may be expected to have resisted modifications to their religious practices. Therefore, the adoption of conformism and the subsequent assimilation of the Huguenot refugees into their host societies by the mid 18th century has been a subject of debate among Huguenot scholars.[5] Explanations offered include the role of the refugees in the production and popularization of luxury goods, the size of the immigrant communities, their distance from France, their success at establishing a well-organized church and the assimilationist tendencies of the host society.[6]

Any explanation of Huguenot assimilation, however, is fundamentally concerned with the nature of Huguenot refugee identity and how it is best understood. Traditionally, the Huguenots have been closely linked with a religious identity: as having been French Protestant refugees who fled persecution in their homeland. Yet, distinguishing between, for example, religious refugees and economic migrants is far from straightforward.[7] Difficulties also arise over whether or not refugees from different territories should be treated as a single group owing to a common language.[8] This has led some researchers to argue that the Huguenot refugee communities are better characterized as a diaspora, having socio-cultural, socio-economic, linguistic and kinship elements.[9] The French Reformed religion, however, is still widely considered to have been a key element in Huguenot identity and evidence for the survival of Huguenot communities frequently depends upon figures that show the duration of Huguenot churches.[10] Yet, the relationship between those refugees who regularly attended Huguenot churches and those who instead attended Anglican services is unclear. To what extent was membership of a French church a prerequisite for Huguenot community membership? If membership of the community was not contingent upon regular attendance of a French church, then the use of the duration of Huguenot churches as an indicator of community assimilation may be misleading. A full examination of these issues is not presented here,[11] but this chapter contributes to this debate by highlighting some of the weaknesses in the data and their interpretation that are currently used to characterize the Huguenot community in London and its assimilation.

THEOLOGICAL CONFLICT AS VISIBLE IN THE LANDSCAPE

Although a problematic definition, the Huguenots are most commonly understood to be French Protestants during the 16th to 18th centuries. Huguenot refugees had migrated to neighbouring countries since the middle of the 16th century and the renewed levels of persecution in the second half of the 17th century increased their number. The Revocation of the Edict of Nantes in 1685 effectively prohibited Protestant worship and required Protestants to convert to Catholicism. Ministers who refused to convert were banished while Huguenot lay-people were prohibited from attempting to leave the country. Following the Revocation, and despite the restrictions on emigration, approximately 200,000–250,000 refugees fled to neighbouring Protestant territories. Approximately 25,000 refugees arrived in England and many of these settled in London.[12]

The first French Reformed church in London was established in the mid 16th century at Threadneedle Street.[13] It consisted primarily of Walloons – French-speaking refugees from the Low Countries. It was nonconformist in that it followed a religious practice that was modelled on the Calvinist French Reformed tradition. It remained the only French church in London until the middle of the 17th century. A second French church was established in 1661 at the Savoy in Westminster. It was independent of the Threadneedle Street church and was funded by the royal bounty. Access to these funds was on the condition that they conformed to the Anglican liturgy. This included the use of a French translation of the Book of Common Prayer, the wearing of vestments and the practice of kneeling during communion.

The two churches became the focus for the main areas of settlement by subsequent refugees, the majority of whom were Huguenots from France. By the end of the 17th century the refugees were primarily concentrated into two main areas: Spitalfields in the east and Soho in the west. The community in the east was largely involved in the textile industry, most notably silk weaving. The members of the western community were primarily involved in trade and service industries relating to luxury goods. One of the differences between these two communities, and one that has been emphasized by Gwynn, is that the eastern community was almost exclusively nonconformist, while the western community had a mix of conformist and nonconformist churches.[14]

Gwynn argues that conformism was a divisive issue among the Huguenot community in London.[15] He claims that resistance to conformism by members of the congregations was downplayed by church elders. His portrayals of nonconformist Huguenots often appear to suggest that theirs was the pure, true form, while the conformists had in some sense become polluted by the imposition of conformism by outsiders. Nonconformists are frequently equated with upholding Huguenot traditions, while the conformists are presented as having sacrificed their religious beliefs for economic gain or personal advancement, for example, through obtaining access to the Court and the upper ranks who attended their churches.[16] In many ways he presents the western suburbs as having been a battleground between the conformist and nonconformist theological positions, and one that can be seen in the spatial and temporal patterning of the establishment of Huguenot churches.

According to Gwynn, this theological conflict was visible in the landscape in the following manner. Between the Act of Uniformity (1662) and the Declaration of Indulgence (1687)[17] the only Huguenot churches that existed in the western suburbs were conformist. Following the Declaration of Indulgence and then the Act of Toleration (1689)[18] the Huguenot community was free to establish churches that followed a form of worship of their own choice, and their preference was for nonconformism. This meant that, after 1690, no new conformist churches were established in the western suburbs. Gwynn offers some figures in support of his case. In 1690 there were seven conformist and only three nonconformist churches. By 1700, however, there was seven of each. Gwynn says that this demonstrates that 'for the majority of Huguenots, the Anglican liturgy was second best'.[19] He also claims in subsequent publications that the western community assimilated into English society more quickly than the eastern community, and cites conformism as being a factor in this.[20]

Gwynn's arguments hold particular interest from an archaeological perspective, most especially his suggestion that a theological or liturgical conflict was visible in the landscape. Also of interest is the argument that conformism was associated with assimilation, as this would establish an association between the adoption of new items of material culture by immigrant groups and their degree of assimilation into their host society. It would also suggest that one might expect to find similar signs of assimilation in archaeological assemblages.

Gwynn's characterization of the London community has become widely accepted by historians, leading some to describe the division between conformism and nonconformism among the Huguenot community as being 'a virtual schism'.[21] Gwynn's original work is

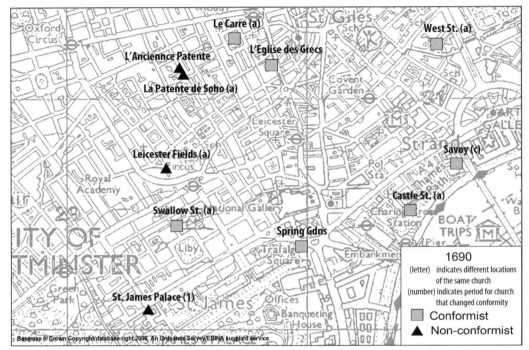

Figure 6.1. The distribution of Huguenot churches in the western suburbs *c.* 1690
(Basemap courtesy of the Ordnance Survey © Crown Copyright).

still widely seen as being the most authoritative statement on the distribution of Huguenot churches within London.[22] Owing to its influence and its potential for directing future research it is important that Gwynn's claims are critically examined.

THE PATTERN OF CHURCH ESTABLISHMENT IN THE WESTERN SUBURBS

Gwynn's original paper attempted to formulate a comprehensive list of the known Huguenot churches in London through the analysis of numerous historical references to French churches in the capital.[23] The current study incorporated this data into a Geographical Information System (GIS) in order to examine the spatial and temporal patterning of church establishment with the aim of comparing variations in the material culture of the Huguenot communities. During this process it became apparent that there were alternative interpretations of these data than that offered by Gwynn. This can be demonstrated by retracing the pattern of church establishment in the western suburbs with the aid of illustrations and statistical analysis.[24]

In the early 1680s a second French church, Les Grecs, was founded in the western suburbs as a satellite of the church at the Savoy. This was due to the inability of the latter to cope with the increasing numbers of refugees attending its services. During 1687, following the Declaration of Indulgence, the first nonconformist church in the west, Leicester Fields, was established. By 1688 there were four conformist churches in the west. Fig. 6.1 shows that by

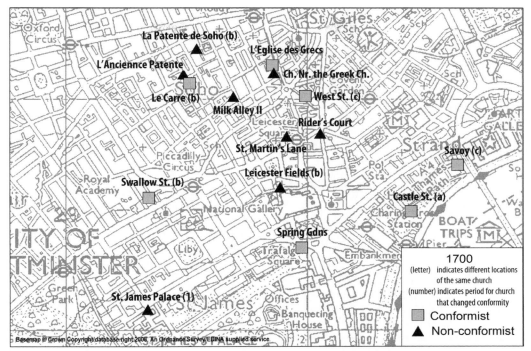

Figure 6.2. The distribution of Huguenot churches in the western suburbs *c.* 1700
(Basemap courtesy of the Ordnance Survey © Crown Copyright).

1690, following the Act of Toleration, seven conformist and four nonconformist churches
were in existence. After this point, Gwynn argues that no new conformist churches were
founded in the western suburbs, and that the only new churches established were nonconformist, thus demonstrating the community's preference for nonconformism. Yet, by 1695
there had been no increase in the number of churches in the western suburbs, somewhat
undermining the impression given by Gwynn that the Huguenot community, when given
the choice, quickly switched to nonconformism.

Fig.6.2, however, does appear to support Gwynn's argument. By 1700 there had been
a dramatic increase in the number of nonconformist churches to a point at which they
exceeded the number of conformist churches.[25] Gwynn interprets this as being proof of the
community's preference for nonconformism. Yet, this interpretation seems less convincing
when the data from subsequent years is considered. By 1705 there was a reduction in
the number of nonconformist churches and an increase in the number of conformist
churches.[26] The decline in the number of nonconformist churches continued, as shown in
Fig. 6.3, so that by 1710 there was only half the number of nonconformist compared with
conformist churches. By 1720 just three nonconformist churches remained in the western
suburbs, while all of the conformist churches survived.

The pattern of church establishment and their duration in the western suburbs is
more clearly illustrated in Fig. 6.4. This shows a significant difference ($t(18) = -2.772$,
$p=0.013$, alpha $= \leq 0.05$) in the duration of conformist churches ($N=10$, $M = 94.3$, $SD =$

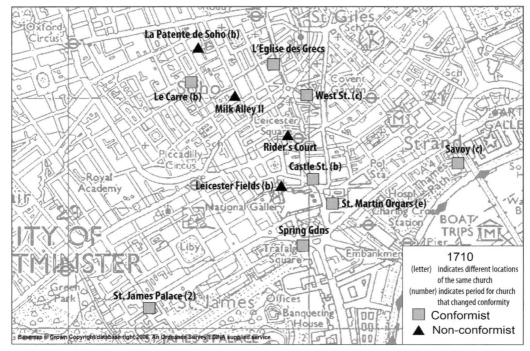

Figure 6.3. The distribution of Huguenot churches in the western suburbs *c.* 1710
(Basemap courtesy of the Ordnance Survey © Crown Copyright).

62.4) compared with that of nonconformist churches (*N=10, M* = 30.7, *SD* = 37.01).[27] While there was a wave of establishment of nonconformist churches at the end of the 17th century, most of these lasted only a few months or years. In all but one case (Swallow Street) conformist churches lasted for more than fifty years after establishment, whereas only two nonconformist churches (Leicester Fields and La Patente de Soho) lasted this long. Is this pattern best explained as being evidence of the preference of the Huguenot community for nonconformism, as Gwynn contends? It is worth considering other factors that may offer alternative explanations.

A comparison between the establishment of churches and the levels of refugee immigration show an apparent association.[28] The immigration figures show sharp peaks at the beginning of the 1680s and around 1687. This is followed by a lull during the first half of the 1690s and then another, smaller, peak in the late 1690s and early 1700s. Gwynn interprets this as being the direct result of changes in royal policy towards the refugees and as further evidence of their preference for nonconformism.[29] However, caution is needed in the interpretation of these figures. The rates of immigration are based on *témoignages* (certificates of good behaviour) and *reconnaissances* (a public statement of faith) at the Threadneedle Street church.[30] Their relationship to absolute numbers of refugees arriving in England is unclear. Gwynn also uses the absence of the establishment of new churches in London during the early 1680s as supporting evidence for the 'almost negligible' number

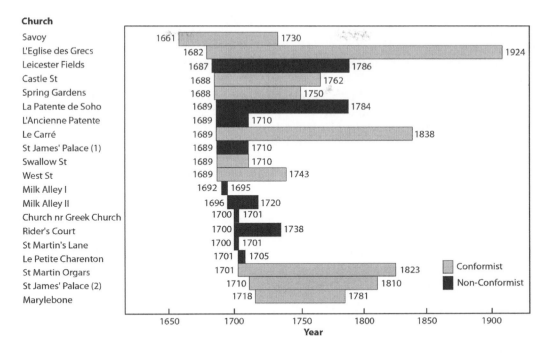

Figure 6.4. Comparison of the date of establishment and duration of Huguenot churches in the western suburbs.

of refugees arriving in the country.[31] Yet in his most recent paper he highlights how it was government policy to deter refugee settlement in London during this period, and that new churches were established in a number of settlements in other parts of the country.[32] The abandonment of this policy in 1687 coincides with the increase in *reconnaissances* at the Threadneedle Street church and the new establishment of nonconformist churches in the capital.

The new and short-lived nonconformist churches may also have reflected new arrivals to London attempting to recreate their previous congregations. It is likely that many of these would have subsequently moved to new areas, joined existing congregations or assimilated. An additional factor to consider is the presence of large numbers of former ministers within the London communities who no longer had a congregation following their expulsion from France. Some of these churches may have been unsuccessful attempts by these ministers to establish new congregations for themselves. A further consideration is that while the refugee community was relatively free to establish new, if sometimes unauthorized, nonconformist churches following the Act of Toleration, they were less free to establish new conformist churches. The existing conformist churches actively opposed attempts to establish new conformist churches and this is probably, in part, due to their concern over who had access to the funds in the royal bounty.[33]

The duration of the churches also does not support Gwynn's claim that the western suburbs assimilated before the eastern community. Gwynn argues that the Spital-fields community maintained its Huguenot identity 'perhaps longer than anywhere else England'.[34] He suggests that the church, and more specifically nonconformism, played a key role in this survival. However, there is no significant difference ($t(37) = 0.573$, $p=0.57$, alpha = ≤ 0.05) between the average duration of churches in the west ($N=20$, $M = 62.5$, $SD = 59.65$) with those in the east ($N=19$, $M = 50.2$, $SD = 73.97$), despite the mean duration of the western churches being greater than the eastern churches.

The use of the duration of the Huguenot churches as a measure of the degree of assimi-lation of the wider community is, perhaps, problematic, and is discussed below. Despite this, it is clear that the duration of the Huguenot churches in London cannot be used to support the contention that the western community assimilated earlier than the east London community, nor that conformism promoted assimilation.

There does, however, remain the apparent difference in the prevalence of nonconformism and conformism between the eastern and western communities. In fact, the arguments put forward in this chapter to some extent suggest that this distinction is even clearer than orig-inally thought, with nonconformism being in the clear minority in the western suburbs. To explain this patterning, the differences between conformism and nonconformism need to be considered.

DIFFERENCES BETWEEN CONFORMISM AND NONCONFORMISM

Many of the differences between conformism and nonconformism related to aspects of church governance and funding, such as the availability of the royal bounty for conformist churches and variations in regulations and the organization of the consistories. Perhaps the key difference in terms of religious practice and theology was the use of a French transla-tion of the Book of Common Prayer by conformists. In theory, the Anglican liturgy of the late 17th century would have resulted in a distinct form of worship from that of the French Reformed church. This would have included the requirement for kneeling during communion, the signing of the cross during baptisms and preaching without the wearing of hats by ministers.[35] The material correlates of these practices included the use of unleav-ened bread during communion, a communion table with rails that was usually located at the eastern end of the church in the chancel and the vestments of conformist ministers. Additionally, while much less ornate than that of the Roman Catholics, Anglican ceremo-nies would have had more ornate liturgical furniture than that of nonconformists.

Yet the reality was much less clear-cut than this. Conformists were often accused of being so 'in name only', by for example, frequently preaching while wearing hats or failing to wear surplices. Nonconformists sometimes did the opposite in order to appease English authorities.[36] It is also misleading to conceive of Anglicanism as a uniform collection of beliefs and practices. This was a period of intense conflict over the correct form of liturgy within the Church of England and there was considerable variation in liturgical layout and use of material culture between Anglican congregations.[37] There is little evidence that the conformists followed 'high church' Anglicanism, and this suggests that the differ-ences between the two liturgies would often have been relatively minor in comparison to their differences with other denominations, such as the Quakers. There is little evidence for architectural differences in the style of Huguenot churches between conformists and nonconformists, although this may be due to paucity of surviving examples. Purpose-built temples were unusual and the majority of congregations met in existing buildings, including churches or meeting houses previously occupied by other religious groups. It is important to note that both conformists and nonconformists considered themselves to be closer to Anglicans than to English Dissenters.[38] The similarities are perhaps illustrated by Noorthouck's mistaken characterization of the nonconformist Threadneedle Street church as being 'in the French tongue, after the manner of the Church of England'.[39] Further evidence for the similarities in liturgical material culture includes the production in 1717 of six communion cups, three for the Threadneedle Street church and three for the Savoy, that were based upon a 16th-century example from Canterbury.[40]

There is also evidence that the conformist and nonconformist congregations had close ties. By the end of the 17th century a General Assembly of French Churches had been established that consisted of all the French churches of London. It was created in order to improve and organize cooperation between the French congregations.[41] At least two conformist and nonconformist churches had a long-lasting pastoral union (the sharing of ministers).[42] There are also several cases where nonconformist congregations became conformist.[43] Additionally, the Threadneedle Street church helped to establish some conformist churches in, for example, Ipswich and Rye in 1681.[44]

It therefore appears likely that the differences in religious practices and theology between Huguenot conformism and nonconformism were relatively minor when compared with the disputes occurring within the Church of England during this period. They also appear to have had more in common with each other than they had with other denominations. This suggests that the division between conformism and nonconformism was, perhaps, not as important as has been claimed, at least for the majority of church attendees.[45] If the accusations of 'conformism in name only' are accurate, then it appears that, for many refugees, conformism was considered a perfunctory requirement to appease English authorities rather than a substantive difference in their form of worship. The French Reformed religion of the late 17th century may be characterized as having emphasized orthodoxy (correct belief) over orthopraxy (correct practice).[46] This enabled the variation in religious practice between conformism and nonconformism to be tolerated. Theological differences, however, were much more controversial and this is reflected in the reaction of the church elders to the spread of Socinianism in the late 1690s.[47] This may also explain why many refugees joined either the Anglican Church or groups such as the English Dissenters relatively soon after their arrival. It would suggest that religions that emphasize orthopraxy are likely to have greater group cohesion owing to the effect of ritualized practices upon group identity.[48]

If the differences between conformism and nonconformism did not correspond to substantive differences in theology, how can the pattern of church establishment between west and east be adequately explained? It is important to note that membership of a congregation was not based solely upon theological considerations. Other influences were related to regional origin in France, geographical location in London, kinship, status, preferences in different ritual practices and even the personalities of the ministers, elders, or other members of the congregation.[49] The religious environment is also likely to have influenced Huguenot religious practices. Spitalfields was an extra-parochial suburb and renowned as a centre of religious dissent before, during and after the Huguenots settled in the area. The religious practices of the refugees are likely to have been considered relatively moderate compared with the Quakers or English nonconformists who also lived in this part of

London. Spitalfields was also close to the Threadneedle Street church, which exerted a strong influence upon the community in both religious and social spheres. In contrast, the western community was under the influence of the Savoy, and later its satellite Les Grecs. It was within parish boundaries, was closer to the court and had more interaction with the higher ranks of society. This would have made their religious practices much more highly visible and more closely monitored. The two areas were also associated with different types of trades and occupations which themselves were associated with either different forms of worship or specific congregations. The pattern of conformism and nonconformism may therefore be largely due to the nature of the reproduction of existing social practices and institutions within society. The apparent division in religious practice may instead relate to only minor differences in the liturgy and theology, differences in church organization and governance and social geography.

HUGUENOT CHURCH MEMBERSHIP AND ASSIMILATION

It may be argued that the conformist churches survived for as long as they did owing to having had access to the royal bounty, rather than having maintained a viable congregation. It is also possible that Huguenots who had assimilated, or Huguenot descendants, supported the churches financially despite attending Anglican churches. It is also possible that the churches in the west had more wealthy, or more generous, contributors than those in the east. Perhaps related to this is the possibility that non-refugees were attending the western churches or making donations to support them.[50]

An alternative to the use of church duration as an indicator of assimilation of the communities may be the sizes of congregations. Gwynn has offered some figures that support his argument that the community preferred nonconformism.[51] He has calculated that during the 1680s the ratio of conformists to nonconformists was 2:3, while by 1700 it had increased to 1:3. Unfortunately, Gwynn fails to supply similar figures for after 1710 and it is therefore not possible to trace the comparative decline in congregational attendance during the 18th century. These numbers seem to suggest that neither the number of churches nor their duration is a good indicator of the overall number of Huguenot church members. This incongruity may be due, in part, to the method used to calculate the size of congregations. This is derived from the number of baptisms registered in each church. Although this may be, as Gwynn argues, the best available means for determining congregation size, there are clearly problems with this evidence. In addition to the difficulty in determining an appropriate birth rate, there are the difficulties in evaluating the reliability and completeness of the surviving church records.[52] Also, there is the fundamental question regarding the relationship between baptism and congregation size. While this relationship may be fairly consistent in a traditional parish setting, it is much more problematic within the Huguenot communities in London. Littleton has argued that baptismal figures tend to greatly overestimate the size of congregations in the French churches.[53] He also highlights the problematic issue of what is meant by membership of the church. During the process of assimilation descendants appear increasingly to have been members of both Anglican and Huguenot congregations. Members supported the church financially and attended the church only on special occasions, often as a sign of solidarity and in remembrance of the persecution of their ancestors.[54]

Other indicators of assimilation may also be used, such as the anglicization of French surnames or the maintenance of the French language. Yet, both of these come with their own problems in reliability and interpretation.[55] Additionally, once these indicators are no longer directly related to religion, the object of investigation subtly, but significantly, changes from the Huguenot church-going community to the wider French-speaking or French descendant community. The French immigrant community did not have a homogenous religious identity. Those who regularly attended the French churches did not form the entirety of the French-speaking immigrant population of London. In fact, the proportion of those attending Huguenot churches to those who were members of other denominations (or non-churchgoers) is difficult to gauge. Their relative place within the community is also difficult to ascertain, but ties such as kinship and occupation often appear to have surpassed those of religion.[56]

CONCLUSION

This chapter argues that the Huguenot community's theological preferences were not visible in the landscape through the temporal and spatial patterning of Huguenot church establishment in the western suburbs of London as Gwynn contends. A more convincing explanation of the pattern of the establishment and duration of the churches in the western suburbs must include a variety of factors relating to levels of immigration, government policy, the behaviour of newly arrived refugees, the over-representation of former ministers in refugee communities and the desire of the established conformist churches to restrict access to the funds from the royal bounty. In addition, statistical analysis of the duration of the Huguenot churches in London does not indicate that the west London community assimilated earlier than the east London community, or that the conformist congregations assimilated earlier than nonconformist congregations.

This suggests that neither the differences between conformist and nonconformist churches nor their material correlates reflected a substantive theological division within the community as a whole. Furthermore, it is argued that the tolerance of variation in religious practices reflects an emphasis upon orthodoxy within the religion. This may suggest that these forms of worship are less likely to maintain strong group cohesion in contexts where there are competing religions with similar theologies. Additionally, more orthodox religions, in comparison to those tending towards orthopraxy, may be expected to show different material culture patterning in a variety of social settings ranging from the liturgical to the domestic. They, therefore, have the potential to be identifiable archaeologically.

NOTES

*   I would like to thank Chris King, Hugh Willmott and Clare McVeigh for their help and support in writing this chapter.

1.   Gwynn 1971–76, 567; 2001, 130; 2006, 35.

2.   Gwynn 1998, 17; 2001, 209–10.

3.   E.g. Fogelin 2007 and other chapters in this volume.

4.   E.g. Burmeister 2000.

5.   E.g. Butler 2003, 200–201; Nash 2003; Van Ruymbeke 2003, 2; Cottret 1991, 263–7.

6.   Parker forthcoming; Van Ruymbeke 2003, 2.

7.   Lomax 1999, 84.

8.   Gwynn 2001, 3.

9.   Joutard 2002; Van Ruymbeke 2003, 18.

10.   E.g. Gwynn 2001, 207; Barrett 2001, 379; Van Ruymbeke 2003, 7–8; Whelan 2001, 472.

11. There is a large body of work that discusses different conceptions of Huguenot identity, e.g. Parker 2009; Lougee Chappell 1999; Joutard 2002.
12. Gwynn 2006, 41.
13. Edward VI granted a petition in 1550 to allow French, Dutch and Italian Protestants to establish congregations in London. These congregations were disbanded during Mary I's reign and subsequently re-established by Elizabeth I.
14. Gwynn 1971–76, 566; 1998, 17; 2001, 130.
15. Gwynn 1971–76, 567; 2001, 130–2; 2006, 28.
16. E.g. Gwynn 1998, 13; 2006, 36.
17. The Act of Uniformity (1662) required churches and religious groups in England and Wales to conform to the rites and ceremonies as set out in the Book of Common Prayer. It also required the Episcopal ordination of ministers. Foreign churches were exempted from the act. The Declaration of Indulgence (April 1687) removed the penalties for non-attendance of Anglican services and permitted freedom of worship to other religious groups. It was reissued the following year with revisions before being revoked in 1688 following the Glorious Revolution and subsequently replaced by the Act of Toleration in 1689.
18. The Act of Toleration (1689) granted limited freedom of worship to other Protestant groups, but not to Catholics or Quakers.
19. Gwynn 1971–76, 567.
20. Gwynn 1998, 17; 2001, 209–10.
21. Loomie 1986, 275.
22. Gwynn 1971–76.
23. Gwynn 1971–76.
24. The churches included in this study are taken from Gwynn 1971–76. Locations are based upon Gwynn 1971–76; Stow 1720; Horwood 1792–99; Sheppard 1957. In some cases the locations are approximate.
25. It may be noted that there is a discrepancy between the number of nonconformist churches shown in Fig. 6.2 (8) and that given by Gwynn (7). This is due to Gwynn's claim that Rider's Court (no. 30) and St Martin's Lane (no. 31) should be considered to be the same church. This is in spite of both having been open concurrently before merging (Gwynn 1971–76, 548), and is inconsistent with how Gwynn has treated other

cases. Whether one treats these two churches as one or keeps them separate does not have a significant effect on the results given in this chapter.
26. The increase in the number of conformist churches is due to St Martin Orgars, one of the oldest and largest of the refugee churches, having moved from the centre of London to a purpose-built location within the western suburbs. Therefore, it was not a *new* conformist church.
27. The *t*-test was used to assess whether there was a significant difference in the average duration of the churches for each group. The *t*-test calculates the mean of each group and then estimates the probability that the two groups originate from the same population. A significant difference is commonly considered to occur when the probability is less than 5%. Two-tailed, independent samples *t*-tests were conducted using SPSS v.16.
28. Gwynn 1965–70, 372.
29. Gwynn 2006, 34.
30. Gwynn 1965–70, 372.
31. Gwynn 2006, 34.
32. Gwynn 2006, 31.
33. Gwynn 1971–76, 546.
34. Gwynn 2001, 210.
35. Murdoch 1991, 3.
36. Gwynn 2001, 127–8; Nishikawa 2001, 359.
37. Benedict 2002, 410–11; Yates 1991, 18.
38. Gwynn 2001, 123.
39. Noorthouck 1773, 566–76.
40. Lomax 1999, 94.
41. Gwynn 2001, 135.
42. Gwynn 1971–76, 561.
43. Gwynn 1971–76, 521.
44. Gwynn 2006, 32.
45. Nishikawa 2001, 360.
46. Bell 1997, 191; Bruce 2004, 10; cf. Collins 2002.
47. Cottrett 1991, 208–10.
48. Fogelin 2007, 58.
49. Gwynn 2006, 214.
50. Strype 2007, I.i.27, 212.
51. Gwynn 2006, 35.
52. Gwynn 2006, 40; 1971–6, 547.
53. Littleton 2003, 91–5.
54. Van Ruymbeke 2003, 9.
55. Gwynn 2001, 204, 221.
56. Lomax 1999, 126.

BIBLIOGRAPHY

Barrett, E. 2001, 'Huguenot integration in late 17th- and 18th-century London: insights from the records of the French Church and some relief agencies', in Vigne & Littleton 2001, 375–82.

Bell, C. 1997, *Ritual: Perspectives and Dimensions*, New York: Oxford University Press.

Benedict, P. 2002, *Christ's Churches Purely Reformed: A Social History of Calvinism*, New Haven (CT): Yale University Press.

Bruce, S. 2004, 'Did Protestantism create democracy?', *Democratization* 11/4: 3–20.

Burmeister, S. 2000, 'Archaeology and migration: approaches to an archaeological proof of migration', *Current Anthropology* 41/4: 539–67.

Butler, J. 2003, 'The Huguenots and the American immigrant experience', in Van Ruymbeke & Sparks 2003, 194–207.

Collins, P. 2002, 'Discipline: the codification of Quakerism as orthopraxy, 1650–1738', *History and Anthropology* 13/2: 79–92.

Cottret, B. 1991, *The Huguenots in England: Immigration and Settlement c.1550–1700*, Cambridge: Cambridge University Press.

Dunan-Page, A. (ed.) 2006, *The Religious Culture of the Huguenots, 1660–1750*, Aldershot: Ashgate.

Finney, P.C. (ed.) 1999, *Seeing Beyond the Word: Visual Arts and the Calvinist Tradition*, Grand Rapids (MI): William B. Eerdmans Publishing.

Fogelin, L. 2007, 'The archaeology of religious ritual', *Annual Review of Anthropology* 36: 55–71.

Gwynn, R. 1965–70, 'The arrival of Huguenot refugees in England 1680–1705', *Proceedings of the Huguenot Society of Great Britain and Ireland* 21: 367–73.

Gwynn, R. 1971–76, 'The distribution of Huguenot refugees in England, II: London and its environs', *Proceedings of the Huguenot Society of Great Britain and Ireland* 22: 509–68.

Gwynn, R. 1998, *The Huguenots of London*, Brighton: The Alpha Press.

Gwynn, R. 2001, *Huguenot Heritage: the History and Contribution of the Huguenots in Britain*, 2nd edn, Brighton: Sussex Academic Press.

Gwynn, R. 2006, 'Conformity, nonconformity and Huguenot settlement in England in the later seventeenth century', in Dunan-Page 2006, 23–41.

Horwood, R. 1792–99, *Plan of the Cities of London and Westminster, the Borough of Southwark, and Parts Adjoining. Showing Every House*, London: London Topographical Society. <http://www.oldlondonmaps.com/horwoodpages/horwoodmain.html> [last accessed 08 January 2009].

Joutard, P. 2002, 'La diaspora des Huguenots', *Diasporas. Histoire et Sociétés* 1: 1–7.

Littleton, C. 2003, 'Acculturation and the French Church of London, 1600–circa 1640', in Van Ruymbeke & Sparks 2003, 90–109.

Lomax, J. 1999, 'Huguenot goldsmiths in London', in Finney 1999, 83–130.

Loomie, A.J. 1986, 'Review of Huguenot heritage and contribution of the Huguenots in Britain by Robin Gwynn', *Albion* 18/2: 274–5.

Lougee Chappell, C. 1999, '"The pains I took to save my/his family": Escape accounts by a Huguenot mother and daughter after the Revocation of the Edict of Nantes', *French Historical Studies* 22/1: 1–64.

Murdoch, T. 1991, 'The Double Ethic: Huguenot Forms of Worship, Belief and Practice', Courtauld: Association of Art Historians Conference paper.

Nash, R.C. 2003, 'Huguenot merchants and the development of South Carolina's slave-plantation and Atlantic trading economy', in Van Ruymbeke & Sparks 2003, 208–40.

Nishikawa, S. 2001, 'Henry Compton, Bishop of London (1676–1713) and foreign protestants', in Vigne & Littleton 2001, 359–65.

Noorthouck, J. 1773, *A New History of London: Including Westminster and Southwark*, <http://www.british-history.ac.uk/report.aspx?compid=46755> [last accessed: 9 January 2009].

Parker, G. 2009, 'Huguenot identity in post-medieval London', *Assemblage* 10: 7–15.

Parker, G. forthcoming, 'Articles of faith and decency: the Huguenot refugees', in Symonds *et al.* forthcoming.

Sheppard, F.H.W. (ed.) 1957, *Survey of London, Vol. 27, Spitalfields and Mile End New Town: the parishes of Christ Church and All Saints and the liberties of Norton Folgate and the Old Artillery Ground*, <http://www.british-history.ac.uk/source.aspx?pubid=361> [Last accessed: 9 January 2009].

Stow, J. 1720, *Survey of the Cities of London and Westminster*, ed. J. Strype, London: Churchill *et al.* <http://www.oldlondonmaps.com/stowpages/stowmain.html> [Last accessed: 8 September 2010].

Strype, J. 2007, *Survey of the Cities of London and Westminster (1720)*, ed. J. Merritt, Sheffield: Humanities Research Institute. <http://www.hrionline.ac.uk/strype/> [Last accessed: 8 September 2010].

Symonds, J., Badcock, A. and Oliver, J. (eds) forthcoming, *Historical Archaeologies of Cognition*, London: Equinox.

Van Ruymbeke, B. 2003, 'Minority survival: the Huguenot paradigm in France and the diaspora', in Van Ruymbeke & Sparks 2003, 1–25.

Van Ruymbeke, B. and Sparks, R.J. (eds) 2003, *Memory and Identity: the Huguenots in France and the Atlantic Diaspora*, Columbia (SC): University of South Carolina Press.

Vigne, R. & Littleton, C. (eds) 2001, *From Strangers to Citizens: the Integration of Immigrant Communities in Britain, Ireland, and Colonial America, 1550–1750*, Brighton: Sussex Academic Press.

Whelan, R. 2001, 'Writing the self: Huguenot autobiography and the process of assimilation', in Vigne & Littleton, 463–77.

Yates, N. 1991, *Buildings, Faith and Worship: The Liturgical Arrangement of Anglican Churches 1600–1900*, Oxford: Oxford University Press.

Part Two

Nonconformity:
Chapels, Landscapes and Communities

Chapels and Landscape in Cornwall

JEREMY LAKE

with ERIC BERRY and PETER HERRING*

Cornwall holds a special place in the development of nonconformity, and in particular Methodism, which was intertwined with the transformation of the county's landscape and communities from the later 18th century. This paper will assert that the cultural value of nonconformist architecture embraces far more than the built environment, and that they are an integral part of the past and present character of the communities and landscapes within which they have developed and are now used. Emphasis will be placed on the need to go beyond purely architectural approaches and present an analysis of chapel buildings as archaeology, both in relationship to the patterns of landscape and settlement inherited from the past and what they reveal about the character and aspirations of their communities and their relationships to external influences – liturgical to architectural.

And Jacob rose up early in the morning, and took the stone that he had put for his pillows, and set it up for a pillar, and poured oil on the top of it. And he called the name of that place Beth-el   (*Genesis*, 28, 18–19)

> To this temple where we call thee,
> Come O Lord of Hosts Today;
> With thy wonted loving kindness
> Hear thy servants as they pray;
> And thy fullest benediction
> Shed within its walls always   (*The Wesleyan Hymn Book*, Hymn 485)

INTRODUCTION

Cornwall holds a special place in the development of nonconformity, and in particular Methodism, which was first established in the west of the county in the 1740s. While the population of Cornwall experienced a 37 per cent increase between 1801 and 1821, Methodist membership rose by 74 per cent, well in excess of the national average.[1] The Census Returns of 1851 demonstrated to the Anglican Church that attendance at dissenting places of worship was most strong in Cornwall and areas of Wales and northern England. They also show that Methodism was the principal denomination in Cornwall at that date, particularly in those areas that had experienced the most rapid settlement growth as a result of the development of the county's extractive industries – notably tin, copper, china clay, slate and granite (see Fig. 7.1). Methodism suffered decline in membership from the

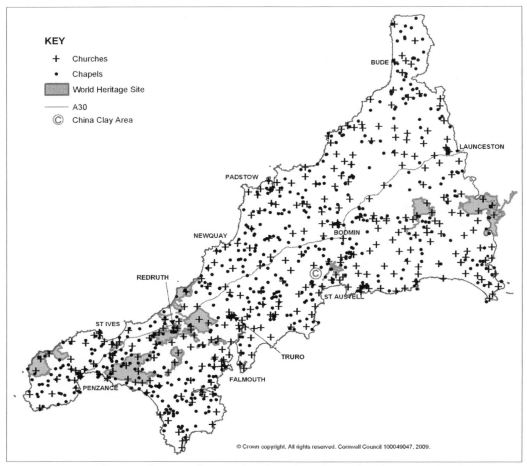

Figure 7.1. Distribution of nonconformist chapels and Anglican churches in Cornwall. The map shows the china clay mining area and the core surviving areas of the tin and copper mining landscapes now selected as World Heritage Sites. © Crown Copyright, Cornwall County Council.

1860s as the pace of emigration, first experienced by Cornwall's farming communities, accelerated in line with the decline of its ore industries.[2] But despite the building by the Anglican Church of chapels of ease, mission rooms and new parish churches (often within newly formed parishes), attendance at chapel continued to outstrip attendance at Anglican churches in both urban and rural areas into the 20th century.[3]

In the late 1990s a project initiated by English Heritage and the Methodist Church sought to better understand these buildings in order to determine their significance and inform future change. The results were published in 2001, alongside a conference that involved all denominations in Cornwall.[4] Much of the discussion focused on the increasing rate of redundancy, the demands of present-day mission and worship and the need to make chapels better suited to serve their communities. Since that date the inventory of 679 surviving nonconformist chapels has been further increased to a total of 914 as a result of the more detailed mapping of settlements and of areas nominated for inclusion in the Cornwall and West Devon Mining Landscape World Heritage Site.[5] Over 80 per cent of these chapels are of Methodist origin. The total of 760 chapels in use by Methodist denominations in 1907 shrank to 662 in 1932, under 400 in 1990 and 250 in 2009.[6] Nevertheless, 12 per cent of the Methodist Church's property is still in Cornwall, and 40 per cent of its recorded surviving buildings within the county are either listed or in a conservation area.[7]

The distribution of chapels reflects the vigour and complex diversity of Methodist societies across the county. This was particularly the case in the area to the west of Truro, which, in the hundred years up to the 1860s, experienced rates in population growth of 79 per cent and over, in contrast to static or even declining rates in the rural north and east: from the early 19th century, mining also developed in the east of the county.[8] It is in west Cornwall that the earliest foundations and chapel fabric, as well as the greatest densities of chapels, are concentrated.[9] The period of rapid economic and population growth that preceded the 1860s had also been accompanied by religious revivals[10] and secessions from the main root of Wesleyan Methodism after John Wesley's death in 1791, which added to the numbers of chapels built. Of 760 chapels in 1907, half (380) were Wesleyan Methodist (a decline of 32 from 1851) and 210 (more than the total of 182 in 1851) belonged to the Bible Christians, who had been founded in 1815 and remained in Cornwall as the most popular and resilient of the divisions from the main stem of Wesleyan Methodism.[11] Meaning can be read into the mapping of chapels with different denominations, with, for example, a marked tendency for non-Wesleyan Methodist chapels around Bodmin Moor to be concentrated away from settlements with medieval churches.[12] However, and given the extent to which chapels changed hands,[13] it is extremely difficult to be sure that denominations as marked on 19th-century Ordnance Survey maps are original to those communities. The picture was further complicated by Wesley's circuit system, for it enabled districts focused on head chapels to be subdivided and expanded as required, facilitating new overlapping networks of place to be adopted by all these various offshoots. How, then, can we approach an understanding of these chapels from a broader perspective, as an integral part of distinct communities and places?

A DEVOTIONAL LANDSCAPE

Popular evangelicalism cannot be considered in isolation from the landscapes and communities within which it developed and of which it formed a part. Memoirs and diaries reveal how members of chapel societies engaged in the social and religious lives of their communities, including inter-denominational work and visits to neighbouring churches and chapels at key dates such as harvest festivals and anniversary celebrations.[14] While specifically nonconformist burial grounds were attached to some chapels within outlying farming hamlets or expanding settlements (such as next to the 1833 chapel at St Just: see (3) on Fig. 7.2), there was no strong tradition (as with the Quakers) of burying the dead away from Anglican churches and burial plots.[15] The memorial of the extraordinary Bible Christian lay preacher Billy Bray stands under the shadow of St Michael's church at Baldhu, one of those commissioned during Bishop Philpott's episcopacy (1830–69), and John Harris (1820–84), the famous miner, poet and Methodist preacher, is buried in Treslothan

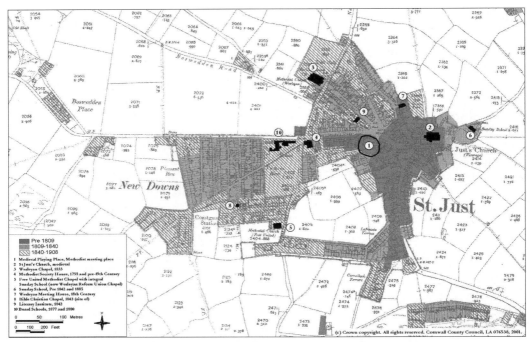

Figure 7.2. Phased plan of St Just, which developed from a small medieval churchtown into a mining town, the population increasing from 2,779 in 1801 to 9,290 in 1861, the most intense period being from the late 1820s to the mid 1840s, when there was a combination of planned and piecemeal development. The former included the laying-out of Chapel Street, at the head of which was placed the chapel (3 on map). The *Plen-an-Gwarry*, or playing place, continued to serve as a focus of community events, including open-air preaching. John Wesley preached here, when he stayed at William Chenhall's Inn close to the church.
© Crown copyright. All rights reserved. Cornwall County Council.

churchyard in Illogan (see Fig. 7.5). Anglican evangelicals played a major role alongside Methodists of all connexions in the promotion of Sunday Observance, the suppression of smuggling and even, in some instances, traditional Cornish sports such as wrestling and hurling: in their place, however, arose a rich and dynamic culture of male voice choirs, new sports (rugby and football) and bands in which chapels played a key part.[16]

Methodism was one of several evangelical revival movements throughout Britain, Protestant Europe and North America that from the late 17th century sought to extend religious activity and worship into the wider landscape, via camp meetings, field preaching, class meetings and an informal domestic setting for religious worship.[17] For John Wesley, for whom Methodism was intended to revive the Anglican Church from within and bring God's grace to all people in all parts of the country, preaching had begun as an addition to, not a substitute for, attendance at the parish church. There has been an understandable focus on the iconic sites of mass evangelicalism, foremost in Cornwall being the specially adapted Gwennap Pit in St Day, where John Wesley famously preached and which became a place of pilgrimage for mining families.[18] Wesley's use of pre-Conquest crosses and communal spaces (such as the medieval playing place or *Plen-an-Gwarry* at St Just – see Fig. 7.2) in part demonstrates that Methodism tapped a rich underpinning seam of earlier spiritual practice and celebration.[19] However, such special places – and the iconic images of mass gatherings – have distracted attention from the combination of 'patient leg work' and 'quiet recruitment along networks of kinship and friendship' that sought to bring Wesley's message to communities in every nook and cranny of the landscape.[20]

By the late 19th century chapels were recognised as focal points of collective identity and performance within Cornwall's landscape, for example for the tea treats and processions which involved all generations of chapel members.[21] Inevitably, different ideas of landscape developed within the context of the diverse places in which Methodism developed. Thus the diaries of tenant farmers who played a prominent role as lay preachers in chapel life, such as John Boaden, who farmed at the top of the Lizard, provide witness to the thrift and 'kind providence' afforded by God's work in nature, contrasting with the 'dread' underground worlds evoked in the poetry and from the pulpit of John Harris and other miner-preachers.[22] Observers often commented upon the extension of religious observance and fervent discussion beyond the walls of church and chapel – into the workplace, whether fishing boat, farmyard or mine, and also into the home, which formed the focus of private prayer, meetings with fellow worshippers and the repository of religious mementos and books.[23] St Just was one of many settlements where the religious revival of the early 1830s had prompted the use of barns and the wider landscape for preaching. An account of the opening of the Wesleyan Methodist chapel in 1833, one of a number built in this rapidly changing mining area in the 1830s, made reference to the landscape of the town – the homes of the poor to whom the remains of the festive dinner were sent, and the 'tents' of the congregation to which they returned 'glad and merry in their hearts, for the goodness the Lord showed to Israel his people'.[24] The chapel had already been enlarged by the time that George Henwood, writing in 1857, contrasted the 'devout attention' that marked the service with the continued enthusiasm of the congregation for singing hymns after the dismissal in the town's public houses.[25] Together with the Greek Revival Literary Institute of 1842 it is the finest 19th-century building in the town, dominating views from the mining landscapes to the north. It is also positioned so that – although located on the edge of the town – its classical façade (see Fig. 7.6) is highly visible from the town's market place. Significantly, this orientation of the chapel was enabled by a disregard for the liturgical norms of the Anglican Church, for the communion area faces west rather than being at the traditional east end.

Such a flexible approach meant that chapel communities were well-placed to assert *en masse* the strength of Methodism in all its diversity as settlements developed, and that builders were able by using available plots to exploit views from highways and public space. New tools, in the form of Historic Landscape Characterisation (HLC) and, for individual settlements, the Cornwall and Scilly Urban Survey (CSUS) and the Cornwall Industrial Settlements Initiative (CISI), have now enabled the mapping of the historic character of Cornwall's landscape and settlement in order to inform future planning, interpretation and recording.[26] Other recent work has shown that historic buildings and sites can be interpreted in relationship to historic landscape character and type, an approach that can be extended to cover the historic distributions of churches and chapels.[27] By the 1830s, the confidence and prosperity of Wesleyan Methodist societies was reflected in a fine group of chapels – all, like St Just, with five-bay classical façades – that had been built in the most fashionable areas of Cornwall's established county towns (Bodmin, St Austell, Truro, Penzance) as well as its new mining landscapes. In total, 679 of the recorded 914 chapels are located within settlements, which occupy just over 4 per cent of the land area of the county: 403 of these are located within the pre-1907 cores of settlements and a further 276 have been absorbed within later settlement expansion.[28] As well as towns, these settlements comprised medieval farming hamlets and villages, the latter usually resulting from post-medieval growth related to highway services, fishing or industry. Analysis of the distribution of Cornwall's churches and nonconformist chapels in relation to historic settlement allows us to gain a subtler understanding of the locational forces determining where chapels were built (Table 7.1):[29] 40.5 per cent of chapels within settlements are located on their edges (including urban suburbs), but they are more likely to be at the hearts of recently expanded towns and villages (79.1 per cent and 65.3 per cent respectively) and at the edges of long-established medieval hamlets (69.2 per cent) and the so-called churchtowns where farmsteads and houses developed around medieval churches (63.2 per cent). Isolated chapels are almost always sited on roads and lanes, 31.6 per cent being placed at road junctions or crossroads.

Analysis against the Cornwall HLC deepens this understanding of how the distribution of surviving chapels relates to the patterns of landscape inherited from the medieval past, which across both the south-west peninsula of England and the north-west of France reflects the reorganisation of land use and settlement between the 7th and 10th centuries.[30] All the isolated medieval churches, in addition to those sited within churchtowns, are located within the HLC zone of Anciently Enclosed Land where isolated farms and farming hamlets (many of which have since contracted into individual farmsteads) formed the basic unit of settlement (Fig. 7.3).[31] Sam Turner has used the Cornwall HLC in order to demonstrate how parish churches developed as focal points within these core productive areas as part of a newly forged and Christian 'ideology of settlement': crosses were placed on the edges of territories and the inland and coastal rough ground which served as vital reserves of winter fuel and summer grazing. In the medieval period this rough ground, which now retains the archaeological remains of earlier communities that preceded this reorganisation of the landscape, occupied around one-third of the land area in Cornwall.[32]

A far smaller proportion of nonconformist chapels is sited within the core medieval farmed areas of Anciently Enclosed Land (62.08 per cent of the land area of Cornwall, with 177 chapels) than within the Recently Enclosed Land, which contains 151 recorded chapels but occupies only 17.44 per cent of the county's land area.[33] Pre-1750 buildings, usually the houses of freehold and wealthier leasehold farmers, are concentrated within the Anciently Enclosed Land, whose fields reflect in their irregular forms and occasional curved boundaries the piecemeal amalgamation and enclosure of medieval strip fields. In contrast, field boundaries are more regular in form and buildings are predominantly of 19th-century date in areas of Recently Enclosed Land, over 95 per cent of which results from the post-medieval enclosure and settlement of coastal and upland rough ground, which now only covers 6 per cent of the county's land area. This transformation was associated with new mining, china-clay working and quarrying activity and the creation of new farms and smallholdings. Fig. 7.4 shows Carharrack, part of the parish of Gwennap, which produced more than one-third of the world's copper ore by the 1820s and whose population had more than doubled to nearly 11,000 in the forty years to 1841. Eleven chapels were joined by a mission church at Carharrack and two new churches at St Day and Lanner in 1826

Table 7.1: Locational analysis of Cornish chapels

Locational sub-type	Total (907)	Percentage of whole sample	Broad type as percentage of total	Sub-type as percentage of broad type
Town: historic core	132	14.5	18.3	79.1
Town: edge/suburb	35	3.8		20.9
Churchtown: heart	29	3.2	8.7	36.8
Churchtown: edge	50	5.5		63.2
Village: heart	206	22.7	34.8	65.3
Village: edge	110	12.1		34.7
Hamlet: heart	36	3.9	12.8	30.8
Hamlet: edge	81	8.9		69.2
Isolated: roadside	152	16.7	24.6	66.6
Isolated: crossroads	72	7.9		31.6
Isolated: open land	3	0.3	0.4	1.4
Isolated: woodland	1	0.1		0.4

This table is based upon an analysis of all the chapels on Cornwall's Historic Buildings, Sites and Monuments Record, excluding an additional seven in the Isles of Scilly. The following are the location types to which chapels were assigned.

Town, historic core = that which was already in place at the first edition of the 1:2500 OS, and normally also in place by the later medieval period.

Town edge/suburb – located on the periphery of the historic core, or (occasionally) in twentieth-century expansion.

Churchtown heart – a churchtown being the cluster of dwellings and other buildings and enclosures forming a hamlet or small village around the parish church – often including a churchtown farm, plus some or all of the parish's rural services (smithy, carpenter, wheelwright etc). Heart here means location either within or between inherited plots.

Churchtown edge – at the edge of a churchtown, but beyond the historic plots.

Village heart – a Cornish village is post-medieval, usually developed in association with industry, fishing or servicing communication networks. Heart here means integrated in the core part of the settlement.

Village edge – either at a village's periphery or within a clearly defined spur or extension of it.

Hamlet heart – hamlets here are those with medieval origins, usually agricultural, typically with Cornish names, and associated with communal and cooperative use of land. Heart here refers to location of a chapel within the pattern of original irregular enclosures and plots.

Hamlet edge – either at a hamlet's periphery or within a clearly defined extension of it.

Isolated roadside – with no other buildings or enclosure immediately nearby (save perhaps a graveyard, a stable and a Sunday School). Alongside any road or lane; often in an enclosure cut out of a field, though sometimes slotted into a pre-existing road-side slip.

Isolated crossroads – as above, but here at a junction or crossroads.

Isolated open land – neither within enclosed land nor beside a road. Usually rough grazing.

Isolated woodland.

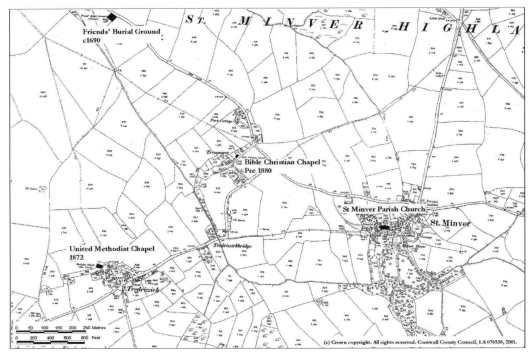

Figure 7.3. Anciently Enclosed Land. Like many churchtowns, St Minver, with its medieval parish church (rebuilt in the late 19th century), grew as the focus of a network of tracks and roads. Later mission work bore fruit in the parish's more isolated settlements. The chapel at Tredrizzick is located on the edge of the medieval hamlet, in contrast to the location of chapels in the heart of the quarrying settlement of Trevanger and the 19th-century coastal and industrial villages of Polzeath and Stoptide. Taken from the 1907 Ordnance Survey map.
© Crown copyright. All rights reserved. Cornwall County Council.

and 1840: a reminder of what Dunstan has termed the 'belated response' of the Anglican Church to the transformation of these settlements.[34]

In contrast, therefore, to the squeezing of chapels into the margins of Anciently Enclosed Land, chapels comprise an integral part of those farming and industrial landscapes created and transformed in the 18th and 19th centuries. Change over time has of course resulted in a diversity of landscape types across and within parishes, but on closer examination these broad distinctions between the two HLC zones still apply. Within the mining parish of Illogan, for example (Fig. 7.5), Methodist societies had developed in a cooperative spirit by the later 18th century in both the anciently settled farmland (centred on the medieval hamlet of Bridge) and in the mining centre of Tuckingmill, which became the head of the Wesleyan circuit.[35] The location of all chapels, included those built as a result of later schisms and separations, is strongly related to their landscape context. Twenty-one of thirty recorded chapels in the parish are located on land within the twelve villages that developed from the mid 18th century along the orefields, including thirteen within their historic

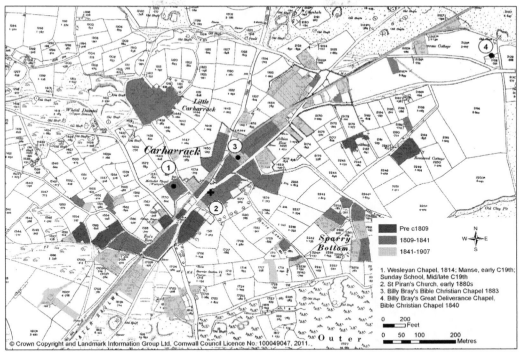

Figure 7.4. Recently Enclosed Land. Carharrack, part of the mining parish of Gwennap, rapidly expanded into a mining village in the first decades of the 19th century, with planned and piecemeal housing development. Small-scale holdings with regular boundaries are clearly visible on the map, part of a transformation of the former moorland, which also retains remnants of prehistoric fields and settlement. The Wesleyan chapel (1) replaced an octagonal one of 1768. The railway bisecting the map was built as a horse-drawn mineral tramway in 1825 to connect the mines to the port of Devoran. Taken from the 1907 Ordnance Survey map, with the phasing of the settlement based on the Cornwall Industrial Settlement Initiative.
© Crown copyright. All rights reserved. Cornwall County Council.

hearts. There is otherwise a very close association between the distribution of chapels and the transformation of the parish's landscape, as noted by one visitor in 1827: 'Cottages and small tenements springing up like mushrooms in every direction ... scattered groups of comfortless cob-houses and numberless single cottages, wretchedly built and damp and dirty in the extreme'.[36] All four of the chapels in Recently Enclosed Land are located in the more densely settled landscapes of the miner-smallholder. Another chapel is located in an area of rough ground adjacent to an area of miners' smallholdings. In striking contrast are the landscapes of Anciently Enclosed Land, whose medieval landscape had been affected by the amalgamation and industrialisation of farms. Enlarged fields and farmsteads rebuilt to regular plans, sometimes with wheelhouses for mechanised threshing, are a notable feature of the ancient and more recent farming landscapes around Tehidy Park, the home of the Basset family, whose fortunes had risen as a result of the exploitation of their estates for mining. One of the chapels in the Anciently Enclosed Land stands on the edge of Bridge,

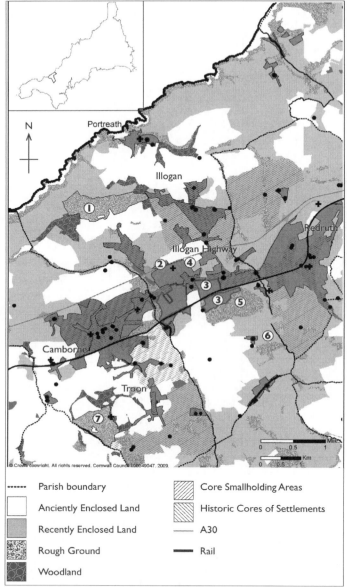

Figure 7.5. The parish of Illogan, showing the relationship of chapels (•) and churches (+) to the patterns of historic landscape character and the adjoining parishes of Camborne and Redruth. Portreath developed as a port for the export of copper ore for smelting to South Wales. Chapels are located in the areas of most dynamic settlement growth, including those areas of Recently Enclosed Land which have smallholdings. Also shown is Tehidy Park, the home of the Bassett family, who played an active role in the development of mining, the encouragement of a smallholder economy from the late 18th century and the provision of Anglican schools in the parish. Hatching within the settlement zones provides a broad indication of those 19th-century areas of smallholdings and dispersed industrial settlement.

Chapels relate to clusters of early 19th-century or earlier housing (as at Pool) or to planned or evolved rows of cottages (as at Tuckingmill), as well as to the roadside development of higher-status detached and semi-detached villas that are a particularly distinctive feature of neighbouring Redruth. The numbers on the map refer to (1) Tehidy Park, (2) Trevenson Church, (3) Tuckingmill, (4) Pool, (5) the rough ground and prehistoric monuments of Carn Brea, whose Basset family monument overlooks the former orefields, (6) Carnkie and (7) the church, school and parsonage of 1841 at Treslothan that adjoins the park and mansion of the Pendarves family.

Redrawn from the Cornwall Historic Landscape Character map by Chantal Freeman.

© Crown copyright. All rights reserved. Cornwall County Council.

one stands on the edge of the mining village of Carnkie, one is located in an area of miners' smallholdings and only one lies in a farming area.

Broadly similar patterns are observable in neighbouring Camborne and Redruth, all being part of the core mining area of Cornwall which had the highest single percentage share of Methodist attendances (79.6 per cent) recorded on Census Sunday in 1851.[37] New chapel societies were being constantly formed against a background of rising population and continuing high levels of schism, crime and prostitution.[38] Different patterns in the location of chapels within the urban settlements of Camborne (nine in the historic heart) and Redruth (three in the heart and six on the edge) reflect historic distinctions between the towns, with the Anglican Church having a far more prominent role and prominence among the professional and middle classes of Redruth than in the solidly mining community of Camborne. Within Illogan, and despite good relations between the Methodists and the Anglican Church (including their patrons the Bassets, who encouraged smallholding on their land), there exists – with the exception of the 1841 mission room at Portreath – a striking distancing of chapel from church. The medieval churchtown at Illogan had continued to serve as the vicinity's rural service centre, and it was buffered on two sides by a large rectory glebe and a vast churchyard recording the names of local and emigrant members of the parish from all denominations. The Anglican church at Trevenson, built in 1806–9 and funded by the Bassets, lies directly opposite the carriage drive of Trevenson House. These distributions follow a trend observable elsewhere in Cornwall, where chapels are either sited at least 500m from the nearest church or form an integral part (as at St Just) of transformed settlement. Such patterns, and the relative proximity of chapels to churches in the non-mining areas, invite questions for future research into the pattern of chapel membership and inter-denominational work.[39]

COMMUNITY AND IDENTITY

The *visible dispersal* of devotional focus away from the parish church thus takes different forms – an *insinuation* of chapel building into areas of centuries-old pre-existing settlement in contrast to its *integration* into areas that experienced the most dynamic change. Early meetings were timed in order to avoid clashing with Anglican services, and there was no intention to form a separate denomination, but by the early 19th century communities that had met in each other's houses and in improvised settings began to build their own chapels, and admit by majority decision the sacraments, in increasing numbers.[40] Members of chapel communities could be elected to be a steward, local preacher, prayer or Class Leader or chapel trustee. Chapel members would lead and form other distinct groups, such as Burial Clubs, Bands of Hope, Sunday School Tea Treats, choirs and Mutual Improvement Classes.[41] Chapels were not simply places where preaching could be heard and worship could take place. They fulfilled just about every social need of their members, from entertainment to the finding of a wife or husband. Space was increasingly required for weekly class meetings, prayer meetings, Bible classes and education in the form of both Sunday and, usually later, Day Schools. The need to educate and nurture children in preparation for life and work was particularly critical, often forming an impetus behind the building of chapels and finding its material reflection in detached or integral schoolrooms: despite the buildings of state schools that followed the 1870 Education Act, Sunday Schools continued as a vibrant expression of Methodist culture (see Fig. 7.2).[42]

As the 19th century and chapel building progressed, the activities of chapel communities – and particularly trustees – were increasingly bound up with managing debt and raising funds for chapel-building projects. Such a process, often prolonged, became a collective commitment that drew all the members of a Society together and made it secure in a way that meetings held in scattered locations could never do. The society at Mousehole, for example, had typically progressed in stages from improvised settings to a place of worship and fellowship: from a house meeting to a salt house, a room accommodating some 200 people over a fish cellar, and a chapel of 1784. This was enlarged in 1813 and soon became 'crowded almost to suffocation' before the move to a 'neat and noble-looking' chapel opened in March 1833: 'The tribes of our Israel came to the dedication with great joy and gladness.'[43] This is one of countless examples that show how the process of building made manifest the *idea of chapel as a community* that incubated within the places within which they developed, serving as an affirmation of Ingold's concept of building – based in turn upon Heidegger's essay 'Building, Dwelling, Thinking'. The process of building (both imagined and real) was thus not simply the result of transcribing 'a pre-existing design of the final product onto a raw material substrate' but instead arose 'within the current of their involved activity, in the specific relational contexts of their practical engagement with their surroundings'.[44] This concept underlines the importance of seeing buildings in the present landscape as part of their lived-in, experienced and perceived environments and to see them as the result of successive and developing demands and requirements.

By the late 19th century the chapel at Mousehole was regarded by its community as 'barn-like', presaging another remodelling and the installation of stained glass in the early 1900s.[45] This critical view of the simplicity of chapel architecture inherited from the earlier 19th century was widespread by this period, and led to considerable discussion concerning the acceptable extent of elaboration and art in the service of God.[46] A predominant characteristic of chapels is evidence for successive rebuilding and refronting, often accompanied by the recycling of building materials and fittings, sometimes from the previous chapel on the site. Enlargement, where the site permitted, was often achieved by an extension at one end, but external rendering and internal plastering can make this very difficult to detect. The façades of chapels were often rewindowed and had porches and vestries added to them. Datestones were often incorporated in such remodellings, and reset examples clearly testify to the antiquity of a chapel society rather than the date of the building. The resiting of foundation stones in later fabric also testifies to the reverence in which past chapel society members and benefactors were held.[47]

The variation in scale and style of Methodist chapels, as shown in Fig. 7.6, is both far broader than for Anglican architecture and a more direct expression of the varied prosperity and aspirations of chapel communities. These range from the mostly high-status five-bay chapels of towns and mining communities, matching the similar bay-widths that typified the houses of merchants and mine captains, to very small chapels seating fifty or fewer people that exemplify the crafts and skills associated with local building materials and techniques. Although documentation has only rarely survived, in contrast to the manner in which the Anglican Church's Faculty system required drawings for all works, it is clear that Methodists could deliberately employ specialist 'chapel architects', James Hicks of Redruth being a well-known Cornish example.[48] There are indeed some examples of direct imitation,[49] and the limited range of chapel types shown in Fig. 7.6 indicates that Trustees, on the ancient vernacular system that certainly operated for some medieval churches, may have asked for a design 'like' an existing chapel (whether vaguely Classical or Gothic in inspiration) rather than seeking to conform to an academic or fashionable notion of a 'correct style'. Thus the 'chaste and beautiful' 1,200-seat chapel at Camborne, whose foundation stone was laid in 1827, was built after members had travelled to Bath and Bristol to inspect other chapels: plans were then drawn up by a Mr Mills, and the chapel built by W. Tuck of Camborne.[50] Chapels of the simplest vernacular style, and those with Gothic or Classical features applied to them, also echo – through their form and use of gabled or hipped roofs – the late Georgian-style three-bay farmhouses and villas (detached and semi-detached) that were being built in the Cornish countryside and urban suburbs into the 1870s. Their panelled front doors and sash windows gave them an overtly domestic appearance that, combined with the use of local materials and styles, distinguishes them from Anglican and Roman Catholic architecture. Their propriety and order also manifests a desire for 'belonging' and conformity to a shared ideal, a direct reflection of the Enlightenment-derived rationalism of Wesley and other evangelical leaders, specifically Wesley's intention that 'Rule, discipline in all things' was the very basis of Methodist devotional life.[51]

This diversity and stylistic range thus reveals a tension between Methodism's centrally regulated system of administration and Wesley's own commendation of a 'pure, scriptural worship of primitive Christianity', echoed in, for example, both familiarity with the Wesleyan Hymn Book and the importance of local hymns for chapel communities.[52] This touches on the significant theme of how these communities have fashioned themselves in relationship to the wider world and, in particular, external rules of governance.[53] The relationship between dissent and popular religion, and the manner in which it incorporated a variety of practices and a type of language not usually tolerated by either the Church of England or Wesleyan Methodism, has been noted elsewhere in England,[54] as also has the conflict between centralised and locally regulated methods of organisation.[55] Such tensions, between the emotive response of many communities and individuals and the Enlightenment-derived rationalism of many of the evangelical movement's founders and leaders, were exacerbated in Cornwall by the exceptionally high ratio of members to ministers.[56] Such vigour and variety provides another counter to Thompson's argument that religious enthusiasm, as seen in the great Methodist revivals, amounted to a centrally controlled 'Chiliasm of Despair'.[57]

These tensions and contradictions are evident in the way in which the builders of Methodist chapels adapted High Classical and Gothic styles. High Classical styles become more prevalent from the 1850s, in part reflecting the growing wealth and confidence of chapel communities.[58] In contrast to the adoption by this period of Gothic Revival by the Anglican Church as the most honest expression of the ritual of the sacraments and of national patrimony,[59] however, it is clear that dissenting congregations viewed their own overall or 'total' approach to Gothic as being fundamentally ornamental. In part this was due to the fact that refronting and adaptation still had to work with the inherited template of the post-Reformation auditory plan, where the siting of the pulpit promoted a liturgy of shared experience and the dissemination of the Word. The Model Plan Committee in 1846 and Jobson's *Chapel and School Architecture*, published in 1850, had recommended the Gothic style to Methodist communities for both chapels and schools. Jobson, however, conceded that the three-dimensional articulation that had already marked out the architectural styles of the Anglican Revival would be very difficult to achieve, given its expense

Figure 7.6. Families of style, all drawn to an approximate comparable scale. The small cob and slate chapel at Boot in Whitstone was built in 1835 for the Bible Christians in an agricultural area. Chapels with side entries were easily capable of extension at one end (Bojewyan), and the windows to middle-sized hipped or gable-roofed chapels often betrayed the position of a gallery to one end. The showfronts to these chapels employed a basic symmetrical template to which a variety of decoration and styles could be applied – Gothick at Tregony and classical of differing degrees of simplicity at Voguebeloth, Tredrizzick and St Just, the latter two with emphasis given to the central bay. Altarnun, Marazion and Penryn provide varied examples of the embellishment given to chapels with projecting central bays and flanking bays which give the outward (albeit deceptive) appearance of aisles – spare, almost Picturesque, Gothic at Altarnun, Middle Pointed Gothic at Marazion and High Classical inspired by the medieval and Renaissance architecture of North Italy at Penryn. Camborne provides an example of the largest 5-bay classical chapels which by the 1830s had been built in urban and industrial settlements. © Keystone Consultants.

and the frequently complex requirements for communal space in chapels. Another key factor was the reliance on the show front for making an architectural statement. The most successful Free Gothic chapels, which achieved a unified approach to the functional requirements of mission and worship, developed within the context of late 19th- and early 20th-century resort towns and suburbs.[60] Full-blooded Gothic Revival chapels, where architectural expression was applied not simply to the façade, are also concentrated in the Anciently Enclosed Land of north-east Cornwall, where foundations were later in date and remodellings of earlier fabric are a far less frequent characteristic of chapel architecture than elsewhere in the county.[61]

CONCLUSION

This analysis offers the concept of landscape and place as a framework that can weave the physical fabric of chapel architecture into inter-disciplinary narratives.[62] By using landscapes of comparable or contrasting type we can also question narratives that have overly relied on concepts of individualism or regional identity to explain patterns of nonconformist activity. While, for example, dispersed settlement elsewhere in England may have provided fertile ground for a strong sense of individualism and pre-1750 dissent, as in the claylands of East Anglia or the Weald of Kent and Sussex, there is little evidence for any straightforward link between Old Dissent and the emergence of a strongly independent class of tenant farmers in Cornwall.[63] Indeed, community relations in farming areas, which display evidence in the inherited patterns of historic landscapes and farmsteads for the erosion and contraction of communal agriculture, continued to be sustained by the need to pool resources, help at harvest time and exchange knowledge and skills.[64] Cornwall's fishing industry and its mining industries were also sustained by high levels of cooperation and independence reflected in, for example, the establishment of Friendly Societies associated with individual mines.[65]

It has been seen that chapels are an integral part of how landscapes and settlements experienced intense change from the later 18th century. This relationship between change (environmental, technological and cultural) and dissent in all its forms as a search for individual and communal meaning has been noted elsewhere in England and other parts of the world.[66] It is significant, when trying to explain the relatively high number – by national standards – of post-1750 dissenting communities in Cornwall, that even those within its Anciently Enclosed Land witnessed high degrees of change in the 19th century – emigration, the emergence of larger farms at the expense of smallholdings and an almost wholesale rebuilding in stone and slate of buildings which were clearly less capable of continued use than those of neighbouring Devon.[67] Such changes observable in the historic landscape are offered as a framework for explaining the strength of nonconformity in broader cultural or geographical terms. Methodism was sustained in part by its remoteness from the core of the nation state – parallels being Jersey, Wales, parts of Scotland, Brittany and Ireland in the same period – but this explanation hides a highly complex interplay.[68] The revival of Protestantism in 19th-century Brittany was thus linked to its strong sense of independent Celtic identity,[69] but in most areas Methodism and other Protestant evangelical movements simply varied in the extent to which they could work their way into changing, established and embattled communities. In Jersey, for example, Methodism was widely adopted by immigrant English military and industrial communities and had a prominent spiritual and physical presence in polite St Helier society: on the other hand, chapels and Sunday Schools also became the foci for the assertion of rural Jersey French language and culture.[70] Jersey Methodists played a minor role in the Protestant evangelical revival in France, which commenced in earnest after 1815, exporting ministers who opened Methodist chapels in Normandy.[71] Similarly, both Methodism and Liberal politics were exported from Cornwall in the 'Great Migration' of the 1870s and onwards, especially to the mining communities of South Australia (known as the 'Paradise of Dissent' soon after its foundation in 1836), South Africa and America.[72] This process of cultural diffusion worked both ways, one early example being a donation from Mexico of £20 towards the cost of Redruth Wesleyan chapel in 1826 and another a donation from a member from Chile that funded the refronting of Lanner Wesley Chapel.[73]

Methodist chapels – indeed all places of worship – thus need to be considered as part of overlapping and interlocking communities of both interest and place, which developed in collaborative as well as contested ways within the framework of regional and global change. Such an approach can complement, enrich and deepen the complex, but overwhelmingly county-based, geographies of political and religious affiliation revealed by recent research.[74] Work on medieval and post-medieval Norfolk, for example, has shown how individual sites and structures – including the crosses which became focal points for recusant groups – were 'woven into a complex and interlocking pattern' within a landscape which provided 'diverse arenas for devotional activities'.[75] In Madagascar the chapels of Evangelical missionaries became an integral part of 'imagined Christian landscapes'.[76] Such work highlights the importance of understanding the archaeology of religion as an integral part of dwelling and landscape, challenging the traditional separation of sacred and secular landscapes and affirming the need – as noted in a recent critique of Methodist histories – for 'intensive local studies ... to test the validity of much grander constructions'.[77] This can help us understand how communities and places have developed in response to the changes around them and how these places will change in the future.[78] Research using the chapels database has already shown how the need for economies of scale, from commerce to education, has led to the foci of investment and housing pulling away from the traditional areas of dispersed rural settlement to areas around the A30 and the larger centres of population.[79]

We need, therefore, to go beyond purely architectural approaches and present an analysis of chapel buildings as archaeology, in terms of both their landscape and settlement context and what they reveal about the relative prosperity and aspirations of their communities and their relationship to the wider world. Recent studies have indicated how such an understanding can reveal and question new, and hitherto unexplored, avenues of historical enquiry for medieval churches.[80] Insoll has argued that archaeologists 'need to recognise the potentially embedded nature of religion as a key building block, if not sometimes *the* key building block of identity', as well as how it expresses ritual, ethnicity and human agency.[81] Geographers have also argued for a better understanding of the temporal and spatial contexts of Methodism and other forms of religious practice, towards which archaeologists and architectural historians can make a valuable contribution.[82]

This chapter has suggested ways in which this can be done, and how we can further enrich and deepen the study of chapels in Cornwall and beyond.

NOTES

*   This article was written by Jeremy Lake, but it would not have been possible without the survey work by Eric Berry and the GIS analysis of chapel distributions by Peter Herring. Their invaluable contribution is reflected in the joint authorship of this article. Jeremy Lake's thanks are also due to Bryn Tapper and Jane Powning of the Cornwall Historic Environment Service for their help in the presentation of the maps and the GIS analysis of chapel distributions.

1.   Probert 1964, 4–5; 27 per cent of those recorded attended Anglican churches and 60 per cent Methodist, leaving only 13 per cent for the other denominations (Soulsby 1986, 106).

2.   Shaw 1967, 98.

3.   Dunstan 2000.

4.   Lake *et al.* 2001.

5.   This mapping was conducted for the World Heritage Site nomination of Cornwall's mining landscapes, which was confirmed in 2007.

6.   Shaw 1967, 133.

7.   The listing of buildings of Special Architectural or Historic Interest was introduced by the Town and Country Planning Act in 1947. Local Authorities have a duty under the Planning (Listed Buildings & Conservation Areas) Act 1990 to identify and designate 'areas of special architectural, or historic interest, the character or appearance of which it is desirable to preserve or enhance'.

8.   Barry 1999a, 116–17; Alexander & Shaw 1999, 120–23; McGuiness 1967.

9.   Lake *et al.* 2001, 239.

10.   For example, Wesleyan Methodist membership in Mousehole had risen from 140 in 1828 to 318 in 1831, anticipating a revival that resulted in March 1832 in a decision by the Circuit Meeting of which it formed part to build five chapels and enlarge two more. When the chapel at Trewellard was opened in November 1833, it was proudly announced that it was the ninth new chapel to have opened in the circuit in the last twelve months (*The Wesleyan Methodist Magazine* 12 (Third Series, 1833), 520–23).

11.   Thorne 1988, 35–47; Currie 1968; Edwards 1964. These offshoots objected in various forms to the centralised control of what came to be called Wesleyan Methodism and sought a more local and democratic system of organisation.

12.   Herring 2008, 166–7.

13.   John Probert, pers. comm., 2001.

14.   Rowe 1996, 42 and 44.

15.   In North Petherwin parish, for example, there were Methodist burial grounds in four outlying hamlets.

16.   See Deacon 2001 for an analysis of these developments.

17.   Ward 1980.

18.   There are later purpose-built preaching pits at Whitemoor, dating from the first half of the 19th century, Newlyn East and Indian Queens (both 1852). Mention could also be made of the reuse of inherited but redundant monuments in remote corners, such as Tregenna Methodist chapel and Chysauster courtyard house hamlet, and the use of distinctive rocks – such as Wesley's Rock, a large rounded boulder between Trewey and Zennor.

19.   Luker 1986.

20.   Walsh 1994, 34.

21.   For the use of landscape features as a part of performative space and routes in tea treats and parades see Harvey *et al.* 2007.

22.   Payton 1992, 216–9 for a summary of the works of the miner preachers; Rowe 1996, 31.

23.   E.g. *The Methodist Magazine* 37, 1814: 397–8; Rowe 1996, 25; Hamilton Jenkin 1970, 165. See also Harvey 1995, 27–37.

24.   *The Wesleyan Methodist Magazine* 12, 1833: 874. There is a biblical (and particularly Evangelical) basis for seeing places of Christian worship as tents (as opposed to the more exclusive temples). The tent was often used as a symbol of God's dwelling simply and in the midst of his people and St Paul himself was a maker of tents (Acts 18.3); Wuest 1973, 39–40. My thanks to Peter Herring for this reference.

25.   Henwood 1857, 658.

26.   Rippon 2004, 100–142; Herring 2007, 19; Thomas 2006; Fairclough 2006a. The Cornwall HLC and its approach is summarised in Herring 1998, and for more on CSUS and CISI see http://www.historic-cornwall.org.uk/csus/.

27.   Lake & Edwards 2006a.

28.   The Cornwall HLC underestimates – owing to its scale of analysis – the numbers of smaller settlements. The total has thus been increased from 435 (3.87 per cent of the land area).

29.   This and subsequent analyses of chapel distributions are based upon an analysis by Peter Herring of 907 chapels in 46 parishes.

30.   Rippon *et al.* 2006; Turner 2006a; Roberts 1990.

31.   Seventy-seven are wholly located within Anciently Enclosed Land, and twenty-four adjoin it.

32. Turner 2006b, 173, 189, 164, 169.
33. The figure for Anciently Enclosed Land includes 4.61 per cent extensively altered in the 18th–20th centuries. Twenty-two chapels are located within unenclosed Upland and Coastal Rough Ground (5.69 per cent), mostly on the edge of Recently Enclosed Land. There are a further three within recreational and ornamental landscapes (1.66 per cent), the remainder of the HLC types being rivers, creeks, steep-sided valleys and other character types with no settlement or chapels.
34. Schwartz & Parker 1998, 197–8; Dunstan 2000, 128.
35. At least one of the chapels (Tuckingmill) in Illogan parish had been first built in the late 18th century. The ground on which the second chapel at Bridge (subscriptions opened in 1814, chapel built in 1816) was built was owned by William Burrall, a blacksmith. He undertook the smithwork for building the new chapel and was a relation of Edward Burrall, at whose house the neighbouring Tuckingmill Society had first met for class meetings in the 1770s (Cornwall Record Office, MR/R (5)/19.
36. Thomas 1990, 69.
37. Coleman 1991, 141.
38. Mudd 1978, 12–23; Tangye 1988, 81–104. Redruth, at the heart of the orefields, saw its population expand from 4,924 in 1801 to 11,504 in 1861 (Barry 1999b).
39. All but two of the top twenty chapels in the sample (see note 26) in terms of proximity to medieval parish churches are in the non-mining parts of Cornwall.
40. Dolbey 1964, 117; Brown 1946, 469–85.
41. For example Schwartz 2008a, 34.
42. Harvey *et al.* 2007, 32.
43. *The Wesleyan Methodist Magazine* 12, 1833: 522, 873–5.
44. Ingold 2000, 186–7.
45. Beckerlegge 1954, 19–22.
46. Jones 1996, 94–5.
47. For more see Lake *et al.* 2001, 77–82, 108–9 & 131.
48. In Leeds, for example, some of the more important chapels were design by architects from Hull and as far afield as Bath and Liverpool (Trowell 1985, 19); for Hicks see Lake *et al.* 2001, 85–6 & 92–3.
49. For example, the two gable-fronted chapels at St Tudy (1869) and Tredrizzick (1872), St Minver Highlands.
50. Lake *et al.* 2001, 85.
51. Dearing 1966, 79. Many chapels, for example, were reordered after 1846 when the Wesleyan Model Plan Committee recommended that the pulpit and reading desk should stand behind the communion-table and not in front, and the consequent development of the rostrum area.
52. Schmidt 1994, 104, 101, 94; Dearing 1966, 24–5. The Christmas carols of Thomas Merritt, a miner and organist to chapels in Illogan Highway, comprise one well-remembered example (Hubert 1988, 66).
53. E.g. Raco 2003.
54. Obelkevich 1976.
55. Ward 1980.
56. Gilbert 1976, 384; Lake *et al.* 2001, 16–19.
57. Thompson 1980, 411–40.
58. As noted in both Wales (Jones 1996, 66) and parts of France (e.g. Pon-Willemsen 1998, 47).
59. See Brooks 1995 for an examination of this theme focused on Devon.
60. Lake *et al.* 2001, 91–6; see Gilg 1999, 125, for urban expansion in this period.
61. Lake *et al.* 2001, 132. The distribution of the range of chapel styles does not otherwise display any strong local differentiation, cutting across the boundaries of chapel circuits. Of the 671 chapels surveyed in the late 1990s, 201 are considered to be vernacular in style; chapels can have features applied to a square or rectangular box (39 classical; 72 Italianate; 51 Gothic; 9 Romanesque; 10 eclectic); chapels remodelled in the post-1860 period are most likely to display an overall approach to a style (Classical 105; Gothic 184. Gothic examples are strongly concentrated in north-east Cornwall).
62. Hicks & Beaudry 2006, 7.
63. Everitt 1972; Payton 1992, 50.
64. Herring 2007, 50.
65. Deacon & Payton 1993, 64–5; Rowe 1953, 151–6, 312–16; Thomas 1965.
66. Armstrong 2001, for example 88.
67. Rowe 1996, 75 & 107; Barnwell & Giles 1997, 96, 98; Lake & Edwards 2006b, 31, 44 & 50; Chesher 1968, 49; see Overton *et al.* 2004 for an analysis of the standards of living in Cornwall against other parts of England; see Lake & Edwards 2007 for an analysis of the 'time depth' of farmstead architecture in relationship to landscape.
68. E.g. Luker 1986, 608; Payton 1992, 92. See also Rule 1998.
69. Vray 1993, 12.
70. Kelleher 1994, 131–2.
71. Mours 1958, 50, 160 and 22; Vray 1993, 207.
72. Payton 1996, 227–8; Schwartz 2008b; as one emigrant at Cornish Settlement later recalled, 'I

was taught to revere two things, John Wesley, and Cornwall' (Payton 1999, 228).

73. Lake *et al*. 2001, 6.

74. Darby 2000; Davie & Hearl 1999; Snell & Ell 2000.

75. Whyte 2009, 39 and 21.

76. Crossland 2006, 109–10.

77. Hempton 1996, 53 and 197; for an argument in favour of a more integrated approach to the geography of religion and place see Kong 2001a and b.

78. Fairclough 2003 & 2006b.

79. Bibby 2009.

80. For example in Stocker & Everson's 2005 study of Anglo-Saxon towers in relationship to communal and manorial space.

81. Insoll 2004, 150–51.

82. As argued by Brace *et al*. 2006, 38.

BIBLIOGRAPHY

Alexander, A. & Shaw, G. 1999, 'Population change, 1811–1911', in Kain & Ravenhill 1999, 119–24.

Armstrong, K. 2001, *The Battle for God. Fundamentalism in Judaism, Christianity and Islam*, London: Harper Collins.

Bailey, A., Harvey, D. & Brace C. 2007, 'Disciplining youthful Methodist bodies in nineteenth-century Cornwall', *Annals of the Association of American Geographers* 97: 142–57.

Barnwell, P.S. & Giles, C. 1997, *English Farmsteads 1750–1914*, Swindon: RCHME.

Barry, J. 1999a, 'Population distribution and growth in the early modern period', in Kain & Ravenhill 1999, 110–18.

Barry, J. 1999b, 'Towns and processes of urbanisation in the early modern period', in Kain & Ravenhill 1999, 413–15.

Beckerlegge, J. 1954, *Two Hundred Years of Methodism in Mousehole*, Penzance: privately published.

Bibby, P.R. 2009, *Churches and Chapels in Cornwall: A Pilot Study Relating Historic Data to their Social and Economic Role*, unpublished report for English Heritage.

Brace, C., Bailey, A.R. & Harvey, D.C. 2006, 'Religion, place and space: a framework for investigating religious identities and communities', *Progress in Human Geography* 30/1: 28–43.

Brooks, C. 1995, 'Building the rural church: money, power and the country parish', in Brooks & Saint 1995, 51–81.

Brooks, C. & Saint, A. (eds) 1995, *The Victorian Church. Architecture and Society*, Manchester: Manchester University Press.

Brown, H.M. 1946, 'Methodism and the Church of England in Cornwall, 1738–1838', typescript in Cornwall County Library, Truro.

Chesher, V. & F. 1968, *The Cornishman's House. An Introduction to Traditional Domestic Architecture in Cornwall*, Truro: Bradford Barton.

Coleman, B. 1991, 'The 19th century: Nonconformity', in Orme 1991, 129–56.

Crossland, Z. 2006, 'Landscape and mission in Madagascar and Wales in the early 19th century: sowing the seeds of knowledge', *Landscapes* 7/1: 93–121.

Currie, R. 1968, *Methodism Divided: A Study in the Sociology of Ecumenicalism*, London: Faber & Faber.

Darby, W. 2000, *Landscape and Identity: Geographies of Nation and Class in England*, Oxford: Berg.

Davie, G. & Hearl, D. 1999, 'Religion and ecclesiastical practices in the 20th century', in Kain & Ravenhill 1999, 234–9.

Deacon, B. 2001, 'The reformation of territorial identity: Cornwall in the late eighteenth and nineteenth centuries', unpublished D.Phil thesis, Open University.

Deacon, B. & Payton, P. 1993, 'Re-inventing Cornwall: culture change on the European periphery', *Cornish Studies* 1: 62–79.

Dearing, T. 1966, *Wesleyan and Tractarian Worship: An Ecumenical Study*, London: Epworth Press.

Dolbey, G.W. 1964, *The Architectural Expression of Methodism: The First Hundred Years*, London: Epworth Press.

Dunstan, A. 2000 'The Church near the People', *Journal of the Royal Institution of Cornwall* New Ser. 2: 3, 125–53.

Edwards, M.S. 1964, *The Divisions of Cornish Methodism 1802 to 1857*. Cornish Methodist Historical Association Occasional Publication No. 7. Truro.

Everitt, A. 1972, *The Pattern of Rural Dissent: The Nineteenth Century*. Department of English Local History Occasional Papers Second Series No. 4. Leicester: Leicester University Press.

Fairclough, G. 2003, 'The long chain: archaeology, historical landscape characterisation and time depth in the landscape', in Palang & Fry 2003, 295–317.

Fairclough, G. 2006a, 'From Assessment to Characterisation: current approaches to understanding the historic environment', in Hunter & Ralston 2006, 253–75.

Fairclough, G. 2006b, 'Our place in the landscape? An archaeologist's ideology of landscape perception and management', in Meier 2006, 177–97.

Foot, S. (ed.) 1988, *Methodist Celebration. A Cornish Contribution*, Truro: Dyllansow Truran.

Gilbert, A.D. 1976, *Religion and Society in Industrial England: Church, Chapel and Social Change, 1740–1914*, Harlow: Longman.

Gilg, A. 1999, 'Population Changes in the 20th century', in Kain & Ravenhill 1999, 125–35.

Hamilton Jenkin, A.K. 1970, *Cornwall and its People*, 2nd edn, Newton Abbot: David and Charles.

Harvey, D.C., Brace, C. & Bailey, A.R. 2007, 'Parading the Cornish subject: Methodist Sunday Schools in West Cornwall, c. 1830–1930', *Journal of Historical Geography* 33: 24–44.

Harvey J. 1995, *The Art of Piety. The Visual Culture of Welsh Nonconformity*, Cardiff: University of Wales Press.

Hempton, D. 1996, *The Religion of the People: Methodism and Popular Religion c.1750–1900*, London: Routledge.

Henwood, G. 1857, 'St Just Feast', *The Mining Journal* XV, 19 September: 658–9.

Herring, P. 1998, *Cornwall's Historic Landscape. Presenting a Method of Historic Landscape Character Assessment*, Truro: Cornwall Archaeological Unit.

Herring, P. 2006, 'Cornish strip fields', in Turner 2006a, 44–77.

Herring, P. 2007, 'Historic Landscape Characterisation in an ever-changing Cornwall', *Landscapes* 8/2: 15–27.

Herring, P. (ed.) 2008, *Bodmin Moor. An Archaeological Survey*, Swindon: Cornwall County Council & English Heritage.

Hicks, D. & Beaudry, M. 2006, 'Introduction: the place of historical archaeology' in Hicks & Beaudry 2006, 1–9.

Hicks, D. & Beaudry M. (eds) 2006, *The Cambridge Companion to Historical Archaeology*, Cambridge: Cambridge Archaeology Press.

Hubert, J. 1988, 'Music in Cornish Methodism', in Foot 1988, 62–7.

Hunter, J. & Ralston, I. (eds) 2006, *Archaeological Resource Management in the UK*, 2nd edn, Stroud: Sutton Publishing.

Ingold, T. 2000, *The Perception of the Environment. Essays in Livelihood, Dwelling and Skill*, London: Routledge.

Insoll, T. 2004, *Archaeology, Ritual, Religion*, London: Routledge.

Jobson, F. 1850 (facsimile reprint 1991), *Chapel and School Architecture*, Methodist Publishing House, Peterborough.

Jones, A. 1996, *Welsh Chapels*, 2nd edn, Worcester: Alan Sutton.

Kain, R. & Ravenhill, W. (eds) 1999, *Historical Atlas of South-West England*, Exeter: University of Exeter Press.

Kelleher, J.D. 1994, *The Triumph of the Country. The Rural Community in Nineteenth-Century Jersey*, Jersey: J.A.B. Publishing.

Kong, L. 2001a, 'Mapping "new" geographies of religion: politics and poetics in modernity', *Progress in Human Geography* 25: 211–33.

Kong, L. 2001b, 'Religion and technology: refiguring place, space, identity and community', *Area* 33: 404–13.

Lake, J. & Edwards, B. 2006a, 'Farmsteads and landscape: towards an integrated view', *Landscapes* 7/1: 1–36.

Lake, J. & Edwards, B. 2006b, *Historic Farmsteads: Preliminary Character Statement, South West Region*, English Heritage and Countryside Agency. Available at http://www.helm.org.uk/rural-development.

Lake, J. & Edwards, B. 2007, 'Buildings and place: farmsteads and the mapping of change', *Vernacular Architecture* 37: 33–49.

Lake, J., Cox, J. & Berry, E. 2001, *Diversity and Vitality: The Methodist and Nonconformist Chapels of Cornwall*, Truro: Cornwall Archaeological Unit.

Luker, D. 1986, 'Revivalism in theory and practice: the case of Cornish Methodism', *Journal of Ecclesiastical History* 37/4: 603–19.

McGuiness, T.W. 1967, 'Changes in population in West Cornwall with the rise and decline of mining', unpublished PhD thesis, University of London.

Meier, T. (ed.) 2006, *Landscape Ideologies*, Budapest: Archaeolingua.

Morrish, P.S. 1983, 'History, Celticism and propaganda in the formation of the diocese of Truro', *Southern History* 5: 238–66.

Mours, S. 1958, *Les Églises Reformées en France*, Paris and Strasbourg.

Mudd, D. 1978, *Down along Camborne and Redruth*, Bodmin: Bossiney Books.

Myles, W. 1813, *A Chronological History of the People called Methodists*, London: Thomas Cordeaux.

Noll, M.A., Bebbington D.W. & Rawlyk, G.A. (eds) 1994, *Evangelicalism. Comparative Studies of Popular Protestantism in North America, the British Isles, and Beyond, 1700–1990*, Oxford: Oxford University Press.

Obelkevich, J. 1976, *Religion and Rural Society: South Lindsey, 1825–1875*, Oxford: Clarendon Press.

Orme, N. (ed.) 1991, *Unity and Variety: A History of the Church in Devon and Cornwall*, Exeter: Exeter University Press.

Overton, M., Whittle, J., Dean, D. & Hann, A. (eds) 2004, *Production and Consumption in English Households, 1600–1750*, London: Routledge.

Palang, H. & Fry, G. (eds) 2003, *Landscape Interfaces: Cultural Heritage in Changing Landscapes*. Landscape Series 1. Dordrecht.

Payton, P. 1992, *The Making of Modern Cornwall*, Truro: Dyllansow Truran.

Payton, P. 1996, *Cornwall*, Fowey: Alexander Associates.

Payton, P. 1999, *The Cornish Overseas*, Fowey: Alexander Associates.

Pon-Willemsen, C. 1998, 'Le patrimoine protestant', in Pon-Willemsen 1998, 17–63.

Pon-Willemsen, C. (ed.) 1998, *Patrimoine de Poitou-Charentes. Architectes et mobiliers*, Paris: Inventaire Général.

Probert, J.C. 1964, *The Sociology of Cornish Methodism: the Formative Years*. Cornish Methodist Historical Association Occasional Publication No. 8. Truro.

Raco, M. 2003, 'Governmentality, subject-building, and the discourses and practices of devolution in the UK', *Transactions of the Institute of British Geographers* New Ser. 28: 78–93.

Rippon, S., with Clark, J. 2004, *Historic Landscape Analysis: Deciphering the Countryside*, York: Council for British Archaeology.

Rippon, S.J., Fyfe, R.M. & Brown A.G. 2006, 'Beyond villages and open fields: the origins and development of a historic landscape characterised by dispersed settlement in South-West England', *Medieval Archaeology* 50: 31–70.

Roberts, B.K. 1990, 'Rural settlement and regional contrasts: questions of continuity and colonisation', *Rural History* 1: 51–72.

Rowe, J. 1953, *Cornwall in the Age of the Industrial Revolution*, Liverpool: Liverpool University Press.

Rowe, J. 1996, *Changing Times and Fortunes. A Cornish Farmer's Life, 1828–1904*, Exeter: Cornish Hillside Publications.

Rule, J. 1998, 'Explaining Revivalism: The Case of Cornish Methodism', *Southern History* 20: 168–88.

Schmidt, L.E. 1994, 'Time, celebration and the Christian year in 18th century Evangelicalism', in Noll *et al.* 1994, 90–112.

Schwartz, S. 2008a, *Voices of the Cornish Mining Landscape*, Truro: Cornwall County Council.

Schwartz, S. 2008b, *Cornwall and West Devon Mining Landscape World Heritage Site: Mining a Shared Heritage: Harnessing the Potential of Cornish Transnationalism*, Truro: Cornwall County Council.

Schwartz, S. & Parker, R. 1998, *Lanner. A Cornish Mining Parish*, Tiverton: Halsgrove.

Shaw, T. 1959, *Methodism in Illogan, 1743–1958*, privately published.

Shaw, T. 1965, *The Bible Christians 1815–1907*, London: Epworth Press.

Shaw, T. 1967, *A History of Cornish Methodism*, Truro: Bradford Barton.

Snell, K.D.M. & Ell, P.S. 2000, *Rival Jerusalems. The Geography of Victorian Religion*, Cambridge: Cambridge University Press.

Soulsby, I. 1986, *A History of Cornwall*, Chichester: Phillimore.

Stocker D.A. & Everson, P.L. 2005, *Summoning St Michael: Early Romanesque Towers in Lincolnshire*, Oxford: Oxbow Books.

Tangye, M. 1988, *Redruth and Its People*, Redruth: privately published.

Thomas, C. 1965, *Methodism and Self-Improvement in 19th Century Cornwall*. Cornish Methodist Historical Association Occasional Publication No. 9. Truro.

Thomas, J. 1990, *Illogan: More Than a Village*, Truro: Dyllansow Truran.

Thomas, R. 2006, 'Mapping the towns: English Heritage's Urban Survey and Characterisation programme', *Landscapes* 7/1: 68–92.

Thompson, E.P. 1980, *The Making of the English Working Classes*, 2nd edn, London: Penguin.

Thorne, R. 1988, 'Chapels in Cornwall', in Foot 1988, 35–47.

Trowell, F. 1985, 'Speculative housing development in Leeds and the involvement of local architects in the design process, 1866–1914', *Construction History* 1: 13–24.

Turner, S. (ed.) 2006a, *Medieval Devon and Cornwall. Shaping an Ancient Countryside*, Macclesfield: Windgather Press.

Turner, S. 2006b, *Making a Christian Landscape. The Countryside in Early Medieval Cornwall, Devon and Wessex*, Exeter: University of Exeter Press.

Vray, N. 1993, *Les Protestants de l'Ouest, Bretagne, Normandie, Poitou, 1517–1907*, Paris: Editions de l'Ouest France.

Walsh, J. 1994, '"Methodism" and the origins of English-speaking Evangelicalism', in Noll *et al.* 1994, 19–37.

Ward, W.R. 1980, 'Power and piety: the origins of religious revival in the early 18th century', *Bulletin of the John Rylands University Library of Manchester* 63: 231–52.

Whyte, N. 2009, *Inhabiting the Landscape. Place, Custom and Memory, 1500–1800*, Oxford: Windgather Press.

Wuest, K. 1973, *Wuest's Words: Studies from the Greek New Testament*, Grand Rapids: William B. Eerdmans Publishing.

Church and Chapel:
Focal Points in Welsh and Manx Landscapes

Harold Mytum

The roles of Anglican churches and nonconformist chapels in 18th- and 19th-century rural communities have been little studied by archaeologists, despite being vibrant cultural and social foci. The distribution of Anglican churches, largely inherited from the Middle Ages, was not always appropriately placed to service later settlement. Nonconformists were often constrained by resources and patronage, though as congregations grew places of worship could be moved or rebuilt. The physical spaces and their associated artefacts were used by rural people to create, re-create, and change their social relations, being actively used in the formulation of cultural structures and identities within their theologically defined parameters.

INTRODUCTION

Most archaeological research has focused on the architectural development of churches, links to changes in style, architects, masons, sources of building materials and techniques of construction.[1] Churches in use have been considered in terms of burial, liturgy and, to a lesser but growing extent, social use of space. This chapter develops the social and spatial context of churches and chapels, but in a wider social and geographical context, following in the tradition of Richard Morris's *Churches in the Landscape*[2] but widening that perspective to include also the participants' cultural, social and economic landscapes within which their church attendance and other church-related activities took place.

Christianity is in the world, but is not of the world. But social activities linked with churches and chapels are of the world as well as in it, and have to be negotiated within existing class, cultural and geographical structures. In the post-medieval period perceptions of that world, and experiences within it, were varied. These were partly reflected in and partly created by the different denominational emphases, and so the first case study area in north Pembrokeshire allows consideration of the role of both Anglican churches and nonconformist chapels in a complex, overlapping set of networks.

This can then be compared with the Isle of Man, where similarities, but also significant differences, emerge both in the denominational dynamics and in the cultural context with regard to language and identity. From these case studies and more general observations it is possible to draw together an archaeological, material perspective on church and chapel in bilingual, culturally diverse parts of the British Isles.

NORTH PEMBROKESHIRE – CHURCHES AND CHAPELS

The study area considered in detail here consists of the four parishes of Dinas, Meline, Nevern and Newport, in effect the small town of Newport and its hinterland stretching along the coast as far as Dinas to the west and along a similar length of coast to the east, and inland into the Preseli mountains to the south. Further surveys not considered here include St Dogmael's and St David's; these provide similar patterning, and it can be argued that the results of the case study apply to the whole of Welsh-speaking Pembrokeshire and western Cardiganshire. Besides the surviving architectural and archaeological remains, several 19th-century travel accounts and censuses provide useful data on all denominations (Table 8.1).[3]

Table 8.1. Places of worship listed in the 1851 Religious Census returns for the north Pembrokeshire study area.

Nevern		
Nevern	Anglican	
Morva Room	Independent	Rented 1843
Gethsemane	Welsh Calv Meth	Erected 1844
Penuel	Baptist	Erected 1824
Glanrhyd	Calv Meth	Erected *c.* 1807
Brynberian	Indep	Erected 1693, last erected 1843
Caersalem Cilgwyn	Baptist	Erected 1841
Newport		
Newport	Anglican	
Bethlehem	Partic Baptist	Erected before 1770
Tabernacle	Welsh Calv Meth	Erected 1815, rebuilt 1837
Ebenezer	Independent	Erected before 1800, rebuilt
Dinas		
Dinas	Anglican	In ruin since 1850 storm
Tabor	Baptist	Erected 1792, rebuilt 1842
Brynhenllan	Calv Meth	Erected before 1800
Gideon	Independent	Erected 1830
Meline		
Meline	Anglican	
Pantgynon	Independent	Erected before 1840

The Anglican churches of North Pembrokeshire were heavily restored or even rebuilt during the 19th century, though much earlier fabric remains at Nevern (Fig. 8.1a) and Newport. These rebuildings were largely financed by the local gentry, but documentation that survives for Newport indicates a wider range of subscribers here, perhaps because this small town contained a range of tradesmen and professionals who could be expected to contribute.[4] Nevern had a school as well as its parish church, and Newport possessed an adjacent chapel that was used by the Wesleyan Methodists until their secession, and a chapel of ease, Capel Cilgwyn (Fig. 8.1b), placed to serve the congregation in the upland part of the parish.[5] The other parish churches had no additional buildings. All the parish churches possessed graveyards, and these were used for burial by all denominations in the 18th century, though a few chapels later had their own grounds. Dinas church lost its chancel to the sea in a storm in 1850 and all but the still-surviving west wall in 1859. This limited services thereafter until a new church was built uphill, near the main road, in the later 19th century.

Three nonconformist chapels stood within the town of Newport: the Independent Ebenezer (1743, rebuilt 1844), the Baptist Bethlehem (1789, rebuilt 1817, 1855) and the Methodist Tabernacle (1811, rebuilt 1838, 1904: Fig. 8.1c). All had some additional accommodation but the Methodists had the most integrated site with their adjoining church room. Outside the town were also Independent Capel y Mynydd and Gethsemane.[6]

The rural areas have a number of nonconformist chapels, some, as at Dinas, situated in the village near the Anglican church, but many others in locations better able to serve the dispersed rural populations or the small villages that grew up from the later 18th century at places such as Brynberian and Felindre Farchog.[7] Unlike in many areas of Wales, several major landowners were sympathetic to nonconformist ideals and allowed the sale of land so that congregations could build chapels, and some provided resources for this. Although Newport St Mary's had its detached Capel Cilgwyn, now deconsecrated and being converted into a dwelling (Fig. 8.1b), the Anglican churches were often poorly located to reach many of their parishioners. For example, Meline was placed at the northernmost extremity of the parish that stretched far south into the Preseli mountains. Within the Cardigan district as a whole at the 1851 Religious Census, the largest group was that of the Baptists, followed in almost equal measure by the Anglicans, Independents and the Presbyterian Welsh Calvinistic Methodists.[8] The Wesleyan Methodists, more closely linked to Anglicanism and much more popular in England,[9] represented a very small minority interest, though they were relatively strong in Newport and Nevern thanks to the support of the Bowens.[10] The attraction of nonconformity was partly theological, partly social – with no gentry involvement and less domination by tenant farmers. It was also partly cultural – with greater acceptance of the Welsh language – but had a geographical component that should be recognized.

While it is clear that denominational affiliation was important to some – and, indeed, within the same family members could disperse on a Sunday to their various places of worship – for many proximity would be major factor. Roads were poor, the countryside far from flat, and services could last a considerable time on the only free day of the week for many. Even the chapels did not easily serve all their members, and a number of farmhouses held monthly services.[11] If numbers increased sufficiently then a chapel could be built, as with Baptist Caersalem Cilgwyn. Many of the chapels gained ancillary buildings over time. Independent Brynberian included an adjacent hall, and the original late 18th-century chapel at Felindre Farchog was used as a school when the larger chapel was built on the other side of the road in 1857.

Nonconformity was represented in the late 18th- and 19th-century landscape by a series of specific, visible structures that proclaimed that denominational allegiance through incised panels that announced affiliation and dates, often with ministers' names as well. It was also represented, however, by a secondary level of buildings used for worship, instruction or prayer, largely known only to those within the sect but creating richer, denser and more integrated religious landscapes for the members. In contrast, Anglicanism was visible through the parish church system, some of the buildings – as at Newport and Nevern – possessing fine medieval towers that dominated the skyline (Fig. 8.1a). The other churches,

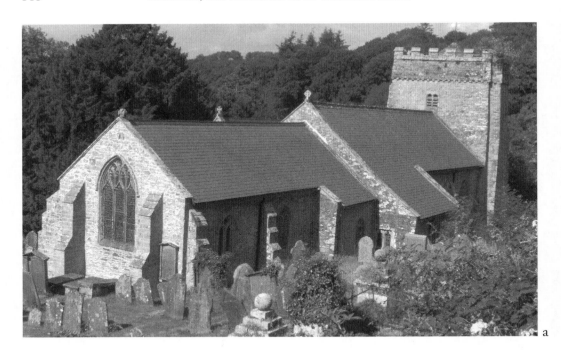

a

b

Figure 8.1. Chapels and churches in north Pembrokeshire. a) St Brynach's, Nevern (Anglican);
b) St Mary's Newport detached Capel Cilgwyn (Anglican); c) Newport (Welsh Calvinist
Methodist) (photographs by H. Mytum).

in contrast, merely enjoyed bellcotes in their gables, were set back within their graveyards,
and generally were less dominating of the landscape and routeways than at least the later
rebuildings of the nonconformist chapels.

NORTH PEMBROKESHIRE – GEOGRAPHY OF ATTENDANCE

Attendance patterns are hard to reconstruct from the churches and chapels, and detailed
work has not been carried out on the parish records to assess this. In Wales this research is
problematic because of numerous people with similar names, variations of spelling of such
names, and many small-scale (under five-mile) movements of much of the population for
employment which are visible in the census but make tracking in parish records problematic. Moreover, nonconformist records have not been consistently preserved.[12] However,
the burial monuments are informative – one of the ways in which popular identification
was ensured was by the use of the epithet of place-name of farm or house as well as name.
Still used in popular speech as an identifier, house or farm names can be seen in use on
gravestones throughout the 19th century.

It is not surprising that for Anglican churchyards the vast majority of people are identified
with particular places in the parish or use of the phrase 'of this parish' on their inscriptions.
This information does not represent the whole population, as only some were provided
with memorials, but half of the numbers indicated in the burial registers are represented on
gravestones from the mid 19th century.[13] In effect the poorer classes were mainly missing

Figure 8.2. Three gravestones at Caersalem Cilgwyn with individuals from other parishes:
a) David Evans from Nevern; b) Margaret Jenkins from Llanllawer; c) Martha Thomas from
Meline; d) Pedimented headstone, Brynberian chapel (photographs by H. Mytum).

from this data set; they would also have been those with least secure tenures, as the census returns show, and these people often had moved between one census date and the next. The parish was the principal structuring unit that affected Anglican church attendance, but not exclusively so; ease of reaching a different church and family ties could affect choice.

Attendance from within the parish was strongly the case for the small town of Newport. Thus, the large sample of over 370 19th-century stones from St Mary's Newport produced fourteen cases where explicit mentions of places outside the parish were given, and the majority of these could be explained by close family relationships with Newport, such as a spouse already buried there or parent living in Newport. It is notable, however, that in the nearby rural village of Nevern a number of memorials note a Newport home for the deceased, perhaps suggesting that for some a rural resting place was preferred to the town, and that further quantification and analysis of rural Anglican catchments might be slightly more comparable to the rural nonconformist pattern described below.

Nonconformist organization was not based on the parish, but it is notable how often the attribution to parish as a location was applied on nonconformist inscriptions also. Many state 'of [house name] of this parish' or just 'of this parish' even though this was meaningless in denominational terms. This shows how one aspect of multiple personal identity was linked to the wider administrative role of the parish beyond that of religion. It also demonstrates that, for some chapels, the catchment could be extensive. For example, Baptist Caersalem Cilgwyn was located in an upland part of Newport (Trefdraeth in Welsh) parish but contains 19th-century gravestones commemorating those also from the parishes of Nevern, Dinas, Llanllawer, Llanychlwydog and Meline (Fig 8.2a–c). Some of these inscriptions are in English but many are in Welsh, indicating a cultural emphasis reinforced in chapel services and activities.

NORTH PEMBROKESHIRE – CULTURAL SIGNIFICANCE

From a young age the inhabitants of north Pembrokeshire experienced the journeys from home to church and chapel each week. For a few enthusiasts there may have been two attendances each Sunday, but for most one was sufficient. In south Cardiganshire such travels – by foot apart from the gentry – were themselves social events, with cottagers and farmers mixing on the basis of age rather than class. Moreover, within tenant farmer households, eating and some social conventions allowed mixing across classes, particularly for younger members of the households.[14]

Two features are important to consider in the Welsh cultural context: class and language. These both affected what material culture was created, how it was used and by whom, within both church and chapel contexts.

Language was an important indicator of class and cultural affiliation in west Wales.[15] English was used only by the gentry and some farmers and professionals at least in some of their business dealings.[16] Even some of the Anglican clergy did not know Welsh, though most did, while all nonconformist ministers were native speakers.[17] While it is not the case that there were no Welsh services in the Anglican churches and only Welsh in the chapels, there was a strong tendency in that direction. More Welsh was introduced into Anglican churches to prevent loss of congregation to chapels in the later 19th century, and as attitudes to the language changed.[18] Chapel Sunday schools employed many volunteer instructors, and these were the only vehicles for formal instruction in Welsh and were

Table 8.2. Use of language on north Pembrokeshire gravestones (after Mytum 2002).

Decade	Newport Anglican				Nevern Anglican				Brynberian Independent				Cilgwyn Baptist			
	Er cof am	Memory	Bedd	Lies body	Er cof am	Memory	Bedd	Lies body	Er cof am	Memory	Bedd	Lies body	Er cof am	Memory	Bedd	Lies body
1810		20		2	1	21		2	1	2		1	1	1		
1820		15		7	1	29		1	2	15	1	3				
1830	1	23		5	2	22		3	7	10		6	1			
1840		50		3	2	13		1	5	5	1	4	5	6		
1850	5	55		2	4	39		1	11	5	9	3	2	7		
1860	4	40		1	5	40		2	10	2	14	1	8	3		1
1870	5	51			7	23			12	1	10		5	13		
1880	7	39			10	17			14	2	15	2	12	4		
1890	12	47			2	14	2	2	18	5	1	1	16	8		
1900	16	41			4	7		1	24	4			23			
1910	17	43			6	17			27	1			14	1		
1920	12	23			5	2		1	30	3						

attended by adults as well as children.[19] Chapel hymn and prayer books were in Welsh, but most families of all denominations used family Welsh language Bibles at home. The extent of bilingualism varied between town and country, and over the period concerned, but in some places, such as the nearby port of Fishguard, Welsh- and English-speaking families rarely intermarried.[20]

While language might be a class indicator, its real importance was to enable access to and participation in a range of cultural activities. The Welsh language was the medium in which various cultural events and competitions took place.[21] Festivals of music, particularly singing, and ones based on chanting Biblical verses followed by questioning on their theological significance were held annually in west Wales, and created competition between all chapels in an area, and between chapels of a particular denomination over a wider area. Larger cultural competitions, the regional and then the national *eisteddfoddau*, were yet another manifestation of local expressions of pride, where choirs, poets and musicians could gain personal or communal prestige.[22] Practice for these activities involved considerable investment of time by people hard-pressed by long hours earning a wage and having to walk to chapel for practice and back home again.

Attitudes to the Welsh language can be seen in the language choices on gravestone memorials.[23] Differences in phraseology between one burial ground and another certainly represent divergent theological emphases. For example, mention of the body, with phrases such as 'Here lies', can be contrasted with the 'In memory' categories, and these indicate differences within nonconformist communities as well as between them and the Anglicans. Thus, the Independents at Brynberian used references to the body (in both English and Welsh) in their introductory phrases through the 19th century, while not a single example of such a phrase was chosen at the Baptist burial ground at Cilgwyn, and Anglican St Mary's Newport contains a small number of these phrases but only to the middle of the century.[24]

Language choice also indicates wider cultural differences. Introductory phrasing indicates the language of the bulk of the stone (Table 8.2). The dominance of Welsh at Independent Brynberian, especially after the 1840s, can be contrasted with the consistent preponderance of English at Anglican Newport. However, many of the English stones at both sites during the 19th century were actually bilingual, with Biblical phrases in Welsh after the biographical details of the deceased. Analysis of the Newport stones reveals some fascinating emphases within these verses, which had formed the subject of the funeral oration.[25] Similar data has been collected on some nonconformist sites, but has yet to be analyzed.

Class was a structuring factor in denominational membership and attendance in that the gentry were all Anglican, but chapels had a mix of all other classes and the Anglican congregations had mixed membership. Indeed, studies of late 19th- and early 20th-century south Cardiganshire by David Jenkins have shown how families could be divided between church and chapel, or between chapels of different denominations. The reasons for this given in his study (carried out ethnographically and so stated reasons could be collected) were largely linked to marriage and movement, but also could be based on personal quarrels.[26] It would seem that quality of preaching or theological differences were not reasons for personal shifts. Therefore, although some schisms could be based on theology, as when the Methodists separated from the Anglicans, and later some of the further Methodist splits, most individuals made decisions largely on allegiance and preference based on cultural and social reasons rather than theological ones. These differences are not easily represented materially on the ground, however, as not all chapels had burial places and so Anglican churchyards were actually multi-denominational. It would seem that clearly middle-class monumental forms such as the pedimented headstones (Fig 8.2d) were used by all denominations,[27] though some others, such as tall pedestal monuments, appear to have been chosen largely by nonconformists.[28]

Class affected the development of nonconformity in terms of the provision of land and resources for the building of chapels. While small groups could and did meet in houses, as soon as a special-purpose structure was required this had to be not only financed but also found a location. In this regard it is worth noting that the Bowens of Llangwair – one of the major landowning families in the region – were very sympathetic to Methodism, and indeed entertained Wesley several times.[29] Their main rivals, the Lloyds of Bronwydd, could also be supportive, although their attitudes to the poor and squatters on the commons were quite different. The Bowens were sympathetic to their plight, the Lloyds not so, and some of the chapels were to serve these populations. Nevertheless, generally the landowners were prepared to help by offering land for purchase, and in some cases also assisted with provision of building materials.

One of the main vehicles by which cultural values were perpetuated across the generations by church and chapel was the education of children. For all their biases and limitations, the Blue Books provide a record and extensive survey of all places of education in Wales, with notes published on individual establishments and tabulated data by location and region.[30] Education can be considered under two headings: formal education during the week, and through Sunday Schools. Nine schools are recorded from within the parishes of Dinas, Meline, Nevern and Newport, with four being linked to the Anglicans and three to nonconformists, and two being private enterprises. Most schools were teaching students in the age range 5–10, with most having no older children. The standards appear low, and facilities meagre, though this may in places have been overstated owing to the clear biases and entrenched attitudes of the surveyors.[31] There were many more Sunday schools, with three being Anglican and fourteen nonconformist. The numbers attending these were much higher, and they also involved many more teachers from a wide range of backgrounds. These figures indicate a vibrant and successful participatory cultural manifestation of religious fervour and desire for education. While Christian teachings dominated, they were almost exclusively mediated through the Welsh language, and could involve poetry, music and song as well as Biblical explication. Many of the other cultural activities linked to chapels and, to a certain extent, churches, as well as those at Sunday schools, were beyond the remit of the Blue Book survey. However, the numbers linked to these places of worship in both the Blue Books and the Religious Census only a few years later testify to their importance within the communities in the middle of the 19th century, a pattern evident from more diverse sources for the whole of the 19th century and beyond.

THE ISLE OF MAN – CHURCHES AND CHAPELS

The Isle of Man contained a largely scattered rural population in the post-medieval period, with small fishing towns at Ramsey and Peel and the administrative and socio-political centre at Castletown. During the 18th century Douglas developed sufficiently to become the major urban centre and with its expanding ferry links with Britain in the 19th century a greater service and tourist industry was encouraged, but the population over most of the island was still largely rural.[32] In 1726 only two parishes contained more than 1,000 inhabitants and the total population was under 15,000; by 1891 over 55,000 people lived on the island, but only Douglas, with 19,000, could be considered a significant town, the next largest being Ramsey, with fewer than 5,000 inhabitants.[33]

Many parish churches are similar in scale to those in Wales, and after considerable neglect were rebuilt in the 18th and 19th centuries under Bishop Wilson's long episcopate and the more dynamic of the later bishops.[34] Most parishes contain at least one substantial Gothic Revival church, usually with a tower (Fig. 8.3a) and occasionally a spire. The mixture of urban and rural centres, together with variations in population density caused by fishing and mining, meant that the attendances within parishes could vary widely (Table 8.3). There were relatively few affluent patrons of the churches, and much investment had to be provided by successive bishops of Sodor and Man.

Table 8.3. Estimated size of congregations from the 1851 Religious Census returns by parish, Isle of Man (adapted from Coakley 2001).

Place	CofE	WM	PM	RC	Pres	Cong	Total
Castletown	562	249	401	183			1395
Douglas	3135	1197	1600	640	190	105	6867
Peel	350	430	386	100			1266
Ramsey	945	646	130		81		1802
Andreas	413	593					1006
Arbory	207	61	139				407
Ballaugh	181	248	237				666
Braddan	441	226	250				917
Bride	38	158	210				406
German	385	259	66				710
Jurby	80	294					374
Lezayre	298	204	168				670
Lonan	207	280	555				1042
Malew	681	368	175				1224
Marown	73	134	141				348
Maughold	65	307	245				617
Michael	292	322	274				888
Onchan	445	298	60				803
Patrick	231	587	94				912
Rushen	545	443	314				1302
Santan	91	90	93				274
Totals	9665	7394	5538	923	271	105	23896

(http://www.isle-of-man.com/manxnotebook/methdism/rc1851/rc_tab.htm)
Key: CofE: Anglican; WM: Wesleyan Methodist; PM: Primitive Methodist; RC: Roman Catholic; Pres: Prebyterian; Cong: Congregational

Note: estimated number in congregations; Peel RC estimated as no service that Sunday; some WM and PM places of worship clearly omitted, but scale of omission hard to estimate.

a   b

c

Figure 8.3. Churches and chapels on the Isle of Man. a) St Paul's, Ramsey (Anglican);
b) Christchurch, Laxey (Anglican); c) Baldrine (Primitive Methodist)
(photographs by H. Mytum).

Nonconformity was generally tolerated on the island in the 17th century, and there was a small Quaker community,[35] though most emigrated before the end of the century. It was the Methodists that were by far the most successful denomination on the Isle of Man, spurred on by visits from John Wesley in 1777 and 1781. The first chapel was opened in Peel in the early 1780s, followed in 1787 by one in Douglas. Primitive Methodism, with its more decentralized system of governance and more democratic structure, was introduced into the Isle of Man in 1822, with figures varying around 800 members for the first part of the 19th century, but with well over 5,000 attendees recorded in the 1851 census (Table 8.3). By 1800 there were around fifteen Wesleyan Chapels, and the 1851 census lists fifty places of worship, more than the Anglicans with thirty-four or the Primitive Methodists with eighteen.[36]

Other denominational groups were largely started by migrants, and most of their congregations consisted of immigrants or their descendants. The Independents were established in the main town of Douglas by the early 19th century, and the Presbyterians appeared in the town in very small numbers from 1825, with another group, largely Scottish and linked to the fishing industry, in the north at Ramsey.[37] Roman Catholics first appear from the 1770s, but in very small numbers, but by the end of the 18th century a few families had settled permanently, particularly in Castletown and Douglas.[38] The first Mass house was in Douglas, though the first substantial church there was opened in 1836, a decade after that of St Mary's Castletown. Missions were established in Ramsey in 1864 and Peel in 1891.[39] Much of the growth in Catholic numbers can be explained by the numbers of Irish migrants that came to the island, which led to some unrest and the first sectarianism experienced on the island, with disturbances and vandalism on the St Mary's of the Isle church under construction in Douglas in 1858, though the full riot that had been feared did not materialize.[40]

THE ISLE OF MAN – GEOGRAPHY OF ATTENDANCE

The dispersed population had led to the establishment of large Anglican parishes, but unlike Wales these were supported by a number of chapels of ease that provided a more dispersed provision. Moreover, in some instances efforts were made to respond to changes in population, such as the construction of Christchurch, Laxey, to serve the mining community (Fig 8.3b) and the provision of additional churches such as those to St Barnabas and St Thomas in Douglas. It was the Wesleyans, however, who were most effective in providing a wide range of small but sufficient places of worship scattered across the island. While there were only twenty-five Anglican places of worship outside the four main towns, there were forty-five Wesleyan and eighteen Primitive Methodist establishments. This ensured relatively short distances for congregations, although travelling could still be difficult. In contrast, the Catholics, Presbyterians and Congregationalists were found only in the towns, presumably as that was where most of the incomers found employment (Table 8.3).

THE ISLE OF MAN – CULTURAL SIGNIFICANCE

The support of the Manx language was a major feature of much 18th-century Anglican churchmanship. Bishops Wilson and Hildesley both encouraged the clergy to use Manx in services, and had gradually translated various items including the catechism (1707) and the

Form of Prayer for the Herring Fishery (1714), an extremely important part of the island's economy at that time.[41] Strangely, the New Testament was fully translated only by 1755 and not published until 1763 – and then only for the clergy. The Old Testament was printed for clergy in 1775, but only in 1819 was a full Bible in Manx available for the population at large. Financial limitations rather than prejudice lay behind all these delays, but the lack of an early and widely available Bible in Manx undoubtedly undermined its likelihood of survival. Although some of the most important examples of vernacular Manx, the Carvals, were carols performed in churches on Christmas Eve in the 18th and 19th centuries, the popular interest in maintaining Manx does not seem to have been strong. By the middle of the 19th century the Manx language was used in Anglican churches only two instead of three Sundays a month, and the last incumbent who regularly provided Manx services died in 1879; by 1900 only English services were available.[42]

Despite Wesley's low opinion of the Manx language, services were largely held at least partly in Manx, although, interestingly, even in 1788 there was an enthusiasm to introduce the singing of at least some English language hymns.[43] This is in contrast to the resolute support of Welsh in the north Pembrokeshire chapels. The Primitive Methodists developed the tradition of using secular tunes for some of their hymns and so were able to attract and motivate attendance and participation owing to the accessibility of their music.[44] Some Carvals had been sung in Anglican churches to such tunes, but not in main services approved of by the Anglican clergy.

Secular attempts in 1672 and 1707 to encourage Anglican Church involvement in education were not met with great episcopal encouragement,[45] but for much of the 18th century the churches were used as schools. Relatively few Sunday School buildings were constructed, though a few, such as those at Spoot Vayne, Michael, St Stephen, Sulby, and Dhoon, Maughold, indicate some attempts at providing an Anglican educational presence of some kind during the 19th century. Unusually, St Peter's, Cregneash, was built in the 1870s with only the chancel consecrated so that the nave could be more easily used as a school, though the latter function did not last long. A Roman Catholic school was established along with the church in Peel, but it was not open for a significant period of time.

Sunday Schools were more significant in both strands of Manx Methodism than in the Anglican tradition, with over 60% of the chapels having schools in 1851.[46] With the assistance of a large number of Sunday School teachers, provision was offered to thousands of Manx children. Schools could take place in the chapel at times other than the service, at with Baldhoon Primitive Methodist chapel, built adjacent to the chapel, as at Lower Foxdale Methodist chapel, or in the original chapel once a larger one was built, as with the Baldrine Primitive Methodists (Fig. 8.3c).

The only separate nonconformist burial ground ever established on the Isle of Man was in Athol Street, Peel, and even that was used only by Methodists from 1845 to 1866, with nineteen interments, a few marked by monuments.[47] Generally, burial provision remained at the parish church graveyards, and this does not seem to have been a cause of any dissatisfaction. Even the clear problems of overcrowding in some graveyards, as revealed in a government report of 1869,[48] did not lead to many separate denominational burial grounds being established but rather to extensions to existing graveyards, and the creation in due course of cemeteries such as that at Douglas, established in 1895.

One of the main common causes across denominations in the last part of the 19th century was the temperance movement, partly because of the excesses of the increasing numbers of summer holidaymakers coming from the industrial towns of the north-west of England.[49] The Independent Order of Rechabites first established themselves on the Isle of Man in 1836 and were successful in setting up branches across the island; in collaboration with the Methodists and others, they offered a strong and articulate alternative to the temptations of alcohol.[50]

CONCLUSIONS

From these two case studies it is possible to draw out some comparative comments that have a wider relevance and finally note the current situation regarding the preservation and use of places of worship in these and other regions.

While the growth of nonconformity is not dissimilar in Pembrokeshire and Man, the dominance of Methodism in the Isle of Man is notable, set beside the more complex multi-denominational model in Wales. In contrast, the Manx language and native culture was not reinforced, supported and maintained through nonconformity, while in Wales this has been the source of its strength that has enabled Welsh to survive and prosper as the most successful Celtic language into the 21st century. Both the Welsh and Manx languages were solidified in a concrete form by the translation of the Bible, but the Welsh cultural survival was more complex. Singing and music also supported the linguistic distinctiveness in the face of considerable discrimination, and while translations of hymns were made into Manx these were insufficiently potent to assist dynamic language survival. Chapels and some of the churches should thus be seen as centres of cultural dissent in Wales, though in both areas they acted thus in a more political sense.

The strength of the Church within the community has meant that there have been relatively few Anglican redundancies in either study area, but in Wales the long-derelict Cilgwyn chapel of ease is now being converted and Meline has been closed, its devoted regular congregation of half a dozen sadly depleted by recent deaths and only augmented by motley archaeologists in recent summers. The Manx situation again reveals some retrench-ment, with sometimes more than one place of worship being retained within the parish but with services concentrated at just one location best suited for access and modern styles of worship.

Some of the Welsh chapels have also been converted or closed – such as Capel Mynydd in Newport parish – but a surprising number still flourish, though whether they will do so after another generation is less certain, as ways in which Welsh identity is manifested move into media such as television and the Internet, and local chapel events are less well supported.

The decline in chapels on the Isle of Man is more like that seen in many parts of Britain. There were about 115 chapels in use at the beginning of the 20th century, with more than five in many parishes, and often with Wesleyan chapels having a Primitive Methodist chapel nearby. Amalgamation in 1932 led to reduction in this duplication, and then in the last forty years many chapels have been sold and converted into commercial premises or private homes. In 1998 there were, for example, only twenty-nine Wesleyan chapels still in use.[51] Here the more limited cultural role of the chapel communities did not assist their viability, though some have clearly survived because of small groups of dedicated individuals with a strong sense of place and chapel heritage.

The pattern of cultural significance attached to places of worship of all denominations, where religion is linked with class and cultural values, became widely established in the later 18th century and was vibrant for about 150 years, since when it has declined. While popular interpretations claim falling religious observance, it is likely that the cultural value of the churches and chapels was more important than has often been recognized in both their rise and their fall. These buildings and burial grounds, their Sunday Schools and halls, represent the physical spaces where people had their most culturally significant education, recreation and socialization. Their place in the physical and mental landscape, the ways in which they concretely represented complex combinations of geographical, denominational, familial and class identities is, through current research, at last being appreciated by archaeologists. The value of this sadly declining resource can be interrogated perhaps just as it disappears.

NOTES

1. Rodwell 1981; 1997.
2. Morris 1989.
3. Lewis 1833; Blue Books 1847; Jones & Williams 1976.
4. Wallace-Hadrill 1989; NLW Llr 17232.
5. Miles 1998a.
6. Miles 1998a.
7. Miles 1998b.
8. Watts 1995, 714.
9. Snell & Ell 2000.
10. Jones 1979.
11. Miles 1998b.
12. Rawlins 1987.
13. Mytum 2002.
14. Jenkins 1971, 214–15; Mytum 2010.
15. White 1997; Davies 1998; Pryce 2000.
16. Moore-Colyer 2000.
17. Howell 1977.
18. Jones, R.T. 2000a.
19. Jones, G.E. 2000.
20. Parry 1999.
21. Jones, R.T. 2000b.
22. Jenkins 1971, 194–207.
23. Mytum 1994.
24. Mytum 2002; Mytum forthcoming.
25. Mytum 1999a.
26. Jenkins 1971, 182–8.
27. Mytum 1999b.
28. Mytum 2002.

29. Miles 1998a.
30. Jones, G.E. 2000.
31. Roberts 1998.
32. Belchem 2000.
33. Coakley 2001 <http://www.isle-of-man.com/manxnotebook/history/pop.htm>.
34. Gelling 1986.
35. Hodgkin 1908; 1909.
36. Coakley 2001 <http://www.isle-of-man.com/manxnotebook/methdism/rc1851/returns.htm>.
37. Davidson & Cuthbertson 1925.
38. Dempsey 1958, 141.
39. Dempsey 1958, 152–3.
40. Harrison 2000, 361–3.
41. Gelling 1986, 5; Thompson 1992, 160–61.
42. Gelling 1986, 35.
43. Coakley 2001 <http://www.isle-of-man.com/manxnotebook/methdism/rise/rise.htm>.
44. Gilchrist & Broadwood 1926.
45. Gelling 1986, 4.
46. Coakley 2001 <http://www.isle-of-man.com/manxnotebook/methdism/rc1851/returns.htm>.
47. McHardy 1980.
48. Moore et al. 1869.
49. Harrison 2000, 363.
50. Franklin 1999.
51. Coakley 2001 <http://www.isle-of-man.com/manxnotebook/methdism/>.

BIBLIOGRAPHY

Belchem, J. (ed.) 2000, *The Modern Period, 1830–1999*. A New History of the Isle of Man 5. Liverpool: Liverpool University Press.

Blench, R. & Spriggs, M. (eds) 1999, *Archaeology and Language III: Artefacts, Languages and Texts*. One World Archaeology 34. London: Routledge.

Blue Books 1847, *Reports of the Commissioners of Enquiry into the State of Education in Wales. Part I Carmarthen, Glamorgan and Pembroke*, London: HMSO.

Coakley, F. (ed.) 2001–2007, *A Manx Notebook. An Electronic Compendium of Matters Past and Present Connected with the Isle of Man*. Unpaginated: individual page compilations are dated. <http://www.isle-of-man.com/manxnotebook/> [accessed March 2009].

Davidson, J. & Cuthbertson, A.B. 1925, *The First Century of Presbyterianism in Douglas, Isle of Man. 1825–1925*, Douglas: Meyer.

Davies, R. 1998, 'Language and Community in south-west Wales, *c*. 1800–1914', in Jenkins 1998, 101–24.

Dempsey, W.S. 1958, *The story of the Catholic Church in the Isle of Man*, Billinge: Birchley Hall Press.

Franklin, A.G. 1999, 'The Independent Order of Rechabites in the Isle of Man: An Account with Some Social Comment on the Influence and Activities of this Friendly Society from 1836 to 1996', MA dissertation, University of Liverpool.

Gelling, J. 1986, *A History of the Manx Church 1698–1911*, Douglas: Manx Heritage Foundation.

Gilchrist, A.E. & Broadwood, L.E. 1926, 'Old primitive Methodist tunes: from the Clague collection and MSS', *Journal of the Folk-Song Society* 7/30: 293–8.

Harrison, A. 2000, 'Religion in the nineteenth century,' in Belchem 2000, 357–64.

Hodgkin, T. 1908, 'Ruillick-ny-Quakeryn: notes on the history of Friends in the Isle of Man', *Friends' Quarterly Examiner* 168: 457–95.

Hodgkin, T. 1909, 'Quakerism in the Isle of Man', *Journal of the Friends' Historical Society* 6/1: 6–11.

Howell, D.W. 1977, *Land and People in Nineteenth-century Wales*, London: Routledge & Kegan Paul.

Jenkins, D. 1971, *The Agricultural Community in South-west Wales at the Turn of the Twentieth Century*, Cardiff: University of Wales Press.

Jenkins, G.H. (ed.) 1997, *The Welsh Language before the Industrial Revolution*, Cardiff: University of Wales Press.

Jenkins, G.H. (ed.) 1998, *Language and Community in the Nineteenth Century*, Cardiff: University of Wales Press.

Jenkins, G.H. (ed.) 2000, *The Welsh Language and its Social Domains*, Cardiff: University of Wales Press.

Jones, F. 1979, 'Bowen of Pentre Ifan and Llwyngwair', *The Pembrokeshire Historian* 6: 25–57.

Jones, G.E. 2000, 'The Welsh language in the Blue Books of 1847', in Jenkins 2000, 431–58.

Jones, I.G. & Williams, D. (eds) 1976, *The Religious census of 1851: A Calendar of the returns relating to Wales, Vol 1, South Wales*, Cardiff: University of Wales Press.

Jones, R.T. 2000a, 'The Church and the Welsh language in the nineteenth century', in Jenkins 2000, 215–38.

Jones, R.T. 2000b, 'Nonconformity and the Welsh language in the nineteenth century', in Jenkins 2000, 239–64.

Lewis, S. 1833, *A Topographical Dictionary of Wales*, London: S. Lewis.

McHardy, A. 1980, 'A Methodist graveyard', *Isle of Man Family History Society Journal* 2/3: available in Coakley, F. (ed.) 2001–2007 <http://www.isle-of-man.com/manxnotebook/famhist/v02n2.htm#31–36> [accessed March 2009].

Miles, D. 1998a, *The Ancient Borough of Newport in Pembrokeshire*, 2nd edn, Haverfordwest: Cemais Publications.

Miles, D. 1998b, *A Book on Nevern*, Llandysul: Gomer Press.

Moore, J.C., Baring Stevenson, W., Farrant, E.C., Goldie Taubman, J.C. & Christian, W.B. 1869, *Report of the Committee of Inquiry into the State of Graveyards*, Douglas: Tynwald.

Moore-Colyer, R.J. 2000, 'Landowners, farmers and language in the nineteenth century', in Jenkins 2000, 81–100.

Morris, R. 1989, *Churches in the Landscape*, London: Dent.

Mytum, H. 1994, 'Language as symbol in churchyard monuments: the use of Welsh in nineteenth- and twentieth-century Pembrokeshire', *World Archaeology* 26/2: 252–67.

Mytum, H. 1999a, 'The language of death in a bilingual community: nineteenth-century memorials in Newport, Pembrokeshire', in Blench & Spriggs 1999, 211–30.

Mytum, H. 1999b, 'Welsh cultural identity in nineteenth-century Pembrokeshire: the pedimented headstone as a graveyard monument', in Tarlow & West 1999, 215–30.

Mytum, H. 2002, 'A comparison of nineteenth and twentieth century Anglican and nonconformist memorials in north Pembrokeshire', *The Archaeological Journal* 159: 194–241.

Mytum, H. 2010, 'Domesticity and the Dresser: An Archaeological Perspective from Rural 19th-Century Pembrokeshire', in Symonds 2010, 87–98.

Mytum, H. forthcoming, 'Faith in action: theology and practice in commemorative traditions', in Symonds *et al.* forthcoming.

NLW Llr 17232, *Book of subscriptions and other fund-raising activities, and estimated costs, for restoration of Nevern Church, c. 1861–63*.

Parry, G. 1999, 'Fishguard (Pembrokeshire)', in Parry & Williams 1999, 237–54.

Parry, G. & Williams, M.A. (eds) 1999, *The Welsh Language and the 1891 Census*, Cardiff: University of Wales Press.

Price, G. (ed.) 1992, *The Celtic Connection*, Gerrads Cross: Colin Smythe.

Pryce, W.T.R. 2000, 'Language zones, demographic changes, and the Welsh culture area 1800–1911', in Jenkins 2000, 37–80.

Rawlins, B.J. 1987, *The Parish Churches and Nonconformist Chapels of Wales: Their Records and Where to find Them. Vol. 1. Carmarthenshire, Cardiganshire, and Pembrokeshire*, Salt Lake City (UT): Celtic Heritage Research.

Roberts, G.T. 1998, *The Language of the Blue Books: The Perfect Instrument of Empire*, Cardiff: University of Wales Press.

Rodwell, W. 1981, *The Archaeology of the English Church: The Study of Historic Churches and Church-yards*, London: Batsford.

Rodwell, W. 1997, 'Landmarks in church archaeology: a review of the last thirty years', *Church Archaeology* 1: 5–16.

Snell, K.D.M. & Ell, P.S. 2000, *Rival Jerusalems: the Geography of Victorian Religion*, Cambridge: Cambridge University Press.

Symonds, J. (ed) 2010, *Table Settings: The Material Culture and Social Context of Dining, AD 1700–1900*, Oxford: Oxbow.

Symonds, J., Badcock, A. & Oliver, J. (eds) forthcoming, *Historical Archaeologies of Cognition*, London: Equinox Publishing.

Tarlow, S. & West, S. (eds) 1999, *The Familiar Past? Archaeologies of Later Historical Britain*, London: Routledge.

Thompson, R.L. 1992, 'Manx language and literature', in Price 1992, 154–70.

Wallace-Hadrill, F.G. 1989, *The Parish Church of St Mary, Newport, Pembrokeshire*, Newport: Newport P.C.C.

Watts, M.R. 1995, *The Dissenters. Vol. II. The Expansion of Evangelical Nonconformity*, Oxford: Clarendon Press.

White, E.M. 1997, 'The established Church, dissent and the Welsh language c. 1660–1811', in Jenkins 1997, 235–87.

ABBREVIATION

NLW Llr   National Library of Wales, Llangwair

'But Deliver Us From Evil': Popular Protest and Dissent in the South-West Woollen Industry *c.* 1760–1860

CLAIRE STRACHAN*

Religion was integral to socialization during the industrial revolution, contributing significantly to the group identity of the working classes by providing security and belonging during social and political instability. In the south-west woollen industry a domestic industry had existed since the 12th century, and industrialization created real concerns for the cloth workers, as their craft traditions were threatened with extinction. This attachment to tradition was emotionalized through increased protest activity from the early 19th century until the industry's eventual decline in the 1850s. Through the analysis of the architecture and spatiality of nonconformist chapels, this chapter illustrates the importance of dissent in the expression of community identity, revealing that nonconformist identities were visible not only in the built environment but also in the social and political actions of the cloth workers.

THE SOCIOLOGY OF DISSENT

Traditional studies of dissent, most famously advocated by social historians and sociologists such as Elie Halévy, Karl Marx and E.P. Thompson, have argued that religion, primarily of a dissenting origin, was crucial in producing a subservient and deferent working class. Halévy's *A History of the English People* argued that dissent was such a stabilizing influence over the English labour force that they lost the desire to revolt.[1] This, he claims, was the reason why there was no revolution in this country during the 18th and 19th centuries. Thompson, in *The Making of the English Working Class*,[2] further developed Halévy's thesis by arguing that Evangelical religion indoctrinated a sense of shame and guilt and focused on preparing the masses for the world of work.[3] Using religion as an instrument to create subordination was not a new idea and was certainly evident in the period under study. Andrew Ure, in his *Philosophy of Manufactures*, claimed in 1835 that 'persons not trained up in moral and religious nurture, necessarily become, from the evil bent of human nature, the slaves of prejudice and vice ... and they are apt to regard their best benefactor, the enterprising and frugal capitalist who employs them, with a jealous and hostile eye'.[4]

In Marx's *Critique of Hegel's 'Philosophy of Right'*,[5] he further argued that religion was fantasy, created in order to ease the pain and suffering of the unjust material world. His famous phrase in which he described religion as 'the opium of the people' illustrates his abhorrence of the influence of religion on the working class, considering it to be a drug that defers true happiness to the afterlife, influencing people to accept their material conditions on earth and blinding them to the inequalities and injustices around them.

However, more recently, this one-sided approach has been criticized. McLeod has argued that in the industrial period joining a chapel was a symbol of independence and a rejection of state control and politics.[6] The theological notion that all men were equal before God disrupted the emphasis on deference within families, local communities and the workplace. James Bradley, in his study of religion and radicalism in the 18th century, similarly argued that nonconformity challenged the system of deference and inequality that the state (and the established Church) advocated, and subsequently argued that dissent was largely associated with urban radicalism and unrest.[7] T.J. Taylor, a government commissioner examining the conditions of the Durham coal mines, stated in 1844 that 'the local preachers, the chief speakers at these prayer meetings were the men, who, by a certain command of language, and by an energetic tone and manner, had acquired an influence over their fellow workmen, and were invariably the chief promoters and abettors of the strike'.[8] Beynon and Austrin's analysis of the Durham coal mines shows that Primitive Methodism from the 1820s became closely associated with early trade union activity in the area.

This chapter supports the hypothesis that dissent and protest activity were closely associated, but develops it further through examining the possible causes of this dual relationship. Although John Wesley and other leading nonconformists did not wittingly promote the erosion of social deference, the by-products of chapel life certainly appeared to contribute to the growth of political and social independence[9] through increased literacy and cohesion. Belonging to a chapel community still promoted a capitalist mindset whereby thrift, hard work and discipline were part of the Christian duty, and traits such as idleness, drunkenness and deceit were not endorsed. However, nonconformity also contributed to a new shape of confidence centred on democracy and, in some more extreme cases, the campaign for civil rights. This paper aims to illustrate that the architectural symbolism and spatial locations of nonconformist chapels reflect this increased group collectivity in the physical landscape, and the physical representation of this group solidarity also manifested itself in the protest activity that occurred in the region during the period under study.

THE SOUTH-WEST WOOLLEN INDUSTRY

This chapter focuses on the woollen industry in Gloucestershire and Wiltshire which had developed from the 12th century, specifically using Trowbridge and Bradford on Avon in Wiltshire and Stroud, Uley, Dursley and Cam in Gloucestershire as case studies. The industry boomed from the 15th century through the migration of Dutch weavers who brought with them far superior cloth manufacturing skills.[10]

The 18th century saw great prosperity, as seen in the elegant houses built by the clothiers in places such as Bradford and Trowbridge, aided in part by the demand for uniform cloth resulting from the revolutionary wars in France and America, and the disruption these wars caused to foreign competition.[11] As the wars ended, however, serious problems in the industry surfaced as demand was stunted and returning soldiers flooded the labour market,[12] and were worsened further by the increasing competition from the Yorkshire cloth trade.[13] By the mid 1820s the industry was in panic. Bankruptcies were common throughout the south-west. Between 1816 and 1825 Wiltshire lost thirty-eight of its woollen companies, Gloucestershire lost eighty-five and Somerset forty-six,[14] and many cloth workers – particularly in Gloucestershire – emigrated to Australia, America and Canada.[15]

In Trowbridge by 1825 employment figures had dropped to a third of the total in the preceding decade. This situation had worsened by 1829–30. A government inspector at the time reported that he had never seen 'such a scene of rags and ghastly faces'.[16] Out of a population of just under 11,000 there were around 3,000 unemployed weavers and shearmen in Trowbridge alone.[17] In Randwick, near Stroud, the situation was desperate by the 1830s and the inhabitants, who were primarily cloth workers, were almost entirely dependent on poor relief.[18] William Miles, a government commissioner, wrote an enquiry on the condition of the handloom weavers in Gloucestershire in 1839 which reported that there were around eighty weavers living in the Cam area and nearly every one of them was ill with measles, whooping cough or consumption, and could find only sporadic work.[19]

The decline in trade, alongside the increasing use of machinery that threatened the employment of the cloth workers, resulted in a rise in protest activity in the 1820s and 1830s, some peaceful, some more violent. In Wiltshire the activity was largely violent, with mobs attacking mills and the clothiers. By 1839 Trowbridge was said to be in a state of almost open rebellion; factories were forced to close, property was attacked and workers reportedly marched the streets with firearms.[20] In Gloucestershire more peaceful activity was dominant, although some rioting did occur. By the mid 1830s military troops had to be stationed in Dursley and Uley to control some of the more aggressive outbreaks. Weavers who were working under price (accepting a lower 'piece-rate' for their cloth than had been agreed in earlier negotiations between the clothiers and the weavers) suffered being stoned by the mob and being ducked in mill ponds.[21]

Combination movements developed, and new union clubs emerged. In Wiltshire in the late 1820s a Union Club was established, favouring selective strikes, some of which lasted over two months.[22] In 1825, during the first stages of economic panic, the membership of the Weavers Union increased from 400 to 5,000 in a matter of days, and subscriptions were paid to fund the infirm, strike action and legal representation.[23] On Selsley Common, near Stroud, and Stinchcombe Hill, near Dursley, 9,000 weavers met to bury their shuttles in peaceful protest against declining wage rates.[24] An enquiry into secret combinations commissioned by the Government recorded that the majority of members of these groups were dissenters and that the meetings were led with hymns and prayers.[25]

IDENTITY AND DISSENT

The south-west woollen industry was based on the putting-out system, where one person (the clothier) organized the processes in the production of cloth. The clothiers would buy the wool and pass it on to the spinners, and from there the spun wool would be given to the weavers to weave. The cloth would then be passed to those in the finishing trades, and finally to a merchant for marketing, either in the domestic market or for export abroad.[26] As a result of this system the cloth workers were scattered across the region, reducing their opportunities to engage in social interaction, which was traditionally considered as an obstacle in creating collective social organization.[27] Naturally, the alehouse has famously been considered to be a central location for social and political interaction; however, as this chapter will illustrate, nonconformist chapels also played an important role.

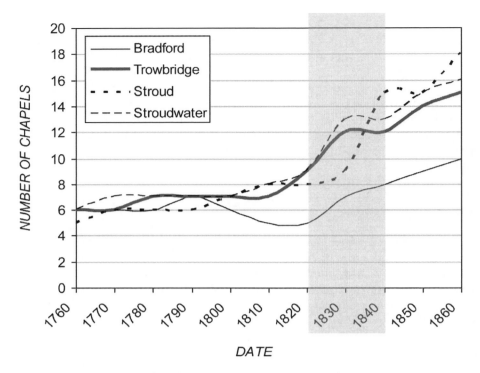

Figure 9.1. The rise in chapel construction, 1760 to 1860 (from RCHME 1986;
Victoria County History 1953; Victoria County History 1976).

The importance of group solidarity is addressed by Cohen, who argues that in periods of change or distress individual identities united to form solid groups in order to cope with a threatened sense of self.[28] Social or economic distress appears to be a great influence on the renegotiation of group collectivity. Gittens states that 'the more economically insecure the household, the greater its reliance on community and kin',[29] which is particularly relevant for the south-west woollen industry, where the traditional domestic industry went into decline. The cloth workers feared the factory for the change in custom that they were used to.

Gilbert has argued that religion was invaluable in developing emotional security, arguing that, in times of crisis, membership numbers of religious sects increased.[30] The years 1832 and 1849, for example, when serious cholera epidemics broke out, saw huge increases in religious observance. Critical situations such as poverty, depression, economic and political stress or social instability had distinct effects on the level of religious observance in a community.

Dissenting religion certainly became more popular during this period of depression in the woollen industry. If the number of chapels constructed between 1820 and 1840 within the case studies are collated, alongside the congregational membership figures of the period, the increase in religious observance during the depression can be clearly iden-tified. In Trowbridge, Bradford, Stroud and Stroudwater (which in this research is the collective name for Cam, Dursley and Uley) there is significant growth in the number of nonconformist chapels constructed in this period – far higher than within any other period (Fig. 9.1). The membership statistics for the chapels also illustrate this further, consistently reflecting a marked increase in numbers disproportionate to the population increase during the period of depression. For example, at John Street Chapel in Stroud the congregation rose from 70 in 1827 to 249 in 1838, while membership at the Old Chapel, which was described as 'scanty' in 1810, reached 210 by 1835.[31]

When the architecture and spatial locations of the nonconformist chapels are consid-ered, further conclusions regarding the increase in group solidarity can be drawn. Architec-ture has been interpreted as an active representation of cultural expression by specific social groups, as famously identified in the work of Henry Glassie, and of Matthew Johnson and Kate Giles,[32] all of whom have concluded that the built environment was a physical expres-sion of social structure and cultural ideology in the wider landscape.

The architecture of nonconformist chapels is highly diverse, ranging from simple vernac-ular styles to classical temples to neo-Gothic 'cathedrals'.[33] What their architecture can symbolize or portray can be highly informative when considered alongside the social and economic context in which they are placed. The form, decoration and embellishment of buildings represent conscious choices, making overt statements about the use and meaning of the building to the people who occupy it. Through a consideration of the development and diversity of nonconformist architecture with reference to the specific economic and social context of the area at the time, this research has identified a growing expression of the social group identity of the working classes at this time, reflecting their increasing concern and involvement in political, social and economic disputes.

ARCHITECTURE AND SPACE

Prior to the 1820s chapel architecture had been relatively plain, with little advertisement of the buildings' function. The Grove Chapel (1698) in Bradford on Avon, Rodborough Tabernacle (1763), near Stroud, and the Water Street Chapel in Dursley (1711) all illustrate this well, with architecture that is subtle, unadorned and domestic in style – one could easily mistake them for private dwellings. There could be numerous reasons for this, not least financial constraints and a desire to remain inconspicuous in order to avoid perse-cution, or even a theological wish to retain tradition Protestant puritanical simplicity of worship. It is remarkable, therefore, to see the change in architectural expression of religious observance in the first half of the 19th century. Take, for example, Bethesda Chapel (1822) and Manvers Street Methodist Chapel (1835) in Trowbridge, or Coppice Hill Chapel in Bradford (1818) (Fig. 9.2). In Stroud, John Street Chapel (1824) and Bedford Street Chapel (1836) (Fig. 9.3) express their religious affiliation through ornate architecture and central locations in the commercial heart of the town, while in expanding suburbs such as Rand-wick and Uplands chapels such as Randwick Wesleyan Chapel (1834) and Stroud Primi-tive Methodist Chapel (1836), although smaller and less ornate, certainly display religious identity enhanced further by name plaques. The use of name plaques in this period was prolific, and in two cases large religious inscriptions further contributed to religious expres-sion in a clear way. Manvers Street Methodist Chapel in Trowbridge displayed the text

Figure 9.2. Coppice Hill Chapel, Bradford on Avon (built 1818).
(Reproduced by permission of English Heritage. NMR).

Figure 9.3. Bedford Street Chapel, Stroud (built 1836).
(Reproduced by permission of English Heritage. NMR).

'Sacred to God', while the Stroud Primitive Methodist Chapel had the inscription 'Thou God Seest Me'.[34]

Text develops meaning when attached to a physical object, identifying the object or process it refers to. This is particularly useful if that object or process is ambiguous.[35] In the case of nonconformist chapels, as a result of their fragmented and late establishment there was no building tradition in place, resulting in great diversity of architectural forms.[36] Name plaques eliminated any ambiguity regarding the building's function, and this concept was becoming more important to the congregations, their religious identity being more visibly expressed. The period 1810 to 1835 witnessed the largest increase in name plaques, which had begun to increase from *c*. 1790. For the first time, chapels were advertising what they were, and their function, in a permanent and obvious way.

The argument that earlier chapels were architecturally plain as a result of financial constraints is not a solid one in this particular context. As already highlighted, the southwest woollen industry was in severe depression. Money was scarce, particularly when considering that funds for the building of chapels were raised largely through public subscription and gifts. Constructing elaborate chapels like these during this period was no easy task. Bethesda Chapel in Trowbridge, for example, was constructed in 1822 and cost £2,100,[37] and the two most elaborate chapels in Stroud (John Street Baptist Chapel, 1824, and Bedford Street Chapel, 1836) were both costly, at £2,000 and £3,000 respectively.[38] Wicks reports that 'there can hardly have been a more unpromising time for the raising of money for a charitable purpose than the second quarter of the 19th century',[39] illustrating the level of commitment and dedication that the community had towards providing a place of religious worship that expressed status, wealth and religious affiliation.

Bedford Street Chapel in Stroud was constructed in the same year that the Stroud Poor Law Union was constituted, and the workhouse was opened the following year. The chapel is particularly ornate, with fluted ionic columns, a Venetian window and a domed circular bell tower with pilasters. To provide £3,000 for the construction of such a magnificent place of worship at this time was 'beyond human comprehension'.[40] Manvers Street Methodist Chapel, designed in an elaborate Grecian style, cost over £4,600 to build, further illustrating the significance of religious identity.

Spatially, the chapels are also more prominent in the landscape during this period than in any previous period. Chapels had often traditionally been constructed in remote locations or behind other buildings. The Old Baptist Chapel (1797) in Bradford on Avon was constructed behind a street-front building through which a small route was inserted to gain access to the chapel. Morgan's Hill Chapel (1741) and Pippet Street Wesleyan Chapel (1756) were constructed in similar locations: behind other buildings with small, concealed access routes leading to their entrances.

The 1820s and 1830s saw moves to construct chapels in more visible positions, often elevated, and in central locations. In Bradford, Zion Chapel (1823) visually dominates not only the adjacent Grove Chapel (1698) but also the wider landscape of the town itself. The congregational chapel in the working-class suburb of Bearfield is located in open grounds, in a central block from which the lanes of the suburb radiate out.

Bethesda Chapel, Zion Chapel and Manvers Street Chapel in Trowbridge continue this trend, having prominent street-front locations in the centre of the town. Fig. 9.4 illustrates the changing nature of spatial locations of chapels in the centre of Trowbridge before and after 1810. The map clearly illustrates that the chapels constructed after 1810 are large and

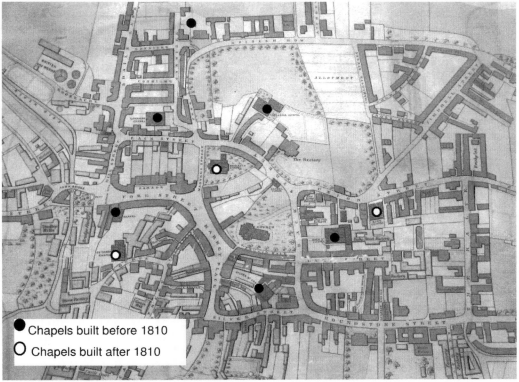

Chapels built before 1810
Chapels built after 1810

Figure 9.4. Distribution map of chapels in Trowbridge before and after 1810 (adapted from J. Howell's map of Trowbridge, *c.* 1860, WSA G15/1/89/PC).

on street fronts, and are more easily accessible. Location maps of this sort are useful to an extent, but when considered alongside the architectural styles and topographical contexts of the structures the visual prominence of these buildings becomes very apparent. The Grecian-influenced Manvers Street Methodist Chapel, for example (probably designed by the same architect behind Coppice Hill Chapel in Bradford on Avon, Fig. 9.2), was elevated on a man-made mound in the centre of the town, indicating that it is of no lesser status than the ornate clothiers' houses lining the streets around it.

For the most part, all the nonconformist chapels in the study area do follow this pattern, becoming more visually dominant as the 19th century progressed, until about 1850, when this trend begins to decline. There are some less elaborate examples of dissenting chapels, but their function is still very apparent and they are situated in central and visible locations in the landscape. Staverton Chapel (1824), just outside Trowbridge, is an example, as are Cam Wesleyan Chapel (1825) and Dursley's Boulton Lane Chapel (1826), illustrating that even the comparably 'simple' structures were still publicly visible as religious buildings during this period. Any doubt as to their function was removed by the name plaques above their doors.

During this period the Church of England also experienced some growth. In response to the decline in popularity of the Church of England in the 18th century Lord Liverpool agreed to the creation of the Incorporated Church Building Society (ICBS) in 1817. The ICBS received £1 million in funding from parliament the following year. Its purpose was to provide densely populated urban areas with Anglican churches with as many free seats as possible in order to attract the poor, partly in response to the growing popularity of nonconformity. By 1835 212 churches had been built using ICBS funds nationally, and a further 208 had received grants.[41] St Matthew's Church (1835) in Ebley, Stroud, was one such church. In the early 19th century the village comprised a small cluster of houses. It was the expansion of Ebley Mill from 1800 that resulted in its growth into a Stroud suburb. The Congregational Chapel was constructed in 1797 and, as discussed further in the paper, Ebley became a centre of political reform movements led by the dissenting congregation, so it is perhaps unsurprising that this was deemed to be an appropriate area for a new church.

Early Victorian Anglican churches were also constructed in other centres of the south-west woollen industry in response to the growing population and the expansion of working-class districts. Christ Church in Bradford on Avon, for example, was commissioned in 1839 to provide Anglican worship to the growing suburb of Bearfield. The congregational chapel had previously been constructed there in 1806. There are further examples in each case studied here. The architecture of the churches was plain compared with the neo-Gothic buildings that were constructed in the late Victorian era; however, the incorporation of towers, spires and religious iconography and symbolism illustrated their function. Their impact on socialization and group activity within this context was not part of this study, and further research into this topic would certainly be valuable. Key areas of research would include a consideration of how the building designs were agreed, the sources of funding for those only partially funded by the ICBS and the demographics and size of the congregations that worshipped there.

SOCIAL BEHAVIOUR AND ACTIVITY

This increasingly visible display of religious affiliation can be interpreted as being associated with enhanced group identity within the chapel community and a desire to advertise this group cohesion and security more overtly in a period when economic and social insecurity were becoming common.

Socialization was enhanced in chapel communities through educational facilities, clubs and social events which all contributed to the group solidarity, cohesiveness and organization which would have echoed into the wider economic context. The Sunday School movement developed from the 1780s, and Walmsley reports that for every child attending a day school in Stroud in 1838 seven more were attending a Sunday School.[42] During the 1820s and 1830s the majority of building ventures of chapel communities were classrooms. Emmanuel, Zion, the Conigre, Silver Street and Bethesda in Trowbridge all built school-rooms in this period, and the Old Meeting in Stroud added two. Literacy was a primary contributor to group behaviour, and was intrinsic in the wider circulation of political pamphlets and newspapers.

Education facilities were provided for adults too, through chapel libraries, Bible and reading classes and lectures. John Burder of the Old Chapel in Stroud developed the British and Foreign Bible Society with the Anglican curate John Williams.[43] Benjamin Parsons, the preacher at Ebley Chapel in Stroud, lectured on animal physiology, mechanics, horticulture, geography, music and elocution, work further enhanced by the opening of the British School there in 1840. The chapel also had benefit societies, literary societies, a library and discussion classes.[44]

Dissenters were intrinsic to political affairs in this period. Petitions against slavery and for the repeal of the Test and Corporation Acts were common in the 1820s, and were often led by dissenters.[45] Benjamin Parsons was notorious for his political campaigns, leading his 1,200-strong congregation to the forefront of politics. He regularly lectured on the French Revolution, Chartism, the anti-slavery movement and the repeal of Corn Laws, and was an active campaigner for social reform. William Yates of the John Street Baptist Chapel in Stroud took a leading role in the anti-slavery movement and lectured on its evils throughout the 1820s.[46] Between 1820 and 1840 419 petitions were produced in the region against slavery, the Corn Laws and others, and although only 35 came specifically from dissenting congregations many more would certainly have been directed by people with dissenting affiliations; Walmsley suggests that they were the primary political activists in the area during this period.[47] Chartism was another popular movement among the dissenters, and in Trowbridge – the heart of Chartism in Wiltshire – a group licensed a building as a 'democratic chapel', although no further evidence of this building could be obtained.[48] Nationally, some nonconformist ministers became leading hymn writers (Charles Wesley and Isaac Watts are two examples), and some expressed their sympathies to the Chartist cause through their hymnody. Thomas Cooper was a leading Chartist in Leicester in the first half of the 19th century and expressed his political opinions in the hymns he wrote. John Bramwich, another Leicester nonconformist, wrote one of the most famous 'Chartist hymns', entitled 'Britannia's Sons':

> All men are equal in His sight,
> The bond, the free, the black, the white:
> He made them all, – them freedom gave;
> God made the man – man made the slave.[49]

Political and union meetings led by nonconformists, with hymns and prayers reflecting the notions of equality and democracy, alongside petitions and campaigns organized by nonconformist groups, all signify the growth of a class consciousness partially nurtured through chapel communities. Combination movements, like those described earlier, were early forms of trade unionism and their links with nonconformity are evident.[50]

CONCLUSION

E.P. Thompson rightly asserts that the working classes during the first half of the 19th century were influenced by the morality and work ethic promoted by nonconformity through its values of self-discipline and industry.[51] However, the growth of nonconformity amidst a backdrop of social and economic unrest had wider implications for group consciousness. Working-class confidence appears to have been raised by chapel membership, resulting in a higher level of industrial challenges and protest activity and a more socially and politically independent working class.

The influence of libraries, lectures and increased literacy through the Sunday School movement enabled further understanding of political issues and it is highly likely that – considering the size and prominence of the industry in the chosen case studies – many who protested against increasing mechanization, unemployment and lowered wage rates had nonconformist affiliations. For a regionally scattered workforce, the significance of growing chapel membership and the activities and learning available there had no small impact on rising political and economic awareness. Moreover, the increasing confidence of the working classes was expressed through the physical landscape via chapel architecture and spatial location. This visible increase in group confidence was further expressed more overtly in the increase in riot and protest activity, alongside inclusion in social and political reform movements. Dissent was consistently associated with liberalism and political and social reform, promoting (albeit indirectly) social freedom. Deference towards employers within this particular economic context appears to have been an unintended casualty of the popularity of nonconformity. It had the effect of creating a more industrious, organized and disciplined working class, who on some occasions focused this group cohesion on fighting the injustices of the system in which they were employed.

Nonconformist chapels have been regarded as 'the foci of the emerging industrial culture',[52] but their importance has been little studied in archaeology. This research is a further contribution to the social archaeology of the industrial revolution in its emphasis on the social role of nonconformity and its impact on working-class communities in the south-west. It highlights the importance of religion to the developing social construction of urban communities and, subsequently, the role of religion in the social context of the industrial revolution is far better understood.

NOTES

*   This research is part of a larger PhD project which has been funded by the Arts and Humanities Research Council, without whom this work could not have been carried out, and my gratitude to them is extensive. I would also like to thank my supervisors, Professor Marilyn Palmer and Dr Sarah Tarlow, for their continuous guidance and support throughout this research. I would also like to extend my thanks to the staff of the Gloucestershire and Wiltshire Records Office for their help in identifying and locating historical documents and sources.

1.   Halévy 1949, 425.
2.   Thompson 1991.
3.   Ditchfield 1998, 86.
4.   Ure 1967, 407.
5.   Marx 1970, 31.
6.   McLeod 2000, 6
7.   Bradley 1990, 5.
8.   Beynon & Austrin 1994, 35.
9.   Gilbert 1976.
10. Child 1995, 16.
11. Perry 2003, 69.

12. Randall 1991, 197.
13. Perry 2003, 111.
14. Mann 1971, 181.
15. Mann 1971, 158.
16. Mann 1971, 164.
17. VCH 1953, 139.
18. Perry 2003, 123.
19. Snelling 2001, 33; also see Miles 1839.
20. Rogers 1994, 66.
21. Perry 2003, 116.
22. Rogers 1994, 100.
23. Moir 1957, 254.
24. Perry 2003, 115.
25. GRO, D4693 14.
26. Palmer & Neaverson 2005, 45–6.
27. Bohstedt 1983, 134; Randall 1988, 33.
28. Cohen 1995, 109–10.
29. Gittens 1986, 251.
30. Gilbert 1976.
31. VCH 1976, 140.
32. Glassie 1975; Johnson 1993; Giles 2000.
33. Powell 1980, 2.
34. NMR, RCHME 143:247/2.

35. Mitchell 2005, 10.
36. Drummond 1934, 43.
37. VCH 1953, 161.
38. Wicks n.d., 6; GRO, D2537 5/1.
39. Wicks n.d., 15.
40. Hoy 1989, 28.
41. Gibson 1994, 60.
42. Walmsley 1990, 119.
43. Walmsley 1990, 45.

44. Walmsley 1992, 621.
45. Walmsley 1990, 54.
46. Wicks n.d., 11.
47. Walmsley 1990, 626.
48. Rogers 1994, 66.
49. Armstrong 1993, 189.
50. Moir 1957, 254.
51. Thompson 1991, 451.
52. Butt & Donachie 1979, 244.

BIBLIOGRAPHY

Archer, J.E. 2000, *Social Unrest and Popular Protest in England, 1780–1840*, Cambridge: Cambridge University Press.

Armstrong, I. 1993, *Victorian Poetry: Poetry, Poetics and Politics*, London: Routledge.

Beynon, H. & Austrin, T. 1994, *Masters and Servants: Class and Patronage in the Making of a Labour Organization, the Durham Miners and the English Political Tradition*, London: Rivers Oram Press.

Bohstedt, J. 1983, *Riots and Community Politics in England and Wales, 1790–1810*, Cambridge (MA): Harvard University Press.

Bradley, J.E. 1990, *Religion, Revolution, and English Radicalism: Nonconformity in Eighteenth-century Politics and Society*, Cambridge: Cambridge University Press.

Butt, J. & Donachie, I. 1979, *Industrial Archaeology in the British Isles*, London: Elek.

Child, M. 1995, *Wiltshire*, Princes Risborough: Shire Publications.

Cohen, A.P. 1985, *The Symbolic Construction of Community*, Chichester: Ellis Horwood.

Ditchfield, G.M. 1998, *The Evangelical Revival*, London: UCL Press.

Drummond, A.L. 1934, *The Church Architecture of Protestantism: An Historical and Constructive Study*, Edinburgh: T. & T. Clark.

Finberg, H.P.R. (ed.) 1957, *Gloucestershire Studies*. Leicester: Leicester University Press.

Gibson, W. 1994, *Church, State and Society, 1760–1850*, Hampshire: The Macmillan Press.

Gilbert, A.D. 1976, *Religion and Society in Industrial England: Church, Chapel and Social Change, 1740–1914*, London: Longman.

Giles, K. 2000, *An Archaeology of Social Identity: Guildhalls in York, c.1350–1630*. British Archaeological Reports Brit. Ser. 315. Oxford: Archaeopress.

Gittens, D. 1986, 'Marital status, work and kinship, 1850–1930', in Lewis 1986, 249–67.

Glassie, H.H. 1975, *Folk Housing in Middle Virginia: A Structural Analysis of Historic Artifacts*, Knoxville: University of Tennessee Press.

GRO, D4693 14 'Reliques of Gloucestershire, chiefly Stroud borough', 1671–1873.

Halévy, E., 1949. *A History of the English People in the Nineteenth Century*. Volume 1: *England in 1815*, London: Ernest Benn.

Hoy, M. & A. 1987, *They Met in a Barn: The Story of Congregationalism in Stroud, 1687–1987*, M. & A Hoy.

Johnson, M. 1993, *Housing Culture: Traditional Architecture in an English Landscape*, London: UCL Press.

Lewis, J. (ed.) 1986, *Labour and Love: Women's Experience of Home and Family, 1850–1940*, Oxford: Blackwell.

McLeod, H. 2000, *Secularisation in Western Europe, 1848–1914*, Basingstoke: Macmillan.

Mann, J.D.L. 1971, *The Cloth Industry in the West of England from 1640 to 1880*, Oxford: Clarendon Press.

Marx, K. 1970 [1844], *Critique of Hegel's 'Philosophy of right'*, Cambridge: Cambridge University Press.

Miles, W.A. 1839, 'Royal Commission on the Condition of the Hand Loom Weavers of Gloucestershire', unpublished, Royal Commission.

Mitchell, W.J. 2005, *Placing Words: Symbols, Space, and the City*, Cambridge (MA): The MIT Press.

Moir, E.A.L. 1957, 'The gentlemen clothiers: a study of the organization of the Gloucestershire cloth industry 1750–1835', in Finberg 1957, 195–291.

NMR, RCHME 143:247/2, archive notes on the Primitive Methodist Chapel, Stroud, written by Christopher Stell for the RCHME Nonconformist Chapels surveys for Gloucestershire.

Palmer, M. & Neaverson, P. 2005, *The Textile Industry of South-West England: A Social Archaeology*, Stroud: Tempus.

Perry, R. 2003, *The Woollen Industry in Gloucestershire to 1914*, Shrewsbury: Ivy House Books.

Powell, K. 1980, *The Fall of Zion: Northern Chapel Architecture and its Future*, London: SAVE Britain's Heritage.

Randall, A. 1988, 'The industrial moral economy of the Gloucestershire weavers in the eighteenth century', in Rule 1988, 29–47.

Randall, A. 1991, *Before the Luddites: Custom, Community and Machinery in the English Woollen Industry, 1776–1809*, Cambridge: Cambridge University Press.

RCHME. 1986, *An Inventory of Nonconformist Chapels and Meeting Houses in Central England*, London: HSMO.

Rogers, K.H. 1994, *Trowbridge: History and Guide*, Stroud: Alan Sutton Publishing.

Rule, J. (ed.) 1988, *British Trade Unionism 1750–1850: The Formative Years*, London: Longman Group UK.

Snell, K.D.M. 2006, *Parish and Belonging: Community, Identity and Welfare in England and Wales, 1700–1950*, Cambridge: Cambridge University Press.

Snelling, D. & J. 2001, *A Faith for the Future*, Cirencester: Dianthus Publishing.

Thompson, E.P. 1991, *The Making of the English Working Class*, London: Penguin Books.

Ure, A. 1967 [1835], *The Philosophy of Manufactures, or, An exposition of the Scientific, Moral and Commercial Economy of the Factory System of Great Britain*, Southgate: Frank Cass and Co Ltd.

Victoria County History. 1953, *The Victoria History of the Counties of England: Wiltshire 7*, Oxford: Oxford University Press.

Victoria County History. 1976, *The Victoria History of the counties of England: Gloucester 11*, London: Oxford University Press.

Walmsley, P. 1992, 'The public face of dissent, Stroud 1830–1852', *The Journal of the United Reformed Church History Society* 4: 619–32.

Walmsley, P.M. 1990, 'Political, Religious and Social Aspects of the Stroud Parliamentary Borough, 1832 to 1852', PhD thesis, University of Bristol.

Wicks, W.O. n.d., *A Desirable Object: the Story of the First 150 Years of Stroud Baptist Church*, Stroud: Downfield Press.

WSA G15/1/89/PC, Plan of Trowbridge by J. Howell c.1860.

ABBREVIATIONS

GRO	Gloucestershire Record Office
NMR	National Monuments Record
RCHME	Royal Commission on the Historical Monuments of England
VCH	Victoria County History
WSA	Wiltshire and Swindon Archives

Meetinghouses of Puritan New England: The Transatlantic Passage, 1630–1800

Peter Benes

The Great Migration of English Puritans to New England required each 17th-century community to build a nonconformist house of worship. Towns erected meetinghouses resembling vernacular barns, forts or even warehouses; but, during the 18th century, these buildings assumed distinct ecclesiastical forms. This chapter provides new evidence to support the view that New England meetinghouses probably derived from 16th- and early 17th-century Scottish kirks, French Huguenot 'temples' and Reformed Dutch churches. It further postulates that 18th-century modifications to the form originated in Anglican church-building practices brought over by later English immigrants and that religious societies inclined toward reinstituting Anglican practices were the first to adopt architectural changes converting the Puritan 'meetinghouse' into a Congregational 'church'.

INTRODUCTION

When John Winthrop boarded the *Arbella* in 1629 to begin his voyage to New England he joined the ranks of approximately 20,000 nonconformist English farmers, tradesmen and gentry who crossed the Atlantic during the great Puritan migration to the New World. 'The eyes of all people are upon us', he wrote in his well-known shipboard sermon as they approached their destination,[1] and indeed the arrival of the 'elect' represented both an opportunity and a dilemma. In England and the northern Netherlands existing Christian churches were available in virtually every parish. During periods of Puritan ascendancy and especially during the Commonwealth period these churches were typically stripped and refitted as meetinghouses for Reformed services. The Westminster Confession of 1645 in fact encouraged congregations to continue services in former Anglican and Catholic churches because these structures were not 'capable of any holiness' regardless of any earlier 'pretence'.[2] In the New England wilderness, on the other hand, the new colonists were not obliged to refit older Anglican or Catholic churches; but because they came in large numbers, they did have to provide houses of worship almost immediately.

Beginning as early as 1639, builders in Hartford, New Haven and Boston made use of old-growth forests to erect wood-frame meetinghouses that alternatively resembled barns, forts and even warehouses. Made of large oak and pine timbers, these structures featured a gathered or 'four square'[3] roof, a high central turret, multiple doorways and windows and a prominent pulpit surrounded on three and sometimes four sides by benches. Their average size ranged between 8 and 10sq m, and while many were one storey in height, about half had posts of 5–6m in height, allowing for one tier of galleries. For example, the 1681 'Old

Figure 10.1. View of the 'Old Ship' wood-frame meetinghouse in Hingham, Massachusetts, built in 1681 by joiner and millwright Charles Stockbridge, as seen in the second half of the 19th century. One of four woodcut illustrations of local meetinghouses by Hosea Sprague of Hingham (First Parish Unitarian Church, Hingham, Massachusetts).

Ship' meetinghouse, built in Hingham, Massachusetts – a structure still standing approximately 28km south-east of Boston – measured 17m by 14m when first built. Enlarged by 4m on two sides in 1731 and 1755, it now seats approximately 600 persons in 80 ground-floor pews and a single tier of galleries on three sides. A 19th-century illustration (Fig. 10.1) shows the gathered roof and central turret; a hypothetical reconstruction based on a recent archaeological study reveals relatively sizable second-storey windows and dormer windows on each side of the roof (Fig. 10.2).[4] Large meetinghouses of this type, such as those raised in Andover and Ipswich, Massachusetts, in 1669 and 1699, measured 15 to 18m on each side with a plate height of 8m or more, allowing a second tier of galleries. Approximately six of these are known before 1714, and they typically seated approximately 750–1,500 persons.

Figure 10.2. Reconstruction of the original appearance of the 1681 Old Ship meetinghouse in Hingham, Massachusetts, based on architectural investigations undertaken in 2006 and 2007 (drawn by Marty Saunders, a member of Hingham First Parish, Hingham, Massachusetts. Courtesy of Brian Powell).

The key question addressed by architectural historians studying these structures is the origin of this form. Did first-period builders simply make up the four-square design as they went along, or did they have a specific precedent or tradition in mind? If the former were the case the design would have been American. If the latter, it would have been English or European and probably related to one of several earlier forms of Calvinist church architecture emerging in the late 16th and 17th centuries. Arguing in favour of an American origin is the lack of any English precedent as there is for domestic architecture.[5] With one important exception (the parish church in Burntisland, Scotland, discussed later), no evidence has been found that gathered and turreted four-square meetinghouses were ever built anywhere in the British Isles in the 17th century either as wood-frame structures or as brick or stone ones.[6] The majority of American scholars, among them Edmund Sinnott and

Kevin Sweeney, subscribe to this point of view.[7] Arguing in favour of a European origin, on the other hand, is a growing body of evidence suggesting that these structures shared many of the characteristics of Protestant meetinghouses built in the 16th and 17th centuries by Calvinist reformers in Scotland, France and the Netherlands. This point of view was first broached by historian Anthony Garvan in the early 1950s and tangentially by Marian C. Donnelly and John Coolidge in the 1960s.[8]

This chapter, based on a study of 2 first-period (1639–1712) and 178 second-period (1713–1800) New England meetinghouse survivals, together with data from approximately 1,470 demolished buildings known now only from historical records and the existence of a few artefacts, presents new evidence supporting a European origin of the form. It suggests that English immigrants brought with them the basic concepts used by Scottish, Huguenot and Reformed Dutch ecclesiastic builders, translating them through the vernacular conduit of post-and-beam barn building. It argues, moreover, that the 'church-like' modifications to these structures made in the 18th and early 19th centuries derived from Anglican practices brought over by later generations of English immigrants after the revocation of the Massachusetts Bay Charter in 1689. Postulating a link between meetinghouse design and Puritan ecclesiology, this study suggests that those New England religious societies most inclined toward reinstituting Anglican and Anglican-derived liturgical and devotional practices were also the first to adopt the architectural changes that converted plain-style Puritan 'meetinghouses' into Georgian and Federal-period Congregational 'churches'.

EUROPEAN TRADITIONS

The conceptual keys to this point of view are set forth in the findings of the architectural historians Per G. Hamberg and (more recently) Andrew Spicer. A Swedish scholar active in the 1950s whose work was translated into English in 2002, Hamberg studied the influence of classical authors such as Marcus Vitruvius Pollio (born c. 70 BC) on the wave of Dutch and French church builders that followed Protestant gains in the northern Netherlands after the formation of the Union of Utrecht in 1579 and the establishment of Huguenot worship in France after the Treaty of Nantes in 1598. Hamberg describes a vibrant Calvinist tradition that was just coming to its peak in Europe in the first decades of the 17th century. Citing Jacques Perret's *Des Fortifications et artifices*, he traces the design of temples and church buildings that used multiple tiers of galleries to bring the congregation as close as possible to the central pulpit. This theatrical layout is seen in circular form in the 1566 Huguenot temple in Lyon, France, called 'Le Paradis', where the congregation sat in a circle on the ground floor surrounding the central pulpit with additional seating for parishioners provided in a circular gallery.[9]

Andrew Spicer in turn describes a surge of temple or church building in Reformed portions of Flanders and the Netherlands after an agreement was reached with regent Margaret of Parma in 1566, temporarily allowing Protestant worship. These churches assumed many shapes (octagonal, square, rectangular), but they typically gave central prominence to the pulpit, segregated women from men and provided one or two tiers of galleries. While many of these structures were demolished in the religious violence that followed, the form persisted and at least one was erected in the British Isles. The four-square form with a four-sided gallery is found in a post-Reformation parish kirk built by seamen and cloth merchants in Burntisland, Fife, Scotland (Fig. 10.3) in 1592. Recent evidence

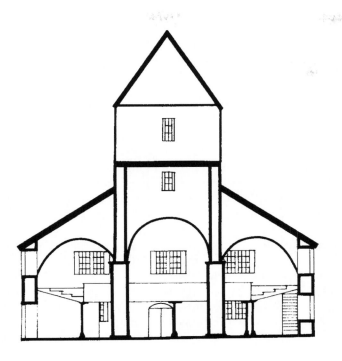

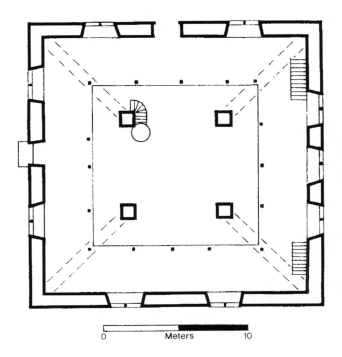

Figure 10.3. Conjectured original elevation and plan of the 18m by 18m Burntisland Parish Kirk, Fife, Scotland, erected by mason John Roche in 1592. Still standing, this house of worship was heavily altered in the 18th and early 19th centuries, with stone buttresses added to each corner and the replacement of a wooden turret with a stone tower. This illustration is based on Hay 1957, 33, and on a 17th-century drawing by John Slezer published in Spicer 2007, 58 (drawn by P. Benes).

has identified the builder as John Roche, a local stonemason. Still standing, Burntisland kirk has an interior dominated by four large masonry columns whose arches support the gathered roof. The structure originally had a wooden turret and a wooden spire, but later renovations in the 18th and 19th centuries added supporting buttresses to each corner and replaced the turret with a central stone tower.[10]

Octagonal and dodecahedral houses of worship also persisted. Willemstad Reformed Church (1596), the first purpose-built Reformed church in the United Provinces, is a surviving single-storey octagon laid out on a centralized plan. At the request of its principal donor it was to be 'built in round or octagonal form'. The design followed Jacques Perret's model and provided benches for men and women on the ground floor and stairs on either side of the pulpit leading to 'three tiers of pews against the walls *en manière de theater*'. A number of these structures were unusually large. The octagonal temple at Ghent measured 46m by 40m; the Huguenot temple at Charenton, near Paris, allowed up to 2,000 people to attend services simultaneously.[11]

By the time of the great Puritan migration to New England some important Huguenot temples and Reformed Dutch meetinghouses were already several decades old. Besides Charenton, these included two temples at La Rochelle, France, illustrated in a 1620 bird's-eye-view map by Martin Zeiller in his *View of La Rochelle*. The Grand Temple (identified as no. 14 in Zeiller) was an elongated, eight-sided masonry structure with a central turret; the second, Le Salle Saint-Michel (no. 13), was a rectangular turreted house of worship with a bank of dormer windows on each side – a reconstituted Catholic meeting hall and possible forerunner of the classic New England style. A dodecahedral half-timbered temple was also raised in Le Petit-Quevilly near Rouen using twelve dormer windows, a central turret and two tiers of galleries. Another illustration of this type of structure is provided by an interior view of Remonstrants' temple in Amsterdam, which again reveals two tiers of galleries with additional benches.[12]

FIRST-PERIOD MEETINGHOUSES

By 1640 square wood-frame meetinghouses similar to Burntisland parish church and Zeiller's no. 13 were being raised in New England. These had centralized interiors like Lyon's 'Paradis' temple and Amsterdam's Remonstrant temple. One of the first was the 1638 meetinghouse raised in Hartford, Connecticut, by the congregation of the Rev. Thomas Hooker (1586–1647), who, with a sizable following, had declined to live in Massachusetts Bay Colony and had resettled along the Connecticut River in 1636. The date of its erection is known from a 'weather cock' (probably meaning a dated flag vane) removed when the house was taken down in 1737 – a fact noted years later in the diary of the Reverend Daniel Wadsworth (1704–1747). While details are sketchy, this was a framed structure (later repairs called for 'new ground sills'). It was covered with clapboards and may have measured 15m by 15m with a 'pyramidical' (meaning gathered) roof, at the top of which was a turret and a bell taken by the congregation from Cambridge. Galleries were installed in 1644, 1660 and 1664, and a covered outside porch led to the 'chambers' upstairs, which were used for trials and meetings of the general court. Repaired many times, the house served the Hartford Church and a variety of civil functions for about ninety-nine years.[13]

A second was a meetinghouse in New Haven, Connecticut, raised by the congregation led by Rev. John Davenport (1597–1670), formerly of Oxford and London. Like Hooker,

this group also declined the opportunity to stay in the Boston area and relocated in Quin-
nipiac, Connecticut, forming an independent government. To meet the immediate housing
needs of the colony, Davenport and his colleagues asked their surveying team to design a
nine-square town slightly offset from the prevailing west winds, a planning system recommended by Vitruvius. In addition, they set aside £500 and built in 1639 the first large
meetinghouse in New England whose dimensions are known from town records. At 'fifty
foot square' [15.24sq m] it was provided with all the essential components of the New
England four-square design: a gathered or bevel roof, gallery seats for about sixty men and
a turret in the centre of its roof surmounted by a banistered and railed platform.[14] The
builder was William Andrews (d. 1675), a joiner of some wealth (he was assessed at £150
in 1639), who became a proprietor of the new colony and was given a lot on one of the
squares. While no images of the 1639 New Haven meetinghouse are known, Andrews and
his son Nathan Andrews replaced it in 1668 with a second meetinghouse that may have
resembled it. This structure is seen in a perspective view taken of New Haven centre.[15] It is
also known from a plan drawn by diarist Rev. Ezra Stiles (1727–95) as a memory aid after
the building was torn down.[16]

A third such structure was the 1640 meetinghouse of the First Church in Boston. No
details survive of the 'Old Meeting House', as it was called by biographer Ebenezer Turell
in 1749, but the building must have been substantial. Gov. John Winthrop's journal notes
that the total cost was £1,000, one-third of which was raised by selling the old building.
This compares to the £400 paid to John Sherman for the 12m by 12m meetinghouse built
in Watertown in 1656 and the £437 (plus the value of the old house) given to carpenter
Charles Stockbridge for the 17m by 14m Old Ship in Hingham in 1681. John Winthrop
also tells us that a young child broke her arm and shoulder in 1643 when she fell 5m from
the gallery to the floor. This was an unusually high gallery, and the structure may have
been fitted with a second gallery in 1675. The house was large enough to accommodate
Boston's First Church for more than seventy years, and the brick structure that replaced it
after the Boston fire of 1711 may have been a masonry equivalent of the original 1640 one.[17]

The four-square form with a rising central turret soon became the dominant meetinghouse in New England in the first period. The meetinghouses in Deerfield, Newbury
and Ipswich, Massachusetts – known from illustrations and maps – differed from these
early prototypes only in the number of galleries, their dimensions and the sophistication
and appurtenances of their turrets. Towns typically imitated one another, distributing the
pattern into every corner of English settlement. Watertown, Massachusetts, voted in 1656
that 'Cambridge meetinghouse shall be our pattern in all points'. Windsor, Connecticut,
in turn voted in 1684 to 'have the form of ... Springfield'.[18] Haverhill, a town on the
Merrimack River in Massachusetts, replicated in 1696 the seats, pulpit, galleries and stairs
of Beverly, 35km to the south, and based the sides of its meetinghouse on Reading, 32km
to the west.[19] Their ultimate source, however, was a new Calvinist architectural radicalism
set in motion by dissenting congregations in Scotland, France and the Netherlands that
saw church services as an exercise in prayer and attentive listening; that denied the special
sanctity of houses of worship and that provided a place for civil uses such as town offices,
court trials, the storage of powder and living quarters for troops on the march.

A parallel European origin also influenced the Reformed Dutch houses of worship built
in Long Island and on the Hudson River area of New York, where both four-square and
eight-sided forms appear. The 1715 stone meetinghouse erected by the Reformed Dutch

Table 10.1. Liturgical innovations by New England's Congregational, Presbyterian and Baptist religious societies by decade, 1691 to 1830, showing the progressive inclusiveness and Anglicization of 18th-century Protestant religious societies.

Date	Relations made optional	Reading Scripture	Men and women seated together
1691–1700	1	1	
1701–1710	2		
1711–1720	2	1	2
1721–1730	10	3	6
1731–1740	8	4	6
1741–1750	7	7	3
1751–1760	11	8	8
1761–1770	6	22	7
1771–1780	6	6	3
1781–1790	4	5	2
1791–1800	4	3	1
1801–1810		4	
1811–1820		3	
1821–1830		1	

Figures represent the number of parishes. Explanation of terms: Column 1: written 'relations' were public confessions required for church membership. Column 2: reading of scripture from the pulpit, previously scrupled in the 17th century as 'rote' worship, was gradually permitted after 1700. Column 3: men and women, initially required to sit apart on opposite sides, were allowed sit with their families in individual pews.

congregation in Albany, New York, virtually duplicated both the 1592 Burntisland Kirk and the 1697 Rotterdam Scottish Church. Eight-sided meetinghouses in turn were built in 1700 in New Utrecht, New York, following what a 19th-century historian called 'the usual octagon form'. Bushwick, New York (now a part of Brooklyn), erected an eight-sided meetinghouse in 1711 that was used until 1840.[20]

An important visual aspect of the outside of these first-period meetinghouses – and one that would come to fruition later in the 18th century – was the ornamental roof fixtures mounted at the gables and on the turret. At least nine meetinghouse 'pyramids' or 'pinnacles' are cited in New England records before 1705. That these were decorative rather than functional is suggested by a vote in Roxbury, Massachusetts, in 1658 'that some pinakle or ornament be set upon each end of the howse'. They also came in multiples or pairs: Haddam, Connecticut, ordered 'tooe pramedyes at each end' of their new meetinghouse in 1672. But their size is uncertain; pinnacles erected on 17th-century domestic dwellings were approximately 0.5m high, but those associated with meetinghouses may have been much larger. Joseph Parsons, a carpenter in Northampton, Massachusetts, hired in 1694 to repair the meetinghouse, was paid for 'sawing two stocks for Preamady [pyramid]', suggesting either that it was formed from two large timbers or that he was making two of them. The one on the turret of the meetinghouse of the 1700 First Church of Newbury, Massachusetts, may have been 7m high and capped by balls. The style (and the use of the term *pyramid*) continued into the 18th century: Norwich, Connecticut, ordered that its

Table 10.2. Singing innovations by New England's Congregational, Presbyterian and Baptist religious societies by decade, 1691 to 1840, showing the increasing importance of formal taste in 18th- and early 19th-century musical liturgy.

Date	New way of singing	Tate & Brady	Watts	Lining out ended	Singers sit together in a pew	Singers sit in gallery	Bass viol	Organs
1691–1700				1				
1701–1710								
1711–1720	3	1		1				
1721–1730	27	1		1				
1731–1740	24	4						
1741–1750	6	1	11	1				
1751–1760		16	25	3	1	1		
1761–1770	1	32	31	7	12	10		1
1771–1780	2	5	17	37	11	29		
1781–1790			10	41	5	23	3	2
1791–1800			8	11		10	26	7
1801–1810			1	4		1	17	5
1811–1820							6	4
1821–1830							5	2
1831–1840								1

Explanation of terms: Column 1: 'New way of singing' represents formal musical training by the congregation. Column 2: 'Tate and Brady' is the introduction of Nahum Tate and Nicholas Brady, *A New Version of the Psalms* (London, 1696). Column 3: 'Watts' is the introduction of Isaac Watts, *Psalms of David Imitated* (London, 1717). Column 4: 'Lining out' means alternating reading by the deacon and singing by the congregation of individual lines from the psalter. Column 5: Trained singers are allowed to sit together in one pew. Column 6: Trained singers are given a special pew in the gallery. Columns 7 & 8: Bass viols and organs are self-explanatory.

pyramid be mended in 1705, and Newbury required a copper weathervane to replace the iron one 'on top of the pyramid' in 1772.[21]

SECOND-PERIOD MEETINGHOUSES

With the revocation of the Massachusetts Bay Charter and the founding of Anglican King's Chapel in Boston in 1686, New Englanders again became exposed to Anglican religious practices. In part through their influence, but also because nonconformists were themselves changing, a number of Anglican practices were reintroduced into the liturgy and into the architecture of dissenting congregations. Practices seen in Trinity Church in Newport, Rhode Island, after 1699, at St. Paul's Church in Narragansett, Rhode Island, after 1707 and St. Michael's Church in Marblehead, Massachusetts, after 1714, resulted in a tug of war between conservative Congregational congregations that wanted to keep intact the spirit of reform and newer, more worldly (and wealthy) Congregational congregations that wished to expand communion and make the church more socially relevant. Reformed congregations now for the first time read scripture in the service and recited the Lord's Prayer. They widened access to communion by introducing the halfway covenant and open admission to the churches, placing increasingly less reliance on 'relations' or 'confessions' spoken to the congregation at large, and more on the appearance of Christian values. They permitted men and women to sit 'promiscuously' in the pews instead of being segregated by gender and age. As indicated in Table 10.1,[22] these liturgical practices reached a tipping point after which those congregations which had not yet adopted them were now seen as conservative. For example, failing to permit the reading of scripture after the decade of 1761–70 characterized a traditional church. In the area of church music (Table 10.2), progressive congregations began singing by rule, adopted new translations of the psalms by Tate and Brady and Isaac Watts and eliminated the old practice of the deacon's 'reading' of each line of the psalm before the congregation attempted to sing it. Trained singers now sat in special seats, and musical instruments such as bass viols or flutes were introduced to accompany psalmody. Even organs – the 'Devil's hornpipes' – eventually made their way into Reformed services.

These liturgical changes were accompanied by innovations in the meetinghouse that dramatically shifted its radical nonconformist or Calvinist orientation into a more 'conventional' English church edifice. One change was to redefine the architectural codes by which meetinghouses were publicly identified. The paired 'pinnacles' or 'pyramids' – which had always marked first-period structures – were converted into a single 'steeple' or 'spire'. The first sign of this critical shift was a debate held in the September 1710 town meeting in Chelmsford, Massachusetts, to determine whether the community would complete the turret of the new meetinghouse raised during the previous summer. After a number of meetings, a consensus was finally reached to go along with the recommendation of a five-man committee to finish everything 'except the steeple'.[23] Use of this term was a crucial turning point. Although Chelmsford finally decided against one, the simple act of considering a steeple held far-reaching religious implications because it publicly designated the meetinghouse as a house of worship – not simply a gathering place for civic and religious life. And it marked a critical conceptual division between the first-period 'pinnacles' and the 'steeples' of the period that followed.

Another change was the introduction of compass windows, a decorative feature that traditionally identified English and European ecclesiastic architecture – regardless of its denomination – throughout the 17th, 18th and early 19th centuries. In New England, compass-topped windows first emerged on early Anglican structures in Boston, in Newport and Narragansett and in Marblehead. But after 1715 they rather suddenly appeared on a number of new meetinghouses raised by dissenting or Reformed congregations in Boston, among them those of the Brattle Square congregation, the New North and the New South. They also appeared selectively in other key port towns, among them Ipswich, Massachusetts, and New Haven, Connecticut. But most rural and inland congregations – possibly because they could not afford them – put compass windows only behind the pulpit; all other windows had rectangular frames.[24] This, too, was an important indicator. What had been a way of distinguishing between a Reformed congregation and an Anglican one had now become a sign of social rank among the Congregationalists.

Equally important were changes to the exterior profile of the meetinghouse. The shift to the so-called pitched roof – as opposed to a traditional Calvinist gathered or bevelled one – began with the same group of dissenting meetinghouses in Boston that first used compass windows. The Brattle, New North, New South and New Brick congregations all built new meetinghouses with pitched roofs between 1699 and 1721. Because of improvements in building techniques, these roofs spread quickly into the countryside, however. Soon after it had approved the building of a new meetinghouse the town of Concord, Massachusetts, was undecided over two alternative designs proposed to the voters on 20 January 1710. One plan was a mostly square structure 16m by 18m in size with two galleries and the usual 'bevel Roof'. The alternative offered what the planners called an 'English Built' roof with end-to-end gables on slightly different, or longer, dimensions of 18m by 15m. To resolve it, the town issued slips of paper marked 'E' for English and 'B' for bevel for the purposes of voting. The count was 66 in favour of the 'English moad' versus 27 for the old style. The resulting meetinghouse, completed in the fall of 1711, was a structure 18m long and 15m wide with a plate height of 8m and two tiers of galleries. Its roof was 'flat', or 'English', and unbroken with the usual dormers or lucarnes.[25]

The Concord pitch-roofed prototype became the standard second-period meetinghouse in New England. Sometimes furnished with a small belfry (but more usually without), these structures retained most elements of the first-period interiors, but radically shifted the profile of the building to conform to the new taste. The town of Lexington, Massachusetts, for example, built a meetinghouse in 1714 'on the plan of the one at Concord' – and, like Concord's, it left enough room to add a second gallery over the first, illuminating it with a set of third-storey windows visible just under the eaves. Nearby Chelmsford built a meetinghouse like Concord's, as did Lynnfield, Massachusetts, located about 30km away. Other towns in New England found their own models and their own descriptive names for a pitched roof. In the Connecticut Valley Hadley, Massachusetts, voted in 1713 for a 'flattish roof'; Westfield, Massachusetts, specified a roof built in 'barn fashion with a bell Coney upon the middle' in 1719; Bridgeport, Connecticut, a 'long roof' in 1716; East Haven, Connecticut, a 'straight roof or barn fashion' in 1717.[26]

A final evolution of the second-period form was the addition of a standing bell tower, a feature that completed the transformation of the meetinghouse into a simulated Anglican church. Again, pioneered by the same Boston congregations that initiated the use of compass windows and pitched roofs, the standing bell tower was introduced in the New North congregation in 1715, the New South in 1716 and the Brattle Street congregation in 1717. While the principal entry still remained on the centre of the long side, the effect was to create an English parish church like those designed by Christopher Wren. For some meetinghouses, the tower that supported the bell also provided a set of exterior stairs leading to the gallery, typically producing a porch on one side and a bell tower on the other (Fig. 10.4).

With these architectural shifts came a new emphasis on Georgian decorative modes. Many of these details were designed to replicate in wood the stonework found in English parish churches. But they also introduced a formality that went far beyond the 17th-century instructions to joiners to provide a 'comely' appearance, and they help amplify our understanding of the full extent of English influence on meetinghouse architecture in the late colonial and post-Revolutionary periods. As early as 1728, joiner Aaron Cleveland's agreement for the third meetinghouse in Malden, Massachusetts, cites 'four oval Windows in the Square' of the steeple, each one decorated with modillions.[27] Bluehill, Maine, voted for 'Covings' at their new meetinghouse in 1792, specifying 'a double Cornish' except for the weatherboards, which were to be single.[28] New terms such as *Doric, Ionic*, and *Corinthian* were cited in meetinghouse contracts; and new colour schemes, stressing 'dark stone color' or 'yellow stone color' marked the outside. Within, marbleizing and mahoganizing finishes

Figure 10.4. Second meetinghouse in Cohasset, Massachusetts,
built 1741 with a belltower added in 1799. One of four woodcuts
displaying Hingham and Cohasset meetinghouses by
Hosea Sprague, second half of the 19th century
(First Parish, Hingham, Massachusetts).

coloured areas such as the columns supporting the gallery, the gallery fronts, the pulpit front and the details of the pulpit windows.

These tendencies all came to a head in 1786 when a young architect named Charles Bulfinch (1763–1844), who had just come back from a European tour, designed a replacement for the Hollis Street meetinghouse in Boston, which had burned down. The result was an unprecedented innovation in early American church building that emerged after the American Revolution. The new Hollis Street meetinghouse was a wood-frame structure with a palisaded entry portico, twin bell towers and domed ceiling, all copied from English

Figure 10.5. 'Old Meeting House, Kingston, Mass. Built 1798. Demolished 1851.' One of three New England meetinghouses that replicated Charles Bulfinch's innovative twin-tower design (illustration from *Report of the Proceedings* 1876, 122–3).

prototypes.[29] While only four such meetinghouses (Fig. 10.5) are known, Bulfinch's design set in motion a new chapter in the history of American houses of worship that inaugurated the third-period, or Federal, style (1789–1830).

These architectural innovations were typically undertaken by wealthy and younger congregations who most actively championed the progressive benchmarks of newer Congregational liturgy and polity. The first 'English roof' was installed on the 1699 meetinghouse of the Brattle Street Congregation, whose 'Manifesto' had repudiated many of the principles of the Cambridge Platform on which most New England Reformed churches were based; the first standing bell tower was raised at Boston's New North Congregation, which had petitioned the town's selectmen in 1713 to allow its wooden bell tower (called 'battlements' in the document); the first compass windows were incorporated into the meetinghouse of the wealthy New Brick Congregation in Boston in 1721. All were recently formed religious societies gathered from the town's huge increase in merchants and tradespeople after 1699.[30] The first standing bell tower in the colony of Connecticut was raised in 1726 by the town of Guilford, which had recently allowed men and women to sit together, one of the first in New England to do so.

Why did progressive congregations in North America introduce architectural changes so dramatically divergent from 16th- and 17th-century Calvinist traditions? First was a shift in perspective. After building a new meetinghouse in 1723 the town of Norwalk, Connecticut, decreed that nothing was to be done with the structure 'but what is consistent with, and agreeable to the most pure and special service of God, for which end it was built and now devoted'. One of many such 18th-century votes emphasizing the exclusive religious use of the meetinghouse in New England, this view became more acceptable as the century progressed. Second was a sense of style. Georgian details were beginning to penetrate civic and domestic buildings, and the men and women who paid for the meetinghouses may have simply expected them. In the words of the Woodbury, Connecticut, town clerk reporting to the New Haven assembly in 1747, the new steepled meetinghouse was 'for its bigness, strength, and architecture ... Transcendantly Magnificent!'

These developments were accompanied by steps toward reacquiring the aesthetics and inclusiveness of the Christian religion their forbears had practised in England that led to the key 18th-century evolutions in the Congregational church experience: allowing all participants in the exercise to share in the sacraments; reading of 'rote' prayers and scripture in the service; and the seating of men and women together in the pews. They also led to new liturgical aesthetics: singing poetic translations of the psalms (Tate and Brady, Watts); singing without a deacon's reading the line; allowing singers to congregate together; and introducing the bass viol and organ. What better way was there to assert the primacy of the Sabbath observance in the community than the 'churchliness' of its meetinghouse?

These innovations took place in the shadow of the physical presence of Anglican churches. The North Society in Salem, Massachusetts, founded in 1770 by a dissident group that aspired to the social ambitions of their Anglican neighbour St Paul's Church, built the first dissenting meetinghouse whose entry was on the short side, a critical architectural decision that 'simulated' an Anglican interior. Now both the outside and interior of their meetinghouse was virtually indistinguishable from their Anglican neighbour. And in 1784 the town of Stockbridge, Massachusetts, possibly humbled by the elegant and expensive Anglican church recently built in Great Barrington (a town immediately to the south of it), did the same thing by placing the pulpit 'opposite the bell tower', in effect transforming the meetinghouse into a church.[31]

CONCLUSION

In closing we will suggest a second question. Are we witnessing an isolated and narrow geographical phenomenon or something larger that forms part of a cultural logic that surrounds the entire Atlantic Protestant experience? Nonconformist practices may have thrived best under conditions where they were in the minority; by the same token, they may have atrophied in an atmosphere of established success. Calvinism, shipwrecked in England by the Restoration, continued to flourish in New England for another half-century. But in the end the movement may have become unsustainable in an American colonial context where virtually the entire population was 'nonconformist' and where exercise of religion was paid through public taxes and served a public agenda. There remained no one to be 'against'. If so, this may explain why it was that the comfortless Huguenot temple had become so quickly softened in America in the 18th and early 19th centuries. Even before their parishioners knew it, stoves heated the bitterly cold New England interior spaces, and the stuffed cushion holding the Bible was now made out of fine Georgian cloth.

NOTES

1. Winthrop 1838, 31–48.
2. Garvan 1951, 141; Spicer 2007, 1–12.
3. The town of Cambridge, MA, voted to repair its meetinghouse 'with a 4:square roof' in 1649. *Records of the Town of Cambridge (formerly Newtowne) Massachusetts, 1630–1703* 1901, 85.
4. Lincoln 1873, 19–41; Corse 1930, 19–31; Coolidge 1961, 435–61; Powell and Gilmore, 2007.
5. Cummings 1979, chap. 6, 'English regional derivations and evolutionary trends'.
6. Stell 1999, 49–81.
7. Sinnott 1963, 16; Sweeney 1993, 61.
8. Garvan 1951, 141; Donnelly 1968, 91–108; Coolidge 1961, 461 & n. 92.
9. Hamberg 2002, 22–3, 36–43, 126–9.
10. Spicer 2007, 111–15, 57–60.
11. Spicer 2007, 134, 198.
12. Hamberg 2002, 40, 128; Laurent 1996, 27; Guicharnaud 1999, 144.
13. Kelly 1948, 1:191–4; *Commemorative Exercises of the First Church of Christ in Hartford, Connecticut* 1883, 143–59.
14. Donnelly 1968, 15.
15. Kensett 1806.
16. Stiles 1916, 264 (13 Nov. 1772).
17. Winthrop 1996, 553; Donnelly 1968, 122; Turell 1749, 179.
18. Watertown (MA) 1894, 1:37; Kelly 1948, 2:305.
19. Hurd 1888, 1:1947–8.
20. Alexander 1991, 309–15; Prime 1845, 341; Stiles 1867–70, 355.
21. Donnelly 1960, 76–7; Trumbull 1902, 1:121; Coffin 1845, 240.
22. Sources for Tables 10.1 and 10.2 are drawn from published parish and church records, town records, clergymen's diaries, and New England town and parish histories. The latter are deemed reliable because most authors had access to the original records.
23. Waters 1917, 677.
24. Benes & Zimmerman 1979, 15–17.
25. Tucker 1985, 306–28.
26. Hudson 1868, 57; Judd 1863, 318; Lockwood 1922, 1:311; Orcutt 1886, 480–82; Havens 1876, 19.
27. Watkins 1911–12, 39.
28. Candage 1905, 44.
29. Kirker 1969, 17–19.
30. Manifesto Church 1902; Thwing 2001, entry 46760; Robbins 1852, 316–19.
31. *First Centenary, the North Church and Society, Salem, Massachusetts* 1873, 21–3; Jones 1854, 184; Taylor 1928, 176.

BIBLIOGRAPHY

Alexander, R. 1991, 'Religion in Rensselaerswijck', in Zeller 1991, 309–15.

Benes, P. & Zimmerman, P. 1979, *New England Meeting House and Church: 1630–1850: A Loan Exhibition Held at the Currier Gallery of Art, Manchester, New Hampshire*, Boston: Boston University Scholarly Publications.

Candage, R.G.F. 1905, *Historical Sketches of Bluehill, Maine*, Ellsworth (ME): Hancock.

Coffin, J. 1845, *A Sketch of the History of Newbury, Newburyport, and West Newbury, from 1635–1645*, Boston: S.G. Drake.

Commemorative Exercises of the First Church of Christ in Hartford, Connecticut. 1883, Hartford (CT): Case, Lockwood and Brainard.

Coolidge, John. 1961, 'Hingham builds a meetinghouse', *New England Quarterly* 34/4: 435–61.

Corse, M.P. 1930, 'The Old Ship Meeting-House in Hingham, MA', *Old-Time New England* 21/1: 19–31.

Cummings, A.L. 1979, *The Framed Houses of Massachusetts Bay, 1625–1725*, Cambridge (MA): Harvard University Press.

Donnelly, M.C. 1960, 'New England pyramids, 1651–1705', *Journal of the Society of Architectural Historians* 19/2: 76–7.

Donnelly, M.C. 1968, *The New England Meeting Houses in the Seventeenth Century*, Middletown (CT): Wesleyan University Press.

Finney, P.C. (ed.) 1999, *Seeing beyond the Word: Visual Arts and the Calvinist Tradition*, Grand Rapids (MI): W.B. Eerdmans.

First Centenary, the North Church and Society, Salem, Massachusetts. 1873, Salem (MA): North Church and Society.

Garvan, A.N.B. 1951, *Architecture and Town Planning in Colonial Connecticut, New Haven*, New Haven (CT): Yale University Press.

Guicharnaud, H. 1999, 'An introduction to the architecture of Protestant temples constructed in France before the revocation of the Edict of Nantes', in Finney 1999, 133–62.

Hamberg, P.G. 2002, *Temples for Protestants: Studies in the Architectural Milieu of the Early Reformed Church and of the Lutheran Church*, Gothenburg: Swedish Research Council.

Havens, W.D. 1876, *Historical Discourse, Centennial Celebration of the Stone Meeting House in East Haven*, New Haven (CT): Punderson & Crisand.

Hay, George. 1957, *The Architecture of Scottish Post-Reformation Churches, 1560–1843*, Oxford: Clarendon Press.

Hudson, C. 1868, *History of the Town of Lexington, Middlesex County, Massachusetts*, Boston: Wiggin & Lunt.

Hurd, D.H. 1888, *History of Essex County, Massachusetts*, 2 vols, Philadelphia: J.W. Lewis.

Jones, E.F. 1854, *Stockbridge Past and Present*, Springfield (MA): Bowles.

Judd, S. 1863, *History of Hadley, Massachusetts*, Northampton (MA): Metcalf.

Kelly, J. 1948, *Early Connecticut Meetinghouses*, 2 vols, New York: Columbia University Press.

Kensett, T. 1806, 'Plan of the town of New Haven, with all the buildings in 1748', copy of a 1744 original by General James Wadsworth, unpublished, Yale University Library, New Haven (CT).

Kirker, H. 1969, *The Architecture of Charles Bulfinch*, Cambridge (MA): Harvard University Press.

Laurent, R. 1996, *Promenade á Travers les Temples de France*, Montpelier: Presses du Languedoc.

Lincoln, C. 1873, *Discourse, First Parish in Hingham, Massachusetts*, Hingham (MA): The Parish.

Lockwood, J.H. 1922, *Westfield and Its Historic Influences*, 2 vols, Springfield (MA): privately printed.

Manifesto Church. 1902, *The Manifesto Church: Records of the Church in Brattle Square, Boston, 1699–1872*, Boston: Benevolent Fraternity.

Orcutt, S. 1886, *A History of the Old Town of Stratford and the City of Bridgeport, Connecticut*, New Haven (CT): Fairfield County Historical Society.

Powell, B. & Gilmore, A. 2007, 'Old Ship Meeting House, First Parish, Hingham, Massachusetts: Historic Structure Report, Volumes I through IV' unpublished, Dedham (MA): Building Conservation Associates.

Prime, N.S. 1845, *History of Long Island*, New York: R. Carter.

Records of the Town of Cambridge (formerly Newtowne) Massachusetts, 1630–1703. 1901, Cambridge (MA): City Council.

Report of the Proceedings and Exercises at the One Hundred and Fiftieth Anniversary of the Incorporation of the Town of Kingston, MA, June 27, 1876. 1876, Boston: Stillings.

Robbins, C. 1852, *History of the Second Church in Boston and the New Brick*, Boston: Wilson.

Sinnott, E.W. 1963, *Meetinghouse and Church in Early New England*, New York: Bonanza Books.

Spicer, A. 2007, *Calvinist Churches in Early Modern Europe*, Manchester: Manchester University Press.

Stell, C. 1999, 'Puritan and non-conformist meetinghouses in England', in Finney 1999, 49–81.

Stiles, E. 1916, *Extracts from the Itineraries*, New Haven (CT): Yale University Press.

Stiles, H.S. 1867–70, *History of Brooklyn*, Brooklyn: published by subscription.

Sweeney, K.M. 1993, 'Meetinghouses, town houses, and churches: changing perceptions of sacred and secular space in southern New England, 1720–1850', *Winterthur Portfolio* 28/1: 59–93.

Taylor, C.J. 1928, *History of Great Barrington (Berkshire) Massachusetts*, Great Barrington (MA): Town of Great Barrington.

Teele, J.W. (ed.) 1985, *The Meeting House on the Green: A History of the First Parish in Concord and Its Church: 350th Anniversary, 1635–1985*, Concord (MA): The Parish.

Thwing, A.H. 2001, *Inhabitants and Estates of the Town of Boston, 1630–1800*, CD, Boston: New England Historic Genealogical Society with the Massachusetts Historical Society.

Trumbull, J.R. 1902, *History of Northampton, Massachusetts*, 2 vols, Northampton (MA): Gazette.

Tucker, E.W. 1985, 'The meeting houses of the First Parish', in Teele 1985, 306–28.

Turell, E. 1749, *Life and Character of the Reverend Benjamin Coleman*, Boston: Rogers & Fowle.

Waters, W. 1917, *History of Chelmsford, Massachusetts*, Lowell (MA): Courier-Citizen.

Watertown (MA). 1894–1939, *Watertown Records, Prepared for Publication by the Historical Society*, 8 vols, Watertown (MA): Historical Society.

Watkins, W.K. 1911–12, 'Malden's old meetinghouses', *Register of the Malden [Massachusetts] Historical Society* 2: 39.

Winthrop, J. 1838, 'A model of Christian charity, written on board the Arbella, in the Atlantic Ocean', *Massachusetts Historical Society Collections* 3rd ser. 7: 31–48.

Winthrop, J. 1996, *The Journal of John Winthrop, 1630–1649*, Cambridge (MA): Harvard University Press.

Zeller, N. (ed.) 1991, *A Beautiful and Fruitful Place*, Albany (NY): New Netherlands.

Part Three

Cemeteries: Funerary Custom, Burial and Identity

The Organization of Post-Medieval Churchyards, Cemeteries and Grave Plots: Variation and Religious Identity as seen in Protestant Burial Provision

Duncan Sayer

Since the Middle Ages the Church has had dominion over the dead, and so it would be fair to assume that religious identities were a strong contributor to post-medieval mortuary behaviour. However, religion is just one part of a selection of different conflicting identities expressed in the act of burial. From the placement of a body within an expensive lead coffin under a church to the rejection of Anglican burial practice in favour of a public or family burial plot, other parts of a person's identity can be visible in the decisions that people made when disposing of their dead. This chapter will outline the history and development of post-medieval burial space in an attempt to define its impact on funerary tradition and begin to understand the differentiation present in the types of site available for burial. Indeed, the 17th, 18th and early 19th centuries saw a considerable amount of variation in burial practice and in context this can be used to understand broader and more subtle social questions.

INTRODUCTION

Society, especially urban society, does not have a single centre and in early modern societies there were overlapping circles of belonging, and identity, the family, household, local community, religious and moral community.[1]

This quotation encapsulates one of the key challenges facing post-medieval archaeologists who want to answer social questions. How do you unpick the mixed identities, social groups, lifestyles and religious organizations that proliferated in cities such as London, Norwich, York, Manchester or Sheffield? Certainly, the ability to draw on textual evidence is important and one of the advantages of historical archaeology. But so too is the vast quantity of data available to study. Just ten years ago I wrote (with James Symonds) an article outlining the problems facing the 'forgotten congregations'[2] – chapels with burial grounds that could be overlooked by development controls. Today the archaeology of post-medieval burial grounds has developed considerably and there is a corpus of good excavation reports from chapels, graveyards, cemeteries and crypts. On superficial examination, post-medieval burial grounds look very similar: lead coffins, wooden coffins, earth-cut graves, iron handles, occasionally some iron, lead, or tin coffin plates, a ring, button or shroud pin all alongside a pile of clay pipe stems left behind by the grave diggers. However, the ability to see broader patterns using local, regional and national comparisons demonstrates that post-medieval burial practices were not only highly varied but can also be used to investigate social differentiation in a far more sophisticated and satisfying way than is the case for many earlier periods. Through this medium it may be possible to see some of the subtle overlapping circles of belonging that made up the identities of people in the past and affected the objects they made and the spaces in which they lived.

In this chapter I will take a broad approach and discuss the burial provision available in the post-medieval period: the cemeteries, burial sites, grave cuts and vaults. I would like this to be a beginning, not an end, as no short article can undertake a complete or satisfying survey; rather, it can highlight more questions and perhaps stimulate some more sophisticated analyses. Taking a long view is problematic where there is so much available evidence and, given that the aim of this chapter is to investigate religion, burial and identity, I will not include institutional burial grounds, but will cover parish churchyards, 'new churchyards', cemetery extensions, chapel and meetinghouse burial grounds and garden cemeteries. The chapter will examine the organization of these burial sites with a particular focus on personal identities, Protestant religious identities and the decisions which went into the act of cutting a grave to make a burial.

ENGLISH BURIAL GROUNDS

Archaeologists primarily study what is left behind by past societies. These remains and how they survive are often thought to be the product of normative social behaviours within those societies and an understanding of these models of behaviour can be used to reconstruct attitudes towards religion, gender, age, social class or wealth. However, these same remains are also the product of choice, or the restriction of choices, made at various levels within society by individuals, family groups or institutions. For much of the medieval and early post-medieval period the Church had dominion over the dead; a mourner, family or community would access their ancestors through the church building and its consecrated ground, binding death and religion together. This is visible within the architecture and trappings of the post-medieval English church. With the paint and finery of the medieval church removed, post-Reformation mortuary monuments dominated the internal space of the buildings. Bronze plaques or stone slabs adorned with names, such as those at Lancaster Abbey, or with images of individuals and their children, such as those at the Abbey in Dorchester-on-Thames, can be found alongside chest tombs and mural monuments with sculpted effigies such as those seen in Westminster Abbey. Within this space, wealthy families could express their status, their identity as a family and their patronage of a church which helped to support the outward appearance of their individual and familial piety. Large stone and wooden funerary monuments often depicted family and professional symbols in post-Reformation mortuary traditions, including coats of arms, invented or real, and guild and trade symbols.[3] However, these monuments were placed within the church space by the wealthiest of families who could afford some choice in their funerary expression. In some cases this choice was quite out of the ordinary: in 1756, Susanna Carteret Webb was placed in a cave she had prepared with her two children, while in 1800 Major Peter Labilliere was buried on Boxhill, Surrey, ten feet deep with his coffin placed on its head.[4] Similar choices were not always available more widely and even though internal church monuments could highlight family identities – such as status – they were still tied directly to religion by association with the church or churchyard space.

The same is not always true of external burial spaces. In medieval and post-Reformation Britain the location of a burial – internal or external – was an important way in which sectors of society indicated their social status. The selection of burial space was also occasionally dependant on religious affiliation: here examples include the Jewish burial ground at Jewbury, York, one of ten known medieval Jewish burial grounds in the UK.[5] Outside of monastery buildings, burials seem to have had general principles governing their organization, allowing commemorative activities to be focused through the presence of spatial markers or objects such as fountains or crosses.[6] In the 16th century, after the English Reformation, burial in many monastic churchyards was abolished and, often for the first time in towns, minor churches[7] and cathedrals took on the responsibility for the majority of burials in Britain.[8] The Act of Toleration of 1689 granted the right of free worship to Protestant dissenters[9] and with these new, if limited, freedoms came the first private cemeteries. Nonconformist groups established meeting houses or chapels and some had burial grounds associated with them. However, the greater part of the nonconformist and Anglican population continued to be buried in parish churchyards until the 19th century. This placed a huge pressure on space in small churchyards as urban populations expanded during the industrial revolution. During the 18th and 19th centuries many of these churchyards were extended or relieved by the establishment of satellite burial grounds on the edge of towns.

The diversification and increasing popularity of nonconformity in the 18th and 19th centuries saw the establishment of new chapel burial grounds and the construction of the Million Act Churches at the beginning of the 19th century also helped to provide new burial space in Britain's growing industrial towns (the 1818 Million Act granted £1 million for church construction around the country). As early as the 1820s and 30s the need for unconsecrated ground for nonconformist funerals and burials contributed to the establishment of new cemeteries on the edge of English towns, mirroring the establishment of French and American cemeteries. However, the diversification of the religious landscape was not the only reason for the extension of burial provision; overcrowding in urban parish churchyards was identified as one of the major risks to public wellbeing by Chadwick's 1843 report on public health.[10] As a result, and starting in London, urban churchyards were systematically closed following the passage of the 1853 Metropolitan Burial Act and the 1855 Burial Act. Although the establishment of new cemetery space had begun among religious dissenters, who established stock management companies to raise the funds needed, the poor state of Britain's urban environments fortified cemetery development within the cause of public health reform.[11] Many of the companies behind these cemeteries experienced financial difficulty, but the new form of burial was established and today the majority of inhumations take place in large municipal burial grounds, crematoria or 'natural cemeteries' on the edges of the urban environment. It is through this process that modern English cemeteries have developed and it is with a combination of French cemetery architecture, the work of John Loudon (see below)[12] and concerns over public health that the reform of burial provision spread across Europe and the New World.

THE ORGANIZATION OF ENGLISH BURIAL SITES

Graveyards

Medieval urban burial sites are usually found associated with major churches, with many, but not all, minor churches also having a churchyard.[13] They were organized around single grave plots with minimal burial superimposition. Using their sample of more than 8,000 graves, from more than 70 burial sites, Gilchrist and Sloane argue that there were no more than 40 examples of double burial where a later burial was deliberately placed into an earlier grave.[14] The same is not true for the deliberate removal of remains to make way for new burials and charnel pits full of bones are often found in medieval and post-medieval burial grounds. Pits of various sizes were used to dispose of the body parts revealed when new graves were cut. The disturbance of remains is partly caused by the overuse of church-yards for burial; and, for many post-medieval sites, such as St Martin's in Birmingham, the ground level was raised up behind a revetment wall as a result of the constant addition of bodies. Indeed, the wall surrounding St Martin's churchyard had to be periodically rebuilt as a result of the volume of earth behind it.[15]

Post-medieval churchyard sites were organized hierarchically, in a similar way to their medieval predecessors, and with little spatial management, at least initially. A single grave cut was usually dug for each individual, resulting in a haphazard and cramped burial ground with much intercutting and charnel (Fig. 11.1). This form of burial can be seen in excavations but also in the styles of gravestones employed. In 17th-century England external commemoration was uncommon and when it was employed monuments carried either initials or had just a single named individual commemorated on them.[16] Like medi-eval burial provision, a single person was interred in a single grave and so commemoration focused on individual identities and personal mortality.

Burial sites were organized hierarchically by wealth, the most expensive locations being inside the church – first the chancel and chapels, then the nave and aisles, followed by the less prominent parts.[17] External burial was also hierarchical, next to the doors and around the building being popular.[18] Gittings[19] and MacDonald and Murphy[20] argue that the manner of a person's death – suicide for example – may have also affected where a body could have been buried, the north side of churches being avoided except in exam-ples of a bad death.[21] Such overtly superstitious ways of organizing a cemetery, however, may have been a local practice or folklore and not a widespread custom, as many early modern cemeteries did not have burials all around them. Some even have burials just in the north of the churchyard: St Pauls, London, or St Martin's, Birmingham, for example. Having said that, even as late as the 1870s some High Churchmen (those Anglican rectors closest to Catholicism) would exclude burial from the parish churchyard for suicides and the unbaptized, banishing them to unconsecrated ground. Events like this were eventually debated in parliament, resulting in nationwide indignation which was reported in the local and national press. A change in the law was made in the 1880s to allow parish churchyard burial, and burial in other consecrated ground, to take place without a Church of England minister.[22]

Later in the post-medieval period some of the superstitions about the organization of churchyards may have been lost as the demand for space became more acute. However, by the 1720s[23] the health hazards and unpleasant experience of disturbing the recently dead had been recognized. Intramural burial was dependant on the space available, and family

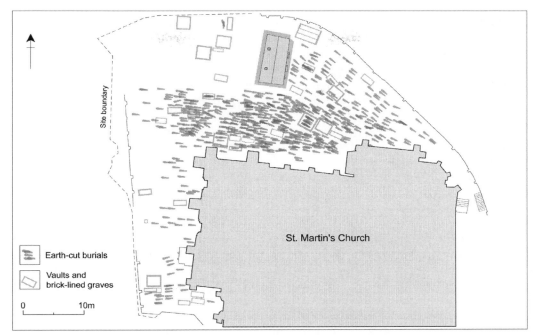

Figure 11.1. St Martin's Church, Birmingham, showing the overall plan of the excavations with earth-cut graves and vaults. The less densely used area to the north-east is the extension. Reproduced with kind permission from Brickley *et al.* 1999, 25, fig. 28.

vaults were constructed inside churches in the 15th and 16th centuries but proliferated both inside and outside them in the 17th and 18th centuries (see Fig. 11.1).[24] Litten argues that these vaults fall into four types: 1) dynastic vaults for aristocratic families; 2) family vaults, often no more than two or three coffins wide with a wall two bricks thick; 3) a single brick-walled grave (as at Bathford);[25] and 4) extensive private and parochial vaults.[26] Importantly, vaults, unlike earth graves, place emphasis on family burial, allowing family commemoration for those who could afford these structures. Despite this, the single earth-cut burial remained the most common form of disposal into the middle of the 19th century and the importance placed on the location of burial continued. For example, the burials in more expressive coffins, often paid for by wealthier families, are found in the most prestigious areas of burial grounds. From the seventy-seven burials excavated at Southwark Cathedral, the single iron coffin and the only three lead coffins identified were all found near to the main south-west door.[27]

New Burial Grounds and Graveyard Extensions
One of the most well-known new burial grounds, and among the earliest, is New Churchyard, London, which was established in 1569. Like those to follow, New Churchyard attracted a stigma as the burial place of the socially marginal because it received poorer people and the itinerant populations who belonged to no particular parish. A similarly non-parochial

site in London, Bunhill Fields, was established in 1665 during a plague outbreak, and because of its non-parochial status it soon became popular among the dissenter communities. Harding argues that these early sites are evidence that by the 16th or 17th century the parish was not an 'inclusive and comprehensive community'. [28] At least in urban environments pan-parish and non-denominational burial sites became more common as the post-medieval period progressed, especially as the pressures on space, wealth and finally public health reform pushed the poorer parishioners away from churchyard burial. This weakening of parochial identity was accompanied by an increasing diversity in religious identity and an increasing indifference to the importance of the parish itself.[29]

Graveyard extensions took on many forms, depending on the local need and the availability of land. Birmingham's St Martin's extended the existing burial ground to the north and east in 1810 (Fig. 11.1). Notably, the new burials were orientated on a slightly different axis to those in the older part of the site (south-east–north-west *vs.* east–west), and seem to be ordered into crude rows, perhaps in an attempt to limit the extensive intercutting which is visible in the older area next to the church. However, the presence of vaults and the continuation of burial adjacent to the church indicate the continuing significance of older types of burial. Simply extending a burial ground was not always an option and, after the 1855 Burial Act, many churches established new burial areas. In London, too, a detached parish burial site was often a solution to the pressures on burial space. Southwark Cathedral established a new churchyard around 1673, later called Cross Bones.[30] Cross Bones developed a reputation for being the burial site for single women and prostitutes, and notably only 23.4% of the excavated burials from the Museum of London (MoL) excavations had decorated coffins. In contrast to this, 42% of the burials excavated at Southwark Cathedral by Pre-Construct Archaeology (PCA), had decorated coffins.[31] This social difference is also reflected in the cost of burial; in 1838 a 4ft grave in Cross Bones cost 12s 20d, a 6ft grave in the churchyard was £1 5s 10d and an 8ft grave in the college ground was £2 10d, while a vault cost £3 13s 8d with an extra charge of 10s for burial in a family vault.[32]

In 1793 the burial ground at St Pancras church was extended to allow for the growing immigrant populations in the north of London, but this burial ground was planned very differently to Birmingham's St Martin's or Cross Bones. An archaeological watching brief on exhumation works was undertaken in this cemetery extension by Gifford together with their subcontractors PCA and MoLSS, and more than 1,300 burials were mapped. The buried population was very different from that at Southwark Cathedral in that it included French Catholics, aristocrats and paupers in an area to the east of the church (Fig. 11.2).[33] From 1793 until at least November 1822 burial practice at St Pancras was characterized by the stacking of multiple coffins within each deep earth-cut grave.[34] The burial registers show that many of these burials were consecutive interments made within a short period of time, often only a few days. The same registers also show that individuals sharing a given grave plot were not generally related. In the latter phase, from at least November 1822 to the closure of the cemetery in 1854 after the Metropolitan Burial Act, the organization was very different and, '[d]uring the later years of the cemetery's use, when overcrowding had reached extreme proportions, coffins had been laid side by side, head-to-toe, in long burial trenches'. [35] The dating of this transition, to after November 1822, is based upon reconstructed stratigraphy and recorded coffin plates.[36] Significantly, 1822 was the year in which the new parish church on Euston Road was opened and the old church lost its parochial status, becoming a chapel of ease primarily used for burial.[37] Following the loss of

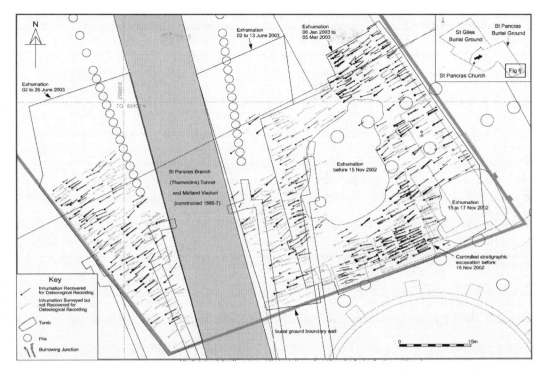

Figure 11.2. St Pancras churchyard extension. Kindly reproduced with permission from Phil Emery and Helen Glass. Emery 2007, 10, fig. 6. Copyright London & Continental Railways Ltd.

the church's status, it would seem that burials interred within the site were of lower-status individuals in flimsy coffins or winding sheets and trenches rather than individual graves. The importance of a parochial church and proximity to a place of worship seems to have been an important factor in a graveyard's usage.

Private Cemeteries

Archaeological intervention when exhuming small private burial grounds has become more commonplace than it once was,[38] which has resulted in a larger collection of recently published material. However, the sites themselves are uncommon in Wales, where in the 1870s nonconformist membership was the highest in Britain, with only 3 of 210 Methodist chapels having burial grounds of their own. Within private nonconformist cemeteries there is evidence to suggest different patterns in monument erection. Protestant dissenters were discriminated against in a number of ways; until the 1830s they had to pay church rates, could not attend university and had to use parish registers for deaths and marriages. These grievances were all addressed except one – nonconformists were not entitled to a lay minister to preside at their funerals until *c.* 1880. The nonconformist community felt disenfranchised and burial grievances were regularly reported in the local and national press. This common sentiment is visible archaeologically and where it is possible to identify nonconformist gravestones (for example, in private cemeteries and unconsecrated ground) their monuments seem to have been deliberately selected because they were less decorated than contemporary Anglican examples. As a result cemeteries took on a uniform, or austere, aesthetic; even where each stone was different they were all of simple design. Each individual expressed their own identity and their membership of a religious group whose doctrinal teaching advocated the ideal of simplicity.[39]

Among the earliest private burial grounds were built by the Quakers, with sites established as early as the 1660s.[40] The Quaker burial ground in Kingston-upon-Thames received its first burial in 1664.[41] Burial at this site was dense and intercut, with inhumations placed in single earth-cut graves with both north–south and east–west orientations to the graves and heads positioned at all of the cardinal points. Within the site was a single brick-built family vault constructed in the middle of the 18th century and containing ten members of the Barnard family.[42] A similar site, the 18th- and 19th-century Quaker burial ground at Bathford, Bath, contained walled graves with room for multiple inhumations.[43] Both of these sites seem to contain intercutting inhumations, but both were well ordered with an efficient use of space. Indeed, the burial records for the 19th- and early 20th-century site of Quakers Friars, Bristol, suggest that interments followed a chronological sequence, with graves both across the site and in loosely arranged clusters.[44]

Burials from the early 19th-century private burial site at Carver Street Methodist Chapel, Sheffield, were stacked horizontally in earthen graves and in one a William and James Simpson were found together, although there is little evidence to suggest that other shafts contained family graves.[45] However, at Upper Chapel, Sheffield, an 18th- and early 19th-century site, the graves seem to have been ordered into family groups and one multiple occupancy grave cluster had a gravestone which recorded a husband, wife and two sons all sharing the same surname.[46] At Bow Baptist churchyard, London, adjacent graves seem to have been chosen for reuse, arguably because of a familial connection between the deceased, a conclusion supported by the coffin plate data.[47]

At St Mary and St Michael, London, a late 18th- to 19th-century Catholic graveyard, burial started at the east end of the site and moved west sequentially. Coffins were stacked in graves up to 4m deep and there was no intercutting of the graves. Within the graves adult burials were found at the lowest levels, children were placed above them and infants were in the uppermost sections. Each stack was filled over a much longer time than at the churchyard extension at St Pancras, but, similarly to St Pancras, the names on the coffin plates did not suggest that they were family plots. For example, 'grave cut [1468] contained thirteen burials, of which five could be dated from coffin plate information giving date of death. The first burial took place in 1846, the second after 25 May 1847, the fourth in October 1847, while the eighth and ninth took place after 20 November 1847.'[48] It would seem that graves were periodically reopened – months or years later – so that further burials could be added.

Landscaped, Planned or General Cemeteries

In England the landscaped, out-of-town cemetery owed its development to several separate ongoing social needs: the nonconformists' desire for unconsecrated burial space; the need to protect corpses (at a time when illicit body snatching, and the fear of body snatching, was at its zenith); and the ongoing public health reforms regarding the cleaning-up of overcrowded cities. Among the first non-denominational (general) cemeteries were Rosary

Cemetery, Norwich (1819), Rusholme Road Cemetery, Manchester (1820), and Low Hill General Cemetery, Liverpool (1825), which were all established by prominent dissenters. Glasgow followed on from these sites and, influenced by the Parisian cemetery of *Père Lachaise* (1804), created a non-denominational cemetery (1832) which 'would harmonize beautifully with the adjacent scenery'.[49] Shortly afterwards London cemetery companies engaged a number of architects to build their cemeteries in the picturesque gothic style – such as Highgate, Kensal Green and Norwood – all of which were divided between conse-crated and unconsecrated ground. These sites also contained catacombs, vaults, brick-lined graves and deep-cut public graves. The success of one of these companies, the London Cemetery Company, empowered it to open other sites in Surrey, Kent and Middlesex, and other municipal cemetery companies were established and set up general cemeteries.[50] Sheffield General Cemetery opened in 1836 as a nonconformist site and in 1846 it was extended to include an Anglican consecrated area. The two sections were divided by a wall. Similarly, York Cemetery, established in 1837, was divided into consecrated and unconse-crated areas,[51] as was Reading Cemetery, established in 1843,[52] among others. These divi-sions, however, were not necessarily the impermeable barrier that they might have seemed and at York Buckham[53] found that some Anglicans were buried in unconsecrated ground, perhaps preferring to be in family clusters, or possibly as a result of the increasing pressure on space that was felt at the end of the 19th and in the early 20th century.

Between 1842 and 1843 John Claudius Loudon wrote about cemetery design, applying gardening and landscaping principles to discuss the laying-out of space in such a way as to positively affect moral sentiment, health and taste.[54] He designed three English cemeteries in 1843 – Cambridge, Bath Abbey and Southampton Cemetery – and developed principles for the laying-out of cemeteries which have had a significant influence on cemetery design to the present day, even though he died in 1843.[55] Loudon disapproved of the reuse of graves and the construction of vaults, catacombs and brick-lined graves, regarding them as unstable, difficult to drain and unhygienic.[56] He advocated a system where the cemetery was removed from a residential area, surrounded by a wall and divided into sectors and plots to allow ease of management and record-keeping.[57] His ideas influenced subsequent cemetery design alongside the public health reforms of the mid and late 19th century. After the closure of urban churchyards from 1855 these general sites became the only burial space available to many. By the 1870s–80s the use of brick-lined graves and catacombs had declined following much criticism of those 'pestilent vaults', although vaults themselves remained popular among the wealthy.[58]

To provide a specific example,[59] in York the general cemetery was divided up into grids composed of series of grave plots. Once paths were laid onto the grids, smaller spaces became available and were used for children. By the 1880s a new type of burial with a separate price had been created for this site: the 'child's burial'. These plots were either adjacent to paths or had been full adult plots divided into four.[60] At about this time smaller, child-sized headstones began to be erected in significant numbers. York cemetery started to see child burials clustered together although it did not have an area just for children, suggesting that there was not a specific movement towards family burial. Similarly, the organization of the cemetery seems to be focused on individual identities, not group ones; where similar gravestones stood next to each other they were usually from the same family, indicating the use of individual rather than family burial plots. Equally, public graves held multiple interments, stacked because of the proximity of their death, and the price of their burial depended on whether the grave was brick-lined or not. In 1848 the York cemetery introduced second-class graves, which would be occupied by only six people who would share a company-supplied memorial.

BURIAL PLACE, SPACE AND IDENTITY

Fig. 11.3 highlights the major changes to urban burial provision that took place within the post-medieval period. This is a generalized view, and there are obvious exceptions; some London non-parochial cemeteries were earlier than depicted, and many minor churches had graveyards in the Middle Ages; furthermore, not all of these options were available in all places or for all people. However, it illustrates neatly the variation present within and changes to burial provision between the 15th century and the end of the 19th century. This history is extremely complex and no two sites are the same. To date, post-medieval mortuary archaeology has usually focused on gravestones across single sites,[61] regional samples[62] or single excavated cemeteries,[63] so comparative studies are still reasonably uncommon,[64] although two notable examples are published in this volume.[65] This may unfortunately be a weakness in helping us to understand complex issues such as religion in post-medieval society. Studies of gravestones have focused on the rise of personal identities, arguing that site-specific patterns were a way for individuals to distinguish themselves from their immediate cemetery neighbours and maintain a sense of individuality, allowing them to feel that their close relationships were unique.[66] However, more subtle identities were also at work. The diversity of expression visible in patterns of gravestone erection peaked during the second half of the 19th century,[67] and it is interesting that it is in this same period that the choice of burial locations available had been reduced significantly; in short, and in slightly crude terms, different ways to express identity had been removed in favour of a 'one size fits all' landscaped cemetery solution.

Archaeological studies are making us increasingly aware of a greater degree of complexity and subtlety behind the selection of funerary monuments, particularly in an environment of mass production and consumption.[68] Funerary material culture may carry complementary and conflicting messages and the placement of stones may simultaneously convey religious and family identities. For example, religious and ethnic identity is sometimes expressed through the selection of gravestones within a particular cemetery space,[69] or, in particular, in situations of social stress such as the oppression of nonconformist funeral rites.[70] However, grave monuments are erected in a context and so must be considered alongside the selection of burial space.

Within this context a middle-class man had the most social, economic, gender-related, age-related and religious advantages or freedoms. Women, depending on their status, had access to the same burial choices as men. Indeed, archaeological excavations have commonly shown that Litten's heraldic principles for selecting coffin furniture – shield motifs for men, diamonds for women – were not exercised in reality.[71] Children may have been buried differently according to the burial site: in special areas, in smaller graves or at the tops/bottoms of public graves. Status and religious affiliation, however, may have reduced the options available. For example, poor widows were more likely to be buried in public graves or in the cemetery extensions such as Cross Bones, and were also less likely to be buried within family groups.[72] This all meant that an adult's social circumstance would

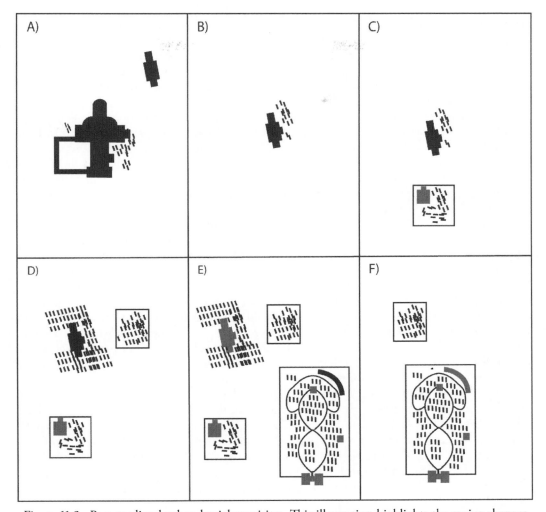

Figure 11.3. Post-medieval urban burial provision. This illustration highlights the major changes to burial sites. A) Late medieval burial provision focused on churches and monasteries with some burials inside church buildings – in black. B) 16th-century burial focused on churchyards and inside churches. C) The 17th century saw the development of some private burial grounds although chapels and meetinghouses did not have internal burials – in grey. D) In the late 17th and 18th centuries churchyard burial was extended and new parochial and non-parochial Anglican burial grounds were established. E) In the early 19th century the general cemetery was added to burial provision, although mid-way though the century burial inside churches was stopped. F) Urban churchyards and private cemeteries were closed, new 'churchyards' were left open or newly established on the edge of towns. The general cemetery became the most dominant burial form; halfway through this period their catacombs were closed.

affect how they were buried, just as religious convictions might dictate which burial ground a person was buried in, or where within a cemetery they were put.

In the 16th, 17th and 18th centuries the parish was not a comprehensive community corresponding with an identity group in life and so was not always an important part of burial choice, but it could be used by some individuals as a way of expressing religious and community affiliations. However, that is not to say that religion was not an important part of burial. By contrast, on the east coast of America, burial sites were often cemeteries and not generally graveyards associated with church/chapel/meetinghouse buildings.[73] In New England burial provision had been influenced by the Puritan, or Calvinist, indifference to the use of sacred space.[74] However, in England religious identity as expressed in burial is found among nonconformists, who fought for their private cemeteries and unconsecrated areas, meaning that their burial was more a statement about their interconnected religious and political identity. By contrast, burial on parish grounds would have taken place among parishioners and Catholics, nonconformists, lapsed Anglicans and strict Anglicans.

Placed within this brief comparison, the presence of a religious building adjacent to a burial space, and the proximity of a person to that building within that burial space, does seem to have been in part a spiritual/doctrinal decision, even if the outward expression of those burials seems to be that of wealth and these individuals were within more expensive coffins. The chancel and chapels were the most sacred parts of a church it was possible to be buried in, and similarly, proximity to the building seems to have been of some spiritual significance. This is especially visible when a church loses its status, as when St Pancras lost its parochial role and the subsequent burials were all from a significantly lower social group. As a result, the spatial organization of Anglican churchyards is a reflection not necessarily of disinterest in spirituality above individual expression of wealth and status, but of the commoditization of the church's sacred spaces. It would seem that even an 18th-century Anglican might try and buy their way into heaven. This may, in part, have resulted from the mixed legacy of post-Reformation concepts of 'sacred space'. Officially Anglicans rejected the idea of one part of the church being more sacred than another – but at least in burial practice there was clearly a hangover of medieval notions of 'degrees of sanctity', something that the High Church Anglican tradition attempted to continue. Material and status considerations were continually bound up with ongoing religious and spiritual concerns.

Where family identity did become significant in England it seems to be among the social classes with dynastic wealth who could afford vaults; while family identity does feature in planned cemeteries the family plot does not seem to be a significant feature for most of the post-medieval period. Instead, where new burial spaces were planned, public graves were dug deep and closed when full; by contrast, individual graves dominated the parish and small private burial sites. Even in landscaped sites such as York Cemetery only a few family clusters were identified from the gravestones. The focus seems to have been much more on religious identity and social status.

CONCLUSION

The question of identity in post-medieval burial practices is a complex one and incorporates many different aspects, including parish identity, religious identity, individuality, household or family identities, gender identity/status and social status (meaning not just wealth or hierarchical position but also age, gender and public service). However, the story of burial space is also a diverse and complex one that is difficult to do justice to in a single short chapter. The 17th, 18th and early 19th centuries were a period of extreme differentiation for burial provision in England even if the individual burials or graves themselves may be very similar. It is interesting that the most notable increases in the diversity of grave monuments come at the same time as the options available for burial itself decrease. Grave goods might not be common, unless coffins are counted, but variation in burial ground types means that social differentiations can be identified through comparison of local, regional or national funerary practices. For example, in the case studies considered here, individual burials seem to have encapsulated social position and religious identity, with family and parish identities becoming secondary; even where individual sites emphasized family identities it was within a religious context – a private cemetery, for example. The archaeology of post-medieval identity is still in its infancy and to advance beyond site-specific questions it will need to develop sophisticated ways to study large amounts of material across different academic disciplines, a challenge that the technologies of the modern world may make possible in future years.

NOTES

1. Harding 1998, 56.
2. Sayer & Symonds 2004.
3. See Finch 2003; Owen 2006.
4. Gittings 2007.
5. Lilley *et al.* 1994, 360.
6. Gilchrist & Sloane 2005.
7. Minor churches in the east of England were often planned with churchyards but this was not always the case in the west, where major churches maintained medieval burial monopolies. Churches in Bristol, Chester, Exeter, Gloucester, Hereford, Worcester and Winchester were not constructed with burial space and many of them did not develop cemeteries until the early modern period: Barrow 1992.
8. Barrow 1992; Gilchrist 2003, 404.
9. Houlbrooke 1999, 174.
10. Chadwick 1843.
11. Rugg 1998.
12. Curl 1993.
13. Barrow 1992.
14. Gilchrist & Sloane 2005, 158.
15. Brickley *et al.* 2006, 16.
16. Mytum & Chapman 2006.
17. Harding 1998.
18. Mytum 2004a; Brickley *et al.* 1999
19. Gittings 1999, 150.
20. MacDonald & Murphy 1990.
21. Gittings 1999, 150.
22. Sayer 2011.
23. Houlbrooke 1999, 193.
24. Litten 1991.
25. Stock 1998.
26. Litten 1991, 211.
27. Divers 2009, 88.
28. Harding 1998.
29. Harding 1998.
30. Brickley *et al.* 1999, 6.
31. Divers *et al.* 2009, 89.
32. Brickley *et al.* 1999, 10.
33. Emery 2007.
34. Emery & Wooldridge forthcoming.
35. Emery 2007, 8.
36. Emery & Wooldridge forthcoming.
37. Lovell & Marcham 1938, 72–95.
38. See Sayer 2010 and Sayer & Symonds 2004.
39. Sayer 2011.
40. Mytum 2004a.
41. Bashford & Pollard 1998.
42. Bashford & Pollard 1998, 161.
43. Stock 1998a.
44. Stock 1998b.
45. Mahoney-Swales *et al.* this volume.
46. Mahoney-Swales *et al.* this volume.
47. Powers & Miles this volume.
48. Powers & Miles this volume
49. Curl 1993, 209.
50. Curl 1993, 224.
51. Buckham 2003, 167.
52. Sayer 2011.

53. Buckham 2003
54. Loudon 1843.
55. Rodgers 2001.
56. Loudon 1843; Curl 1993, 245, 251.
57. Loudon 1843.
58. Curl 1993, 236.
59. Although there may not be a typical organization for general cemetery sites.
60. Buckham 2003.
61. Mytum 2004a; 2004b for examples, although some of his comparisons are more regional; Buckam 2003.
62. Tarlow 1999; Sayer 2011.
63. For example Brickley et al. 2006; Divers et al. 2009; Emery 2007; Stock 1998a.
64. See Sayer & Symonds 2004.
65. Mahoney-Swales et al. this volume; Powers & Miles this volume.
66. Jalland 1996; Tarlow 1999.
67. Tarlow 1999; Mytum 2004a.
68. Veit 2009.
69. Chenoweth 2009; Stone 2009.
70. Sayer 2011.
71. See Litten 1991.
72. Harding 1998, 59.
73. Stannard 1979.
74. Sweeney 1993; Walsh 1980.

BIBLIOGRAPHY

Barrow, J. 1992, 'Urban cemetery locations in the High Middle Ages', in Bassett 1992, 78–100.

Bashford, L. & Pollard, T. 1998, '"In the burying place" – the excavation of a Quaker burial ground', in Cox 1998, 154–166.

Bassett, S. (ed.) 1992, *Death in Towns: Urban Responses to the Dying and the Dead, 100–1600*, Leicester: Leicester University Press.

Brickley, M., Buteux, S., Adams, J. & Cherrington, R. 2006, *St. Martin's Uncovered: Investigations in the Churchyard of St. Martin's-in-the-Bull Ring, Birmingham, 2001*, Oxford: Oxbow.

Buckham, S. 2003, 'Commemoration as an expression of personal relationships and group identities: a case study of York Cemetery', *Mortality* 82, 160–175.

Burgess, C. 2000, '"Longing to be prayed for": death and commemoration in an English parish in the later Middle Ages', in Gordon & Marshall 2000, 44–65.

Chadwick, E. 1843, *Report on the Sanitary Condition of the Labouring Population of Great Britain. A Supplementary Report on the Results of a Special Inquiry into the Practice of Interment in Towns*, London: HMSO.

Chenoweth, J.M. 2009, 'Social identity, material culture and the archaeology of religion: Quaker practices in context', *Journal of Social Archaeology* 93: 3, 19–340.

Cox, M. (ed.) 1998, *Grave Concerns: Death and Burial in England 1700–1850*, York: Council for British Archaeology Research Report 113.

Curl, J S. 1993, *A Celebration of Death*, London: Batsford.

Divers, D., Mayo, C., Cohe, N. & Jarrett, C. 2009, *A New Millennium at Southwark Cathedral*, London: Pre-Construct Archaeology Monograph 8.

Emery, P.A. 2007, 'Cracking the code: biography and reconstructed stratigraphy at St Pancras burial ground', in Zakrzewski & White 2007, 6–13.

Emery, P.A. & Wooldridge, K. forthcoming, *St Pancras Burial Ground*, London, Gifford Monograph.

Finch, J. 2003, 'A Reformation of meaning: commemoration and remembering the dead in the parish church, 1450–1640', in Gaimster & Gilchrist 2003, 437–49.

Gaimster, D. & Gilchrist, R. (eds) 2003, *The Archaeology of Reformation 1480–1580*, Leeds: Maney.

Gilchrist, R. 2003, 'Dust to dust: revealing the Reformation dead', in Gaimster & Gilchrist 2003, 399–414.

Gilchrist, R. & Sloane, B. 2005 *Requiem: the Medieval Monastic Cemetery in Britain*. London: Museum of London Archaeological Service.

Gittings, C. 1999, 'Sacred and secular: 1558–1660', in Jupp & Gittings 1999, 147–173.

Gittings, C. 2007, 'Eccentric or enlightened? Unusual burial and commemoration in England,1689–1823', *Mortality* 12: 4, 321–49.

Gordon, B. & Marshall, P. (eds) 2003, *The Place of the Dead: Death and Remembrance in Late Medieval and Early Modern Europe,* Cambridge: Cambridge University Press.

Harding, V. 1998, 'Burial on the margin: distance and discrimination in early modern London', in Cox 1998, 54–64.

Houlbrooke, R. 1999, 'The Age of Decency: 1600–1760', in Jupp & Gittings 1999, 174–201.

Jalland, P. 1996, *Death in the Victorian Family*, Oxford: Oxford University Press.

Jupp, P.J & Gittings, C. (eds) 1999, *Death in England: An Illustrated History*, Manchester: Manchester University Press.

Lilley, J.M., Stroud, G., Brothwell, D.R. & Williamson, M.H. 1994, *The Jewish Burial Ground at Jewbury*. The Archaeology of York 12/3, York: York Archaeological Trust.

Litten, J. 1991, *The English Way of Death: The Common Funeral since 1450*, London: Robert Hale.

Loudon, J.C. 1843 (1981 reprint), *On the Laying Out, Planting & Managing of Cemeteries*. Redhill, Surrey: Ivelet.

Lovell, P. & William, M. 1938, 'St. Pancras Old Church', *Survey of London: Volume 19: The parish of St Pancras Part 2: Old St Pancras and Kentish Town,* Victoria County History, 72–95.

MacDonald, M. & Murphy, T.R. 1990, *Sleepless Souls: Suicide in Modern England*. Oxford: Clarendon Press.

Mytum, H. 2004a, *Mortuary Monuments and Burial Grounds of the Historic Period*, New York: Kluwer Academic/Plenum Publishers.

Mytum, H. 2004b, 'A long and complex plot: patterns of family burial in Irish graveyards from the 18th century', *Church Archaeology* 5–6, 31–41.

Mytum, H. & Chapman, K. 2006, 'The origin of the graveyard headstone: some 17th-century examples in Bedfordshire', *Church Archaeology* 7–9, 67–78.

Owen, K. 2006, 'Iconographic representations of mortality and resurrection in 17th-century Gloucestershire', *Church Archaeology* 7–9, 79–96.

Rogers, E.B. 2001, *Landscape Design: A Cultural and Architectural History*, New York: Harry N. Abrams.

Rugg, J. 1998, 'A new burial form and its meanings: cemetery establishment in the first half of the 19th century', in Cox 1998, 44–53.

Sayer, D. 2010, *Ethics and Burial Archaeology*. London: Duckworth.

Sayer, D. 2011, 'Death and the dissenter: group identity and stylistic simplicity as witnessed in 19th-century nonconformist gravestones', *Historical Archaeology*, 45.

Sayer, D. & Symonds J. 2004, 'Lost Congregations: the crisis facing later post-medieval urban burial grounds', *Church Archaeology* 5–6, 55–61.

Stannard, D.E. 1979, *The Puritan Way of Death*, Oxford: Oxford University Press.

Stock, G. 1998a, 'The 18th- and early 19th-century Quaker burial ground at Bathford, Bath and north-east Somerset', in Cox 1998, 144–53.

Stock, G. 1998b, 'Quaker burial: doctrine and practice', in Cox 1998, 129–43.

Stone, G. 2009, 'Sacred landscapes: material evidence of ideological and ethnic choice in Long Island, New York, gravestones 1680–1800', *Historical Archaeology* 43: 1, 142–59.

Sweeney, K.M. 1993, 'Meetinghouses, town houses, and churches: changing perceptions of sacred and secular space in southern New England, 1720–1850', *Winterthur Portfolio* 28: 1, 59–93.

Tarlow, S. 1999, *Bereavement and Commemoration: An Archaeology of Mortality*, Oxford: Blackwell.

Veit, R.F. 2009, '"Resolved to Strike Out a New Path:" consumerism and iconographic change in New Jersey gravestones, 1680–1820', *Historical Archaeology* 43: 1, 115–41.

Walsh, J.P. 1980, 'Holy time and sacred space in Puritan New England', *American Quarterly* 32: 1, 79–95.

Zakrwewski, S.R. & White, W. 2007, *Proceedings of the Seventh Annual Conference of the British Association for Biological Anthropology and Osteoarchaeology*. British Archaeological Reports 1712.

ABBREVIATIONS

MoLSS   Museum of London Specialist Services

The Hidden Material Culture of Death: Coffins and Grave Goods in Late 18th- and Early 19th-Century Sheffield

Diana Mahoney-Swales, Richard O'Neill and Hugh Willmott*

Since 1997 there have been excavations in a number of graveyards in Sheffield that pre-date the 1855 Burial Act. These sites have yielded an important, if limited, resource of coffins, coffin furnishings and grave goods. This material provides an important insight into a broad cross section of the social and religious classes present in Sheffield during the late Georgian and early Victorian period. The purpose of this chapter is to assess the archaeology within the grave in late 18th- to early 19th-century Sheffield to observe what can be inferred about funerary ritual and trade at this time.

INTRODUCTION

In the last decade a number of graveyards pre-dating the 1855 Burial Act, which prohibited further interment within inner-city cemeteries, have been excavated within the centre of Sheffield. These sites – Sheffield Cathedral, St Paul's Church and the two nonconformist burial grounds of The Upper Chapel and Carver Street – provide a limited, but nevertheless important, resource of coffins, coffin furnishings and grave goods. The majority of studies addressing the material culture of the grave in the late 18th and early 19th century concern London, with rare exceptions including St Martin's (Birmingham), Glasgow Cathedral and West Butts Street (Poole).[1] Such paucity of published information from outside of London elevates the importance of the recently excavated cemeteries from Sheffield. The Sheffield excavations were of extra-mural interments, contrasting with the majority of published reports from London and the St Martin's and Glasgow Cathedral publications, which concentrate on the elite burials within crypts and vaults. The archaeological material recovered from within the graves of the Sheffield cemeteries also provides a valuable insight into the burial practices of a broad cross section of the social and religious communities present in Sheffield during the late Georgian and early Victorian period.

The present study builds upon the paper 'Lost congregations: the crisis facing later post-medieval urban burial grounds' in which Sayer and Symonds identified, from a brief appraisal of sites from Sheffield and Barnsley in South Yorkshire, that 'the study of later post-medieval urban burials would benefit from synthesis and analysis at a regional level' to 'establish variations in … funerary practices and associated material culture within and between different congregational groups and different localities'.[2] The purpose of this chapter is to implement such a synthesis and analysis of the mortuary practices visible in the graves of late 18th- and early 19th-century Sheffield to determine whether regional, religious or social variations are identifiable. This chapter demonstrates, via the similarities and differences observed within cemeteries of different denominations, that the archaeology of the grave, particularly in a regional context, is fundamental to studies of post-medieval funerary behaviour. However, such archaeological analysis must be included within a multi-disciplinary approach incorporating osteological research and documentary research of both mortuary behaviour and the social and cultural environment in which it occurred.

HISTORICAL BACKGROUND

Sheffield Cathedral

There has been a parish church on the site of the current cathedral in Sheffield since at least the 12th century. The earliest recorded dedication of the church is to St Peter, although at some point after the Reformation its dedication was changed to Holy Trinity, and in the early 19th century it was changed again, this time to St Peter and St Paul, the name by which it continues to be known. The parish church was granted cathedral status with the formation of the new Diocese of Sheffield in 1914 and further rebuilding and extension followed.[3] Surviving church registers date from 1560 but it is a certainty that, as the only parish church in Sheffield, there was a longer history of burial at the site. There are 34,186 records of burials at the church between 1813 and 1855 alone, the last registered burial being that of Mary Wagg, a widow, on 10 April 1855.[4]

A total of 100 graves containing the articulated remains of 186 individuals, including adult males and females and children, was recovered from a series of archaeological works undertaken between 1999 and 2006. The burials were predominantly earth-cut graves orientated west–east with some distinct north–south rows visible. Owing to later truncation, often all that remained to be excavated was the base of the grave, from which no skeletal remains were recoverable. As a result of the constant recutting of the graves and reworking of the graveyard soil it was not possible to assign sub-phases within the cemetery based on stratigraphic relationships alone or to phase graves on the basis of artefacts contained within them. Analysis of the skeletal remains and coffin furnishings has suggested that this part of the cemetery served a predominantly working-class population. This inference is supported by the burial register, which lists labourers, joiners, file-cutters and scissor-smiths among the dead in this area.

Carver Street

The Methodist chapel was built between 1804 and 1805 and was subsequently extended in 1883. The chapel, now a Grade 1 Listed Building, quickly gained a reputation as a centre for Methodism and hosted the National Methodist Conference eleven times during the 19th century. The burial records date from 1806 to 1855. Carver Street represents the only major burial ground for the nonconformist population of Sheffield for the first half of the 19th century, and contained an estimated 1,600 inhumations.[5] The burial registers indicate that the Carver Street inhumations represent a good cross section of Sheffield's 19th-century population, with both significant public figures and members of the working class being interred there. Burial within this cemetery slowed with the opening of the General Cemetery, an extra-mural burial ground, in 1836 and ended with the passing of the 1855 Burial

Grounds Act. Archaeological work undertaken in 1999 recovered the articulated remains of 101 individuals and a minimum of 25–30 disarticulated skeletons from 47 earth-cut graves.

The Upper Chapel

The Unitarian chapel was constructed in 1700 and is believed to have been the earliest brick building in Sheffield, although most of the present building dates from its enlargement in 1848. Analysis of the Burial Register and a survey of the inscriptions on the surviving gravestones suggest that burial occurred in The Upper Chapel burial ground between 1717 and 1858. An archaeological watching brief and evaluation carried out during 2006 and 2007 resulted in the excavation of four earth-cut graves that were previously disturbed by construction work, or were at risk of such disturbance. These represent a very small proportion of the 160 graves recorded by the burial plans and registers.[6] However, the small size of this assemblage does not invalidate its importance in terms of identifying aspects of status and burial provision.

St Paul's

By the beginning of the 18th century the parish church of St Peter was considered insufficient for Sheffield's expanding population and a Protestant dissenter and local goldsmith, Robert Downs, funded the construction of a new church, which was completed in 1720. The church was constructed in a baroque style reminiscent of many London and continental churches. Following disputes over patronage with the parish church, Downs applied for permission to use the building as a nonconformist meeting house in 1739. The church was consecrated in 1740 and burials commenced in 1743.[7] Records suggest that St Paul's was well funded, with contributions from many of Sheffield's wealthier families. Many well-known local figures were interred in the graveyard, including at least three former Master Cutlers and Thomas Boulsover (inventor of Old Sheffield Plate).[8] In excess of 8,000 burials had been undertaken in this burial ground by the 1850s, the majority of which were transferred to the Abbey Lane cemetery in the 1930s.[9] Archaeological work undertaken in the late 1990s recovered the skeletal remains of sixteen individuals and wooden coffins from both earth-cut and brick-lined shaft graves.[10] The locations of these burial grounds within Sheffield City Centre are displayed in Fig. 12.1.

BURIAL ARCHAEOLOGY OF THE SHEFFIELD CEMETERIES

The majority of burials within the Sheffield cemeteries consisted of earth-cut graves. However, from Sheffield Cathedral, Carver Street and St Paul's occasional brick- or stone-lined shaft-graves, containing both single and occasionally multiple interments, were unearthed. All of these cemeteries have produced examples of grave cuts containing individuals stacked horizontally, which may represent either a necessity due to limitations of available space or a desire to bury related individuals within the same grave. Shaft graves are often associated with family groups, and the family focus of such structures is represented at Carver Street by the interment of William and James Simpson, identified by their coffin plates, within the same grave cut. At The Upper Chapel there was also evidence for large burial plots for the interment of several individuals, probably family groups. For example, the backfill of one large grave contained two later burials, which were deliberately cut within the outline of the original grave. A large stone slab structure covered the two later

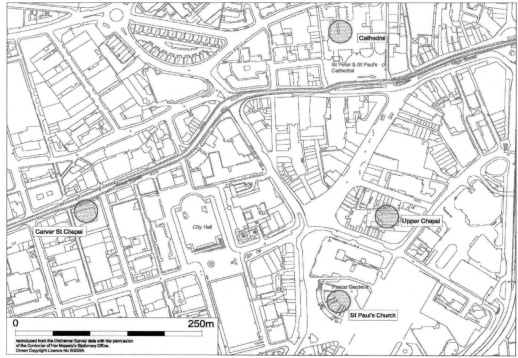

Figure 12.1. Map showing the location of the Sheffield Burial Grounds.
© Ordnance Survey (Swales Geomatics 2010).

graves, indicating that it was desired that the graves be regarded as one feature, if not a single event. The well-organized and spacious layout of this cemetery demonstrates that it had a larger capacity for burial than it contained; therefore, the recutting was not a consequence of overcrowding but of the personal choice of family burial. This interpretation is supported by the inscription upon a gravestone associated with one multiple occupant grave, which recorded the death of five individuals: a husband, wife and two sons sharing the same surname, and an additional individual with a different surname described as a widow.

All the coffins from the Sheffield cemeteries that could be identified were single-case, single-break wooden coffins, which were characteristic of this period.[11] These coffins consisted of single wooden cases which were widest across the shoulders, from which point they narrowed towards the opposing extremities of the head and feet with a single break. The majority of coffins recovered from Sheffield Cathedral were manufactured from elm, whereas those recovered from Carver Street and The Upper Chapel were mostly made with oak lids and sides and scot's pine or elm base boards.[12] The burials recovered from St Paul's were all interred in wooden coffins but no further interpretation of the type of wood or construction was possible owing to the poor levels of preservation. Elm was traditionally used for the manufacture of coffins, whereas oak, which was less accessible and therefore more expensive, was used only occasionally 'for exceptionally important interments'.[13]

Therefore, the use of oak at Carver Street and The Upper Chapel on what would have been the only visible surfaces of the coffins during the funerary process may be indicative of a 'display' purpose intended to project an image of wealth.

The excellent preservation of wooden coffins recovered from The Upper Chapel enabled detailed observations of their construction to be made. The shoulders of the side panels were made by kerfing, which involved the removal of a triangular wedge of wood from the inner surface so that the wood could be bent inwards, forming an invisible joint. No dovetailing or mortise and tenon joints were observed. This, and the scarcity of nails, may indicate the use of a pitch or glue to adhere the sides, base and lids together. A separate ridge of wood located upon the outer rim of the superior edge of the side panels of the coffin[14] would have formed a seal, securing the lid without the use of nails. There is also evidence that coffins from three of these sites were upholstered externally. Textile was adhered to the surface of depositum plates recovered from both Sheffield Cathedral and Carver Street. The fabric recovered from Sheffield Cathedral was sufficiently well preserved to be identified as a dark green velvet or baize with the outline of a lid motif or escutcheons stained onto its surface. Round-headed upholstery studs, typically used to affix upholstery to the outside of the wooden coffin, were recovered from Sheffield Cathedral, Carver Street and The Upper Chapel. Black coffin-lace, made from thin rolled-out lead or, occasionally, composed of copper alloy, was also recovered from Sheffield Cathedral.

When the type of coffin fitting recovered from the Sheffield cemeteries was discernable, the Christ Church, Spitalfields catalogue was consulted.[15] The nearly 1,000 coffin fittings recovered from the crypts at Christ Church, Spitalfields, constitute an important corpus from which to identify contemporary styles of coffin furnishings and fittings. However, it is not a comprehensive list and, therefore, any new styles observed in the Sheffield cemeteries were documented and compared with objects from other contemporary cemetery sites.

Grips and grip plates (the coffin handle and the decorative plate attached to the coffin behind the handle) were a common feature of burials within the Sheffield cemeteries. Both objects ranged from plain geometric shapes to highly decorative designs, depicting such images as cherubs and flowers. All the grips recovered from the Sheffield cemeteries were made of iron. The grip plates were also predominantly iron, save for occasional tin-alloy examples recovered from Sheffield Cathedral.

Only five grips and three grip plate designs were identifiable from Sheffield Cathedral. The majority of grips recovered from Sheffield Cathedral were undecorated and consistent with grip types 1, 2a and 2b from Spitalfields. One grip displayed a partial fragment of a cherub motif, and a second displayed a flower motif comparable with those recorded on grip types 4 and 5 within the Spitalfields catalogue, respectively. The fourth grip type displayed a large sphere in the centre of the horizontal bar, and was directly comparable to grip type 3 from Kingston-upon-Thames. The final grip type was similar, but possessed two smaller spheres on either side of the larger central sphere (Fig. 12.2a). This design was comparable with grip type 6 from Kingston-upon-Thames.

The most commonly occurring grip plate recovered from Sheffield Cathedral was a plain design comparable to type 13 from Kingston-upon-Thames. This grip plate consisted of a simple disc located at either end of the grip, to which the stop of the grip socket was attached.[16] Although this grip plate was visible in sixteen graves and one unstratified deposit its prevalence may be more a consequence of selective preservation than individual choice. The smaller surface area, smooth surface and thickness would result in less oxidisa-

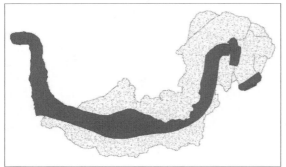

Figure 12.2. a) Grip displaying
central sphere with adjacent spheres.
b) Cherub motif grip plate.
© Swales Geomatics 2010.

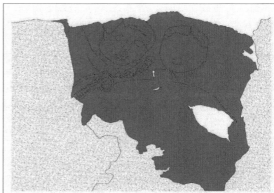

tion, corrosion and fragmentation, making this grip plate more likely to survive than the more fragile patterned grip plates. The three remaining grip plate types recovered from Sheffield Cathedral were comparable with types 5, 3 and 17 from Spitalfields. These plates consisted of a plain plate with an undulating outline and a more decorative patterned plate featuring the aforementioned cherub motif seen upon the grips from Sheffield Cathedral (Fig. 12.2b). Only fragments of unrecognizable iron grip plates – owing to their extreme corrosion – were recovered from Carver Street, and no evidence for grips or grip plates was recovered from The Upper Chapel or St Paul's.

Breastplates, or depositum plates, were plain or decorated plates placed upon the wooden or upholstered surface of the coffin lid, in the chest area. These plates documented the identity of the deceased. There appear to have been two types of depositum plates circulating within South Yorkshire during the period of occupation of the Sheffield cemeteries. The first were ornate die-stamped plates made from iron or tin or, alternatively, iron coated with tin, which gave a silvered effect. These decorative plates documented the name of the deceased, the date of death and, in some instances, occupation or a brief memorial inscription. The second type consisted of plain base-metal plates which simply provided the name of the deceased and date of death.

The depositum plates from Sheffield Cathedral were made predominantly from iron, but some were tin or displayed tin-plating. Fragments of plain base-metal plates were also recovered. The depositum plates from Sheffield Cathedral were similar to the designs present at Spitalfields, but none were exact matches. For example, the crown and tree pattern from Sheffield Cathedral was very clearly visible and resembled several examples from Spitalfields, but was not identifiable as any one specific design from that assemblage. Fragments of a depositum plate recovered from an evaluation trench resembled plates 5, 48 and 103 from Spitalfields, but did not match any of these designs absolutely. From Sheffield Cathedral only one of the burials could be identified from epigraphic evidence. A lead depositum plate was discovered belonging to Selina Webster, a spinster of Scotland Street, who died on 13 September 1845 aged 51 years (Fig. 12.3a). A further two name plates exhibited discernable fragments of text which were possibly surnames. Leaf patterning and the letters **WSNA / - Years** were etched upon one lead depositum plate and painted black (Fig. 12.3b). Analysis of the burial register suggested this was from the surname 'Dewsnap' or 'Dewsnapp', for which there were eighty entries and one entry respectively. These individuals were recorded as being buried within this cemetery between 1813 and 1849. **GOS** was etched upon a lead plate fragment recovered from a second grave. Analysis of the burial register suggested these letters represented the surname 'Gosling' or 'Gossling', for which there were only nine entries and one entry respectively, recorded as being buried within this cemetery between 1828 and 1851.

The most common depositum plates recovered from Carver Street were thin iron plates die-stamped with complex designs. Unfortunately, only unidentifiable fragments of the patterns survived, preventing further interpretation. However, three plain rectangular tin depositum plates with cut-out corners and rolled-under edges were recovered, upon which the identity of the deceased could be discerned as William Simpson, James Simpson and Mary Rowbotham (Fig. 12.3c). William and James Simpson were interred within the same grave cut, further supporting the interpretation that multiple interment graves were often family groups. Fabric was adhered to the reverse of Mary Rowbotham's depositum plate, confirming the presence of upholstered coffins at Carver Street.

The depositum plates recovered from St Paul's were made from tin and displayed no form of decorative pattern upon the surface. From them the names of five individuals were discernable (John Froggatt, John Pye, George [Hi]gginbotham, Thomas Jepson and Peter Milner). The plain tin depositum plates interred with these individuals varied in outline, including a round-edged rectangle, a shield shape and a square plate with cut-out corners (Figs 12.3d–e). Several of the St Paul's depositum plates were similar in profile to what Litten describes as 'heraldic provision'. The use of heraldic imagery could be interpreted as emulation of the wealth and respectability of the social elite. However, the age and sex of the deceased rarely matched the heraldic shape of the depositum plate, a common occurrence at the time according to Litten.[17] An example of such inconsistency was the provision of the shield plate for Thomas Jepson, who died at the mature age of 67. In heraldic tradition the shield is associated with boys or young men, not elderly males, suggesting that its inclusion within the graves of St Paul's was a consequence of aesthetics, not heraldic meaning.

Numerous small fragments of thin die-stamped plate were recovered from Sheffield Cathedral and Carver Street; however, they were undiagnostic and too small to determine if they represented depositum plates, lid motifs or escutcheons. There was no definitive evidence of lid motifs and escutcheons, but owing to the poor levels of preservation at Sheffield Cathedral and Carver Street this does not prove their non-existence. No plate fragments of any form were recovered from The Upper Chapel.

a

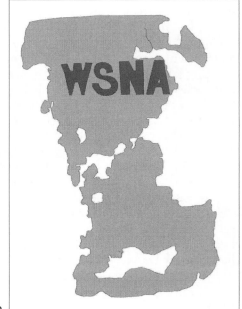

b

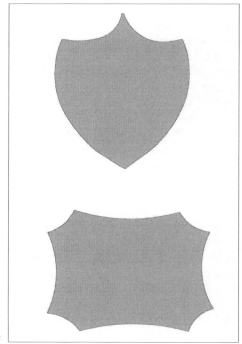

c

Figure 12.3. a) Selina Webster depositum plate. b) Depositum plate for 'Dewsnap' or 'Dewsnapp'. c-e) Variation in depositum plate designs recovered from Sheffield cemeteries. © Swales Geomatics 2010.

d-e

ARTEFACTS WITHIN THE GRAVE

An important aspect of burial archaeology is the inclusion of material within the coffin and the grave. Typically the term 'grave goods' refers to objects placed deliberately within the grave as part of the funerary process. Examples include objects such as Bibles and heirlooms. However, within this paper the term 'grave goods' is used to represent *any* object present within the grave or coffin which is not directly associated with the construction and decoration of the coffin. Therefore, objects such as buttons are included because they are associated with the funerary practice of dressing the deceased and are not a physical component of the coffin.

A deposit of wood chippings found below the coffin in a grave from The Upper Chapel may have been employed to absorb any odours or liquid matter that may have exuded from within the coffin into the surrounding grave fill. This would have kept the interior of the coffin clear for purposes of display, if the body was to be laid out in the open coffin prior to burial. The coffins from St Paul's, however, were almost completely filled with sawdust and wood-shavings.[18] There are several possible alternative explanations for this. The visibility of sawdust within the open coffin while the body was lain out perhaps did not concern the bereaved, or the sawdust may have been contained within the upholstery lining or a mattress within the coffin, which no longer survived. Alternatively, the remaining space in the coffin may have been filled with sawdust and wood shavings when the coffin was sealed, immediately prior to burial. Further evidence for the inclusion of organic matter within burials was observed in the form of laurel and ash leaves included in one grave from St Paul's. These possibly represented the remains of a wreath.[19]

All of the shroud pins recovered from Sheffield Cathedral, Carver Street and St Paul's were standard copper-alloy globular- or wrapped-headed dressmaker's pins. In several graves from Sheffield Cathedral and Carver Street shroud pins were found alongside small fabric fragments and minor dress accessories such as small bone buttons. A testament to the level of preservation of archaeological material recovered from The Upper Chapel is the recovery of seven perfectly preserved gold-coloured wrapped-headed shroud pins. X-ray fluorescence analysis of one of the pins revealed they were composed of a brass type commonly utilized for the manufacture of thin wire and pins, colloquially described as 'yellow brass' because of its golden colour.[20] A number of shroud pins recovered from Carver Street were recorded as 'copper alloy ... with a tinned surface', which would have resulted in a silvered effect, as seen among the depositum and grip plates from Sheffield Cathedral and Carver Street.[21] Within published site reports for this period there is either no mention of the shroud pins or they are described simply as being made of copper alloy.[22] The dearth of detailed published information on 'yellow brass' and 'tinned' shroud pins prevents definitive assessment of whether the use of such materials was an economic or stylistic decision, or whether the 'yellow brass' and 'tinned' appearance may simply have been lost in the archaeological record. It is probable that other copper-alloy shroud pins recovered during excavations in Sheffield and beyond were made from these materials, but were too heavily eroded and oxidized to determine their original colour. Consequently, the recovery of 'yellow brass' and 'tinned' pins from The Upper Chapel and Carver Street may be a consequence of the exceptional levels of preservation.

Buttons found at both Carver Street and Sheffield Cathedral may have derived from both day-clothes or fastening shrouds, both of which have been found in graves throughout

England, with shroud burials being the more common.[23] Of the twenty-one graves from Sheffield Cathedral which contained buttons, fourteen had only a single example. The buttons were made predominantly from bone, but wood and copper-alloy examples were also recovered. The same types of button were recovered from seven graves at Carver Street. It is probable that these buttons derived from the front of a shroud, which was typically cut to the central chest area and secured by either cloth ties or buttons.[24] In ten of these graves from Sheffield Cathedral and four from Carver Street shroud pins were found alongside buttons, supporting the interpretation that the buttons derived from shrouds. In one instance from Sheffield Cathedral the button was clearly located upon the left wrist, suggesting either that it derived from the sleeve of a tailored sleeve shroud, examples of which were recovered from Spitalfields,[25] or from the cuff of a shirt. Litten states that the body of the deceased was normally clothed in textiles provided by the undertaker and that it was unusual for the deceased to be buried in their own clothes.[26] However, at Christ Church, Spitalfields, sixteen individuals were recorded with their own garments, sometimes under a shroud.[27] In addition, an adult burial from the Cross Bones Burial Ground, Southwark, was buried in a shirt, trousers and boots.[28] These examples suggest that burial in normal clothes, or normal clothes and a shroud, although not a frequent occurrence, was not wholly exceptional. Therefore, it is possible that buttons recovered from the Sheffield Cemeteries represent either burial in normal day clothes, burial in shrouds or a combination of the two. No buttons were recovered from The Upper Chapel, only shroud pins, which may suggest that the shrouds used in Sheffield may not have utilized buttons as fastenings, implying that the buttons recovered from Sheffield Cathedral and Carver Street do in fact represent clothed burials. Alternatively, the lack of buttons from The Upper Chapel either may be due to the small sample size or is a feature specific to the burials within this burial ground. Therefore, any inference is highly speculative and requires more evidence.

Several graves from Sheffield Cathedral contained jewellery that had been placed with or adorned the deceased. The most common jewellery artefacts recovered were glass beads (Fig. 12.4). Two coffins from within the same grave cut contained 30 and 34 opaque rose-coloured small glass beads. A further two graves contained 76 and 30 black beads each. These beads indicated necklaces and bracelets, but without the preservation of the clasps or the total number of beads, it was impossible to clearly ascertain which. An almost complete necklace recovered from St Martin's cemetery in Birmingham was made up of approximately 300 glass beads similar to those observed at Sheffield Cathedral.[29] Jewellery was also recovered from Sheffield Cathedral in the form of a small metal plate closely resembling the backing of a brooch. A single copper-alloy earring with an undeterminable wave or leaf pattern upon it and two silver or silver-plated hoop earrings (too eroded to determine which) were also recovered from Sheffield Cathedral. The inclusion of silver or silver-plated earrings does not necessarily denote that the deceased individual was wealthy, as they may have been an heirloom. No evidence of jewellery was recovered from Carver Street, St Paul's or The Upper Chapel.

Poorly preserved copper-alloy coins and an identifiable George III penny were found within graves at Sheffield Cathedral. The George III penny, dating from 1760–1820, had been placed over the right eye socket of an elderly adult male. Four copper coins were found in graves in both the Carver Street and St Paul's cemeteries. It is possible that these are redeposited material; however, the group of four copper coins found adjacent to the head

Figure 12.4. Beads. © R. O'Neill 2010.

of one skeleton at St Paul's appeared to the excavator to have been deliberately placed.[30] Could this be the standard value of money expected to be interred with the deceased for this period? It is interesting that both cemeteries contain graves containing four copper coins when little or no coinage was recovered during the rest of the excavations.

At Sheffield Cathedral several graves contained objects that may have been placed with the deceased, including a bone knife handle, bone comb and a large thin key. Some graves contained ceramic wig curlers and ceramic and stone marbles. A bone knife handle was also recovered from Carver Street. From St Paul's the remains of a chisel were found within a coffin beneath the head of the deceased. However, it is unclear whether this was an oversight on the part of the coffin-maker or a tribute to the trade of that individual. No grave goods were recovered from The Upper Chapel.[31]

DISCUSSION

Cultural trends, industrialization, technological developments, morality, economic pride, religious doctrine and attitudes to public health have all been argued as being major influences upon burial ritual in the late 18th and early 19th century.[32] Julie Rugg and James

Stevenson Curl emphasise the influence of Romantic, Evangelical and Gothic literary and artistic movements upon attitudes towards death.[33] However, both these authors concentrate their discussions upon standing sculptures, monuments and mausoleums, with no reference to the comparable advances occurring within the grave. Such idealization of death was visible within the grave in the Sheffield cemeteries by the use of Romantic images such as the cherub, tree, crown and flowers upon grips and grip plates from Carver Street and Sheffield Cathedral. The artefacts recovered from Sheffield are comparable to those recovered from cemetery sites throughout Britain. Therefore, the choice of upholstered coffins and the cherub motif recovered from Carver Street and Sheffield Cathedral reflect a larger, national cultural trend, possibly influenced by the aforementioned artistic and literary movements of the period, rather than a regionally distinct practice.[34]

It has been claimed by authors such as Bell and Richmond that the onset of industrialization was responsible for the increased elaboration in funerary display for a number of reasons.[35] Firstly, industrialization resulted in increased urban mortality rates and, consequently, the demand for coffins and their associated furnishings. These demands were met by technological developments such as Thomas Pickering's 1769 patented power-assisted method for raising patterns in sheet iron.[36] This enabled the mass production and subsequent reduction in cost of the more elaborate coffin furniture designs, making them more affordable for the common burial. Such technological developments are represented by elaborate stamped designs on fragments of depositum and grip plates from Sheffield Cathedral and Carver Street. The presence of the cherub motif and identical grips at these sites and others – including Glasgow Cathedral, Spitalfields and St Martin's, Birmingham – demonstrates the availability of these objects throughout Britain.[37] The ubiquity of this cherub motif, the production of trade catalogues advertising coffin furnishings and improved transport links promoted the spread of specific designs across the country, increasing their accessibility spatially as well as economically.[38] The increased economic availability is witnessed in Sheffield through the common presence of fragments of die-stamped plate iron from Carver Street and Sheffield Cathedral which, according to the burial registers, served a contributing population predominantly of skilled workers and labourers, not landed gentry and aristocrats.

Secondly, industrialization created a prosperous middle class who utilized death as an 'exhibition of material success'.[39] Affluence was, it has been suggested, equated with respectability, and therefore a sequence of emulation arose, with the upper classes being emulated by the middle classes who in turn were emulated by the lower classes.[40] Elaborate mass-produced coffin furniture displayed aspirational, as well as actual, wealth, imparting in death an impression of wealth and, therefore, respectability not attainable in life. It must be considered, however, that the presence of die-stamped grip plates displaying the cherub motif in the burial assemblages of Sheffield Cathedral and Carver Street may be representative of higher- and middle-class burials included within these burial grounds, even if these social groups were not the dominant contributing population. All the sites documenting elaborate coffin furnishings contain high-status intra-mural burials, which bias interpretation of the archaeology of the grave. For example, the data presented in the St Martin's publication represents the vaults and brick-lined graves only, as the iron material from the extra-mural earth-cut graves was too corroded to enable analysis.[41] It may be that the desire and potential to emulate the social elite was confined to the middle classes. Testimonies of paupers and the poor in Hulme, Lancashire and Brixworth, Northamptonshire, in the

1830s reveal that they fought strongly for their 'rights' to a pauper funeral. Such a funeral included 'the provision of a woollen shroud, nursing expenses incurred to wash and lay out a body, a basic wooden coffin, a simple Christian service and the burial itself'.[42] This implies that such pauper funerals were deemed sufficient, and emphasizes the importance of such practices as the laying-out of the body to the poorer classes.

Religious doctrine was, theoretically, influential in the choice of burial provisioning. For example, it has been suggested that overt displays of wealth through elaborate coffin furnishings opposed nonconformist Quaker, Baptist and Methodist doctrine.[43] However, highly decorated coffins have been observed at several nonconformist sites, such as the Quaker burial grounds at Kingston-upon-Thames and Bathford, Somerset.[44] The contrasting cemeteries of Sheffield Cathedral and Carver Street share similar burial practices, including the use of the cherub motif on grip plates. The ubiquity of decorative grips and grip plates and their relative inexpense, enabled by mass production, meant that such grips may not necessarily have been regarded as any more ostentatious than their unadorned equivalents. It is possible that both conformist and nonconformist burials in Sheffield were provided by the same tradesmen, and therefore each denomination chose similar burial provision. Alternatively, the nonconformist Methodist burials may have occurred in the Sheffield Cathedral cemetery prior to the establishment of the Carver Street burial ground, and possibly afterwards, creating a similar archaeological material assemblage.

The Baptist burial ground of West Butts Street, Poole, does appear to display discipline in the plain nature of the burial assemblage, which employed six unadorned or modestly decorated grip and grip plate designs, in contrast with those at Kingston-upon-Thames and Bathford.[45] The coffin furnishings from Poole were utilitarian, not decorative. For example, the grips are the same as those used in the area for household furnishings.[46] Similarly, the Baptist burials from the Unitarian Upper Chapel also appear very plain. However, the contrast with funerary display in other cemeteries should not be overstated. Indeed, the Anglican burial ground of St Paul's also lacks elaborate coffin furnishings, while the most commonly occurring grips and grip plates from Sheffield Cathedral and Carver Street are in fact plain geometric shapes. In the Anglican cemetery at St Martin's, Birmingham, a popular design of grip plate was also a plain geometric shape (dated to 1837), which the excavators propose reflects the late Victorian trend towards less ornate funerals. Such a cultural shift, symbolizing the rejection of increasingly elaborate ostentation, befits Cannon's cycle of 'Expressive Redundancy' whereby a shift towards simplicity by higher-status social groups occurs as part of a long-term cycle of expressive elaboration, redundancy, decline and development.[47] Consequently, it is difficult to ascertain whether the choices observed represent religious, social, economic or cultural influences. However, the lack of phasing for the Sheffield interments and the scarcity of identifiable coffin furnishings prevents further discussion of the decline in elaboration over time during the cemeteries' periods of use.

Bashford and Sibun suggest that wealth may be expressed in the materials used in the construction of the coffin and in the presence of family vaults and shaft-graves in nonconformist cemeteries.[48] Such use of expensive materials in nonconformist burials is apparent in the construction of the coffins at Carver Street and The Upper Chapel. Support for the argument that such materials are used for display and not their functional benefits is provided by the use of pine bases, indicating that the oak lids and sides were solely for display. The populations interred within these oak coffins may have been connected with cabinet makers and the other industries associated with the construction of coffins and their furnishings. Such connections with skilled tradesmen would have reduced the cost of coffin hardware and workmanship. The material utilized appears to be a greater indicator of wealth than the actual designs employed in both the Anglican and nonconformist burial assemblages from Sheffield. The predominantly labouring classes buried at Sheffield Cathedral, as suggested by the entries in the Burial Register, may have utilized iron grips, grip plates and depositum plates, whereas the wealthier denizens of St Paul's, as suggested by the high class of individuals documented to have been interred within its cemetery, still constructed functional features of the coffin, such as grips, from iron but used a tin alloy for the depositum plates. However, such generalizations about the cemetery populations as a whole cannot be proven until artefacts are recovered from named individuals of known occupation and status. Nevertheless, some support for this argument is provided from St Martin's, where the grips and grip plates from the crypts were predominantly made from copper alloy, whereas those recovered from the extra-mural earth-cut graves were all iron.[49]

Finally, common attitudes to public health and infection may have influenced late 18th- and early 19th-century burial practices. The absence of lead coffins from the Sheffield cemeteries may be because such coffins were generally used only in high-status burials until they became compulsory for intra-mural burials from 1813 because of health fears associated with the smell released during the reopening of burial vaults and brick-lined graves.[50] The biggest health fears at this time revolved around diseases, such as cholera, which were then believed to be airborne. Infection in general was believed to 'hang in the air like an invisible mist' and, therefore, the detection of smells emanating from the deceased 'caused great concern'.[51] As the Sheffield interments are extra-mural the odours would have been less contained and able to dissipate into the soil and surrounding fresh air more readily. Nonetheless, the attempted airtight construction of coffins from the Upper Chapel and the presence of sawdust from the Upper Chapel and St Paul's may indicate alternative solutions for such concerns.

CONCLUSION

The archaeology of the grave is an often neglected, under-documented aspect of post-medieval archaeology, owing to poor preservation of the material itself and perhaps limited post-excavation budgets. However, it is apparent from the present study and those mentioned throughout this chapter that the provisioning of burials in Britain was influenced by factors including socio-economic status, religious doctrine, cultural trends, pragmatism and the increased availability of burial materials. These influences appear to be united by two main factors in the Sheffield cemeteries: the *accessibility* of the financial, practical and decorative resources for the burial and the *desire* to utilize them. The work presented here is very much in its embryonic stages and this chapter presents an introduction to the material recovered from Sheffield. This material, though limited, is an important resource, because it includes not only nonconformist burial grounds, of which few have been published, but extra-mural burials as well. To understand further the development of the funerary trade, it is important that the archaeology of the grave is studied in a regional and multi-disciplinary context. Future research on the Sheffield cemeteries needs to incorporate examination of burial registers, trade catalogues, local newspapers and literary sources; evidence for trade links with other towns needs to be addressed; and analysis of memorial stones needs to be combined with the related osteological data to truly determine the factors influencing burial practices in South Yorkshire. As more regional studies are undertaken and published a greater understanding of the factors influencing burial choices in the 18th and 19th century will be attained.

NOTES

*   The archaeological excavations which provided the material for this paper were undertaken by ARCUS (Archaeological Research and Consultancy, University of Sheffield) and were funded by Tilbury Douglas; P.J. Brown and Son Ltd, Sheffield Cathedral Church of St Peter and St Paul and Sheffield City Council. The authors would like to thank Chris Swales, Paul Belford, Annsofie Witkin, Dawn Hadley, Jim Symonds, Bridget Mosley, Lauren McIntyre, Maarit Katila, Christie Cox, Sheffield Local Studies Library, Sheffield Archives, South Yorkshire Archaeology Service, Chris Moore and ARCUS staff who helped with the excavations and post-excavation analysis.

1.   Brickley & Buteaux 2006; Richmond 1999; McKinley 2008.
2.   Sayer & Symonds 2004, 55.
3.   O'Neill *et al.* 2007.
4.   O'Neill *et al.* 2007.
5.   Hunter 1869; Belford & Witkin 2000.
6.   Baker 2008.
7.   Sayer & Symonds 2004, 56.
8.   Belford & Witkin 2000.
9.   Belford & Witkin 2000.
10. O'Neill *et al.* 2007.
11. Hancox 2006, 152.
12. McIntyre & Willmott 2003; Baker 2008.
13. Litten 1991, 90–2.
14. Baker 2008.
15. Reeve & Adams 1993.
16. Stock 1998, 150.
17. Litten 1998, 15.
18. Belford & Witkin 2000, 38.
19. Belford & Witkin 2000, 38.
20. Baker 2008.
21. McIntyre & Willmott 2003, 21.

22. Fritz 1995; Litten 1991; Reeve & Adams 1993; Cowie *et al.* 2008, 35–7.
23. Reeve & Adams 1993; Janaway 1998, 18; Brickley & Miles 1999, 27.
24. McIntyre & Willmott 2003, 32; Janaway 1993, 107.
25. Janaway 1993, 104–12.
26. Litten 1991.
27. Reeve & Adams 1993; Janaway 1998, 18.
28. Brickley & Miles 1999, 27.
29. Hancox 2006, 180.
30. Belford & Witkin 2000, 38.
31. Baker 2008.
32. Bell 1990; Rugg 1999, 202; Curl 2000, 1–5; Mytum 1989, 295; Richmond 1999.
33. Rugg 1999, 202; Curl 2000, 1–5.
34. Bell 1990.
35. Bell 1990; Richmond 1999.
36. Litten 1991, 106.
37. Richmond 1999; Reeve & Adams 1993; Brickley & Buteaux 2006.
38. Fritz 1995; Gale 2006, 163.
39. Mytum 1989, 295.
40. Richmond 1999, 145.
41. Brickley & Buteaux 2006, 152.
42. Hurren & King 2005, 325.
43. Stock 1998, 133; McKinley 2008.
44. Bashford & Sibun 2007, 130; Boore 1998.
45. McKinley 2008.
46. McKinley 2008, 47.
47. Cannon 1989; Parker-Pearson 1999, 43.
48. Mahoney 2005; Bashford & Sibun 2007, 130.
49. Brickley & Buteaux 2006, 152.
50. Cox 1996; Adams & Reeve 1987; Litten 1991, 101.
51. Wood 1995, 119; Mytum 1989, 288–9.

BIBLIOGRAPHY

Adams, M. & Reeve, J. 1987, 'Excavations at Christ Church, Spitalfields 1984–6', *Antiquity* 61, 247–56.

Baker, S. 2008, 'Upper Chapel, Norfolk Street, Sheffield', unpublished ARCUS rep. 732f.3(1).

Bashford, L. & Sibun, L. 2007, 'Excavations at the Quaker Burial Ground, Kingston-upon-Thames, London', *Post-Medieval Archaeology* 41:1, 100–54.

Belford, P. & Witkin, A. 2000, 'Archaeological Recording and Osteological Analysis of Human Remains from the Site of the Graveyard of St Paul's Church, Pinstone Street, Sheffield', unpublished ARCUS rep. 323f.

Bell, E.L. 1990, 'The historical archaeology of mortuary behaviour: coffin hardware from Uxbridge, Massachusetts', *Historical Archaeology* 24:3, 54–78.

Boore, E. 1998, 'Burial vaults and coffin furniture in the West Country', in Cox 1998, 67–84.

Brickley, M. & Buteux, S. 2006, *St Martin's Uncovered: Investigations in the Churchyard of St. Martin's-in-the-Bull-Ring, Birmingham,* Oxford: Oxbow Books.

Brickley, M. & Miles, A. 1999, *The Cross Bones Burial Ground, Redcross Way Southwark London: Archaeological Excavations (1991–1998),* MOLAS Monograph 3, London: Museum of London Archaeology Service.

Cannon, A. 1989, 'The historical dimension in mortuary expressions of status and sentiment', *Current Archaeology* 30:4, 437–47.

Cowie, R., Bekvalac, J. & Kausmally, T. 2008, *Late 17th- to 19th-Century Burial and Earlier Occupation at All Saints, Chelsea Old Church, Royal Borough of Kensington and Chelsea,* MOLAS Archaeology Studies Series 18, London: Museum of London Archaeology Service.

Cox, M. 1996, *Life and Death in Spitalfields 1700–1850,* York: Council for British Archaeology.

Cox, M. (ed.) 1998, *Grave Concerns: Death and Burial in England 1700–1850.* Council for British Archaeology Research Report 113, York: Council for British Archaeology.

Curl, J.S. 2000, *The Victorian Celebration of Death* Stroud: Sutton Publishing.

Downes, J. & Pollard, T. (eds) 1999, *The Loved Body's Corruption: Archaeological Contributions to the Study of Human Mortality,* Scottish Archaeological Forum: Cruithne Press.

Fritz, P. 1995, 'The undertaking trade in England: its origins and early development, 1660–1830', *Eighteenth-Century Studies* 28:2, 241–53.

Gale, R. 2006, 'Coffins and coffin furniture', in Brickley & Buteux 2006, 161–3.

Hancox, E. 2006, 'Coffins and coffin furniture', in Brickley& Buteux 2006, 152–161.

Hunter, J. 1869 (revised by A. Garry from 1819 edition), *Hallamshire: The History and Topography of the Parish of Sheffield in the County of York,* Sheffield, Pawson and Brailsford.

Hurren, E. & King, S. 2005, 'Begging for burial': form, function and conflict in nineteenth-century pauper burial', *Social History* 30:3, 321–41.

Janaway, R. 1993, 'The textiles', in Reeves & Adams 1993, 93–119.

Janaway, R. 1998, 'An introductory guide to textiles from 18th and 19th century burials', in Cox 1998, 17–32.

Jupp, P.C. & Gittings, C. (eds) 1999, *Death in England: An Illustrated History,* Manchester: Manchester University Press.

Litten, J. 1991, *The English Way of Death: The Common Funeral since 1450,* London: Hale.

Litten, J. 1998, 'The English funeral 1700–1850', in Cox 1998, 3–16.

Mahoney, D.L. 2005, 'Analysis of Quaker Inhumations from the Friends' Burial Ground, Vancouver Centre, Kings Lynn Excavation Report', unpublished Oxford Archaeology rep.

McIntyre, L. & Willmott, H. 2003, 'Excavations at the Methodist Chapel Carver Street Sheffield', unpublished ARCUS rep. 507.

McKinley, J. 2008, *The 18th Century Baptist Chapel and Burial Ground at West Butts Street, Poole,* Salisbury: Wessex Archaeology.

Mytum, H. 1989, 'Public health and private sentiment: the development of cemetery architecture and funerary monuments from the eighteenth century onwards', *World Archaeology* 21:2, 283–97.

O'Neill, R., Baker, K. & Swales, D. 2007, 'Assessment Report of Archaeological Excavations at Sheffield Cathedral NW Car Park, Sheffield, South Yorkshire', unpublished ARCUS rep. 546d.1.

Parker-Pearson, M. 1999, *The Archaeology of Death and Burial,* Stroud: Sutton Publishing.

Reeve, J. & Adams, M. 1993, *The Spitalfields Project: Across the Styx, Vol.1,* Council for British Archaeology Research Report 85, York: Council for British Archaeology.

Richmond, M. 1999, 'Archaeologia Victoriana: the archaeology of the Victorian funeral', in Downes & Pollard 1999, 145–58.

Rugg, J. 1999, 'From reason to regulation: 1760–1850', in Jupp & Gittings 1999, 202–29.

Sayer, D. & Symonds, J. 2004, 'Lost congregations: the crisis facing later post-medieval urban burial grounds', *Church Archaeology 5–6, 55–61.*

Stock, G. 1998, 'Quaker burials, doctrine and practice', in Cox 1998, 144–153.

Wood, A. 1995, *Nineteenth century Britain 1815–1914,* 2nd edn, Essex: Longman Group.

Nonconformist Identities in 19th-Century London: Archaeological and Osteological Evidence from the Burial Grounds of Bow Baptist Chapel and the Catholic Mission of St Mary and St Michael, Tower Hamlets

Natasha Powers and Adrian Miles*

Between 2005 and 2007 Museum of London Archaeology carried out developer funded excavation in two post-medieval burial grounds: the Catholic Mission of St Mary and St Michael, Tower Hamlets and the Baptist Chapel, Bow. Presenting the preliminary results of the examination of over 1,000 burials, coffin furniture, clothing, artefacts and accompanying documentary data, this chapter discusses whether religious affiliation, location or socio-economic circumstances were the greatest influence on the living population and how they treated their dead. It examines whether wholesale differences could be used to infer religious affiliation for other buried populations or individuals.

INTRODUCTION

This chapter introduces and compares archaeological evidence from developer-funded excavations of two post-medieval burial grounds, carried out from 2005 to 2007 in East London. Excavation resulted in the recovery of more than 1,000 individuals and associated coffin furniture, clothing and artefacts. Outlining the historical background and results of the excavations before discussing the archaeological and osteological differences between the two sites, this chapter seeks to determine whether religious affiliation was the primary factor determining differences in life and death or rather that geographic location and socio-economic circumstances proved the greater influence; examining key differences to determine if religious identity could be inferred where historic or documentary sources are not available. The data presented here represents preliminary conclusions and provisional prevalence rates following MAP 2 assessment by the authors.[1] Detailed analysis of the human remains, the grave goods, the typology of the coffin furniture and the biographic information they contain is currently ongoing.

BOW BAPTIST CHAPEL

Bow Baptist Chapel was founded in the late 18th century when Bow was a large village. The first congregation met in a derelict granary and members were baptized in the nearby

Figure 13.1. Bow Baptist Chapel burial ground under excavation © M. Cox, MOLA.

river. In 1800 construction began on a New Chapel, completed within the year at a cost of just over £2,000. Land adjoining the site was purchased and 'part of this additional land, planted with trees of lime, willow and lilac, and alder was set aside as a burial ground'.[2] In the first ten years the congregation increased from 100 to over 600. Despite the construction of an extension to the New Chapel, space was insufficient to cope with the demand from the local population and the congregation maintained a waiting list for places.

By the time Mrs Basil Holmes wrote in 1896, the Chapel burial ground had been partly turned into a private garden. Several tombstones remained in their original locations, but others had been moved and placed against the boundary walls.[3] The original church was replaced in 1866, but this second building was bombed in 1940–41 and the congregation were left worshipping in a hut until 1948. In the 1950s a brick building replaced the hut and this remained at the time of excavation.

Museum of London Archaeology (MOLA) undertook archaeological excavations within 50% of the area of a proposed development (Fig. 13.1), the archaeologically excavated sample representing approximately one-quarter of the original extent of the burial ground. In total, 351 individuals were retained for osteological assessment.[4] Forty-four legible coffin plates were recovered during excavation and by cross-referencing against plans of the burial ground which had been maintained by the chapel it was possible to provide identities for just over 100 burials. The burial sample dated from 1816–54, though it is known that burials continued on occasion until 1870.

Figure 13.2. The burial ground of the Catholic Mission of St Mary and St Michael
© M. Cox, MOLA.

In 1837 nonconformist churches of all denominations were invited to deposit their registers for authentication by a commission initiated in advance of the 1840 Non-parochial Registers Act.[5] Over 3,500 volumes were deposited with the Registrar General in London.[6] As a result, well-maintained burial registers for Bow are extant for the period from 1800 to 1837 and show the increasing use of the burial ground over this period. Subsequent records were lost in the Second World War.

THE CATHOLIC MISSION OF ST MARY AND ST MICHAEL, TOWER HAMLETS

In 1842, the Catholic mission of St Mary and St Michael purchased a plot of land on Commercial Road for £3,000. The Catholic Emancipation Act of 1829 had lifted many restrictions, allowing Catholics to worship freely for the first time in centuries.[7] Part of the land was immediately set aside as a burial ground and consecrated on 24 July 1843. Perhaps surprisingly, the foundation stone of the church (which remains to this day) was not laid until a decade later and the church was not opened until 8 December 1856. By this time the burial ground had been closed for two years.

Excavation revealed a heavily used burial ground to the south of the church; 747 individuals were retained for assessment (Fig. 13.2), the burials spanning just eleven years (1843–54). Partially legible coffin plates were recovered from 194 contexts.[8]

No burial registers were located for St Mary and St Michael and, while it is possible that no register was kept, before 1850 the Catholic Church was based on missions (rather than fixed geographical parishes) and records moved with individual priests.

MIGRATION AND IMMIGRATION

The first congregation at Bow was formed by eight people on 21 June 1785. The pastor, Mr John Knott, was associated with the 'Particular' Baptists of Sussex and Kent. In 1780 the Knotts moved to Bow to be closer to his wife's relatives.[9] With industrial development in the early 19th century, the village of Bow quickly became unrecognizable. Factories producing soap, rubber, hemp cloth and matches were constructed and contributed to a massive increase in population: by 1862, Bow was covered with dense housing and a network of railways. The 19th century was also a period of rapid growth for the Baptist church, with the formation of the Baptist Union, who held their first assembly in 1813.[10] Surprisingly, the coming of the factories resulted in an initial decline in the size of the congregation at Bow, as many of the founding members emigrated to the colonies. However, this exodus did not persist and in 1864 the Chapel celebrated its thousandth member.[11]

Among those exhumed in the 2007 excavations were a husband and wife from the Parnell family (d. 1853 and 1870). The 1851 census results show the family birthplaces as a microcosm of this migration (Table 13.1).

Table 13.1. The 1851 census for the Parnell family, buried at Bow Baptist Chapel.

Name	Relation to head	Age	Occupation	Parish of birth
William Parnell	Head	60	Watchmaker	Canterbury, Kent
Elizabeth Parnell	Wife	56		Sudbury, Suffolk
Thomas Parnell	Son	30	Watchmaker	Bow
Henry Parnell	Son	21	Watchmaker	Bow
Frederick Parnell	Son	16	Watchmaker	Bow
Mary Parnell	Daughter	18		Bow

The picture at St Mary and St Michael is equally of a population in flux. Initial examination of the epigraphic data showed that of 49 individuals whose surnames could be confidently established, 32 names were of probable Irish origin. Master Alphonso [266] and Mr Miguel Penethera [1349] suggest that the larger Catholic community was also served by the burial ground and raise the question of the distance individuals might travel for burial in what was then one of the few Catholic burial grounds in London.

The failure of the potato crop and subsequent famine in 1847–8 initiated mass migration from Ireland to England, further encouraged by the cheap travel available on steamboats and the higher wages available in England. In 1851, at the peak of the population movement, 257,372 people left Ireland. Commercial Road, off which the burial ground lay, was the main communication route between the docks and the city and a focus of Irish Catholic settlement.[12] Surname evidence cannot definitively determine whether those buried at St Mary and St Michael or their forebears were born outside England. By the 1840s the Irish 'Cockneys' had long established themselves in the East End, but researchers at the University of Bradford are currently examining stable isotope data from the site and have found carbon and nitrogen signals that support the presence of recent migrants.[13]

BURIAL PRACTICES AND BURIAL GROUND MANAGEMENT

Excavation demonstrated that Bow Baptist churchyard was neat and ordered. Within the excavated area, 127 grave cuts were arranged in parallel north–south rows. The deceased were buried east–west with their head to the west end of the grave. Most were contained in wooden coffins within earth-cut graves. Just seven lead coffins and two brick vaults were seen.

The first entry in the registers for Bow relates the interment of Penelope Huntley from Mile End, Stepney on 13 April 1816. Intriguingly, Penelope had been moved from 'the other burial ground to this' and was originally buried on 27 April 1814. Following 27 November 1822, ten entries refer to burials from the previous decade. A change in handwriting indicates that a new person had become responsible for completing the register and it may be that they were correcting a previous error but it is tempting to speculate that these were also earlier burials moved from burial grounds elsewhere.

Some burials were disturbed by later interments within the same grave cut: the bones of the first occupant were found disarticulated and moved aside to accommodate the later coffin. Specific plots were chosen for reuse, presumably because of a familial connection between the deceased, an interpretation which is supported by the coffin plate data.

At St Mary and St Michael burial started in the eastern part of the site and moved west. Burial took place within wooden coffins, of which organic residue and metal fittings survived. These coffins were stacked in graves up to 4m deep. There was no intercutting of the graves, which were aligned east–west with the heads of the deceased placed to the east end of each grave. Adults were found in the lowest levels of the stacks while older children were placed above this and infants lay uppermost.

It was initially thought that each stack represented deaths occurring over a short time, such as a week, gathered together for a single, planned burial event. No indications of family plots were gleaned from the biographic data and the sorting of the burials by size seemed to confirm this interpretation. Further examination of the coffin plates revealed this was not the case. Within some stacks the dates of death did not follow a short chronology. Grave cut [1468] contained thirteen burials, of which five could be dated from coffin plate information (giving date of death). The first burial took place in 1846, the second after 25 May 1847, the fourth in October 1847, while the eighth and ninth took place after 20 November 1847. There is no suggestion of the reopening of family plots, though extended family connections which would not be demonstrated by surname evidence cannot be completely ruled out. It is possible that the individuals had previously been interred elsewhere and were moved to the Mission in one event, but the scale of this practice suggests that graves were periodically reopened to receive additional burials.

BURIAL CLOTHING

Copper-alloy pins were recovered from sixteen contexts at Bow, indicating burial within a shroud. A further thirty-one individuals had copper-alloy staining on the cranium or mandible resulting from contact with shroud pins. One copper-alloy, two bone, two glass and four shell buttons from eight further contexts, along with two tortoiseshell hair combs [263] and an iron hairpin [661], show that a small number of the deceased were clothed.

The evidence for clothed burial is much greater at St Mary and St Michael. A large

Figure 13.3. St Mary and St Michael: adult male [755] interred wearing leather shoes or boots © A. Miles, MOLA.

number of bone and brightly coloured glass buttons, sets of shirt and trouser buttons and hook and eye fastenings and a large quantity of textile were recovered. Preservation of hair enabled limited observation of hairstyles, such as a well-preserved 'bun' held together with a series of hairgrips from a 13–17 year old [1174]. Adult female [1505] was found wearing a pair of finely knitted gloves, while adult male [755] had been interred wearing sturdy shoes or boots (Fig. 13.3).

GRAVE GOODS

The archaeological evidence from St Mary and St Michael is of a great number and variety of grave goods. Crosses, chains and rosaries were recovered. The rosaries were made of bone, glass or wooden beads. One large cross was stamped DE LA MISSION (to remember the Mission). This came from the burial of an adult male [1057] who had been suffering from a pulmonary (lung) infection at the time of his death. Pendants with religious figures were recovered from four burials while a heart-shaped pendant with remains of ribbon was found (with a cross) placed in the grave of a 13–17-year-old adolescent [621]. One unusual find was a ceramic crucifix with an integral cup used to contain holy water and decorated with a lion's head motif. This household object was found in the grave of an adult female [1237]. Coins were found in eight burials from Bow Baptist church, though it is unclear whether these were deliberate inclusions.

THE HUMAN REMAINS

The assessment data was utilized to examine whether cultural, economic or other influences affected the demography or health of the two groups. Assessment involved the rapid scanning of the remains, and age at death was determined by permanent molar eruption and/ or the completion of fusion of the long bones.

Basic quantification and scanning of the remains indicated an almost even distribution of adults and subadults at Bow: 182 adults (those aged over 18 years with erupted third molars and/or fully fused long bones (52%)) and 169 subadults (48%) were recorded. Sixty per cent of the subadults had died aged less than seven years, the largest proportion dying between one month and six years. In contrast, at St Mary and St Michael subadults significantly outnumbered adult burials: 293 adults and 454 subadults (61%) were noted. Nearly three-quarters of the subadults were under seven years old at the time of their death (as indicated by the absence of the first permanent molars).

Of the 166 adults from Bow for whom sex could be estimated, there was a slightly larger proportion of females (52%) than males (48%). In contrast, at St Mary and St Michael 58% of the adults for whom sex could be estimated were male and 42% female.

Differing attitudes to medicine and surgery may be reflected in the osteological record. Autopsies were carried out in London from the 1760s,[14] but attitudes towards the scientific investigation into cause of death varied greatly in the 18th and 19th centuries. By the end of the 18th century autopsy, carried out to reassure the living as much as to establish the cause of death, was gaining acceptance.[15] By the 19th century it formed a common part of the coroner's inquest.

At Bow, adult male [800] had been subject to a craniotomy (1/356: 0.3%). A single sweeping cut ran around the vault of the skull. The blade had not passed cleanly through both tables of the skull and separation had required the bone to be snapped apart. Rib cuts showed that the viscera had also been removed. Seven individuals from St Mary and St Michael had undergone craniotomy (7/750: 0.9%): three males, one female, two adolescents (aged 13–17 years) and one infant under five years at death. Cuts to the manubrium were present in an adult male [606]. Again, there was evidence of irregular and poorly located saw cuts (adult male [1491]).

Evidence of medical treatment was suggested by successful fracture healing at St Mary and St Michael and surgical intervention seen in male [1392]. He had suffered multiple fractures (lower leg, face and spine) and his right leg had been amputated above the knee (Fig. 13.4). At Bow, adolescent [281] had survived amputation of the right lower leg, although with subsequent infection which may have led to their death. Male [313] had also undergone surgery, with the amputation of the right leg in the mid-shaft of the femur (thigh). Striations caused by the surgeon's saw were clearly visible in the cut surface, indicating that no healing had occurred, and it is quite probable that the operation resulted

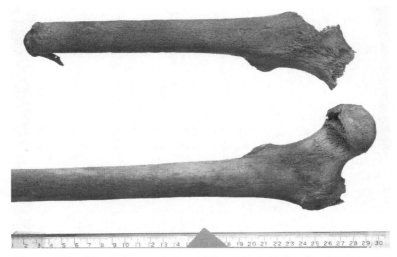

Figure 13.4. A healed amputation of the right leg of male [1392] buried
at St Mary and St Michael © A. Chopping, MOLA.

in death. Post-operative mortality rates of 46% were reported prior to the introduction of antiseptics.[16]

Dental treatment is most clearly demonstrated by the presence of fillings and dental prostheses and a number of archaeological examples have been found in archaeological contexts dating from the 18th and 19th centuries.[17] A partial denture was recovered from the mouth of adult male [123] from Bow. Constructed from shaped human teeth and set into a rose gold plate via a series of screw posts, the metal extended to form a clip around two remaining teeth and hold the denture in place. Extreme wear suggested prolonged use.

Rickets, caused by a deficient diet or a lack of exposure to sunlight (ultraviolet) required for vitamin D synthesis, can inform us about past child-rearing practices.[18] From the late 18th century increased urban poverty necessitated an early return to work for many mothers, while the middle classes considered breastfeeding unfashionable.[19] Artificial or 'farinaceous' feeds became popular.[20] These were purchased ready-mixed, boiled with water, sweetened and mixed with cows' milk before being placed in a feeding bottle.[21] Any infant fed solely artificial feeds would have been deficient in vitamin D.[22] Coupled with this, the practice of swaddling children reduced skin exposure to sunlight and increased the chances of acquiring rickets. Ironically, this practice was supposed to keep infant limbs straight.[23]

Rickets was prevalent at both sites, with greatest numbers of those affected dying in early childhood (1 month–6 years). At Bow church, fourteen subadults, thirteen under the age of six years, were vitamin deficient at the time of death (13/73: 18%). Thirty-seven rachitic children (7%) were noted during assessment at St Mary and St Michael. The crude prevalence of the condition in the subadult assemblage from Bow was 8% (13/169), slightly higher than at St Mary and St Michael. However, it is important to consider this difference in conjunction with the overall demographic profile of the two sites: a greater proportion of children was found in the Catholic burial ground, suggesting that overall child health was poor.

At St Mary and St Michael 50% of the assemblage (316 individuals) had evidence of dental disease. Sixty per cent of the observable adult dentitions (156/259) and 2% of the subadults (7/376) had caries and even young children (those under seven years) were affected, reflecting a high carbohydrate (sugar and starch) intake.[24] Fifty-one per cent of individuals from Bow church had evidence of dental disease (180/351) with caries affecting 56% (92/163) of adult and 12% (15/129) of subadult dentitions.

Finally, it is interesting to examine social behaviour as reflected by the skeletal record. 'Immorality' was given frequently as the reason for expulsion of members of the Baptist congregation, such as 'a very Lyeing man' and a woman ejected for 'marreing a Profane man'.[25] Accounts of the Irish population of the East End suggest a population who engaged in drunken brawling, and that religious conflicts between the immigrants continued, though these reports should be viewed with caution since anti-Papist feeling ran high in the mid 19th century. Contemporary references also refer to the chastity of the Irish Catholics: young girls did not attend social events unless chaperoned and adultery was uncommon, but immigrants were 'corrupted' by a long stay in London.[26]

Some injuries and injury patterns may be indicative of assault. At St Mary and St Michael suggestions of interpersonal violence affected men alone (12/149: 8.1%) and included nasal fractures, in one case associated with broken teeth and head injuries. Just one individual from Bow had injuries which could be suggested to have resulted from conflict, though an accidental cause is more likely: male [816] had healed fractures of the right ribs, left fibula, left first and second metatarsals and left third metacarpal and nose.

Smoking was a popular pastime from the mid 19th century and the contrast between the two sites is marked. At Bow, adult male [342] was the only individual in whom notches resulting from habitual smoking of a clay pipe could be seen during assessment. Recent work on St Mary and St Michael showed that 40% of male dentitions (139) and 3% of females (102) had pipe notches and a large number had tobacco-stained teeth (Fig. 13.5).[27]

By the 1840s restrictive undergarments were commonly worn, and pointed footwear was fashionable for both sexes. At Bow, four females (4/87 females: 5%) and an adult with intermediate sexual characteristics demonstrated clear evidence of rib deformity of a type resulting from the wearing of stays or corsets. Four adult females from St Mary and St Michael had thoracic changes indicating the routine wearing of restrictive garments (4/109 females: 4%). Eleven males and six females from Bow (17/182 adults: 9%) had evidence of *hallux valgus*, a deformity of the great toe which may be caused, or exacerbated, by restrictive footwear.[28] In twelve cases the condition could be observed in both the right and left feet. The proportions of individuals affected at St Mary and St Michael were considerably lower: *hallux valgus* was seen in just twelve adults (12/293: 4.1%), seven males and three females, with indications of bunion formation in two cases.

DISCUSSION

Burial Practices

No excavation reports yet exist for Catholic burial grounds and there are few comparative samples from Baptist burials grounds. A group of forty Baptist individuals was recovered from Commercial Road, Hereford in 2001 but is as yet unpublished, and a small group from Kings Lynn have also been examined.[29] The largest Baptist assemblage currently known is from West Butts, Poole, and dates from the late 18th to early 19th century.[30] However, the

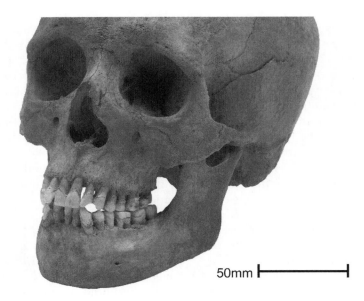

50mm

Figure 13.5. Male [1099] from the burial ground of St Mary and St Michael with notches in his left canines and first premolars caused by habitual smoking of a clay pipe © A. Chopping, MOLA.

existing comparative data does enable examination of any identifiable differences between these sites and Anglican burial grounds of the same date from within London.

In both burial grounds graves were aligned east–west, following standard Christian burial practice.[31] Although north–south-aligned nonconformist burials have been found elsewhere,[32] there was no evidence of this practice at Bow, but the 'back to front' burials of St Mary and St Michael remain intriguing. No pattern has been found to the occurrence of west–east burials in the medieval period[33] and, at this stage, no religious significance can be ascribed to the occurrence here. The alignment appears to be particular to this burial ground and individual human error or variability appears the most probable cause.

The evidence relating to the management of the burial ground at Bow suggests that burial location and the gathering of the family together in death was of great importance to the congregation. This is perhaps unsurprising in a group working to establish their religious identity, where maintaining a sense of community and belonging to support a collective identity is vital. At West Butts Street, Poole, intercut graves suggested that early graves were not marked or that these markers had gone. Later graves were in rows and seemed to indicate more efficient burial ground management. Several graves had been used for multiple burials and five grave groups had been recut to enable later interments above existing ones,[34] though this did not involve the wholesale movement of the original occupant, as seen at Bow. One grave had no human remains, but an impression of a coffin at the base, and was interpreted as the result of deliberate exhumation for burial in another ground or perhaps repatriation.[35] In contrast, the reopening of plots at St Mary and St

Michael was due to a lack of space for new graves, suggesting huge pressure on burial space consistent with the surprisingly short use of the burial ground and cholera epidemics.[36]

The indications are that while shrouded burial was the standard form for the congregation at Bow, a number of those interred at St Mary and St Michael were fully dressed.[37] Shrouded burial appears to have been standard practice at West Butts Street, where 77% of individuals were contained in shrouds and almost no evidence of clothing was recovered. The *Act for Burial in Wool* (requiring use of a woollen shroud) was not repealed until 1814,[38] and a purely temporal explanation is possible, but perhaps clothing also reflects the practice of an open casket and the importance of the display of the funeral ceremony to the Catholic community, in contrast to the simplicity of the Baptist edicts. Although many migrants were in the lower classes and some references suggest that burial within a Catholic burial ground would have been beyond their means,[39] others state that even the poorest Catholics would ensure that their friends and relatives were afforded a full wake and funeral.[40] Even the poorest in Victorian society felt the importance of being 'fashionable', to the point of incurring unaffordable expense.[41] Perhaps this extended to ensuring that the deceased was buried in good clothing? The Catholic burials were also furnished with grave goods and decorative and symbolic objects, including a ceramic stoop which appears to have been taken from around the home for inclusion in the burial and perhaps belonged to the deceased or a relative. Few objects were found at Bow and the small number of coins seen has a parallel at West Butts Street.[42]

The Living Population

Within the Baptist population at West Butts Street there was a high proportion of females (61% female, 36% male) and a female bias is reported in early nonconformist congregations, influenced by the Corporation Act of 1661 which required any man who was a member of a municipal corporation to swear an oath that they received Church of England communion.[43] McKinley concluded that the demographic imbalance was enhanced by the 18th-century General Baptist practice of endogamy, and the transient male population of Poole.

The data from Bow indicated a slight female bias, in contrast to the results from many other recent excavations in the capital where men consistently outnumber women (St Marylebone: 54% male, 46% female, St Luke's, Old Street: 56% male, 44% female).[44] This pattern of male excess was repeated at St Mary and St Michael, where a ratio of 1.4:1 was seen, representing a slight male bias when compared to the ratio of live births expected in any population of 1.06:1.[45] As variables such as the transient nature of the male population in a seafaring settlement can be excluded when discussing Bow (in fact the economic migration known to have occurred in the 19th century should result in a male bias), this suggests that the pattern seen at West Butts Street and repeated here may indeed have been influenced by religious practices.

At King's Lynn an under-representation of subadults contrasted with the number of children evident in the parish registers, suggesting that the buried population were genuinely different from the larger population group from which they came.[46] Such a disparity is not evident at Bow. Although the proportion of the buried population composed of subadults was significantly smaller than that seen at St Mary and St Michael, smaller numbers of subadults have been noted at other contemporary sites; for example, they made up just 26% of the population buried at St Marylebone.[47] Rather, then, it seems that the child mortality rate at St Mary and St Michael may be unusually high. Separating the effects of fertility (birth rate) and mortality requires further work, but at the present time the cholera epidemics of 1848–54 and child mortality issues relating to child rearing (as manifest in prevalence of rickets),[48] appear to have been of greatest influence on the differences in demographic pattern.

Religious humanitarianism was directly linked to the anti-slavery movement and from the late 18th century the General Baptists supported a boycott on sugar owing to the links with the slave trade.[49] The intake of refined sugar can, to some extent, be examined by a comparison of the prevalence of dental disease, yet rates for both sites appear similar, particularly among the adult populations. This may indicate that there was no major difference in diet. Dental health is known to have been generally poor in this period.[50] Juvenile dental disease may indicate the influence of sugary foods, drinks and the use of comforters in infant rearing. The results are also consistent with poor dental health seen at West Butts Street.[51]

Although it may be problematic to interpret long-term behaviour or identify a change in practices during adulthood, such as might follow religious conversion, it does appear that there were marked contrasts between the number of smokers in the Baptist and Catholic populations. The contrast is so marked that further investigation into the interplay of cultural and economic influences on this behaviour is required. Contemporary accounts indicated that social status was important in determining the levels of smoking, and gender was critical. Males smoked, most females did not.[54] The high number of smokers at St Mary and St Michael may simply reflect economic status. The sole example of dental treatment from the two sites reflects the economic status of the individual: dentures were extremely expensive,[52] and this may contradict the assertion that early Baptist congregations were predominantly poor.[53] The implication is that the Catholic population was poorer since, despite the slightly later emphasis of the date and the greater numbers of adults present, no dental treatment was seen.

Rates of interpersonal violence at Bow, as indicated from skeletal trauma, contrast with those from Commercial Road, Hereford, where 10% of the individuals had suffered nasal fractures and reportedly high rates of trauma at King's Lynn, Norfolk.[55] This suggests that social factors independent of religious background were the primary influence on levels of assault.

While confirmation following analysis is necessary, there also appears to have been a difference in the footwear used by the two populations as suggested by the rate of hallux valgus. Perhaps this is a reflection of migration from rural Ireland?

Compared with St Mary and St Michael and other contemporary sites,[56] there appear to be fewer incidences of post-mortem intervention at Bow than might be expected considering the date of use. At West Butts Street only one individual with a craniotomy was seen, a 5-year-old child buried in 1813,[57] but the question remains as to whether the initially rural location of Bow and later emphasis in the date of burials at St Mary and St Michael, rather than religious beliefs, resulted in such a difference.

CONCLUSIONS

Although the data presented here remains only the provisional conclusions following assessment, clear differences between the two populations studied are manifest.

The Baptist congregation at Bow appears to have been highly organized with methodical record-keepers who planned for the expansion of both their living congregation and their burial ground. In contrast, the Mission of St Mary and St Michael appears to have been unprepared for the demands on their burial ground and found themselves returning to reopen and fill grave stacks until the space was completely filled.

The demographic data suggests a female bias at Bow which could potentially be used to identify Baptist groups, and, while epidemics and child-rearing practices appear to be the greatest influence on the child mortality rate, these may in turn be influenced by cultural or religious beliefs.

Osteological indicators of social behaviour also demonstrate the disparity between the two groups and, though separating the social, economic, temporal and religious influences on a population is by no means simple, further comparison with contemporary sites and examination of the historical record may yet provide definitive answers. As work progresses, examination of epigraphic data and burial registers giving date of death or burial will enable the temporal and geographic influences to be separated from the cultural.

The examination of these two groups raises important considerations for the interpretation of post-medieval burial grounds, demonstrating that secondary burial and the reuse of graves may be more commonplace than previously suspected. The complexity of post-medieval burial practices demonstrates the importance of archaeological evidence as the identifier of variations from expected (documented) procedures. The wealth of artefactual evidence found at St Mary and St Michael opens up new opportunities for examining funerary ritual on an individual level and, with the increasing volume of post-medieval material available, the potential to study correlations between grave inclusions, age, sex and religious beliefs will increase further.

Though there is much work yet to be done, this study shows that an holistic approach to the analysis of historic burial-ground assemblages, drawing together artefactual, funerary and osteological evidence, can demonstrate the variety in the human experience of death and burial more vividly than the written word can do alone.

NOTES

*   The authors wish to thank the following organizations and individuals for their assistance: Galliford Try, TCS Exhumation Services Ltd, Archdiocese of Westminster Education Service, The Berkeley Consultancy, Durkan Pudelek, Teevan, Modebest, David Divers of the Greater London Archaeological Advisory Service; MOL Archaeology specialists Michael Henderson, Don Walker, Nicola Powell and Beth Richardson; Robin Wroe-Brown for his editorial assistance; photographers Andy Chopping and Maggie Cox; Dr Janet Montgomery, and Julia Beaumont, University of Bradford and, of course, all the excavation and processing staff.

1. English Heritage 1991.

2. Lynn 1935, 28.
3. Holmes 1896, 144.
4. Miles & Powers 2007a.
5. WYAS 2008, 3.
6. London Metropolitan Archives 1999.
7. WYAS 2008, 3.
8. Miles and Powers 2007b.
9. Lynn 1935, 13.
10. Baptist Union of Great Britain.
11. Lynn 1935, 36.
12. Garwood 1853; Mayhew 1861–62.
13. Julia Beaumont pers. comm.
14. Lane 2001, 48.
15. Moore 2005, 75, 232.
16. Porter 1997, 372.

17. Powers 2006, 462.
18. Mays 2003, 144.
19. Lane 2001, 36.
20. Redfern and Roberts 2005, 125.
21. Beeton 1861, 1038.
22. Molleson and Cox 1993, 45.
23. Beeton 1861, 1039.
24. Hillson 1996, 278.
25. Lynn 1935, 13.
26. Mayhew 1861–62; Garwood 1853.
27. Walker and Henderson 2010.
28. Mays 2005, 139.
29. Archenfield Archaeology Ltd.; Boston 2005.
30. McKinley 2008.
31. Gilchrist and Sloane 2005, 152.
32. McKinley 2008, 21.
33. Gilchrist and Sloane 2005, 153.
34. McKinley 2008, 17.
35. McKinley 2008, 28, 21.
36. Wilson 2003, 36.
37. Sixty-four burials had buttons and a further eight had other possible clothes fastenings (72/747: 10%), 27 had shroud pins, the archaeological evidence suggesting a ratio of 1:2.7 shrouded to clothed burials. A small number of burials contained the remains of textile which could have originated from either clothes or a shroud.
38. McKinley 2008, 24, 46.
39. Garwood 1853.
40. Mayhew 1861–62.
41. Stevens Curl 2000, 197.
42. McKinley 2008, 46.
43. McKinley 2008, ix, 102.
44. Miles *et al.* 2008, 104; Boyle *et al.* 2005, 187.
45. Rousham & Humphrey 2002, 128.
46. Boston 2005, 124.
47. Miles *et al.* 2008, 104.
48. Wilson 2003, 36.
49. McKinley 2008, 5, 75.
50. Roberts & Cox 2003, 327.
51. McKinley 2008, 75.
52. Powers 2006, 462.
53. McKinley 2008, 75.
54. Walker and Henderson 2008.
55. Archenfield Archaeology Ltd.; Boston 2005.
56. Miles *et al.* 2008; Boyle *et al.* 2005, 180, 251; Brickley *et al.* 2006, 146.
57. McKinley 2008, 95.

BIBLIOGRAPHY

Archenfield Archaeology Ltd., <http://www.archenfield.com> [accessed 28/03/07].

Baptist Union of Great Britain, <http://www.baptist.org.uk/baptist_life/baptist_history.html> [accessed 18/01/09].

Beeton, I. 1861, *Mrs Beeton's Book of Household Management*, London: S.O. Beeton.

Boston C. 2005, 'Appendix 10: human bone - Baptist inhumations', in Brown 2005, 121–159.

Boyle, A., Boston, C. & Witkin, A. 2005, 'The archaeological experience at St Luke's Church, Old Street, Islington', unpublished Oxford Archaeology report.

Brickley, M., Buteux, S., Adams, J. & Cherrington, R. 2006, *St Martin's Uncovered: Investigations in the Churchyard of St Martins-in-the-Bull Ring, Birmingham, 2001*, Oxford: Oxbow Books.

Brown, R. 2005, 'Vancouver Centre and Clough Lane car Park, King's Lynn, Norfolk. Post-excavation assessment and research design', unpublished Oxford Archaeology report.

English Heritage, 1991, *Management of Archaeological Projects*, London: Historic Buildings and Monuments Commission for England.

Garwood J. 1853. *The Million Peopled City*. London: Wertheim & MacIntosh <http://www.victorianlondon.org> [accessed 18/01/09].

Gilchrist, R. & Sloane, B. 2005 *Requiem: the Medieval Monastic Cemetery in Britain*. Museum of London Archaeological Service, London.

Hillson S. 1996, *Dental Anthropology*, Cambridge: Cambridge University Press.

Holmes, B. 1896, *The London Burial Grounds: Notes On Their History From The Earliest Times To The Present Day*, London: T. Fisher Unwin.

Lane, J. 2001, *A Social History of Medicine: Health, Healing and Disease in England 1750–1950*, London: Routledge.

London Metropolitan Archives 1999, *Records of Nonconformists in London*. Information Leaflet no. 27. London: London Metropolitan Archives.

Lynn, J.E. 1935, *"Three Jubilees": A Brief Outline of the Story of Bow Baptist Church Written in Commemoration of the 150th Anniversary*, Grays: Thameside Printers.

Macbeth, H. & Collinson, P. (eds) 2002, *Human Population Dynamics: Cross-disciplinary Perspectives*. Cambridge: Biosocial Society Symposium Series.

Mayhew H. 1861–62. *London Labour and the London Poor*, London: Griffin, Bohn & Co. <http://www.victorianlondon.org> [accessed 18/01/09].

Mays, S. 2003, 'The rise and fall of rickets in England', in Murphy & Wiltshire 2003, 144–53.

Mays, S. 2005, 'Paleopathological study of hallux valgus', *American Journal of Physical Anthropology* 126: 139–49.

McKinley, J.I. 2008, *The 18th century Baptist Chapel and Burial Ground at West Butts Street, Poole*, Salisbury: Wessex Archaeology.

Miles, A. & Powers, N. 2007a, 'Bow Baptist Church Burial Ground, 2–25 Payne Road, London, E3, London Borough of Tower Hamlets: A post-excavation assessment and updated project design', unpublished MOL Archaeology assessment report.

Miles, A. & Powers, N. 2007b, 'Bishop Challoner Catholic Collegiate School, Lukin Street, London, E1, London Borough of Tower Hamlets: A post-excavation assessment and updated project design', unpublished MOL Archaeology assessment report.

Miles, A., Powers, N., Wroe-Brown, R. with Walker, D. 2008, *St Marylebone Church and Burial Ground: Excavations at St Marylebone Church of England School, 2005*, MOLA Monograph Series 46

Molleson, T. and Cox, M. with Waldron, A.H. & Whittaker, D.K. 1993, *The Spitalfields Project. Volume 2: The Anthropology - The Middling Sort*, Council for British Archaeology Research Report No. 86

Moore, W. 2005, *The Knife Man: Blood, Body-snatching and the Birth of Modern Surgery*, London: Bantam.

Murphy, P. & Wiltshire, P.E.J. (eds) 2003, *The Environmental Archaeology of Industry*. Symposia of the Association for Environmental Archaeology 20, Oxford: Oxbow.

Porter, R. 1997, *The Greatest Benefit to Mankind: A Medical History of Humanity From Antiquity to the Present*, London: Harper Collins.

Powers, N. 2006, 'Archaeological evidence for dental innovation: an eighteenth century porcelain dental prosthesis belonging to Archbishop Arthur Richard Dillon', *British Dental Journal* 201: 459–63.

Redfern, R.C. & Roberts, C.A. 2005 'Health in Romano-British urban communities: reflections from the cemeteries', in Smith *et al* 2005, 115–29.

Roberts, C. & Cox, M. 2003, *Health and Disease in Britain: from prehistory to the present day*, Stroud: Sutton.

Rousham, E.K. & Humphrey, L.T. 2002, 'The dynamics of child survival', in Macbeth & Collinson 2002, 124–40.

Smith, D., Brickley, M. & Smith, W. (eds) 2005, *Fertile Ground. Papers in Honour of Susan Limbrey*. Symposia of the Association for Environmental Archaeology Symposia 22, Oxford: Oxbow.

Stevens Curl, J. 2000, *The Victorian Celebration of Death*, Stroud: Sutton Publishing.

Walker, D. & Henderson, M. 2010, 'Smoking and health in London's East End in the first half of the 19th century', *Post-Medieval Archaeology* 44:1, 209–22.

West Yorkshire Archive Service 2008, 'Collections Guide 5. Roman Catholic Registers', unpublished West Yorkshire Joint Services guide.

Wilson A.N. 2003, *The Victorians*, London: Arrow Books.

ABBREVIATIONS

MOLA   Museum of London Archaeology
WYAS   West Yorkshire Archive Service

The General Baptists of Priory Yard, Norwich

ANWEN CEDIFOR CAFFELL AND RACHEL CLARKE*

Excavations undertaken in 2002 at the former Jarrolds Printing Works, Norwich, revealed parts of the medieval Carmelite friary, including an area later used as a burial ground by the Priory Yard Baptists. The sixty-three skeletons recovered from this cemetery display extraordinary levels of pathological conditions and provide a rare opportunity to study a nonconformist population, many of whom appear to come from the poorer levels of Norwich society. This chapter presents some of the key results of the osteological analysis, concentrating on evidence predominantly relating to childhood stress, maternal health, infectious disease and dental health.

INTRODUCTION

The site of the former Jarrolds Printing Works on Whitefriars, Norwich (TG 235 098) was excavated in 2002 by AF Howland Associates (AFH) and the Norfolk Archaeological Unit (now NAU Archaeology) prior to redevelopment (Fig. 14.1). Large parts of the medieval Carmelite friary, which occupied the site from 1256 until the Dissolution, were revealed, including an area later used as a burial ground by the General Baptists of Priory Yard. Post-excavation analysis was conducted by Cambridgeshire County Council's Archaeological Field Unit (now Oxford Archaeology East), with the human skeletal remains analysed by one of the authors (ACC) on behalf of York Osteoarchaeology Ltd in 2006. A full report on the site is in progress.

This paper is concerned with the human remains excavated from the Priory Yard Baptist cemetery, which lies to the north of the extant St James' Yarn Mill, built 1836–9.[1] To place them in context, the historical background to the development and use of the chapel and burial ground is outlined. The demography of those buried is examined, comparing osteological data on age and sex with documented evidence for known burials. It is beyond the scope of this paper to report in detail on the many pathological conditions observed, which included traumatic injuries, joint disease and evidence for corset wearing. Consequently, aspects of health and disease are considered in relation to social status. Those selected predominantly relate to childhood stress, maternal health, infectious disease and dental health.

Ideally, the Priory Yard skeletons would be compared to a post-medieval Norwich population from a Christian burial ground, but owing to the lack of such a collection this was not possible. Instead, information on the post-medieval sites to which the Priory Yard population was compared is given in Table 14.1.

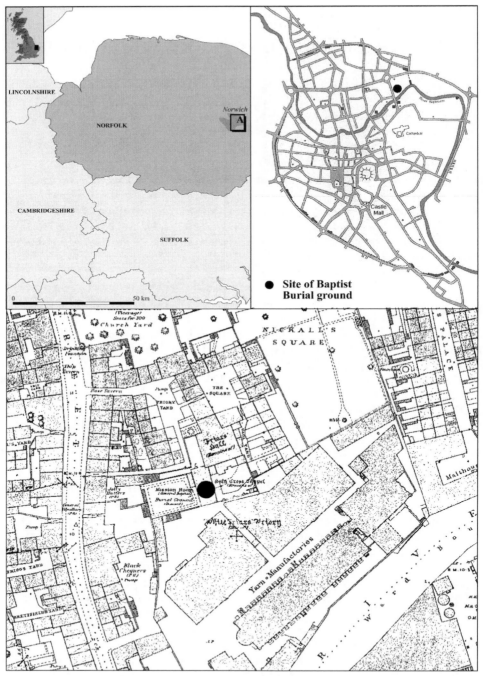

Figure 14.1. Priory Yard, Norwich site location, showing the cemetery in relation to the 1885 Ordnance Survey map (drawn by Crane Begg © Oxford Archaeology East. Top right insert after Shepherd Popescu 2010, Fig. 1.1).

Table 14.1. Comparative sites

Site	Date	No. of skeletons	Religion	Social Status	Source
St Martin's Church, Birmingham	c. 1720–1863	857	Protestant	Majority working-class; small no. middle-class	Brickley *et al.* 2006
St Marylebone Church, London	1767–1859	301	Protestant	Wealthy	Miles *et al.* 2008
St-Mary-and-St-Michael, London	1843–1854	705	Catholic	Poor, Irish immigrant descent	Powers 2006
Christ Church, Spitalfields, London	1729–1852	987 (387 named)	Protestant	Middle-class, French Huguenots	Molleson & Cox 1993
West Butts Street, Poole, Dorset	1735–1855	83	Baptist	Middle-class, trades people	McKinley 2008

PRIORY YARD CHAPEL

The Priory Yard Chapel was founded by Thomas Grantham, who moved to Norwich in 1686.[2] In April 1697 the upper storey of one of the remaining Friary buildings was leased for use as a meeting house, with land to the south ('41ft long by 30ft wide') used as a burial ground.[3] The latter was extended a further '27ft to the south' in 1726, when Grantham Killingworth (member of the congregation, and grandson of Thomas Grantham) acquired the leasehold.[4] The meeting house was demolished in 1817 and a new enlarged chapel and ancillary buildings were built, which included a Sunday school-room/vestry and baptistry.[5] Despite these improvements, the congregation remained concerned over the condition of their facilities. In the mid 19th century the auxiliary buildings were described as 'a long low room, little better than a shed, running along one side of that burial ground'.[6] Between 1851 and 1856 the congregation briefly relocated to another chapel in Tombland, Norwich, and in 1864 it was decided that a new place of worship was required.[7] A description of Priory Yard chapel in 1874 illustrates the unacceptable nature of the surroundings: 'we were worshipping in Priory Yard literally in a yard, a back yard, surrounded by buildings which totally shut it out from public view and the approach to which is a narrow dark passage flanked on the right by the Jolly Hatters public house and on the left by a succession of dustbins'.[8]

The last recorded burial at Priory Yard took place in 1854, which coincided with the opening of the nearby non-denominational cemetery in Earlham Road in 1855. However, the burial ground was not closed officially until 1876, when the chapel was sold and the congregation purchased and moved to St Clement's Chapel, Colegate.[9]

Priory Yard was located north of the River Wensum in one of the poorest areas of the city. However, not all those attending would have been poor, or lived in the immediate area. Some of the members were wealthy, or relatively so, such as Grantham Killingworth, who arranged financial assistance for the chapel in his will.[10] However, there is evidence that the chapel struggled financially prior to Grantham Killingworth's bequest in 1778,[11] and it seems unlikely that many of the members were as wealthy as Killingworth. By the early 19th century there are clear indications that some of the lowest social classes in Norwich were included in the congregation: thirty-six births in central Norwich were

Figure 14.2. Burial of skeleton 10466 containing a transfer-printed tea cup, with a design
of peacocks (photograph © NAU Archaeology).

recorded in the chapel register between 1821 and 1836, of which fifteen occurred in either
the Workhouse or in 'yards' (areas of poor housing later classified as slums).[12]

Membership of the chapel fluctuated considerably during the 18th and 19th centuries,
but ranged from 20 (1831) to 96 (1709) and 97 (1851).[13] Of course, 'membership' was
restricted to those adults baptized as a believer, and applications for membership were carefully considered before being granted, refused or deferred. Children could not be baptized
and become members, as they were considered too young to understand and make a full
commitment to the faith.[14] The actual number of the congregation was often considerably higher than the number of members,[15] and 150–200 people (including children)
were estimated to have attended the services in 1851.[16] In 1736, it was agreed that only
members should be allowed burial in the chapel's burial ground.[17] However, in 1789, the
costs charged for digging a child's grave were half those for an adult's grave, indicating
that burial of non-members (children) was taking place.[18] In 1852, a scale of charges for
preparing the graves of adults, children, members and non-members was introduced.[19] Not
all members were buried in the chapel's burial ground, the most notable example being
Thomas Grantham (the founder), who was buried in St Stephen's Church amidst fears his
body might be abused.[20] Unfortunately, no burial register survives for Priory Yard, so the
information available is limited.

THE EXCAVATED BURIALS

Part of the southern extension to the Baptist burial ground, encompassing an area *c.* 15m by 9m, was investigated, although not all of this was exposed. Flint walls of the former friary's north-east range formed the western and southern boundaries. The excavated skeletons probably date between *c.* 1726 and 1854 and, given the intensive use of the cemetery, much of the surviving material probably dates to the later period. Graves were tightly packed within the available space; many were cut through underlying masonry and were consequently quite shallow. The alignment of both the earthen graves and a brick-lined vault generally followed a south-west–north-east axis, as dictated by the surrounding walls. Many individual grave plots were used repeatedly, with the number of burials in each ranging between one and six, the latter probably indicating family plots.

Most if not all of the burials appear to have been interred in coffins, indicated by the presence of nails, wood-staining, handles/grips and plates in many of the graves; possible shroud pins were also recovered. All articulated burials were supine with heads to the west and arms to the side. Tentative evidence for the inclusion of 'grave goods' was found. A small but complete transfer-printed tea cup (Fig. 14.2) appears to have been placed within one coffin ([sk10466], a probable female aged 17–18), and was found resting on the ribcage, while a pistol-grip penknife was also found close to the left forearm of [sk10321] (a probable male aged 26–35).

DEMOGRAPHY

The remains of sixty-three individuals were excavated (forty-two by NAU and twenty-one by AFH). In general the skeletons were well preserved, with only slight fragmentation of the bones and clear surface detail, but they tended to be incomplete owing to the intercutting of graves. Sex determination was carried out in adult skeletons through examination of pelvic and skull morphology, supplemented by post-cranial measurements.[21] Age at death was estimated according to standard osteological techniques,[22] employing as many methods as possible; see Table 14.2 for age categories. Determining age at death in adult skeletons is difficult, with the age of older adults frequently underestimated.[23] The defined categories provide a guide to relative physiological age, rather than being an accurate portrayal of chronological age; no doubt many of those aged '46+ years' would in actuality have been decades older when they died.

Of the sixty-three individuals, thirty-nine were adults (61.9%) and twenty-four were non-adults (38.1%). This proportion of non-adults is high, but not as high as the *c.* 50% of the population thought to have died before the age of 20 in the 18th and 19th centuries.[24] The proportion of non-adults in excavated samples is often lower than suggested by documentary sources: at St Martin's Church, Birmingham, 30.3% of the skeletons were under 20, compared with the 53.8% expected from burial register analysis.[25] Poor preservation and recovery of non-adult remains may account for some of this discrepancy, as may the practice of burying infants within a particular location outside the excavation area.[26] The proportion of non-adults among the NAU-excavated skeletons (22/42, 52.4%) was considerably greater than among the AFH-excavated skeletons (2/21, 9.5%), although whether this relates to a genuine preference for burial of non-adults in a certain part of the cemetery or reflects differences in excavation methods between the two units is unclear. At

Table 14.2. Age categories

Fetus	Up to 38 weeks *in utero*
Neonate	c. birth
Infant	1–12 months
Juvenile	1–12 years (subdivided where necessary)
Adolescent	13–17 years
Young adult	18–25 years
Young–middle adult	26–35 years
Old–middle adult	36–45 years
Mature adult	46+ years
Adult	18+

Table 14.3. Non-adult age-at-death

Age Group	No.	(%)
Fetus	1	4.2
Neonate	1	4.2
Infant	3	12.5
1–3 years	8	33.3
4–6 years	4	16.7
7–12 years	4	16.7
13–17 years	3	12.5
Total	24	

St Martin's Church non-adults made up 32.8% of all burials in the lower-class earth-cut graves, but only 20.2% of the middle-class vault burials.[27] The proportion of non-adults at Priory Yard was greater than both, and higher than that observed in the comparatively wealthy population of St Marylebone Church, London (25.9%).[28] This suggests that the Priory Yard sample may have come from among the poorer sections of society.

The non-adults ranged in age from fetus (30–32 weeks *in utero*) to older adolescent (16–18 years). However, over half (54.2%) were under three years old, and nearly three-quarters (70.8%) were under six years (Fig. 14.3a; Table 14.3). These figures compare with the proportion of non-adults under seven at St Mary and St Michael, London (72.2%), and with the data from St Marylebone, where child deaths peaked below three years of age.[29] It has been suggested that 30% of the population in this period died before the age of two years.[30] However, at Priory Yard 20.6% of the total sample died before the age of three. The relative lack of individuals younger than twelve months suggests under-representation of this age group, a trend noted at St Martin's Church and Christ Church Spitalfields, London.[31]

Of the adults that could be sexed, twenty were female (60.6%) and thirteen were male (39.4%). This sex ratio contrasts with that observed at other post-medieval cemeteries, where males predominate: the proportion of males at both St Mary and St Michael and St Martin's Church was 58%, and at St Marylebone it was 55%.[32] However, there are similarities with the Baptist burial ground of West Butts Street, Poole, Dorset, where 61%

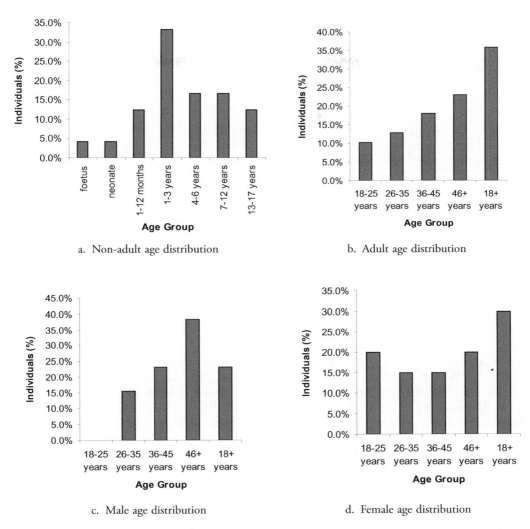

a. Non-adult age distribution

b. Adult age distribution

c. Male age distribution

d. Female age distribution

Figure 14.3. Age distributions amongst the excavated individuals.

of the skeletons were female.[33] Women commonly outnumbered men in early Baptist congregations, perhaps owing to the 'political, social, and economic consequences for males joining a Dissenting congregation'.[34] However, the possible presence of sailors (who may have died at sea) among the Poole congregation may have influenced the demography of the skeletal sample.[35]

Two-thirds of the adults that could be aged were placed in the two older age groups (Fig. 14.3b; Table 14.4), which corresponded to the distribution at St Marylebone.[36] Differences were apparent between the sexes: no young adult males were present, most being found in the two older age groups, whereas the females were evenly distributed between the four categories (Fig. 14.3c and d; Table 14.4). Most skeletons had well-preserved pelvic

Table 14.4. Adult age-at-death

Age Group*	Males No.	(%)	Females No.	(%)	Unsexed No.	(%)	Total Adults No.	(%)
YA (18–25)	0	0.0	4	20.0	0	0.0	4	10.3
YMA (26–35)	2	15.4	3	15.0	0	0.0	5	12.8
OMA (36–45)	3	23.1	3	15.0	1	16.7	7	17.9
MA (46+)	5	38.5	4	20.0	0	0.0	9	23.1
Adult (18+)	3	23.1	6	30.0	5	83.3	14	35.9
Total	13		20		6		39	

* YA = young adult; YMA = young–middle adult; OMA = old–middle adult; MA = mature adult; see Table 14.2

bones, lessening the likelihood that they had been mis-sexed.[37] The deaths of young adult females might be linked to the dangers associated with first pregnancy and childbirth. During this period maternal mortality was around five deaths per 1,000 births, and the risks to lower-class women in particular were high.[38] Repeated pregnancies and breastfeeding (if the mother was able) would have weakened her health, making her more susceptible to undernutrition and infectious diseases.[39] However, numerous possible causes of death exist, and the prevalence of lung infection (possibly tuberculosis) among the young women was notable. It is possible that younger men were concerned by the legal disadvantages of association with a nonconformist group,[40] and so were less likely to join one. However, this may not have been a strong consideration among the lower classes.

The osteological evidence was compared with data from burial memorials, supplemented by additional historical sources; unfortunately no burial registers survive. Twenty-four people are known to have been buried at Priory Yard (Appendix 1), but only one named skeleton could be positively identified.[41] The ages of nineteen individuals were given, and these range from 23 months to 83 years, with a mean of 51.3 years. Although some adults lived into their 70s and 80s, the majority died in their 50s and 60s (Fig. 14.4); this is broadly consistent with the osteological results. However, few child burials were recorded, and non-adults are severely under-represented when compared to the archaeological evidence. The mean female age at death was fourteen years lower than that for males, at 42.7 years (range: 23 months to 65 years) compared with 56.7 years (range: 6–83 years). This supports the osteological findings that females tended to be younger and males older.

However, burial memorials are a limited and biased source of information on those buried at Priory Yard.[42] No doubt many memorials have been lost: they span a considerable number of years, representing births between 1668 and 1829 and deaths between 1725 and 1843. They may not correspond with the period for which the most skeletal evidence was recovered. Presumably memorials were only affordable by relatively wealthy members of the congregation,[43] and since much of the congregation probably derived from the lowest socio-economic level, it is unlikely that the majority would be represented. Cost may also be an explanation for the general exclusion of children from memorials.[44] Despite the marked female bias of the excavated skeletons, the number of memorials to males slightly outnumbers those to females, and in three cases wives were included on their husbands' memorials.[45] The age at death was provided for twelve of the thirteen males (92.3%), but

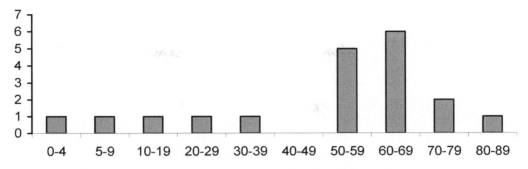

Figure 14.4. Age distribution of known burials at Priory Yard, Norwich.

only eight of the eleven females (72.7%);[46] one did not even have her first name reported, simply being recorded as the 'mother of Grantham Killingworth'. This suggests that the lives of males, especially older men, were considered more worthy of marking through a memorial.

STATURE

The stature of adult skeletons was calculated from measurements of intact long bones.[47] Although the potential stature of an individual is governed by genetics, the actual height achieved can be influenced by environmental factors. Consequently, short adult stature may reflect episodes of poor nutrition and disease during childhood sufficient to cause stunting of growth.[48] The mean stature for ten males was 167.9cm (5ft 6in), and for eleven females it was 155.1cm (5ft 1in); ranges are given in Table 15.5. Both sexes were below average height for the period, falling at or below the lower end of the range of means for eleven post-medieval sites: 168–174cm for males, and 156–164cm for females.[49] They were also short compared with three post-medieval sites not included in that study (Table 14.5).

Table 14.5. Comparison of adult stature

| Site | Males | | Females | | |
	Mean (cm)	Range (cm)	Mean (cm)	Range (cm)	Source
Priory Yard	168	157–175	155	145–163	
St Martin's Church	172	156–185	159	139–171	Brickley *et al.* 2006, 101
St Marylebone	170	154–182	159	145–169	Miles *et al.* 2008, 108
West Butts	169	157–186	158	140–174	McKinley 2008, 64–7

It has been suggested that socio-economic status in this period is not reflected in stature,[50] a finding corroborated at St Martin's Church, where no significant difference in stature was observed between the two class-groups.[51] However, this contrasts with documentary sources, which often report a noticeable difference in height between classes.[52] The sample size for Priory Yard was small, which may have influenced the results, but it seems likely that the short statures observed reflect poor nutrition and childhood disease (see below). It is possible that in this case short stature was connected with lower socio-economic status.

CHILDHOOD HEALTH

... their children are being stunted and starved and breeding disease[53]

Enamel defects take the form of pits, lines or grooves in the teeth, termed dental enamel hypoplasia (DEH). These can occur if a child experiences stress, such as poor nutrition and/or disease that causes a temporary halt in growth. Since tooth enamel is not remodelled, the evidence is retained throughout life.[54]

DEH was observed in the deciduous (milk) teeth of two non-adults (15.4% of thirteen with deciduous teeth present), and 16.5% of deciduous teeth were affected (23/139). The latter prevalence was higher than that observed at both St Martin's Church (10.4%) and St Marylebone (3.2%).[55] Deciduous teeth form while the baby is in the womb and during the first few months after birth,[56] so the presence of DEH implies stress during these periods of growth. In turn, this implies poor levels of maternal health, leaving mothers unable to supply essential nutrients to the baby during pregnancy or through breastfeeding.[57] Breast milk is the most nutritious food for a baby, and it also provides protection against disease.[58] Undernourished mothers will have had difficulty breastfeeding, and if working outside the home they may have found it impossible. Many working-class women resorted to feeding their infants unsuitable foods, such as sweetened condensed milk or flour mixed with water, which lacked adequate nutrition for a baby. Furthermore, the risk of infection from unsterilized feeding utensils or from the food itself was often high.[59] Evidence that some of the infants and children from Priory Yard were bottle-fed with sweetened milk, or given sweetened comforters to suck, was suggested by the presence of dental caries in the upper deciduous incisors (see below).

The presence of DEH in the permanent teeth of many individuals attested that malnutrition and poor health probably continued throughout childhood. DEH was observed in 66.7% of the non-adults with at least three teeth present (4/6), affecting 28.2% of their teeth (34/110). Among the adults, DEH was observed in 50.0% of those with permanent teeth present (9/18), and 22.6% of their teeth were involved (Table 14.6). The proportion of teeth affected was broadly comparable with St Marylebone (20.1%), but lower than at St Martin's Church (29.7%).[60] The highest prevalence (30.4%) occurred in the young adult teeth (Table 15.6), and was comparable with a peak in the same age group at St Martin's Church (35%), and in the 26–35 year group at St Marylebone (31.2%).[61] This may indicate a shorter life expectancy among individuals experiencing childhood stress.[62]

Six non-adults showed signs of a nutritional deficiency, giving a crude prevalence rate (CPR) of 27.3%.[63] However, since all six were under three years of age, 54.5% of those under three were affected (including all three infants).[64] It is possible, and indeed likely, for an individual to suffer from more than one deficiency at the same time, and these conditions are difficult to diagnose in skeletal remains.[65] Five non-adults (22.7%) had probably been suffering from scurvy (vitamin C deficiency), suggesting that insufficient fresh fruit and vegetables were being consumed.[66] Potatoes were probably the main source of vitamin C for the lower classes,[67] and a connection between localized episodes of potato blight

Table 14.6. Prevalence of DEH, adult teeth affected

Age group	Teeth with DEH	Total teeth present	(%)
18–25	14	46	30.4
26–35	26	123	21.1
36–45	9	41	22.0
46+	1	5	20.0
18+	12	59	20.3
Total Adult	62	274	22.6

and scurvy among the poor has been suggested at St Martin's Church, where evidence for scurvy was seen only in the working-class section of the population.[68] A similar cause can be postulated for the occurrence of scurvy at Priory Yard.

One 1–2-year-old child (4.5%) had probably suffered from rickets, a deficiency in vitamin D which prevents the bone from mineralising correctly (Fig. 14.5).[69] Evidence for healed childhood rickets was also observed in the flattened and bowed tibiae of a 36–45-year-old female, and in a disarticulated femur, tibia and fibula. The body produces most of the vitamin D it needs, but requires sunlight in order to do so. Rickets became prevalent among the poor in the industrialized cities of Europe, when narrow streets, overcrowded living conditions and polluted atmospheres prevented sunlight from reaching children,[70] yet skeletal evidence for rickets is less common than might be expected from documentary sources.[71] With 41.7% of births between 1821 and 1836 recorded in the chapel register occurring in the Workhouse or in yards (slums),[72] it is likely that such conditions encouraged the development of rickets in the Priory Yard population. The appalling conditions within these dwellings were described by Samuel Clarke, sanitary inspector in Norwich during the late 19th century, in letters he wrote to the *Norfolk Chronicle*.[73]

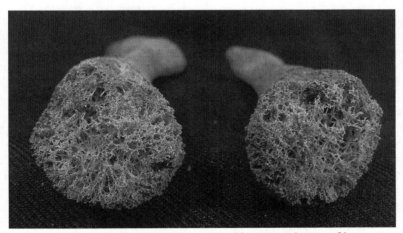

Figure 14.5. Skeleton 10874, 1–2 years old, proximal view of humeri, showing an expanded 'honeycomb' appearance, with no firm cortical bone present, resulting from poor mineralization of the bone. Probable childhood rickets (photograph by A. Caffell).

Cribra orbitalia, or porosity affecting the orbital roof, has recently been associated with megaloblastic and haemolytic anaemias, the causes of which are complex.[74] It is often used as a general indicator of stress during childhood.[75] At Priory Yard the prevalence in both adults and children was close to 30% (Table 14.7), providing further evidence for childhood ill-health and poor nutrition. In only one individual did cribra orbitalia coincide with scurvy, which may reflect the involvement of the orbital roofs in both conditions: it is possible that in the remaining individuals the new bone formation associated with scurvy obscured any evidence for cribra orbitalia. However, Ortner *et al.* suggested that individual skeletons rarely display evidence for multiple deficiency diseases.[76]

Table 14.7. Prevalence of cribra orbitalia, individuals and orbits affected

	Individuals*		Right orbit		Left orbit	
	(n)	(%)	(n)	(%)	(n)	(%)
Non-adults	5/16	31.3	5/14	35.7	5/16	31.3
Adults	9/31	29.0	6/31	19.4	8/31	25.8

* Prevalence among individuals with at least one orbit present

INFECTIOUS DISEASE

Twenty adults and eight non-adults showed evidence for infection, manifested as deposits of woven or lamellar bone. The former indicated an infection active at the time of death, whereas the latter indicated that the lesion had healed.[77] In most individuals the lesions were non-specific – that is, of unknown cause – and will not be discussed further here. Endocranial new bone formation (on the internal surface of the cranium) occurred in seven non-adults (six under the age of 6, and a 16–18-year-old adolescent) giving a CPR of 29.2%. It is believed to result following inflammation or haemorrhage of the meningeal blood vessels, and possible causes include chronic meningitis, trauma, anaemia, cancer, metabolic diseases, venous drainage disorders and tuberculosis.[78] Interestingly, 14-year-old Frances Scott was recorded as having died from a 'brain fever'; unfortunately her remains were not recovered.

Tuberculosis was particularly common among the poor, who lived in overcrowded dwellings and suffered from poor nutrition.[79] It affects the skeleton in a small percentage of cases and consequently archaeological evidence is uncommon.[80] The reported prevalence in post-medieval skeletons was just 0.47%, yet documentary evidence suggests that *c.* 25% of deaths in London may have been attributable to tuberculosis in the late 18th and early 19th centuries.[81] Tuberculosis was diagnosed in an 18–20-year-old female from Priory Yard (CPR 2.6%), who had destruction of the lower thoracic and upper lumbar vertebrae, bone formation on the lower ribs, a probable psoas abscess and widespread periostitis.[82] Deposits of new bone on the pleural surfaces of the ribs have been associated with tuberculosis, but it also occurs with other respiratory diseases.[83] Such deposits were observed in 20.5% (8/39) of the adults, all of which (bar one) were female. The CPR among females (35.0%) was higher than that among males (7.7%), and most of those affected were young or young–middle-aged adults. Considering the dominance of the textile industry in Norwich during the 18th and 19th centuries, it is notable that female textile workers have been identified as a group particularly susceptible to tuberculosis.[84]

Maxillary sinusitis can also indicate respiratory infections, this time affecting the upper respiratory tract. It could indicate exposure to polluted or smoky environments, although it can result from dental abscesses.[85] It occurred in adults and non-adults and was most common among males (Table 14.8). This may be connected with the higher prevalence of dental abscesses observed in the male adults. In relation to both rib lesions and sinusitis, it is interesting that there was evidence of pipe-smoking in the Priory Yard population, with 57.1% of men (4/7) and 12.5% of women (1/8) showing pipe-wear-facets on their anterior teeth. These facets were most common on the right, which may reflect handedness, and in the anterior teeth, suggesting that a long curved-stem pipe was smoked.[86] At St Martin's Church, 10/11 individuals (all male) with pipe-smoking wear were from the earth-cut graves, suggesting that smoking was associated with the lower classes.[87]

Table 14.8. Prevalence of maxillary sinusitis, individuals and sinuses affected

	Individuals*		Right maxilla		Left maxilla	
	(n)	(%)	(n)	(%)	(n)	(%)
Non-adults	3/11	27.3	3/10	30.0	2/9	22.2
Males	4/9	44.4	4/7	57.1	4/9	44.4
Females	5/14	35.7	3/9	33.3	3/10	30.0
Total Adults	10/24	41.7	8/17	47.1	8/20	40.0

* Prevalence among individuals with at least one maxillary sinus present

DENTAL HEALTH

Analysis of the teeth and jaws provided evidence for health, diet and oral hygiene. If dental plaque is not removed from the teeth effectively, or on a regular basis, then it can mineralize and form concretions of calculus. Calculus formation can also be common when the diet is high in protein and/or carbohydrates.[88] It was observed in 87.5% of the adults, and affected 82.8% of the teeth (Tables 14.9 and 14.10); it was also seen on the deciduous and permanent teeth of non-adults. The proportion of individuals affected was considerably higher than the 21.4% average for the post-medieval period,[89] but that figure was based largely on samples from crypts which were likely to represent the middle or upper classes. The data from St Martin's Church, where 81.4% of those buried in earth-cut graves had calculus, compared with 69.7% of those buried in the vaults,[90] suggests that lower-class individuals were more likely to have calculus deposits on their teeth. The various abrasive dentifrices and tooth powders available during this period would typically have been used by the middle and upper classes.[91] No evidence for their use, which would have stripped teeth of enamel as well as plaque and calculus, was seen at Priory Yard. The light nature of most calculus deposits could suggest either that some form of oral hygiene (though ineffective) was attempted or that proteins/carbohydrates did not form a significant part of the diet.

Dental caries (tooth decay) forms when bacteria in the plaque metabolize dietary sugars, producing acid which causes the loss of minerals from the teeth and eventually leads to the

Table 14.9. Prevalence of calculus and dental caries (teeth affected), antemortem tooth loss and dental abscesses (tooth positions affected)

Age group	Calculus (n)	(%)	Caries (n)	(%)	AMTL (n)	(%)	Abscess (n)	(%)
18–25	41/46	89.1	4/46	8.7	1/62	1.6	0/62	0.0
26–35	111/123	90.2	37/123	30.1	22/156	14.1	6/156	3.8
36–45	39/41	95.1	10/41	24.4	109/184	59.2	3/184	1.6
46+	4/5	80.0	2/5	40.0	231/248	93.1	2/248	0.8
18+	32/59	54.2	10/59	16.9	133/238	55.9	5/238	2.1
Total	227/274	82.8	63/274	23.0	496/888	55.9	16/888	1.8

Table 14.10. Prevalence of calculus and dental caries (adults with teeth affected), antemortem tooth loss and dental abscesses (adults with tooth positions affected)

Age group	Calculus (n)	(%)	Caries (n)	(%)	AMTL (n)	(%)	Abscess (n)	(%)
18–25	2/3	66.7	3/3	100.0	1/3	33.3	0/3	0.0
26–35	5/5	100.0	5/5	100.0	4/5	80.0	2/5	40.0
36–45	5/6	83.3	5/6	83.3	7/7	100.0	2/7	28.6
46+	3/3	100.0	1/3	33.3	8/8	100.0	2/8	25.0
18+	6/7	85.7	4/7	57.1	9/11	81.8	3/11	27.3
Total	21/24	87.5	18/24	75.0	29/34	85.3	9/11	26.5

Table 14.11. Prevalence of caries in non-adults – individuals and teeth affected (deciduous and permanent)

Age group	Deciduous teeth (n)	(%)	Permanent teeth (n)	(%)	Individuals (n)	(%)
1–5	21/108	19.4	0	–	4/8	50.0
6–12	13/31	41.8	6/25	24.0	4/4	100.0
13–17	0	–	5/85	5.9	3/3	100.0
Total	34/139	24.5	11/110	10.0	11/15	73.3

formation of a cavity.[92] Dental caries was observed in 73.3% of the non-adults, affecting all those over, and half of those under, six years (Table 14.11). Nearly a quarter of deciduous teeth had cavities, and the upper deciduous incisors (particularly the central incisors) of three children were affected. Caries in this location has been associated with bottle-feeding with sweetened milk, or sucking on sweetened comforters, and the latter may have been used to quieten sick children.[93] The presence of DEH may also have contributed to the high caries prevalence.[94] The older juveniles experienced the highest overall caries frequency, with 33.9% of their total teeth (deciduous and permanent) showing at least one cavity.

Three-quarters of the adults with at least one tooth present had cavities in their teeth, and all adults between 18 and 35 years were affected (Table 14.10). The proportion of teeth involved (23.0%, Table 14.9) was double the post-medieval average of 11.2% and the 11.1%

of teeth affected at St Martin's Church.[95] A general increase in prevalence with age was observed from adolescence onwards (Tables 14.9 and 14.11), consistent with the fact that cavities cannot be remodelled and accumulate throughout life. Consumption of a diet high in sugar and refined carbohydrates, coupled with ineffective oral hygiene, were the likely causes of the high caries prevalence. The increased availability and dramatic drop in the price of imported sugar in the 18th and 19th centuries enabled the poor to include it as a staple part of their diet.[96]

A considerable portion of the adults (85.3%) had lost teeth during life, and all adults over 35 years were affected (Table 14.10). The mature adults had lost a staggering 93.1% of their teeth (Table 14.9), and eight adults (six mature, two unaged) had completely tooth-less mandibles (26.7% of mandibles). The frequency of antemortem tooth loss (AMTL) in both individuals (85.3%) and teeth (55.9%) was exceptionally high compared with the post-medieval averages of 60.6% (individuals) and 23.4% (teeth).[97] Dental caries was probably a leading cause of AMTL at Priory Yard, and carious teeth could have been lost as the natural culmination of the disease process or through deliberate extraction. Another cause of AMTL, periodontal disease (the result of untreated gingivitis),[98] was also prevalent – fourteen individuals had moderate to considerable loss of bone surrounding the teeth, and in some cases little more than soft tissue would have remained to hold the tooth in place. Extraction may have been the only treatment available for the poor, who would have been unable to afford fillings or dental prostheses.[99] No evidence for either was observed at Priory Yard, in contrast to the relatively wealthy crypt burials of Christ Church, Spital-fields, where three individuals had fillings and nine had bridges or partial dentures.[100] At St Martin's Church the only evidence for fillings was observed in vault burials, and while both a vault and an earth-cut burial contained dentures, those of the former were more expensive and of better quality.[101]

CONCLUSION

Until relatively recently few post-medieval cemeteries had been excavated and, at the date of analysis, few had been published. Those that have are usually of the middle or upper classes, such as Christ Church, Spitalfields, and St Brides, London.[102] Cemeteries belonging to a religious minority are also scarce, although, again, more have recently been excavated, such as West Butts Street, Poole, and the cemeteries of St Mary and St Michael and the Baptist burial ground in Bow.[103] The Priory Yard population, although small, provides an invaluable insight into life and health in post-medieval Norwich. As such, it adds to the geographical range of urban samples, as most are from London.

Various aspects of the Priory Yard population suggest that they were probably of low socio-economic status. Poverty is invariably associated with poor nutrition and increased vulnerability to disease, and the health of mothers and children is closely linked. The impact of poor nutrition and disease on women would have been exacerbated by the demands of pregnancy and lactation, and the presence of enamel defects in the deciduous teeth of young children suggested that mothers were unable to provide adequate nutrients to sustain the normal growth and development of their babies. Undernourished mothers would have found it difficult to breast-feed, and those working long hours outside the home would have found it impossible to do so. Consequently many working-class women resorted to feeding unsuitable foods to their babies, and evidence for bottle-feeding with sweetened milk was present in the form of cavities in the upper deciduous incisors. The possibility that many of these women were employed as textile workers may correlate with the prevalence of lung infections and tuberculosis in the young women; such chronic infections would have been a further drain on their physical resources.

That poor health and nutrition continued through childhood was indicated through the prevalence of cribra orbitalia and enamel defects in the permanent teeth. A high proportion of the non-adults had suffered from scurvy, suggesting a diet lacking in fresh fruits and vegetables, which may be linked to potato availability. Rickets was also observed, suggesting overcrowded living conditions and polluted atmospheres. The high frequency of dental caries implied consumption of a diet high in sugar and refined carbohydrates from a young age, consistent with the low cost and wide availability of sugar in the 19th century. The volume of sugar consumed may also have contributed towards malnutrition.[104] The large proportion of non-adult burials, particularly those under three years of age, attests that many probably succumbed to a combination of poor nutrition and/or infectious disease. The short stature of those that survived to adulthood indicates the long-term effect on growth. Short women are more likely to give birth to stillborn or underweight babies, and the latter are in turn predisposed to undernutrition and vulnerable to disease.[105]

The absence of any form of dental treatment, such as fillings, dental prostheses or the use of tooth powders, implied a low social status. Tooth-extraction may have been the only affordable treatment for dental caries, and could have contributed to the high prevalence of AMTL.

It has not been possible to address the full range of pathological conditions observed within the scope of this paper, nor to consider the limitations of the data,[106] and the data has been interpreted solely in relation to socio-economic status. Interesting questions are raised concerning the impact nonconformist religions had on the lives of those who adopted them, and the relationship between non-conformism and social class. To what extent are the pathological and demographic patterns observed influenced by religious belief, and to what extent do they reflect social status? With the recent increase in the number of excavated nonconformist and 'normal' cemetery populations of varying status, it may be possible to begin to consider such issues (see Powers and Miles this volume). It is anticipated that the Priory Yard population will provide a vital contribution to future studies in this area.

APPENDIX

Known burials at Priory Yard Baptist Cemetery, Norwich

Name	Age	Year of birth (approx)	Date of death	Occupation	Relationship	Other
Daniel Killingworth	57	1668	4th Nov 1725		Father of Grantham Killingworth	Before steps up to the meeting house
William Barron	52	1678	7th Feb 1730	Minister		
Thomas Ives	52	1698	29th May 1750	Minister		
Martha Barnham	65	1700	11th Aug 1765		Wife of John Barnham	
John Barnham	63	1709	10th Feb 1772	Worsted weaver	Husband of Martha Barnham	St George, Tombland
___ Killingworth	?	?	before Nov 1777		Mother of Grantham Killingworth	Before steps up to the meeting house
Grantham Killingworth	79	1699	24th Jan 1778		Son of Daniel Killingworth	Before steps up to the meeting house; memorial erected 1816
Ann Humphrey	?	?	before Sep 1783		First wife of William Humphrey	
Catherine Humphrey	?	?	before Sep 1783		Second wife of William Humphrey	
Mary Cawston	?	?	13th Oct 1783		Wife of Joseph Cawston	
William Humphrey	75	1712	20th Mar 1787	Woolcomber	Husband of Ann & Catherine	
John Ropkins	65	1730	29th Nov 1795			
Samuel Bell	6	1790	20th Jul 1796			
Mary Barnham	65	1741	18th Apr 1808		Wife of Richard Barnham	
Eleanor Barnham	1y 11m	1815	1st Feb 1817			
Mary Tillyard	63	1754	25th Dec 1817		Wife of Abraham Tillyard	

Mary Bagstaff	57	1764	7th Oct 1821		Wife of John Bagstaff	
Matthew Watts	52	1775	21st Mar 1827	Deacon		
Henry Green	?	?	after Jan 1829			
John Ward	69	1760	19th Jul 1829			
Frances Scott	31	1802	9th Feb 1833		Wife of Thomas Scott, minister	
Abraham Tillyard	83	1751	5th Oct 1834	Deacon	Husband of Mary Tillyard	
James Ward	25	1817	21st Dec 1842	Cabinet maker		Died of carditis
Frances Smithee Scott	14	1829	26th Jan 1843		Daughter of Thomas and Frances Scott	Died of brain fever

NOTES

* We would like to thank Malin Holst, York Oste-oarchaeology Ltd, for her support and advice during the skeletal analysis and preparation of this paper. We are grateful to Elizabeth Rutledge for her research into the historical and documentary sources relating to Priory Yard chapel and its congregation. Matthew Champion drew our attention to the letters written by a 19th-century sanitary inspector for Norwich to the *Norfolk Chronicle*. Thanks are also extended to Crane Begg for producing Fig. 15.1 and preparing the other figures for publication. Support for the final stages of article preparation was provided by Elizabeth Shepherd Popescu (Oxford Archaeology East).

1. NHER 26226.
2. Oldfield 1829, 358.
3. We have drawn heavily on the documentary research carried out by Elizabeth Rutledge for the historical background to Priory Yard chapel. White 1845, 121, refers to the congregation first meeting in 1686 in a 'hired building', location not given.
4. NRO NRS 5821 18 D3, cited in Rutledge forthcoming.
5. Rutledge forthcoming; although White 1845, 121, gives a date of 1812 for the erection of the 'present chapel'.
6. Hewett n.d., 15, cited in Rutledge forthcoming.
7. NRO FC 12/2, cited in Rutledge forthcoming.
8. Hewett n.d., 16, cited in Rutledge forthcoming.

9. Rutledge forthcoming.
10. NRO ANW 1778 ff.13d–18d, cited in Rutledge forthcoming; White 1845, 121, refers to an endowment of c. £75 per annum bequeathed by Grantham Killingworth.
11. Rutledge forthcoming.
12. NRO MF 1152/652, cited in Rutledge forthcoming.
13. Rutledge forthcoming.
14. Bebbington 1992, 10–11; Briggs 1994, 27–30, 43–53, 59–60.
15. Briggs 1994, 257–61.
16. Rutledge forthcoming.
17. NRO FC 12/1, cited in Rutledge forthcoming.
18. Rutledge forthcoming.
19. Rutledge forthcoming.
20. Oldfield 1829, 360–61.
21. For an overview see Mays & Cox 2000; Buikstra & Ubelaker 1994, 16–21.
22. For an overview see Cox 2000; Scheuer & Black 2000a; 2000b.
23. E.g. Molleson & Cox 1993, 167–72; Molleson 1995; Miles *et al.* 2008, 105.
24. Roberts & Cox 2003, 304.
25. Brickley *et al.* 2006, 98–9, Table 92.
26. Lewis 2007, 23–33.
27. Brickley *et al.* 2006, 98.
28. Miles *et al.* 2008, 104
29. Percentage calculated from figures given in Powers 2006, 8, Table 3; also see Powers & Miles this volume; Miles *et al.* 2008, 104–6.

30. Roberts & Cox 2003, 303.

31. Brickley *et al.* 2006, 67–70; Molleson & Cox 1993, 209–10.

32. Powers 2006, 8; see also Powers & Miles this volume; Brickley *et al.* 2006, 99–100; Miles *et al.* 2008, 104

33. McKinley 2008, 64.

34. McKinley 2008, 64, 103–4; see also Powers & Miles this volume.

35. McKinley 2008, 63–4, 5–10.

36. Miles *et al.* 2008, 104.

37. See Walker 1995.

38. Roberts & Cox 2003, 315–18.

39. Wohl 1984, 12–3.

40. McKinley 2008, 64 103–4; see also Powers & Miles this volume.

41. Frances Scott, the wife of minister Thomas Scott. Her stone memorial plaque was found with that for her daughter Frances Smithee Scott, but the daughter's remains were not identified. Copper-alloy coffin plates were also recovered for John Ward and James Ward, although these could only be tentatively associated with excavated skeletons.

42. Limitations of documentary evidence have been discussed by, e.g., Cox 1995; Molleson & Cox 1993, 189.

43. Mr. Grantham Killingworth (benefactor of Priory Yard), his mother and father, and two other men entitled 'Mr.' (Henry Green and John Barnham) all had memorials. A church connection is also evident with two ministers (William Barron and Thomas Ives), the wife and daughter of a minister (both Frances Scotts), and two deacons (Matthew Watts and Abraham Tillyard) all accorded a memorial. Occupation is given for only three other individuals, including a worsted weaver, a woolcomber and a cabinet-maker.

44. Although Samuel Bell (6 years) apparently had his own memorial, the young Eleanor Barnham (1 year 11 months) was presumably added to that of John and Martha Barnham (relationship unknown, possibly grandparents).

45. Martha Barnham shared a memorial with her husband John Barnham; William Humphrey shared his memorial with his first and second wives (Ann and Catherine); and Mary Tillyard shared a memorial with her husband Abraham Tillyard.

46. However, in one case the age given was illegible, so age was known for only seven females.

47. Trotter 1970.

48. Bogin 1988, 268–328.

49. Roberts & Cox 2003, 308, Table 6.7.

50. Roberts & Cox 2003, 308.

51. Brickley *et al.* 2006, 101.

52. E.g. Wohl 1984, 57–8.

53. Clarke 1864.

54. Provided teeth are not lost or the surfaces obscured by calcified plaque; Hillson 1996, 165–77; Roberts & Manchester 2005, 75–7.

55. Brickley *et al.* 2006, 144; Miles *et al.* 2008, 111.

56. Hillson 1996, 121–4, Table 5.2.

57. Lewis 2007, 98; 105; Wohl 1984, 12–13; 20–33.

58. Lewis 2007, 97–9; Fauve-Chamoux 2000, 626.

59. Wohl 1984, 20–33; Fauve-Chamoux 2000, 629–33.

60. Miles *et al.* 2008, 114; Brickley *et al.* 2006, 144, calculated from Table 115.

61. Brickley *et al.* 2006, 144; Miles *et al.* 2008, 114.

62. Lewis 2007, 106.

63. Of 22 non-adults, excluding the fetus and neonate from the calculation.

64. Lewis 2007, 2, defines neonates as between birth and 27 days, and infants as between birth and one year. In this study, neonates were identified as an important subcategory of infant as they may be subject to different causes of death and/or funerary treatment to post-neonatal infants (Lewis 2007, 84 and 33). It was decided to represent the two age groups as 0–27 days and 1–12 months to prevent overlapping data groups where the second category is referred to as infants in the text.

65. Brickley & Ives 2006, 170–71; Lewis 2007, 97.

66. See Ortner 2003a, 383–93; Aufderheide & Rodríguez-Martín 1998, 310–14; Ortner & Ericksen 1997; and Ortner *et al.* 2001 for diagnostic criteria and detailed discussion of aetiology.

67. Roberts & Cox 2003, 306.

68. Brickley & Ives 2006, 171; Brickley *et al.* 2006, 131.

69. See Ortner 2003a, 393–404; Aufderheide & Rodríguez-Martín 1998, 305–10; and Lewis 2007, 119–26 for diagnostic criteria and detailed discussion of aetiology.

70. Roberts & Manchester 2005, 238; Lewis 2007, 121.

71. Roberts & Cox 2003, 308–10.

72. Rutledge forthcoming.

73. Clarke 1864.

74. Walker *et al.* 2009.

75. Lewis 2007, 111–15.

76. Ortner *et al.* 2001, 349.

77. Roberts & Manchester 2005, 8.

78. Lewis 2004; 2007, 141–3.

79. Roberts & Cox 2003, 338; Roberts & Manchester 2005, 183.

80. Roberts & Manchester 2005, 188, report skeletal involvement in 3–5% of cases; Aufderheide & Rodríguez-Martín 1998, 133, suggest 5–7% of cases.
81. Roberts & Cox 2003, 338–340, table 6.23, graph 6.16; although some of the diseases attributed to 'consumption' will have been respiratory diseases other than tuberculosis.
82. Diagnostic criteria described by Aufderheide & Rodríguez-Martín 1998, 133–40.
83. Roberts *et al.* 1994; Santos & Roberts 2001; 2006.
84. Aufderheide & Rodríguez-Martín 1998, 130.
85. Roberts & Manchester 2005, 174–6.
86. Capasso *et al.* 1999, 157.
87. Brickley *et al.* 2006, 145.
88. Roberts & Manchester 2005, 71–3; Hillson 1996, 255–60.
89. Roberts & Cox 2003, 324–7, table 6.16.
90. Brickley *et al.* 2006, 143.
91. Hillam 1990; Roberts & Cox 2003, 324–5, fig. 6.15.
92. Zero 1999, 636.
93. Williams & Curzon 1986, 208–10.
94. Williams & Curzon 1986, 208.
95. Roberts & Cox 2003, 324–6, table 6.13; Brickley *et al.* 2006, 141, figure calculated from data provided in table 110.
96. Hardwick 1960, 14; Corbett & Moore 1976, 412–13.
97. Roberts & Cox 2003, 324–7, table 6.15.
98. Hillson 1996, 260–69.
99. Hillam 1990; Roberts & Cox 2003, 321–4; Bishop *et al.* 2001.
100. Cox 1996, 87–92; Molleson & Cox 1993, 53–60.
101. Brickley *et al.* 2006, 139; Hancocks 2006, 140.
102. Molleson & Cox 1993; Scheuer & Bowman 1995.
103. McKinley 2008; Powers 2006; Powers and Miles this volume
104. Hobhouse 1999, 57–9.
105. Wohl 1984, 13.
106. E.g. Wood *et al.* 1992.

BIBLIOGRAPHY

Aufderheide, A.C. & Rodríguez-Martín, C. 1998, *The Cambridge Encyclopedia of Human Palaeopathology*, Cambridge: Cambridge University Press.
Bebbington, D. 1992, *Victorian Nonconformity*, Bangor: Headstart History.
Bishop, M.G.H., Gelbier, S. & Gibbons, D. 2001 'Ethics – dentistry and tooth-drawing in the late eighteenth and early nineteenth centuries in England. Evidence of provision at all levels of society', *British Dental Journal* 191: 575–80.
Bogin, B. 1988, *Patterns of Human Growth*. Cambridge Studies in Biological Anthropology 3. Cambridge: Cambridge University Press.
Brickley, M. & Ives, R. 2006, 'Skeletal manifestations of infantile scurvy', *American Journal of Physical Anthropology* 129: 163–72.
Brickley, M., Buteux, S., Adams, J. & Cherrington, R. 2006, *St. Martin's Uncovered: Investigations in the Churchyard of St. Martin's-in-the-Bull Ring, Birmingham, 2001*, Oxford: Oxbow Books.
Briggs, J.H.Y. 1994, *The English Baptists of the Nineteenth Century*. A History of the English Baptists 3. Didcot: Baptist Historical Society.
Buikstra, J.E. & Ubelaker, D.H. (eds) 1994, *Standards for Data Collection from Human Skeletal Remains*. Arkansas Archaeological Survey Research Series 44. Fayetteville (AR): Arkansas Archaeological Survey.
Capasso, L., Kennedy, K.A.R. & Wilczak, C.A. 1999, *Atlas of Occupational Markers on Human Remains*. *Journal of Paleontology* Monographic Publication 3. Teramo: Edigrafial.
Clarke, R. forthcoming, *Norwich Whitefriars: Excavations at Jarrold's Printing Works, Norwich, 2002–03*, East Anglian Archaeology. Cambridge: Oxford Archaeology East.
Clarke, S. 1864, 'Unhealthy homes in Norwich', *Norfolk Chronicle* (18 Jan).
Corbett, M.E. & Moore, W.J. 1976, 'Distribution of caries in ancient British populations IV: the 19th century', *Caries Research* 10: 401–14.

Cox, M. 1995, 'A dangerous assumption: anyone can be a historian! The lessons from Christ Church, Spitalfields', in Saunders & Herring 1995, 19–29.

Cox, M. 1996, *Life and Death in Spitalfields, 1700 to 1850*, York: Council for British Archaeology.

Cox, M. 2000, 'Ageing adults from the skeleton', in Cox & Mays 2000, 61–82.

Cox, M. & Mays, S.A. (eds) 2000, *Human Osteology in Archaeology and Forensic Science*, London: Greenwich Medical Media.

Fauve-Chamoux, A. 2000, 'Breast milk and artificial infant feeding', in Kiple & Ornelas 2000, 626–35.

Foley, R.A. & Cruwys, E. (eds) 1986, *Teeth and Anthropology*. British Archaeological Report Int. Ser. 291. Oxford: British Archaeological Reports.

Hancocks, A. 2006, 'Dentures', in Brickley *et al.* 2006, 140.

Hardwick, J.L. 1960, 'The incidence and distribution of caries throughout the ages in relation to the Englishman's diet', *British Dental Journal* 108: 9–17.

Hewett, Rev. M.F. n.d., 'Collection of material in preparation for an historical record of the Baptists of Norfolk and their churches, vol. 3, NRO MS 4261.

Hillam, C. (ed.) 1990, *The Roots of Dentistry*, London: British Dental Association.

Hillson, S.W. 1996, *Dental Anthropology*, Cambridge: Cambridge University Press.

Hobhouse, H. 1999, *Seeds of Change: Six Plants That Transformed Mankind*, 2nd edn, London: Papermac.

Kiple, K.F. & Ornelas, K.C. (eds) 2000, *The Cambridge World History of Food 1*, Cambridge: Cambridge University Press.

Lewis, M.E. 2004, 'Endocranial lesions in non-adult skeletons: understanding their aetiology', *International Journal of Osteoarchaeology* 14: 82–97.

Lewis, M.E. 2007, *The Bioarchaeology of Children: Perspectives from Biological and Forensic Anthropology*, Cambridge: Cambridge University Press.

McKinley, J.I. 2008, *The 18th Century Baptist Church and Burial Ground at West Butts Street, Poole, Dorset*, Salisbury: Wessex Archaeology.

Mays, S.A. & Cox, M. 2000, 'Sex determination in skeletal remains', in Cox & Mays 2000, 117–30.

Miles, A., Powers, N., Wroe-Brown, R. & Walker, D. 2008, *St Marylebone Church and Burial Ground in the 18th to 19th Centuries: Excavations at St Marylebone School, 1992 and 2004–6*. MoLAS Monograph 46. London: Museum of London Archaeology Service.

Molleson, T. 1995, 'Rates of ageing in the eighteenth century', in Saunders & Herring 1995, 199–222.

Molleson, T.I. & Cox, M.J. 1993, *The Spitalfields Project Volume 2: The Anthropology of the Middling Sort*. Council for British Archaeological Research Report 86. York: Council for British Archaeology.

Oldfield, E. 1829, *A Topographical and Historical Account of Wainfleet and the Wapentake of Candleshoe, in the County of Lincoln*, London: Longman, Rees, Orme, Brown and Green.

Ortner, D.J. 2003a, 'Metabolic disorders', in Ortner 2003b, 383–418.

Ortner, D.J. (ed.) 2003b, *Identification of Palaeopathological Disorders in Human Skeletal Remains*, San Diego (CA): Academic.

Ortner, D.J. & Ericksen, M.F. 1997, 'Bone changes in the human skull probably resulting from scurvy in infancy and childhood', *International Journal of Osteoarchaeology* 7: 212–20.

Ortner, D.J., Butler, W., Cafarella, J. & Milligan, L. 2001, 'Evidence of probable scurvy in subadults from archaeological sites in North America', *American Journal of Physical Anthropology* 114: 343–51.

Powers, N. 2006, *Assessment of Human Remains Excavated from Bishop Challoner School, Lukin Street*, unpublished MoLSS rep. HUM\ASS\05\06.

Roberts, C.A. & Cox, M. 2003, *Health and Disease in Britain: From Prehistory to the Present Day*, Stroud: Sutton.

Roberts, C.A. & Manchester, K. 2005, *The Archaeology of Disease*, 3rd edn, Stroud: Sutton.

Roberts, C.A., Lucy, D. & Manchester, K. 1994, 'Inflammatory lesions of ribs: an analysis of the Terry Collection', *American Journal of Physical Anthropology* 95: 169–82.

Rutledge, E. forthcoming, 'Documentary and Historical Evidence', in Clarke forthcoming.

Santos, A.L. & Roberts, C.A. 2001, 'A picture of tuberculosis in young Portuguese people in the early 20th century: a multidisciplinary study of the skeletal and historical evidence', *American Journal of Physical Anthropology* 115: 38–49.

Santos, A.L. & Roberts, C.A. 2006, 'Anatomy of a serial killer: differential diagnosis of tuberculosis based on rib lesions of adult individuals from the Coimbra Identified Skeletal Collection, Portugal', *American Journal of Physical Anthropology* 130: 38–49.

Saunders, S.R. & Herring, A. (eds) 1995, *Grave Reflections: Portraying the Past through Cemetery Studies*, Toronto: Canadian Scholars.

Scheuer, J.L. & Black, S. 2000a, *Developmental Juvenile Osteology*, San Diego (CA): Academic.

Scheuer, J.L. & Black, S. 2000b, 'Development and ageing of the juvenile skeleton', in Cox & Mays 2000, 9–21.

Scheuer, J.L. & Bowman, J.E. 1995, 'Correlation of documentary and skeletal evidence in the St. Brides' Crypt population', in Saunders & Herring 1995, 49–70.

Shepherd Popescu, E. 2010, *Norwich Castle: Excavations and Historical Survey 1987–98, Parts I & II*, East Anglian Archaeology 132.

Stewart, T.D. (ed.) 1970, *Personal Identification in Mass Disasters*, Washington DC: National Museum of Natural History, Smithsonian Institution.

Trotter, M. 1970, 'Estimation of stature from intact long limb bones', in Stewart 1970, 71–83.

Walker, P.L. 1995, 'Problems of preservation and sexism in sexing: some lessons from historical collections for palaeodemographers', in Saunders & Herring 1995, 31–47.

Walker, P.L., Bathurst, P.R., Richman, R., Gjerdrum, T. & Andrusko, V.A. 2009. 'The causes of porotic hyperostosis and cribra orbitalia: a reappraisal of the iron-deficiency anaemia hypothesis', *American Journal of Physical Anthropology* 139: 109–25.

White, W. 1845, *History, Gazetteer and Directory of Norfolk, and the City and County of the City of Norwich*, Sheffield: R. Leader.

Williams, S.A. & Curzon, M.E.J. 1986, 'Observations on dental caries in primary teeth in some medieval British skull material', in Foley & Cruwys 1986, 201–13.

Wohl, A.S. 1984, *Endangered Lives: Public Health in Victorian Britain*, London: Methuen.

Wood, J.W., Milner, G.R., Harpending, H.C. & Weiss, K.M. 1992, 'The osteological paradox: Problems of inferring prehistoric health from skeletal samples' *Current Anthropology* 33: 343–70.

Zero, D.T. 1999, 'Dental caries process', *Dental Clinics of North America* 43: 635–64.

ABBREVIATIONS

AMTL	antemortem tooth loss
CPR	crude prevalence rate
DEH	dental enamel hypoplasia
MoLSS	Museum of London Specialist Services
NHER	Norfolk Historic Environment Record
NRO	Norfolk Record Office

Maidens' Garlands:
A Funeral Custom of Post-Reformation England

Rosie Morris

This chapter examines the phenomenon of mortuary garlanding – the custom of making maidens' garlands in commemoration of young, mainly female virgins. It is also work in progress because of the questions it raises. The prime objective is to uncover and record a chronological history of the practice, including manufacture, popularity and various geographic and theological contexts. The ultimate aim is to discover whether maidens' garlands were simply part of popular religious culture, or were sanctioned within the formal practices of the established Church.

BACKGROUND

From the late Middle Ages to relatively recent times garlanding was an established aspect of the Anglican funeral rite. Although detailed accounts of this practice are sparse, funeral garlands have been recorded in most parts of Britain. All extant examples date from the post-Reformation period. They were similar in construction, composed of greenery and flowers – which were common elements of English calendrical decorative custom whether celebrating chimney sweeps and milkmaids on 1 May or local miners and fishermen on 29 May – and also of semi-permanent elements such as textiles, paper and gloves. Children took a central part in their making, decorating and carrying (Fig. 15.1).

Of course, floral tributes have always been widespread in European society, examples varying from the medieval May Day garland to the massed floral tributes which accompanied the burial of the late Princess of Wales[1] to smaller ones in contemporary society seen at the sites of road accidents. Other garlands are associated with seasonal celebration and festivity such as Christmas, Easter, May Day,[2] Rogationtide and Whitsun.[3] But the particular custom of funeral garlanding – which stressed the importance of the deceased individual and their immediate family – was a popular custom throughout Europe. The English version, the so-called 'maidens' garlands' or 'virgins' crowns', have a cultural significance that invites us to think about wider contexts such as class, religion, geography and gender. As their name indicates, these were special garlands, looking like crowns, used at funerals to celebrate the lives of those who died in a 'state of virginity'. They left a visible record, albeit ephemeral, in the church fabric.

Distinct recurring ideas lie behind the custom, therefore, which involve virginity, flower symbolism and a reward for the innocent life. The virginity symbol was personified during the Middle Ages in the Cult of the Blessed Virgin Mary. The flowers derive from medieval legends, though there is a confused etymology involving the word 'rosary' from a mythic

Figure 15.1. Garland day, Abbotsbury, near Weymouth, Dorset. Garlanding was a widely accepted form of celebration. These garlands are made by the children then blessed in the church before being cast into the sea as a votive of the Feast of Neptune on 13 May in the hope of a year of abundant fish harvest (Sir Benjamin Stone Collection, Central Library, Birmingham: Courtesy of Birmingham Archives and Heritage).

story about St Dominic and both French and German versions involve a crown of roses ('chapelet' and 'Rosenkranz').[4] It is possible that the crown of roses, or 'chapelet' in the context of the medieval cult of the Blessed Virgin Mary, was a forerunner of the maidens' garland. The reward was symbolized by the 'crown' awarded to those who died in youth, usually female virgins, celebrating their 'triumphant victory over lusts of the flesh'.[5]

The terms 'maidens' garlands', 'virgins' crowns' or 'crants' (the latter derived from the German word 'kranz', Dutch/Danish/Swedish word 'krans' or 'cranstes' in Derbyshire) were by the late 17th century in general use to signify a garland, chaplet or wreath.[6] In 1879 the *Shropshire Word Book* defined them as 'chaplets of white paper-flowers, with a pair, sometimes more than one pair, of gauntlet-shaped gloves – likewise of paper – suspended from them'.[7] According to the folklorist Charlotte Burne, 'these garlands were formerly laid on the coffin of the deceased maiden before her burial, borne by her companions before the corpse to the grave, and finally hung over her seat in church to keep her memory green'.[8] The custom was well known to Shakespeare: in *Hamlet* (c. 1601) a priest protests at the burial of Ophelia, a suicide, in the churchyard:

Yet here she is allowed her virgin crants,
Her maidens strewments and the bringing home
Of bell and burial.[9]

CONSTRUCTION

The maidens' garland generally took the form of a bell, similar to the shape of a bishop's mitre or an old-fashioned bee hive, measuring approximately 0.3m in height. They were made of two strips of wood, intersecting each other at the top and secured at the base and again at mid-height with a hoop of bent wood. They were then bound with wool or felt and covered with paper flowers attached by stitching to the felt or wool. A paper hand-kerchief or collar was suspended inside, together with gloves made of parchment which usually bore the name of the deceased and favourite hymns or readings from the Bible. Localized and regional variations were evident. Some were made entirely of paper, such as those found at the entrance to St Bartholomew's chapel, Holy Cross, Ilam, in Staffordshire, while another awarded to Mary Boyce in 1685 at St Mary, Walsham-le-Willows, Suffolk, took the form of a plain wooden disc of similar thickness to a plank of elm used for coffins. Several had remnants of cloth, and one, recently conserved by the York Archaeological Trust (2002) from St Michael's church, Theydon Mount, has paper decoration and sprigs of box (*Buxus sempervirens*) attached to the wooden framework.[10] This evergreen is often associated with funerals[11] and its use is mentioned by William Wordsworth in 'The Child-less Father' (1800).[12]

Their decoration varied as well. For example, at Holy Cross, Ilam, Staffordshire, and St Giles, Matlock, Derbyshire, garlands were fashioned with fringed paper similar to the decoration of the Wassail Bough carried around the parish at Christmas.[13] The similarity in design suggests a Derbyshire custom crossing over the borders of Staffordshire. Yet those found at St Stephen's, Fylingdales, Yorkshire, combine cloth, wood and gloves in a spherical shape. To have remained intact, in some cases for over 300 years, shows that all the surviving examples have one thing in common – they are extremely robust.

Writing about her childhood in Oxfordshire in the 1880s, Flora Thompson described the construction of a May garland of fresh flowers upon a wooden frame.[14] Funeral garlands, too, could be decorated with fresh flowers, as recorded in a letter from Sir Thomas Browne to John Evelyn (*c.* 1657–8).[15] Two hundred years later, fresh flowers were still being used. The Reverend Vaux, writing in 1894, described the spring-time funeral of a 'maiden friend of his' who was buried twelve months earlier at Teignmouth: 'She lay in her coffin with a chaplet of Eucharis (lily) and lilies of the valley on her brow and the sides of the grave were lined with moss.'[16] Eventually fresh flowers were replaced by artificial ones. The rosettes, crosses and cockades found on the 18th-century garlands at Holy Trinity, Minsterley, Shropshire, were made from wallpaper. Conservation work has identified the wallpaper as matching a design used to line a deed box *c.* 1700, found at Bewdley, Worcestershire.[17] Artificial flowers made of dyed horn were used for the decoration of Susannah Perwich's '*costly*' garland at St Augustine of Hippo, Hackney, Middlesex, in 1661.[18]

The inclusion of gloves within the garland and their symbolism requires closer scrutiny. They symbolized cleanliness, honesty and integrity. Gloves worn by mourners were part of the funeral accoutrement.[19] They were associated with the legal profession, and played

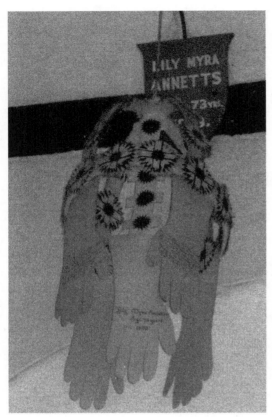

Figure 15.2. Garland, St Mary, Abbotts Ann, Hampshire. The most recent virgin's crown will hang permanently in the nave until it will naturally decay and fall as dust to the floor. It was made by the village carpenter and decorated by Jessie Threadgill (church warden) and his wife for Lily Myra Annett, died 24 May 1973 (photograph by R. Morris).

a conspicuous role in the binding of pre-contracts and legal betrothals. They were also a commitment of faith, a symbol of confidence and a sign of trust, sent as pledges of safe conduct in times of truce.[20] Within the Anglican Church, gloves of white linen were used to ensure clean hands, free from all impurity,[21] and were part of the liturgy of Episcopal investiture.[22] Funeral garlands in nearly all cases included white gloves. At a time when fresh flowers were used, white kid gloves belonging to the deceased were always included in garland construction.[23] At St Mary's, Abbotts Ann, Hampshire – as is reported in the description visible in the church today – the glove is fashioned like a gauntlet, and is reported by participants to have symbolized a challenge made to anyone who might question or deny the deceased's virginity (Fig. 15.2).

Who made the garlands? At St Mary's, Abbotts Ann, in the 1950s and 1970s local men were commissioned to cut the wood and the 'local carpenter – who refused to divulge his trade secrets – made the crown, and the churchwarden and his wife decorated them'.[24] In 1661 Susannah Perwich's 'rich and costly garland of gum work' was most likely to be the work of girls 'of choice breeding' attending her parents' school, where wax and gum work were curriculum subjects, as well as 'silver, silk, straws and glass'.[25] In 1789 the Rev Gilbert White of Selbourne recollected having seen the 'clerk's wife cutting in white paper the resemblance of gloves and ribbons twisted into knots and roses to decorate these memorials of chastity'.[26] In 1841 William Howitt recalled his mother making the floral decoration for a garland in Derbyshire.[27] At St Calixtus, Astley Abbotts, Shropshire, the garland awarded to Hannah Phillips, who died in 1709 on the eve of her marriage, was felt to be such a poignant symbol that it was completely renewed in 1860 and included the white gloves of the vicar and his wife. Yet at St Mary the Virgin, Shrawardine, Shropshire, the funeral garlands that hung in the church were believed by villagers to be the work of giants.[28]

DISTRIBUTION

To date, 140 locations have been documented and 70 extant garlands have been found. Extant collections are small in number with the exception of St Mary's church, Abbotts Ann, Hampshire, where 43 garlands hang from hooks, each displaying the name and date of the person to whom they were awarded. At St Andrew's, Alfriston, Sussex, in 1894, 70 garlands are recorded,[29] and at St Mary, Ilkeston, Derbyshire, 50 or more were documented in the mid 19th century.[30] More recently, in 1923, an elderly resident of West Hallam, Derbyshire, remembered at least 30 hanging in St Wilfred's church.[31]

Regional distribution in England and Wales was considerable: from County Durham to Hampshire, from Llandovery to Lincoln. Widespread adherence to the practice has been noted from the late medieval period to the First World War and after (Fig. 15.3 illustrates the geographical spread of documented and extant garlands by county). In 1982, Gereth Spriggs tabulated a gazetteer of fifty-six churches and mapped their distribution.[32] To date I have doubled Spriggs' listing of churches and have documented further information including patronal dedication, patronage and lists of incumbents for each church. For example, 20% of churches are dedicated to St Mary, and 10% were peculiar chapels. The heaviest concentration for extant garlands is to be found in Derbyshire where, perhaps significantly, the customs of Ascension Day observance and Rogation-tide well dressing was widespread, as was the oak apple garlanding custom on 29 May.[33]

The earliest extant garlands date from the 17th century and are located in Sussex and Yorkshire. (In every case we are dependent on historical dating rather than any other scientific method.) In St Mary's church, Walsham-le-Willows, Suffolk, is a disc with the name of 'Mary Boyce' carved on the side facing the altar and, on the reverse, the date she died: 15 Nov 1685. Five years earlier, at St Mary's church in Beverley, Yorkshire, a maidens' garland awarded to Elizabeth Ellinor, who died 14 August 1680 aged 21, can be found in the priest's room of the church. The process of construction involved both the three-dimensional craft skills of the carpenter, wheelwright trug or basket maker and decoration in the form of calligraphic design.

Among the garlands documented or extant there are wide variations in frequency and popularity. The most popular period for funeral garlanding seems to have been during the 18th and 19th centuries, but at Bromley, Kent, the custom was 'dying out' at the beginning of the 18th century.[34] Yet it was thriving at the close of the same century at St Helen, Eyam, Derbyshire.[35] In the mid 18th century at St Peter's, Hope, Derbyshire, the churchwarden's accounts of 1749 record 'paid 1/6d for removing of the garlands to make the church look lighter'. This rigorous cleaning was later recorded to 'signalise the advent of a new incumbent'.[36] Yet at St Stephen's, Fylingdales, Yorkshire, maidens' garlands began to appear in 1760.[37]

Figure 15.3. Map showing distribution of number of churches
with surviving or recorded maidens' garlands.

THEOLOGICAL TENSION

The Church of England did not always welcome garlanding – the spectres of idolatry and profanity always loomed large – and in many cases local clergy, it must be assumed, took the opportunity of a 19th-century restoration to dispose of them.[38] For example, at St Helen, Darley, Derbyshire, an eyewitness account records eleven garlands '30 years ago, prior to the church being restored in 1877'.[39] At St Helen, Eyam, Derbyshire, the church was repaired in the early 19th century and 'the garlands taken down and destroyed'.[40] During the restoration and reseating of St Cuthbert's, Satley, Derbyshire, the last one was destroyed by 'an iconoclastic clergyman'.[41] In 1819 Holy Trinity and Virgin Mary, Clee, Lincolnshire underwent a 'thorough repair' during which 'these emblems of innocence and friendship were finally removed'.[42]

Episcopal opposition was significant. As early as 1662 Matthew Wren, bishop of Hereford, Norwich and Ely, described the garlands in his Ely Visitation as 'gew gaws',[43] linking them with magic and superstition and suggesting that only 'the fonder sort of people' would participate in such a custom.[44] Canon Law was silent on their sanction, but interpretation of Canon 88 in particular[45] – 'churches not to be profaned' – was an ecclesiastical argument used, especially by Evangelicals during the 19th century, to defend the lawful exclusion of such objects in the ceremonial of the church.[46] During the 1820s at St Giles, Matlock, Derbyshire, Philip Gell (curate and well-known Evangelical) forbade the hanging of them. A letter dated 15 September 1879 from Robert Bull to John Talbot Coke, the Lord of the Manor and patron of the parish church of All Saints, Trusley, Derbyshire, described the garlands there and their destruction. Bull suggested that the incumbent Rev. William Copestake considered them 'a waste of paper',[47] and that Mr W. Pole of Radbourne Hall (related to the Gell family) described them as 'remnants of Popery and superstition … and ordered their destruction.'[48]

Yet there are exceptions to this trend. In 1661 Dr William Spurstowe, Presbyterian minister and one of Charles II's chosen Divines, permitted garlands at the funeral of the Presbyterian Susannah Perwich. And in 1879 the rural dean of Trusley and Radbourne is said to have 'begged Mr Pole by all means to treasure them'.[49] More work will be required to uncover the full complexities of this particular occurrence, which are clearly bound up in the local history of this part of Derbyshire, where the Gell family had long been the dominant landed interest. But clearly garlands had an emotional and no doubt aesthetic appeal.

Garlands that no longer hang in the church nave have in some cases remained within the church building, but hidden away. For example, at St Giles, Matlock, Derbyshire, five garlands remain in a cupboard just inside the entrance (a further garland has recently been conserved). At St Mary, Abbotts Ann, garlands from the previous church were kept in cupboards of the new one, but no longer exist. Rev. Parker informs readers of *Notes and Queries* (18 October 1911) of the location of a garland 'in a cupboard on the north side of the tomb of St Alban behind the High Altar'.[50] Yet other parish churches have had them included in large exhibitions. For example, the garland from St Mary's, Acton Burnell, Shropshire, was displayed at Shrewsbury at the Ecclesiastical Art Exhibition of the Church Congress in 1896. It was listed in the catalogue as 'A Maiden's Garland on loan from Rev W. Serjeantson MA Acton Burnell Rectory' (numbered 173).[51] Reference was also made to the display of later exhibits 311–317, which were 'A fine specimen set [7] of "Love Tokens"

Figure 15.4. 'Two Unfortunate Lovers or a True Relation of the Lamentable End of John True and Susan Mease', *c.* 1640, London: Henry Gosson. British Library C.20.f.7 [428]. This early woodcut illustrates the custom of female bearers, each dressed similarly; a maidens' garland is placed on the coffin. (Courtesy of the British Library. All rights reserved Roxburghe Coll. 1.428).

or "Maidens Garlands" on loan from Rev R.W. Williams PhD, Minsterley Vicarage'.[52] A note added 'These at Minsterley (the centre of Christianity in these parts, a very old Collegiate Church, if not the oldest in Salop) are considered to be unsurpassed.'[53] One of the Minsterley garlands was also displayed at a later Congress at Stoke-on-Trent in 1911.[54]

The custom of funeral garlanding came to be associated with the cult associating chastity and the divine. Exploration of the religio-sexual psychology behind this cult is beyond the scope of this paper, but the sadness at the young women's demise is genuine. Early ballads and broadsheets found in the Roxburghe and Bagford collections offer visual evidence for contemporary attitudes towards virginity/chastity/death. Titles such as 'The Bride's Burial – to the tune of The Lady's Fall', 'Two Unfortunate Lovers' and 'The Pining Maid – or A Pattern for Lovers' evoke images of a poignant nature.[55]

Theological inconsistencies can also be found here and there. In 1661, a year before the introduction of Charles II's Book of Common Prayer, at Hackney, London, Susannah Perwich organized her own funeral. It included a garland carried for her by 'two maidens who entirely loved her' (Fig. 15.4).[56] Susannah 'had the advantage of choice breeding',[57] and was deeply pious and intelligent. She was highly accomplished at music, and described as a 'rarity of England'.[58] She spent four to five weeks from her death bed organizing her funeral readings and meeting with the minister, Dr Spurstowe, who was to carry out her

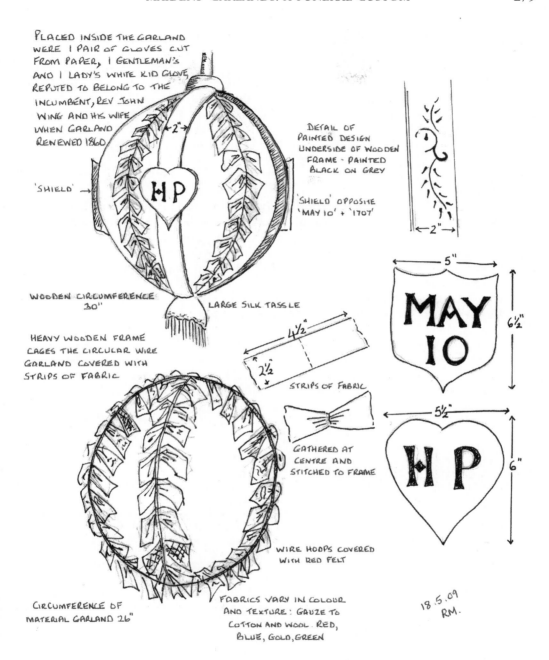

PLACED INSIDE THE GARLAND WERE I PAIR OF GLOVES CUT FROM PAPER, I GENTLEMAN'S AND I LADY'S WHITE KID GLOVE REPUTED TO BELONG TO THE INCUMBENT, REV JOHN WING AND HIS WIFE WHEN GARLAND RENEWED 1860

'SHIELD'

2"

HP

WOODEN CIRCUMFERENCE 30"

LARGE SILK TASSLE

HEAVY WOODEN FRAME CAGES THE CIRCULAR WIRE GARLAND COVERED WITH STRIPS OF FABRIC

DETAIL OF PAINTED DESIGN UNDERSIDE OF WOODEN FRAME - PAINTED BLACK ON GREY

'SHIELD' OPPOSITE 'MAY 10' + '1707'

2"

5"

MAY 10

6½"

4½"

2½"

STRIPS OF FABRIC

GATHERED AT CENTRE AND STITCHED TO FRAME

5½"

HP

6"

WIRE HOOPS COVERED WITH RED FELT

CIRCUMFERENCE OF MATERIAL GARLAND 26"

FABRICS VARY IN COLOUR AND TEXTURE: GAUZE TO COTTON AND WOOL. RED, BLUE, GOLD, GREEN

18.5.09 RM.

DETAILS OF HANNAH PHILLIPS' GARLAND ST CALIXTUS, ASTLEY ABBOTTS SHROBHIRE

Figure 15.5. Details of the renewed (1862) garland for Hannah Phillips who died on the eve of her marriage, 9 May 1707, at Astley Abbotts, Bridgnorth, Shropshire (drawn by R. Morris).

wishes. These included the carrying of a 'rich and costly garland of gum work'.[59] Here a Presbyterian minister legitimized the use of a garland at a virgin's funeral.

It is impossible to determine any class exclusivity among recipients of the garlands. Susannah Perwich, the person awarded the silver filigree garland at Bromley, Kent, and the young maiden from Glossop who had a garland costing £30 could be argued to have connections with the upper classes.[60] Yet the garlands made for Lily Annetts, or even her nephew, William George Annetts, from Abbotts Ann, or those of Ann Swindell (Ashford-in-the-Water) or Mary Hill (Springthorpe) were clearly more modest (Fig. 15.5).

CONCLUSION

I shall continue to explore the implications of local attitudes and responses. Eamon Duffey, David Cressy, Ronald Hutton and Bob Bushaway, to name but a few, have underlined the importance of post-medieval popular religion in furthering our understanding of community behaviour in England and Wales.[61] There is no doubt that maidens' garlands represent an aspect of popular religion. Working families and communities in the provinces firmly adhered to their own distinctive styles of religion and practice as a result of their received mentality. These customs regulated ethical behaviour and provided a system of symbols whereby the individual and community made sense of the world.

How reluctantly were maidens' garlands sanctioned by the Church? They appear to endorse the theological concept of a celibate death, something which might be seen as heretical in the context of the Anglican Creed. But the issue is hugely complex and also lies beyond the scope of this paper. What can be said is that their survival as a 'beautiful and simple hearted custom of rural life'[62] shows the strength of their appeal.

NOTES

1. Evans 1998, 101–4.
2. Hazlitt 1905, 400.
3. Brears 1989, 178–9.
4. Addis & Arnold 1954, 703–4.
5. Steele 1747, 264–5.
6. *Oxford English Dictionary* 1989, 1117.
7. Jackson 1879, 465.
8. Burne 1883, 312.
9. Shakespeare 1959 [1601], Act 5, Scene 1, line 255–7.
10. Spriggs *et al.* 2002, 280–87.
11. Vickery 1984a, 180–201.
12. 'The basin of box wood just six months before, Filled at Timothy's door, A coffin through Timothy's threshold had passed, one child did it bear and that child was last', Wordsworth 1827, 203–4. In several parts of the North of England, when a funeral takes place, a basin full of sprigs of boxwood is placed at the door of the house from which the coffin is taken up.
13. Brears 1989, 192.
14. Thompson 1948, 190–97.
15. Browne 1962 [*c*.1657/58].
16. Vaux 1894, 127.
17. Storey 2001, 4–6; Jenkinson 1925, 237–53.
18. Batchilor 1661, 40.
19. Jack & Jack 1909, 779.
20. Beck 1883, 196.
21. Beck 1883, 17.
22. Beck 1883, 17.
23. Hone 1888, 272.
24. George King pers. comm..
25. Batchilor 1661, 40, 2, 7.
26. White 1789, 315–16.
27. Howitt 1841, 484.
28. Thistleton Dyer 1891, 163.
29. Hare 1894, 194.
30. Moutrey-Read 1911, 292–329.
31. Cox 1932, 306.
32. Spriggs 1982, 12–32.
33. Boyes 1993, 105–19.
34. Boyes 1993, 105–19.

35. Seward 1792.
36. Cox 1932, 306.
37. Harrison 1966.
38. Tyack 1899, 88.
39. Brushfield 1899, 54–74.
40. Andrews 1890, 143–4.
41. Fawcett 1937.
42. Oliver 1829, 413–17.
43. *Articles of Enquiry*, Cambridge University Library B125:2.9 reel 324:1 7.
44. *Articles of Enquiry*, Cambridge University Library B125:2.9 reel 324:1 7.
45. Harford & Stevenson 1913, 147.
46. Goode 1851; Perry 1857.
47. Robert Bull 1879.
48. Robert Bull 1879.
49. Robert Bull 1879.
50. Parker 1911.
51. Auden 1896, 106.
52. Auden 1896, 117.
53. Auden 1896, 117.
54. Burne 1911, 496.
55. Roxburghe Ballad Coll.
56. Batchilor 1661, 40.
57. Batchilor 1661, 2.
58. Batchilor 1661, 7.
59. Batchilor 1661, 40.
60. Jewitt 1860, 61.
61. Duffy 1992; Cressy 1997; Hutton 2001; 1994; Bushaway 1982.
62. S.M.M. 1882.

BIBLIOGRAPHY

Addis, W.E. & Arnold, T. 1954, *Catholic Dictionary*, 15th edn, London: Virtue.

Andrews, W. 1890, *Curiosities of the Church*, London: Methuen.

Articles of Enquiry (with some directions intermingled) for the Diocese of Ely in the 2nd Visitation of the R. Reverend Father in God, Matthew, Lord Bishop of the Diocese, anno Dom 1662, London: Timothy Garwaite.

Auden, Rev. T., 1896, *Illustrated Guide to the Church Congress and Ecclesiatical Art Exhibition, Shrewsbury, 1896*, London: Maltravers House, Arundel St, Temple.

Batchilor, J. 1661, 'Virgins' Pattern', Printed Simon Dover.

Beck, S.W. 1883, *Gloves their Annals and Associations*, London: Hamish, Adams.

Boyes, G. 1993, 'Dressing the part: the role of costume as an indicator of social dynamics in the castleton garland ceremony', *Folklore* 22: 105–19.

Brears, P. 1989, *North Country Folk Art*, Edinburgh: John Donald.

Browne, T. 1962 [*c.* 1657/58], *Of Garlands and Coronary or Garland Plants. Thomas Browne to John Evelyn, Esq., F.R.S.* (No. 2 of 'Certain Miscellany Tracts'), Northhampton (MA): Gehenna Press.

Brushfield, T.N. 1899, 'Derbyshire Funeral Garlands', *The Journal of the British Archaeological Association* 6: 54–4.

Bull, R. 1879, Letter to John Talbot Coke 15th September 1879, unpublished notes from John Talbot Coke's notebook, copied by David Coke-Steel, Trusley.

Burne, C. (ed.) 1883, *Shropshire Folkore – A Sheaf of Gleanings from the Georgina Jackson Collection*, London: Trubner & Co

Burne, C. 1911, 'Virgins garlands', *Folklore* 22/4: 496.

Bushaway, R. 1982, *By Rite: Custom, Ceremony and Community in England 1700–1880*, London: Junction Books.

Cox, J.C. 1932, *English Church Fittings, Furniture and Accessories*, London: Batsford.

Cressy, D. 1997, *Birth, Marriage & Death Ritual, Religion and the Life-Cycle in Tudor and Stuart England*, Oxford: Oxford University Press.

Duffy, E. 1992, *The Stripping of the Altars: Traditional Religion in England 1440–1580*, New Haven (CT): Yale University Press.

Evans, M. 1998, 'The Diana phenomenon reaction in the East Midlands', *Folklore* 109: 101–4.

Fawcett, J.W. 1937, 'Old funeral customs: bachelor's garlands', *Notes and Queries* 24 April 1937: 302–3.

Goode, W. 1851, *Aids for Determining Some Disputed Points in the Ceremonial of the Church*, London: Thomas Hatchard.

Hare, A.J.C. 1894, *Sussex*, London: G. Allen.

Harford, G. & Stevenson, M. 1913, *Prayer Book Dictionary*, London: Sir Issac Pitman.

Harrison, M.S. 1966, 'Fylingdales Old Church: A Small Guide', unpublished church guide.

Hazlitt, W.C. 1905, *Dictionary of Faiths and Folklore Beliefs, Superstitions and Popular Customs*, London: Reeves & Turner.

Hone, W. 1888, *The Every Day Book or a Guide to the Year*, London: Ward Lock.

Howitt, W. 1841, *The Rural Life of England*, London: Carey and Hart.

Hutton, R. 1994, *The Rise and Fall of Merry England*, Oxford: Oxford University Press.

Hutton, R. 2001, *Stations of the Sun*, Oxford: Oxford University Press.

Jack, T.C. & Jack, E.C. 1909, *Jack's Reference Book for Home and Office*, London: T.C. & E.C. Jack.

Jackson, G. 1879, *Shropshire Word Book*, London: Trübner.

Jenkinson, H. 1925, 'English wallpapers of the sixteenth and seventeenth centuries,' *Antiquaries Journal* V: 237–53.

Jewitt, L. 1860, *The Reliquary*, London: John Russell Smith.

Moutrey-Read, D.H. 1911, 'Hampshire folklore', *Folklore* 22: 292–329.

Oliver, G. 1829, 'Account of Clee, Co Lincoln', *Gentleman's Magazine* 1: 413–17.

Oxford English Dictionary, 1989, 2nd edn, Vol III, Oxford: Clarendon Press.

Park, Rev. 1941, 'Maidens' garlands or love tokens', *Notes and Queries* 18 October 1941.

Perry, T.W. 1857, *Lawful Church Ornaments: Being an Historical Examination of the Judgement of the Right Hon Stephen Lushington in the Case of Westerton v. Lidell, etc*, London: Joseph Masters.

Roxburghe Ballad Collection, British Library C.20.f.7–10.

Seward, A. 1792, 'Elegiac Ode', *The Oricle* 25 September 1792.

Shakespeare, W. 1959 [1601], *Hamlet* (ed. G. Rylands), Oxford: Clarendon Press.

S.M.M., 1882, 'Minsterley Church', *Eddowes' Shrewsbury and Salopian Journal* 10 May 1882.

Spriggs, G. 1982, 'Maiden's garlands', *Folklife* 21: 12–32.

Spriggs, M., Spriggs, J.A. & Spriggs, S. 2002, 'Maidens' garlands: an Essex example of ancient church folklore', *Essex Archaeology and History* 33: 280–7.

Steele, E. 1747, 'Burial garlands', *Gentleman's Magazine* 17: 264–5.

Storey, G. 2001, 'Maiden's garlands: decorated papers found in unusual circumstances', *The Wallpaper History Review* 2001: 4–6.

Thistleton Dyer, T.F. 1891, *Church Lore Gleanings*, London: A.D. Innes.

Thompson, F. 1948, *Lark Rise to Candleford*, London: The Reprint Society.

Tyack, G.S. 1899, *Lore and Legend of the English Church*, London: William Andrews.

Vaux, J.E. 1894, *Church Folklore*, London: Griffith, Farran.

Vickery, R. 1984a, 'Plants, death and mourning', in Vickery 1984b, 180–201.

Vickery, R. (ed.) 1984b, *Plant-lore Studies*, Botanical Society of the British Isles Conference Report 18, London: Folklore Society.

White, G. 1789, 'Letter 3', in *The Natural History and Antiquities of Selborne, in the County of Southampton: with engravings and an appendix*, London: B. White & Son, at Horace's Head, Fleet Street, 314–16.

Wordsworth, W. 1827, *The Poetical Works of William Wordsworth, Vol. I*, London: Longman, Rees, Orme, Browne & Green, Paternoster Row.

INDEX